For many years, the Roman Catholic Church has used the term 'transubstantiation' to express the presence of Christ in the Eucharist. Of late, however, although proposed replacements have not found favour, the term itself no longer has the place and setting it once had, and debates about transubstantiation have died down. This book is written in the belief that reflection upon the matter is indispensable. It submits that transubstantiation and its proposed replacements are fundamentally similar in their confusions – they divorce appearance from reality because they fail to do justice to the Eucharist as a rite. The changes in Roman Catholic worship have sharpened the need for an account that will do justice to this, and the book is an attempt to provide one. It is also an endeavour to discuss problems which affect all Christians.

IN BREAKING OF BREAD

IN BREAKING
OF BREAD

The Eucharist and ritual

P. J. FITZPATRICK

Emeritus Reader in Philosophy
University of Durham

 CAMBRIDGE
UNIVERSITY PRESS

Published by the Press Syndicate of the University of Cambridge
The Pitt Building, Trumpington Street, Cambridge CB2 1RP
40 West 20th Street, New York, NY 10011–4211, USA
10 Stamford Road, Oakleigh, Melbourne 3166, Australia

First published 1993

Printed in Great Britain at the University Press, Cambridge

The author and publisher are grateful to the Marvell Press for permission
to reproduce lines from 'Church Going' by Philip Larkin.

A catalogue record for this book is available from the British Library

Library of Congress cataloguing in publication data

FitzPatrick, P. J.
In breaking of bread: the Eucharist and ritual / P. J. FitzPatrick.
p.   cm.
Includes bibliographical references and index.
ISBN 0 521 35111 1
1. Transubstantiation.   2. Lord's Supper – Catholic Church.
3. Catholic Church Doctrines.   1. Title.
BX2220.F58   1993
234′.163–dc20   92–23174   CIP

ISBN 0 521 35111 1 hardback

*To my mother; and to
the memory of my father*

Natis in usum laetitiae scyphis
pugnare, Thracum est –

Wine-cups were made for joy;
only barbarians use them as weapons.
Horace, *Odes* i. 27

Ἦσαν δέ τινες Ἕλληνες ἐκ τῶν
ἀναβαινόντων ἵνα προσκυνήσωσιν
ἐν τῇ ἑορτῇ

Now there were certain Greeks among
those that went up to worship at the feast.
John xii 20

Contents

ix

Preface

Years ago, back in the seventies, I wrote a book on the eucharistic presence. In it I expressed my dissatisfaction with the account associated with transubstantiation, and my belief that recent attempts at other accounts had not succeeded. The book was given a friendly turn-down by a publisher, on the grounds that its theme was too much tied to Roman Catholicism to interest Christians of other traditions, while the Church of Rome itself would regard its contents as offensively heterodox. The verdict did not surprise me, the typescript went into honourable retirement on the upper shelf, and I turned my attention to other matters. But I was wrong to think myself rid of the topic. In the eighties, Stephen Sykes (now bishop of Ely) was editing a volume on sacrifice. The contributors were for the most part colleagues of his in the Department of Theology at Durham, but he asked me too for an essay, on eucharistic sacrifice in the middle ages, and I accepted the invitation. The topic – to my surprise – turned out to be rather a snakes-in-Ireland business, but I learned a good deal in the process, not least about the setting of the Eucharist. And then the Cambridge University Press, which was publishing the volume, expressed interest in publishing my book. And so it was that I set out upon a lengthy journey. The length was due in part to matters wholly alien to the life of the mind – administrative offices that were as uncongenial as they had been unsought. It was due in part to the need to complete other pieces of writing on which I had embarked. But it was due most of all to the need for a radical refashioning and extension of what I had written. What I offer the reader now is another book.

What it offers – and what it does not offer – I have tried to hint at in the two mottoes prefixed to it: one from Horace, the other from St John's Gospel. Horace remonstrates with some friends who were turning an occasion for fellowship and happiness into a brawl.

Disagreement about the Eucharist is only one of the many disagreements among Roman Catholics today. That disagreement should
touch the Eucharist is natural enough – it is meant to be a sign of
unity among those who celebrate it, and sign and signified go
together. But I shall be submitting that disagreements here point to
the widespread unease there is in the Roman Church, an unease
which has many causes and shews itself in many ways; and that not
only do eucharistic disagreements point to this unease, they indicate
the morals to be drawn from it, and ways in which it might be
mended. But if Horace provides me with a motto for the task I have
undertaken, the Fourth Gospel has given me a text which shews
something of how I have undertaken it. The verse I cite refers to
Greeks who had come up to Jerusalem to worship at the feast, and I
understand from the commentators that these for St John are not
Greek-speaking Jews but 'God-fearers', people outside the law like
other pagans, but seekers after the true God. I do not think it is
pretentious to take the text as describing my own undertaking,
because I know that many others would see themselves described
there as well. I have come up, as they have, to Jerusalem to worship
– I take part in the Eucharist that is done in memory of Him, and I
join in its unique thanksgiving for the redemption He came to bring.
But I am, as they are, 'a Greek': I inherit a tradition of debate and
enquiry that goes back to Athens, not to Jerusalem. These pages are
a contribution from outside to the various theological debates that
will be met in them. I neither am nor wish to be regarded as a
theologian, and this observation is not a personal quirk, it touches the
course that the book will take.

I have come to see, in the reflexions which have led me to the new
book, that debates about the Eucharist point to themes that go far
beyond what is eucharistic. Or – and this is better – because the
Eucharist is what it is, disagreements here in speculation and in
practice are bound up with what human beings are and with what
they seek to be. In the first two chapters, I give an exposition and
critique of older and newer accounts, finding fault with them both for
much the same reasons. But the reasons touch topics like human
knowledge, the relationship between present and past for us, and the
language which we inherit and develop – and so in the third chapter
I am obliged to think on these things. And thinking on them demands
in its turn that I take the thoughts further. Knowledge, time and
language are bound up here with a tradition which is valued and to

which those who are disagreeing all claim to belong. The tensions
and differences which have arisen about the Eucharist are examples
of what can arise and does arise in any temporally extended activity,
where past and present both matter. My disagreement with older
and newer accounts turns out to be a disagreement with a style of
thought that appears in many places: in particular, a style that
appears in eucharistic speculation and practice, and in the life of the
Church.

I have given various names to the style, and just what is bound up
with it the book itself must shew; here and now I give one of the
words, which is *insulation*. I claim to detect, in what is written of
Eucharist and of Church alike, a propensity to isolate and to fence off
what is most precious. The propensity is understandable, and it leads
to what seems comfortingly definite; in my submission, the definiteness and the comfort alike are deceptive, and the propensity must be
resisted. When I turn in the fourth chapter to distinguish between
signs and disguises, and make the former into the path towards the
Eucharist, not the latter, I claim to see a confusion made between the
two by older and more recent accounts alike; and I claim that old
and new fail to take the eucharistic ritual on its own terms: I claim
that ritual must not be reduced to what is in another category.

The fifth chapter is in consequence devoted to what I have called
'The Way of Ritual', an approach to the Eucharist that I see as
respecting the irreducibility of ritual to anything else. But I have
already disabled myself for offering any account that can compete
with those I have rejected, if to compete means to offer anything as
definite. My rejection of insulation, whether in eucharistic theology
old and new, or in the relations between present and past, or in the
nature of language, condemns me – and condemns readers who
agree with me – to a posture that is awkward. Once more, the
awkwardness will appear as the book goes on, but the phrase 'The
Way of Ritual' points to where the awkwardness lies and points to
the nature of the whole book. Ritual is of its nature incomplete: it
resists translation without remainder into language, it both builds on
and surpasses that which it puts to ritual use, it has links with what
has gone before and with what is still to come. It is a way, a journey,
and the book is meant to be one as well; but the journey is one where
each stage calls for the others. My dissent from older and newer
accounts leads to reflexion on time and on language; but those
themes were already present in the first two chapters, as was the

theme of insulation, and the confusion between signs and disguises. Just so, the Way of Ritual I put forward, while it does not possess the apparent definiteness of what I oppose, does have consequences for time and language in religious belief, and for the need to accept what I have called an uncomfortable posture. And so it is that the sixth and final chapter draws out these consequences for the setting of the eucharistic celebration: the Church, of whose unity in Christ the Eucharist is the sign. Present and past, the tensions between them and the attempts to ease the tensions; language and its temporal spread; the place of language in worship and the place of worship in the Church, and the place of the Church in the wide world – all our themes come together, as our journey comes to its end.

Which means that the book needs to be read as a whole, whether or not the whole proves more persuasive than the parts which make it up. The bibliography is already too long, but it would be very much longer if I were to include all the material I have examined. As it is, some readers will regret the absence of this or that theme – for instance, there is little about oecumenical matters, and nothing about the celebration of the Eucharist in Christian traditions other than that to which I belong (I am a Roman Catholic priest). Conclusions can, I think, be drawn from many things I have written, but I have deliberately refrained from drawing them, just as I have deliberately held back from entering into many topics that invited entry. I have tried to give, if I may take up the phrase again, a perspicuous concreteness to what I have written, concentrating upon specific matters and endeavouring to draw from them morals just as specific. If there be any methodological lesson that writing the book has taught me, it is not to say what must be the case, but look and see. The wisdom of Wittgenstein's command (cf. *Philosophical Investigations* §66) is matched by the extreme difficulty of obeying it: I have tried, but I dare say I shall be seen to have tried at times in vain.

The etymology of 'Eucharist' connotes the giving of thanks, and here it is not only meet and right but a pleasure so to do. I know that my family and friends will be glad to see me released and restored to human society: I also know that their gladness is as nothing compared with my own. The Syndics of the Cambridge University Press have shewn me a confidence and a patience for which I am most grateful, and I give here a special word of thanks to Alex Wright at the Press – the completion of the book is due as much to *mon raseur sympathique* as it is to myself. Many people have over the years discussed topics of the book with me. I mention Professor Eric Mascall and Fr Herbert McCabe, O.P., with whom I exchanged views in *New Blackfriars* when writing the earlier version; and I was both touched and grateful in 1987 when Fr McCabe gave a place to my side of the exchange in *God Matters*, a collection of his own writings. Their two names I give, because our discussions were printed, but after some deliberation I have decided to limit myself to a general acknowledgment to the many others. Some of them were in agreement, but others were not, and I do not wish to mention names in a setting where some of those named might not wish to find themselves. I assure them all that I much value the trouble they took, and that – whatever be thought of the result – I pondered their comments.

The book called for the obtaining a wide range of material, and I was given much help in my search for it. Most of the texts by Schillebeeckx that I translate and discuss come from his book on the eucharistic presence (Schillebeeckx 1967 (1968)). The Dutch original, *Christus' tegenwoordigheid in de Eucharistie*, is published by H. Nelissen of Bilthoven, and here I am obliged to Mr Dick Boer for his helpful kindness. Mr Thomas Downie supplied me with a variety of cuttings and other printed matter. The Librarian of the University of Nijmegen provided microfilms of articles not otherwise obtainable. And, inevitably but with a feeling of personal gratitude for willing help, I extend my thanks to five libraries in England: to the British Library obviously, and I am grateful in particular for the trouble taken there in photocopying or microfilming materials I needed; to the library of Heythrop College London, where the wealth of periodicals was of special value; to the Warburg Institute, the range of whose holdings is an education in itself, and to which I am indebted for – among many other things – a much needed inter-library loan; to the University Library at Durham, both for material and for the help so readily given over the years; and – last of all and most of all – to the library of Ushaw College, Durham, and to its Librarian, the Revd Michael Sharratt: without the facilities there, the book would have been neither begun nor ended.

I was glad to receive assistance from among my students in the Department of Philosophy. Miss Sabine Scharnagl checked some of my translations from the German, and Miss Tineke van Putten and Miss Maaike Liebert checked some of my translations from the Dutch. But none saw all my versions, and any readers who can improve what I have provided will' be thanked in (any) future editions. Miss Sharon Elizabeth Ney generously undertook the word-processing of collateral writings, and bravely undertook the initiation of myself into the mysteries of that art. To all four, my grateful thanks. I add something that indeed I hope does not need adding. I have preferred to work whenever possible from original texts and to make my own translations. This is a personal choice, it is no reflexion upon the worth of what translations I have seen; their worth is real, and I have profited by those I have read. In some cases, the original could not be obtained – I have been glad then to use a translation, and have made an acknowledgment at the appropriate point.

The preparation of the book spanned that great turning-point in civilisation, the transition from typewriting to word-processing. On both sides of the divide I was given good help. Mrs P. A. Dryden undertook much of the work involved in the first drafts; for work later on I am indebted to Mrs C. Dowson, Mrs E. Soley, and (as at other times) to Mrs H. Coppen. Then, for the word-processing of the final drafts, I am glad to express my appreciation of Computerised Document Preparation Services (CDPS, 79 Broadmeadows, Sunderland). Mrs K. I'Anson had to work from material that was both complex and recondite; time and again, she proved better than I at seeing what I had written or even what I ought to have written.

On this occasion as on so many other occasions, Mrs C. M. L. Smith gave generous help – in the obtaining of photocopied material, in the typing of earlier drafts and of collateral work, and above all in the monumental task of preparing the index. I express to her my deep appreciation. I also express my gratitude to her, and to Sister Mary Francis of the Convent of Mercy, Sunderland, and to Miss Angela McAllister for reading the proofs, so patiently and so inexorably.

I hope it is in order to end this giving of thanks with an acknowledgment to two groups. The first group is made up of the numerous authors – popes, theologians, fathers, councils, Thomas Aquinas and all the rest of it – who appear in the pages ahead. They tend to appear when I disagree with them, for such is the way of books. But let us not forget what is the way of disagreement. As a philosopher of our time has reminded us, profitable disagreement calls for a background of massive agreement among those who are disagreeing. (I can differ from Snooks about the strengths and weaknesses of Eden, because Snooks and I share beliefs about the course of history in this century; the disagreement collapses if Snooks turns out to associate the word only with a garden in the Old Testament.) 'We know in part and we prophesy in part' is a quotation that occurs more than once in the book, and I acknowledge that the phrase applies to arguing as well. That I disagree does not mean that I have not learned in the process; nor does it mean that there is nothing to these authors except what has provoked my disagreements.

The second group I thank comes to my mind because of what the book is and how it has come to be. Its composition has called for a survey and critique of a wide range of specialised material; but I like to think – and indeed I have reasons for thinking – that the result is not some professional speculation remote from the common concerns of those who think. I hope it interests theologians, for I suspect that at times they are hard up for things to interest them; but I should be sorry if it interested nobody else. And that is why I express my thanks to this second group, which is simply all those with whom over the years – nearly forty of them now! – I have celebrated the mysteries. For that is where all reflexion here must start, and that is where all reflexion here needs to return, if there is to be any life in the thoughts we have. Be it said in favour of what follows that it admits as much.

Department of Philosophy, pjf
University of Durham

Abbreviations

(Where needed, fuller details are available in the References)

AAS	*Acta Apostolicae Sedis*
AG	Abbott, W. M. and Gallagher, J. (eds.), *The Documents of Vatican II*
ARCIC	Anglican/Roman Catholic International Commission
ASS	*Acta Sanctae Sedis*
DD	*De defectibus*: section in Missal on defects
DS	Denzinger, H. and Schönmetzer, A., *Enchiridion Symbolorum*
DTC	*Dictionnaire de théologie catholique*
ET	English translation
F	Flannery, A. (ed.), *Vatican Council II: the Conciliar and Post Conciliar Documents*
H	Jedin, H., *Geschichte des Konzils von Trient*
J	Jorissen, H., *Die Entstehung der Transsubstantiationslehre bis zum Beginn der Hochscholastik*
MG	Migne, J. P. (ed.), *Patrologiae cursus completus: series Graeca*
ML	Migne, J. P. (ed.), *Patrologiae cursus completus: series Latina*
RCM	*Ritus celebrandi missam*: section in Missal on rite of celebration
RG	*Rubricae generales*: section in Missal on general rubrics
SM	*Sacramentum mundi: an encyclopedia of theology*
ST	Aquinas, *Summa Theologiae*
SzT	Rahner, K., *Schriften zur Theologie* (collected writings)
TI	Rahner, K., *Theological Investigations* (translation of the above)
W	Wohlmuth, J., *Realpräsenz und Transsubstantiation im Konzil von Trient*
ZkT	*Zeitschrift für katholische Theologie*

Methods of citation

All citations are listed in the References, and I give them by author and year of publication. I attempt to mitigate the oddities of this method ('Aquinas 1935' and the like) by what I write in the text. Whenever I could find the original, I have made my own translation from that – I renew here the thanks, already expressed in the Preface, to the librarians who made access possible. In one or two cases the original was not to be had, and I acknowledge at such points the translation I have used. I have tried to give references, whenever I could, in a way that is in some measure independent of the edition or translation available to the reader – for example, my references to Jungmann's work on the Mass apply to the English version as well. Some items by Rahner I found reprinted in his collected *Schriften zur Theologie*; I have added when I could the corresponding reference to the English translation of the collection, *Theological Investigations*. Readers might care to note that the numeration of the volumes in the two series diverges for some reason after a while; and that the items are in some cases revised versions of what Rahner originally wrote. I add when I can the date of first appearance. Some of my own early items in the References bear an asterisk. This means that they originally appeared under the pseudonym 'G. Egner'. For Egner's origin, achievements and eventual demise, see FitzPatrick 1987c. References to patristic and early medieval authors I give by title, book and the rest; and I add the location in Migne's Latin or Greek series: ML or MG, preceded by volume number and followed by column number.

Two kinds of reference call for separate treatment, those to ecclesiastical documents and those to Aquinas.

References to ecclesiastical documents

The official source for documents from Rome is the *Acta Apostolicae Sedis* or '*Acta*', which continues the *Acta Sanctae Sedis* begun in the pontificate of Pius IX. Whenever possible, I have translated texts from this and given references by volume and page number. A standard anthology of ecclesiastical documents is Denzinger and Schönmetzer 1963 (DS) which replaced Denzinger and Umberg, itself the last of a long line of new editions of a work going back to the last century. DS is very helpful, but it needs to be used with caution. The critical accuracy and the arrangement of the texts printed are much superior to what went before, but the editors, while inserting some items not previously present, have tactfully removed other items that now embarrass – I notice one in the text.

The *Acta* classifies the documents it prints according to their source, whether the pope or this or that 'Congregation' – 'Ministry' more or less – in the Roman curia (civil service). It also classifies them according to their status, and there is often a time-lag between a document's date and its printing in the *Acta*. Matters are further complicated by the fact that there was a re-ordering of the curia some years ago in which various congregations were re-named. I have given some appropriate cross-references. One re-naming was of something already re-named. 'The Congregation for the Doctrine of the Faith' is what used to be 'The Holy Office', and 'The Holy Office' is what used to be 'The Roman Inquisition'. I am reminded of what an aged economist said to my brother Desmond about J. M. Keynes: 'very brilliant man of course...funny sort of chap, though – always changing his address'. And I have left it as 'The Roman Inquisition'.

I give reference by name of pope or of congregation, together with year of printing. References to councils are under their place of meeting. Many papal documents have been given English translations published by the Catholic Truth Society, and where I knew such a translation to exist, I added '(C)' to the item in the References. There are of course other translations accessible. The *Acta* prefixes descriptions – usually ponderous and sometimes misleading – to the documents it prints, and the documents are or were often referred to by the opening words of the (usually Latin) original. I have in some cases given these words; in all cases I have inserted in square brackets a standardised description of date, topic, language (if other than Latin) and place of issue or delivery (if other than Rome).

The decrees of the Second Vatican Council appeared in the *Acta* (its proceedings are also published, but they do not concern us here). Translations of the decrees were again published by the Catholic Truth Society, and there are two collections that deserve separate mention. Abbott and Gallagher (1967) gives the decrees and other material, each decree preceded by an introduction, and then followed by a response from someone not a Roman Catholic. Flannery (1975) is wider-ranging. It gives the decrees, but also post-conciliar documents connected with them. It has gone to sources other than the *Acta* for some of these, and in an appendix gives references to yet more documentation. This admirable book is a mine of information and an excellent guide to material. Its one defect is a preface by somebody signing himself 'John Cardinal Wright', who takes occasion to comment unfavourably upon earlier translations, and upon the salutary arrangement – found in Abbott and Gallagher – of having conciliar documents followed by comment from an outsider. For him, the book he introduces 'is *the* collection of Council documents and their authentic interpretation'. The pompous silliness of all this is well matched by its hermeneutical stupidity. I add 'AG' and/or 'F' to items in the References, whenever a translation may be found in one or both of these two helpful collections.

I have naturally cited the service-books of the Roman Church. Although these exist in many editions, their arrangement is standard and references may be followed up without difficulty.

References to Aquinas

Most references to Aquinas are to his *Summa Theologiae*. This work of his maturity – begun it would seem because he was dissatisfied with available manuals – is divided into three parts. The first treats of God and creation. The second treats of human acts and of the good and evil in them (with general principles laid down in the first division of the part, and their applications in the second). The third part – which principally concerns us – treats of the redemptive work of Christ, and of the sacraments. Each part is divided into questions, and each question into articles. Each article begins by asking whether a given proposition is true; gives objections against its truth; gives reasons for its truth; and concludes by giving responses to the objections. This structure makes references easy to give. '*ST* 3.75.4' is '*Summa Theologiae*, part 3, question 75, article 4'; '*ST* 1/2.13.2 ad 3' is '*Summa Theologiae*, first division of the second part, question 13, article 2, response to objection 3'. And so on. Aquinas also composed *Quaestiones Disputatae*, in which arguments for and against a given opinion are surveyed, a general solution offered, and the conflicting opinions assessed (for more information, sources like van Steenberghen 1966 and Knowles 1962 can be consulted). The arrangement here, by question and article, is that followed in the *Summa Theologiae*.

Matters are more difficult in an early work of Aquinas, his Commentary on the *Sentences* of Peter the Lombard. We must not lose sight of the fact that the Commentary on the *Sentences* is an early work, and it would be an interesting exercise to compare its treatment of eucharistic questions with that given them in the *Summa Theologiae*. The later work is immeasurably more impressive, in the 'architectonic' of its composition and in the economy with which it deals with its topics. But the earlier Commentary does have an interest of its own – and, I shall be suggesting, does have the advantage in one place over the *Summa*.

Some information about the nature of the earlier work may be useful, and some information about the way of interpreting references to it will be more than useful. Peter the Lombard ($+c.$ 1160) composed the *Sentences* at Paris about 1150, a skeletal work of theology, where texts from the fathers were accompanied by a meagre commentary. It became the custom to write 'Commentaries' on Peter's *Sentences*, where the writer would in fact simply use Peter's divisions in order to set out his own opinions. The custom lasted into the sixteenth century, giving the original a curious 'Nachleben by proxy'.

Reference to the Commentary of Aquinas on the *Sentences* is complicated, and can best he explained by the imaginary example 'In 4 *Sent.*, dist 1, q. 2, art. 3, qu.la 5, obj. 6 and ad 6; 789/101, 793/124'. This means: go to his Commentary on the fourth book of the *Sentences*, and to the first of the 'distinctions' into which Peter divided each book. Inside this distinction, go to the second question which Aquinas puts, and inside that to the third Article into which the question is divided. Inside that, go to the fifth quaestiuncula ('mini-question'), and inside *that* to the sixth of the objections Aquinas raises, and to the reply he offers. All that is bad enough, worse is to follow. Not all the distinctions divide into questions; not all the articles divide into quaestiunculae; and (particularly foxing) all the quaestiunculae of an Article with their objections are printed first, only then come the responses Aquinas offers. All the more welcome then is the edition by Moos of the third and fourth books of Aquinas' work, in which everything under a given distinction is divided into continuously numbered paragraphs (the first and second books, with another editor, unfortunately lack this help). In the imaginary reference, the two numerals divided by a solidus give the page and the paragraph on it where the texts begin.

I use also the commentary of Aquinas on the *Metaphysics* of Aristotle. Each book of Aristotle's work is divided by Aquinas into *lectiones*, or passages for comment, and then each *lectio* is expounded. Reference is therefore by book and lectio (notice, not by chapter). The much-used edition by Cathalà (Aquinas 1935) divides the · Commentary into numbered paragraphs; I add the number to all references I give.

CHAPTER I

Against transubstantiation

I THE DECLARATION AND THE DECREE

'The Spanish Armada, the Battle of Waterloo, and the doctrine of Transubstantiation': such were the three topics of conversation favoured by Ruskin when, as an awkward and inexperienced youth, he was thrown into the society of an elegant, convent-bred young lady from France. In choosing at least the third theme he was in good company. For over more than two hundred years, every English sovereign had to profess his belief that 'in the sacrament of the Lord's Supper there is not any transubstantiation of the elements of bread and wine into the body and blood of Christ at or after the consecration thereof by any person whatsoever.' To those who wished to safeguard the Protestant succession to the throne, there seemed to be no more distinctively popish a doctrine for the monarch to repudiate in the presence of his first Parliament.[1] If times be thought to have changed, one sign of the change would be found in the 'Final Report' of a commission of Anglican and Roman Catholic theologians published in 1982. In the part of this devoted to eucharistic belief (first produced in 1971), 'substantial agreement' is claimed, and the word 'transubstantiation' is relegated to a footnote, where we are told that in contemporary (presumably this means 'recent') Catholic theology the word is not understood as explaining

---

[1] For Ruskin here, see his *Praeterita* I.x.207 (Ruskin 1983: 170). An account of the Royal Declaration is in Williams (1967), and the story of its eventual replacement is in the thirty-fifth chapter of G. Bell (1938). This is the biography of Randall Davidson, who as Archbishop of Canterbury was involved with the modification (the monarch now declares himself 'a faithful Protestant'). As I read Bell's account, the Declaration caused annoyance among Catholics, not only by its denial of their beliefs, but by its elaborate verbal safeguards. Their presence exhibited the presupposition that Romanists are allowed by the rules of their persuasion to equivocate when using plain language on solemn occasions, and to go back on their sworn word if given papal permission. I hope that this book will in places throw light on the justice of this presupposition.

I

how the eucharistic change takes place (ARCIC 1982: 16, 14). And yet perhaps times have not changed so much after all. Reservations about the report were expressed in a letter from no less than the Roman Inquisition (its latest change of name is into 'Congregation for the Doctrine of the Faith'). One reservation touches some expressions in the report, 'especially some of those which attempt to express the realisation of this [real] presence'. They do not, the letter claims, 'seem to indicate adequately what the Church understands by "transubstantiation"' (Inquisition 1982: 1066).[2] And the letter goes on to explain what is understood there by the word, by citing the account given in the decree of the Council of Trent on the Eucharist. Which was, of course, a notorious origin of the association of transubstantiation with the old religion, and of its denial with the reformed. So let us start by seeing something of the decree.

The passage to which the Inquisition refers is found in the council's decree on the Eucharist, promulgated on 11 October 1551. There will of course be more to say of Trent later on, but I set down here for convenient reference the general course of the specific claims made by the part of the decree concerning transubstantiation. The decree was cast into the form of 'Canons', condemnations of propositions judged to be heretical, and the canons were preceded by 'chapters', in which true belief was given a positive expression. The first of the canons here condemns any who deny the true, real and substantial presence of the whole Christ in the Eucharist, or who would reduce it to no more than a presence in terms of sign or figure or power (DS 1651). Then follows the canon on transubstantiation:

If anyone should say that, in the most holy sacrament of the Eucharist, there remains the substance of the bread and wine together with the body and blood of our Lord Jesus Christ, and should deny that wondrous and unique conversion of the whole substance of the bread into the body, and of the whole substance of the wine into the blood, with only the appearances of the bread and wine remaining, a change which the Catholic Church most fittingly (*aptissime*) calls transubstantiation – let him be anathema. (DS 1652)

---

[2] There appeared in December 1991 yet another statement from Rome, declining to accept that substantial agreement has been reached beween Anglicans and Roman Catholics – not only in eucharistic matters, but in others. I have not investigated this document; for my purpose, what I have cited will prove amply sufficient.

The fourth of the chapters goes with this canon, and it runs thus:

Because Christ our redeemer said that what he offered under the appearance of bread was truly his body [see Matt. xxvi 26f.; Mark xiv 22f.; Luke xxii 19f.; 1 Cor. xi 24f.], it has always been believed in the Church of God, and this holy Council now declares it again: – that by the consecration of the bread and wine there is effected the conversion of the whole substance of the bread into the substance of the body of Christ our Lord, and of the whole substance of the wine into the substance of his blood. This conversion has been suitably and properly [*convenienter et proprie*] called transubstantiation by the holy Catholic Church. (DS 1642)

So much for the texts of the canon and the chapter. I offer some preliminary observations. We can notice first that the Council allots to belief in transubstantiation a canon and a chapter to itself, over and above what was allotted to belief in the real, true and substantial presence of Christ asserted in the first canon and chapter. What more is involved can be seen in the greater elaboration of the terminology: we have 'substance', 'conversion of the whole substance', and 'the appearance alone remaining'. But we can now notice something about this more elaborate terminology – its resemblance to what Aquinas writes of transubstantiation in his *Summa Theologiae*:

The whole substance of the bread is converted into the whole substance of the body of Christ, and the whole substance of the wine is converted into the whole substance of the blood of Christ. Consequently, this conversion is not formal but substantial. Nor does it fall under any of the kinds of natural change, but can be given its own name of transubstantiation. (*ST* 3.75.4)

Here the terminology is richer still, with 'formal' and 'substantial' distinguished from each other, and the latter linked with transubstantiation in its apartness from all natural change. But the resemblance is still worthy of note, and it becomes still more worthy when we consider the place which Aquinas then held in theological speculation in the Church of Rome, and which until recently he held in the training of the clergy there. The history and interpretation of the expressions used at Trent, like the place of Aquinas in theology, will turn out to harbour unsuspected complications. But the presence of terms common to his account and to the council's decree demands that we examine what he makes of the terms and how he uses them in the account he offers. To examine Aquinas' account will give some background to the formulation used by the Council, and some idea of the theological reflexion on the Eucharist there has been in the Church of Rome. I go for the account to the *Summa Theologiae*, reminding the reader that I cite it, and other works by Aquinas, according to the conventions explained at pp. xxi–xxiii where I also say something of the general form into which Aquinas casts what he writes.

Aquinas devoted eleven questions to the Eucharist in the third part of his *Summa Theologiae*. That part (left unfinished by him at his death in 1274) deals with the Incarnation, the life of Christ, and the sacraments by which that life is shared with us. After two questions on the Eucharist in general and on the material for it (73, 74), four consider the eucharistic conversion: the conversion itself (75); Christ's manner of existence in the Eucharist (76); the accidents or appearances of the elements after the consecration (77); and the formula to be used in the eucharistic celebration (78). From the conversion, the questions pass to the consequences and setting of the conversion: the effects of the sacrament upon recipients (79); the right use of it (80), and the first use of it at the Last Supper (81); the minister of the Eucharist (82). A final question examines the whole eucharistic rite as practised in the Church, and here Aquinas also asks whether Christ can be said to be immolated in the Eucharist (83). The last five among these questions, touching the institution, the use and the sacrificial character of the Eucharist, I shall consider later on. It is the questions to do with the eucharistic conversion that we must start to examine here and now.

But as soon as we go to the first of them, question 75, we find that we need to travel still further afield. We saw that the passage I cited from it sets transubstantiation apart from all natural changes. Earlier in the same question Aquinas states where the distinction lies – natural changes touch the *form* of things, transubstantiation touches the *whole reality (totius entis)* of what is converted. So we must first see what Aquinas makes of natural changes in the terminology he uses, for only in this way shall we be able to see what he has in mind when he insists upon the 'apartness' of transubstantiation. And to his account of natural change we turn in the next section.

2 AQUINAS' ACCOUNT OF NATURAL CHANGE

Aquinas wrote as he did within the part of medieval tradition that welcomed and built upon Aristotle's speculations, which had become known in the West since the whole *corpus* of his writings and the commentaries on them began to be translated towards the end of the twelfth century.[3] I go to the Commentary of Aquinas on Aristotle's *Metaphysics* for texts in which the account of change can be found. The fidelity of Aquinas as a commentator does not concern us here, and there are other texts to which I might have gone, but the Commentary by its nature abstains from the theological applications we shall be meeting in the next section. Moreover, what we meet in the Commentary touches something that is going to be one of the preoccupations of this book. Aquinas, like the author on whom he is commenting, is writing about change, but the concerns and the limitations of what he writes stand apart from what we ourselves would ask on the subject. Not wholly apart, of course; but the gap between past and present is real, and coming to appreciate it will be an important part of what this chapter can help us to see.

Aquinas follows Aristotle in finding it easiest to discuss change in terms of the fashioning of an artefact, and the working of bronze into a statue or ball is an example (VII 2; 1277. VII 7; 1418). I will take something more manageable and suppose that I have a cube of plasticine in my hand. If I rotate it gently between my palms, I shall get what the geography primers used to call an oblate spheroid – a ball flattened at the poles. For Aquinas, we are to distinguish in such examples between the subject of the change and the two extremes of it (VIII 1; 1688): that is to say, we began with one shape and ended with another, but we still have the kind of stuff with which we started, namely plasticine. The plasticine is the *matter* or *subject* of the change, while the shapes are the successive *forms* of the matter (VII 2; 1277). I notice at once a limitation in this account: it does not furnish the very kind of information we ourselves like, namely *how* the change takes place – why for instance reversing the direction in which I revolve the palms of my hands will not restore to the plasticine its original shape. But I also notice an implicit danger in the account: it

---

[3] For the advent of Aristotle's works in the West, and for the different responses to them, van Steenberghen 1966 is a detailed and masterly account – his earlier work of 1955 gives a usefully brief survey of a complicated topic. Knowles 1962 is a helpful presentation of the 'academic machinery' of medieval thought – what it inherited from the past, how universities worked and so on. The tone of the book is at times tediously pious, but readers should persevere. Those who would like to go to Aristotle for themselves will find close translations of parts of his *Physics* and *Metaphysics* in the 'Clarendon Aristotle' series, with commentaries on the translation. Ackrill 1981 is a lucid introduction to Aristotle's thought, and gives further references. Aquinas had no Greek, and used a translation by William Moerbeke, who rendered the Greek into Latin word for word, to so odd an effect that learning Greek seems a minor chore compared with deciphering so hermetic a crib. It is a tribute to the power of Aquinas that he was able to achieve what he did in this commentary.

may tempt us to make *things* out of matter and form, to *reify* them. We might, for example, fall into asking what shape the plasticine was all the time; answer that it was no particular shape all the time; and conclude that the plasticine in itself inhabits some topological limbo, and is given a shape only by the forms that successively characterise it, rather as a piece of stuff might be given different colours by the successive application of different dyes.

Aquinas, like Aristotle, was aware of the dangers in reification, as is easily seen from his insistence that what changes, what comes to be such or such, is 'the composite', the object composed of matter and form, and that neither the matter nor the form can be so spoken of (VII 7; 1419–21, 1431). The whole context of those paragraphs elaborates the point. Replacing the work of Aristotle's coppersmith with my moulding the plasticine, we must say that I make a ball out of plasticine, not that I make the plasticine or that I make its shape. That I do not make the plasticine is obvious – what I achieve by rotating my palms presupposes that there is something for them to work on (1419). But neither do I make the form – I make the plasticine be of such a form. The distinction between matter and form is drawn as part of construing all change in terms of matter that is first of all of one form and then of another form; so if I now make the *form* change as well, I must make the same distinction there, and have a matter and form of the form itself; and so shall be involved in an infinite regress (1420).[4]

Let us supplement this account by seeing (still in the same *lectio* of the Commentary) two errors that Aquinas points to as consequences of confusion here. We have seen him insist that forms do not change or come into being, but that it is the composite, the individual object,

---

[4] This is a suitable point at which to remind ourselves that Aristotle's vocabulary here – where *hylé* is 'matter' and *eidos* or *morphé* is 'form' – was given a Latin dress by writers like Lucretius and Cicero into *materia* and *forma*, from which our own words are derived. 'Materia' has the associations of 'wood' that *hylé* has; 'form' echoes as *eidos* does the Platonic vocabulary. If we find the use of 'wood' here eccentric, we must bear in mind that every language needs a word to indicate in a non-specific way that of which something is composed, be it an artefact or a living being, and that the notion of composition here can be extended from objects to things like discussions or pieces of writing. Just so, a word doing that job will be naturally complemented by another type of word. This other word will record the distinction between one object and another when the ingredients are the same – will distinguish our ball of plasticine from the cube with which we started, or distinguish words arranged in one way from the same words arranged in another. 'Matter' and 'form' are only one such pair; 'stuff' was used in the main text, but 'stuff' is no less odd in its origin than 'matter' – it is simply the Italian *stoffa*, 'cloth'. We need such pieces of verbal *passe-partout*, and Aristotle's creations have long outlasted their original setting.

which comes to be of such a form. Suppose we reject his warning, and want the forms themselves to come into existence. If so, we must give them an origin. So either there will have to be a special creation of them (God creates the roundness just as I stop rotating my palms); or the forms will in some way have to pre-exist or lurk in the matter – the various shapes of the plasticine are in some fashion tucked away in it (1430). Aristotle excludes both these errors, says Aquinas, by making the composite, not the form, come to be. The forms are not themselves caused by some external source, nor do they pre-exist in the matter. They are potentially there, and they are brought out from the potentiality of the matter – that is, the matter was originally only *potentially* of such or such a form, and is now *actually* of that form (1431, 1423).

We noted earlier that talking in terms of matter and form did not explain *how* the change takes place. We must now note the same limitation in these warnings against saying that the forms themselves come to be. If we follow Aquinas and exclude 'Where does the shape come from?' as an improper question, we are not thereby prohibited from asking in mechanics why an unladen clothes-line assumes the shape we call a catenary, or indeed why I end with an oblate spheroid of plasticine rather than with a sphere. The exclusion is a matter of logic and language: express change in terms of matter and form, and you cannot consistently make those in their turn change in the same way. You can, of course, say things like 'the shape (form, if you prefer) has changed'; but this is only a paraphrase (by synecdoche, I suppose) of saying that the plasticine was cubic and is now spherical. The oddness of the accounts rejected by Aquinas – the special creation of forms, or their lurkingness (*latitatio*) – come from *reifying* forms and then asking of them the questions asked of the plasticine. Just so, we avoid these odd accounts, not by suggesting some third origin for the form (as we might suggest another origin for some natural phenomenon), but by rejecting reification, and so the vocabulary of 'origin', altogether. We saw in the preceding paragraph how Aquinas writes that forms are 'brought out from the potentiality of the matter' (1423). But when he does so, he is not offering yet another starting-point for them – and he shews he is not, by at once elucidating the phrase he has used: 'in as much as the matter, which was potentially of such a form, becomes actually of it; and this is to make the composite'. We are, in other words, being sent back to our plasticine and to our manipulation of it; we are forbidden

to treat its successive shapes as if they were independent things; we
are forbidden to pass from admitting the capacity of the cube to be
moulded into a ball to believing that the spherical shape is in some
fashion already inside the cube. The error may seem too recondite to
need attacking, and indeed is of an age other than ours. However,
readers acquainted with wilder flights of fancy in recent speculations
over 'possible worlds' may feel that the warning is not wholly out of
date even now.

I have spelt out laboriously something (only something) of how
Aquinas introduces the terms Matter and Form. The labour has been
necessary, because there is another setting for their use, and to this we
must now turn.

The account so far has been concerned with changes of a limited
sort, changes where we end up with the same kind of stuff as that with
which we began. Not all changes are so limited, some are more
profound. What if we burn the plasticine? Presumably we end up
with something charred and unpleasant – let us call it 'residue'.
What are we to say if we want to apply to this more profound change
the distinction between matter and form, in terms of which was
expressed the moulding of the cube of plasticine into a sphere? The
application will at all events have to be cautious, because the dangers
of misunderstanding are so much greater. 'What shape is the
plasticine all the time?' we rejected as a badly put question, but there
was at least something identifiable for the question to be wrong
about. 'What is it that is first plasticine and then residue?' has not
even that much. (If we prefer a culinary example, we can consider a
carafe of wine that has turned to vinegar and ask what was in the
carafe all the time.) But there is now yet another danger, if we still
decide to say of the new change that matter is qualified first by one
form (that of plasticine) and then by another (that of residue). Logic
teaches us to beware of confusing the order of words like 'some' and
'every', it warns us against passing from 'every journey has *an end*' to
'there is *one end* to all our journeyings'. Such confusion of order can
entrap us here. Our present claim is that, in every change of the
profounder sort, matter is qualified first by one form (such as that of
plasticine, or of wine) and then by another (such as that of residue or
of vinegar). This claim is no more than our decision to extend the
distinction between matter and form, first drawn about moulding the
plasticine, to profounder changes like burning it. But it is all too easy
to rearrange the order of words, and so slip from this claim into

another and much stronger claim: that there is *one matter* which, in every change of the profounder sort, is qualified first by one form (such as that of plasticine or of wine) and then by another (such as that of residue or of vinegar). And once we do *that*, we are claiming that there is some indefinitely adaptable substratum that can be plasticine, residue, wine or vinegar. And whatever we make of such a claim, it goes much further than the distinction we originally drew between form and matter.

I have already prescinded from estimating the fidelity of Aquinas as a commentator on Aristotle. I now prescind further from deciding how far Aquinas, let alone Aristotle, was affected by these confusions. It is enough for my purpose to notice that he does accept what I have just called 'one matter'. He calls it *materia prima* – 'prime matter' – and its place in his account of change must now be stated.

He holds that the way to understanding it lies through what, following Aristotle, he calls generation and corruption. We have just seen an example in the burning of the plasticine. Generation and corruption are the sort of change in which what we end with is a different *kind of thing* from what we started with, changes that are in *substance* (VIII 1; 1688–9). 'Substance' can mean either an individual object or the nature of something (x 3; 1979). The latter answers the question 'What is this?', and that question cannot be answered by naming properties that the object happens to have. You may be educated, but 'educated' is not an answer to such a question; the question calls for a reply that states what you are *as such* – a human being, an animal, and the rest (VII 3; 1309–10). And it is to change touching the 'What is it?' of things – substantial change – that Aquinas, in his talk of *materia prima*, extends the distinction between matter and form. The distinction embodies the principle already laid down: that in all changes there is a subject common to the two extremes, which is qualified first by one and then by the other. The principle which was applied in the first place to *accidental* change, where 'accident' lacks the associations of fortuitousness or calamity, and simply means an attribute that something can have. Accidental changes include change in place and growth as well as alteration, and in each of these a subject is first such and then such. Aquinas, we have seen, extends the principle to *substantial* change, where we end with a different kind of thing from that with which we began: here too there must be a subject common to the two extremes. This common subject, this matter, is *prime* matter, and the nature of substantial

changes shews that prime matter must be *purely potential*. That is to
say, prime matter must have no form of its own, distinct from the
forms which characterise the origin and the terminus of a substantial
change (such as the burning of the plasticine). Because if prime
matter did have such a form of its own, it would be 'something in its
own right', independently of the end-points of the change. And if this
were so, the change would no longer be substantial, no longer be a
change that begins with one kind of thing and ends with another. All
we should have would be an 'independent' prime matter, having first
one form and then another (VIII 1; 1688–9) – just as our plasticine
was, while still remaining plasticine, first cubic and then spherical.

It is no part of my concern at this point to ask whether the
extension to substantial change of the distinction between matter and
form is worth the complications it brings with it. What counts for us
is the extension itself, and the claim by Aquinas that it is substantial
change that provides the way of understanding the rôle of prime
matter. There is more to say about the terms in which Aquinas talks
about change. But this much will do for the present, and we can turn
to the eucharistic employment of the terms.

3   HIS ACCOUNT APPLIED TO THE EUCHARIST

An account of change in terms of a matter or subject that is
successively qualified by different forms; the account illustrated by
an analogy drawn from the making of an artefact; the analogy
extended to changes of a more profound sort, and so the introduction
of prime matter: all this we have seen in what Aquinas writes about
natural changes, and we have also seen how, following Aristotle, he
persistently warns against reifying the distinctions drawn, warns
against treating matter and form as so many things. Let us keep that
much in mind as we move to the use made in eucharistic theology of
this broadly Aristotelian speculation.

I write 'broadly Aristotelian', not only because I believe the
description justified, but because it can serve to place my general
contention about what Aquinas writes here and to enable us to keep
a sense of proportion. There is no question (how could there be?) of
Aquinas (or of anyone else) finding adequate expression for a mystery
of the Christian religion in the speculations of a Greek philosopher
who had been dead three centuries when Christ was born. Still less is
it my intention to blame (how could I blame?) the speculations of

that philosopher for being inadequate here. At the same time, the phrase can keep the general drift of this section apart from what others have written about transubstantiation. My thesis here is not going to be that Aquinas gives a formulation of eucharistic belief in Aristotelian terms, a formulation which might be regarded now as outmoded. Some theologians do indeed say this, as we shall see in due course, but that is not what I say myself. For me, transubstantiation is a eucharistic application of Aristotelian terms which abuses them to the point of nonsense – it is 'Aristotelian' only in the sense that forged money is 'money'. I begin my submissions by shewing how Aquinas sets about revealing the unique character of transubstantiation.

For him, the body of Christ becomes present by the substance of the bread's being converted into it.[5] The conversion he considers in *ST* 3.75.4, the article I cited to shew the resemblance between what he wrote and what Trent decreed. I now print most of the article, inserting paragraph-letters:

(a) This conversion is unlike any natural conversion; it is wholly supernatural, and brought about by the power of God... [some texts of the fathers]

(b) Whatever acts, obviously does so to the extent that it is itself an act. Any created agent, being of a determinate kind, is determinate in its act; and so its action ends in some determinate act.

(c) But the determination of anything in its actual existence is through its form. So no natural or created agent can act except for the changing of a form...

(d) But God is Infinite Act... and so his action extends to the whole nature of that which is.

---

[5] Aquinas used 'conversion' (*conversio*) and cognate words about the Eucharist, not 'change' (*mutatio*). At the same time, *conversio* is used to cover both the Eucharist and natural changes, nor does Aquinas deny that *conversio* is 'a certain change' (*quaedam mutatio*; *ST* 3.75.4; and obj. 1 and ad 1). I add two things before going any further. The first is that readers who would like to see a 'standard' account of what Aquinas makes of the eucharistic conversion will find one in Aquinas (1965). This is one of the volumes in the 'Blackfriars' edition of the *Summa Theologiae*, where the original Latin is given with an English translation *en regard*, and where notes and appendices provide useful guidance. The second thing I add concerns the presence of *qualifications* in the language Aquinas uses. *Quoddam, quasi, aliquomodo* – 'a kind of', 'as it were', 'to some extent' – are only a few among many, and they can easily be missed. The elevation by Rome of Aquinas into an oracle made them be missed all too often. Times have changed, and a computer-assisted concordance has been made to his works: someone should set about examining these phrases.

(e) And so, not only can he effect a formal conversion – that is, bring it about that different forms succeed one another in same subject; he can also effect the conversion of the whole reality – that is, so that the whole substance of *this* is converted into the whole substance of *that*.

(f) Which is what happens by divine power in this sacrament. The whole substance of bread is converted into the whole substance of Christ's body, and the whole substance of wine is converted into the whole substance of his blood. That is why this conversion is not formal but substantial. It does not fall under any kind of natural change, but can be called by its own name of transubstantiation. (*ST* 3.75.4)

To this translation I now add a brief preliminary comment on each part.

In (a) there is yet again the assertion that we have here something unique. In (b), the expression of natural change found in the preceding section is briefly stated. Things are seen as determinations of matter by form, and the activity of things is seen as a piece with their form – bread nourishes us because of its form, but does not have the magnetic properties that come from the form of iron; just as iron's form, while making it magnetic, does not make it nutritive. (c) draws the conclusion that, since determination comes from form, natural change is concerned with forms – as we have seen, the form may be accidental (moulding gives the plasticine a new shape) or substantial (burning turns the plasticine into residue). We pass in (d) to the infinite power of God, who is not limited to the pattern of change in which a pre-existent matter is 'informed' in a new way. (e) spells out what divine power can do – effect the conversion of one whole substance, matter and form, into another whole substance. And (f) applies this to the Eucharist, and says that the conversion there 'can be called' (the phrase is worth noticing) 'transubstantiation'.

I offer a first ration of objections to all this; not for the last time, it will be Aquinas himself who provides me with a starting-point for the difficulties I raise. He makes an objection in the same Article:

Conversion is a kind of change. But in every change there must be a subject which is first potentially and then actually [this or that]... So it cannot be that the whole substance of bread is converted into the body of Christ – a substance is by definition not in any further subject. (*ST* 3.75.4 obj. 1)

The reply Aquinas offers reiterates that transubstantiation does not have a subject, unlike changes that touch the form. Obviously this is an answer that only refuses the objection, it does not solve it. But this is not surprising, for Aquinas has gone in his objection here to the heart of the problem. The apparatus of terms and distinctions we saw him use in the preceding section amounts to conceiving change as the qualifying of a subject or matter by successive forms. Think as we please of the apparatus, that is what it rests on; there is simply no sense in taking its terms and then combining them in a way which denies what is their foundation. To make this objection is in no sense to object to the mystery in the Eucharist. My objection here – and repeatedly as the book goes on – is directed rather against conundrums of our own making. It insists that a set of words used systematically cannot be combined without more ado in a way that contradicts the system, as if the words had semantic luggage-labels on them indicating their new destination. They can be juxtaposed, of course; but the combination is no more guaranteed sense than is talk about the floor of the bottomless pit.

What gives an appearance of sense to the new combination here – gives it an appearance of indicating the unique conversion called 'transubstantiation' – is its disregard of the warnings given against *reification*, against making *things* out of matter and form. We can notice that Aquinas is even more scrupulous about reification in his commentary on the *Metaphysics* than was Aristotle in what he wrote. He writes, in a *lectio* we have already met:

Although the text [of Aristotle] has 'the form comes to be in the matter', the phrase is not correct. What comes to be is not the form but the compound. Just as the form is said 'to be in the matter', even though it is not the form that exists, but the compound through the form. The proper way of putting it is to say 'the compound comes to be from the matter into such or such a form' (VII 7; 1423)

It is ominous that already in the text from the *Summa* I have printed, Aquinas is shewing less care in his language. Paragraph (c) there has 'the changing of a form'; (e) describes natural change as bringing it about that 'different forms succeed one another in the same subject'. In a later Article of Question 75, Aquinas rejects the suggestion that the substantial form of the bread remains after transubstantiation, and one ground is that were this so, 'only the matter of the bread would be converted into the body of Christ' (*ST* 3.75.6) – and now matter has become something that can itself change, instead of being the result of a distinction drawn in the first place about changing things, and so excluded from having change predicated of it. Nor are we better served in the eighth Article, where we are told that 'in natural change, the matter of one thing *lays aside* the form of that thing and *receives* the form of another' (*ST* 3.75.8).

These are not simply verbal infelicities. They are symptoms of the reification that is taking place, and of the transformation of distinctions into dissections. The process turns form, matter, substance and accident into so many *constituents* of objects, and turns the whole question into one of *power*. This or that constituent can remain while others do not; human power is confined to some; divine omnipotence can replace or interchange them at will. When power is put at the centre of things, all the oddities in the phrases we have met fall into place: power is exercised upon these constituents, and the infelicities I have noticed become occasions for its exercise. Aquinas is prepared even to institute comparisons between transubstantiation, natural change and creation. Transubstantiation is said to resemble creation in having no subject common to its two extremes; it is said to resemble natural change in that what was there first passes into (*transit in*) what is there afterwards; and indeed also to resemble natural change in that in both something remains the same – in natural change the matter or subject, in transubstantiation the accidents (*ST* 3.75.8). And (naturally enough, once he has gone so far with reification) Aquinas asks in the same Article which is the more *difficult*, creation or transubstantiation (*ST* 3.75.8 ad 3 – for the record, the latter). We are invited in all this to think in terms of constituents or components, and of the divine power which alone can manipulate them.

Now it is not that appeals to divine power are wrong – any religious reflexion is conducted within the context of that power – the trouble comes from making the appeal a substitute for raising questions of intelligibility. When not under theological pressure, Aquinas writes with great lucidity on omnipotence, and effectively analyses in the *De Potentia* the hoary question as to whether God can make things like square circles. I give extracts:

What is said to be impossible in itself is so called because the terms will not hold together (*discohaerentia terminorum*): any such impossibility involves the simultaneous affirmation and denial of something... So God cannot make an affirmation and negation simultaneously true... not because of a lack in his power, but because of a lack of something possible. (*De Potentia* 1, 3)

(Or, as we might put it within another tradition, the 'impossibility' here is the impossibility of judging a nonsense). The eucharistic employment of terminology drawn from natural change suffers, I have submitted, from *discohaerentia terminorum* – suffers indeed in the very way Aquinas describes here, because it simultaneously affirms and denies what the terminology amounts to. No appeal to omnipotence can by-pass the question as to whether what God is being asked to do makes sense in the first place.

We shall be meeting consequences of the *discohaerentia*, enough and to spare of them. For the moment, I give two examples of it: the mode of Christ's presence, and the survival of the accidents of the bread when its substance has gone. Concerning the former, Aquinas writes:

Christ is present by way of substance (*per modum substantiae*), which is the way in which substance is under its dimensions; he is not present by way of dimensions (*per modum dimensionum*), which is the way in which the dimensive quantity of a body is under the dimensive quantity of a place. (*ST* 3.76.3)

Let us pass the double use of 'under' – one for the placing of a thing, one for the relationship between a thing's substance and its dimensions (reification again!) – and appreciate the general drive of what Aquinas is saying, leaving details for a later chapter. He wants to exclude the *commensurability* of Christ with the dimensions of the host, and so laudably sets himself against grotesques which eucharistic belief has at times thrown up (and which we shall be encountering). But the presence *per modum substantiae* is made to do more, it is made to account for the fact that, however many hosts there may be, the one Christ is present in each; that he is present as much in a small portion as in a large; and that, even before a host is broken, the whole of Christ is in each part. For this purpose, he continues,

It is obvious that the whole nature of a substance is in [literally 'under'] any part of the dimensions containing that substance; that in any portion of air the whole nature of air is contained, and that in any portion of bread the whole nature of bread is contained. It makes no difference whether the dimensions are actually cut – as when air is divided or bread sliced – or whether they are actually undivided, but potentially divisible. (*ST* 3.76.3)

The argument, unfortunately, will not work as Aquinas wants it to. True enough, a slice of bread is as truly bread as a whole loaf, and slicing up a loaf does not touch its substantial nature, does not stop it being bread. But 'being bread' is not a predicate like 'being Christ' or 'being Aquinas'; Christ and Aquinas are determinate individuals, not kinds of thing. And so the proper equivalent in the argument ought to be 'being *this slice of bread*'. But then, of course, the argument collapses: nothing else can be as much this slice of bread as this slice of bread is, the project does not make sense.[6]

As for the *discohaerentia* I detect in the survival of the accidents when the substance has gone, Aquinas himself can once again provide the starting-point for my objection. He devotes question 77 to the accidents, and in its first Article he states forcefully the objection that there cannot intelligibly be talk of accidents that survive the subject (*ST* 3.77.1 obj. 2) – that is, whiteness when there is nothing white, roundness when there is nothing round, and so on. He makes the objection thus:

Not even by a miracle can the definition of something be separated from it, or the definition of something else apply to it – a man cannot, while remaining a man, be an irrational animal: the consequences of that would be that contradictories were simultaneously the case...But the definition of an accident involves existing in a subject; and the definition of a substance involves existing in itself and not in a subject. So it cannot miraculously be the case that there be in this sacrament accidents without a subject. (*ST* 3.77.1 obj. 2)

The objection, notice, specifically goes beyond appeals to divine power, goes to the intelligibility of that power's exercise. How does Aquinas answer this objection he has himself raised?

Being (*Ens*) is not a genus; and so existence as such (*hoc ipsum quod est esse*) cannot be [part of] the essence of a substance or of an accident. So the definition of a substance is not 'something existing in itself without a subject'

---

[6] Some readers will already have been drawing distinctions here between mass-nouns and count-nouns ('bread'/'slice'), and this note is primarily for them. My 'the whole nature of air' translates *tota natura aeris*, and the use by Aquinas in these questions of examples involving air makes the rendering acceptable. But a similar passage in a previous Article may give us pause. Claiming there that the whole Christ is present in the Sacrament, he puts the objection that Christ's body is much larger than the host; and his answer is similar to what we have just met. But see how he goes on: 'The specific totality of a substance is contained indifferently in a small or large quantity – such as the whole nature of air in much or little air, and the whole nature of man in a big or little man' (*ST* 3.76.1 ad 3). 'Much or little air' here translates *magno vel parvo aere*, where *magno* should be 'big' or 'large' rather than 'much'. Now *aere* and *aeris* are cases of the noun *aer* ('air') that it has in common with the noun *aes* ('copper' or 'bronze' or 'coin'); see how the English 'copper' has the same ambiguity as the Latin '*aes*', meaning both the metal and the countable objects supposedly made of it.) If we so take *aere* and *aeris* in what I translate in the main text, we might render the whole phrase as: 'the totality of a substance is contained indifferently in a small or large quantity – such as the whole nature of copper in a large or small copper, and the whole nature of man in a large or small man'. Could Aquinas have been tempted to confuse individuals with kinds because of the ambiguous resonances of *aeris* and *aere*? I am quite prepared to be told that this note is no more than fantasy.

(*ens per se sine subjecto*); and the definition of an accident is not 'something existing in a subject'. Rather... to the essence of a substance it *pertains* to have existence in itself; and to... the essence of an accident it *pertains* to have existence in a subject. But it is not because of their essence that accidents in this sacrament are given to exist without a subject. They are given it [that mode of existence] by the divine power which sustains them. So they do not stop being accidents; the definition of accident still applies to them, and the definition of substance does not. (*ST* 3.77.1 ad 2)

The answer may strike some readers as an odd inversion of the Ontological Argument. There, an attempt is made (or so its opponents claim) to smuggle existence into definitions. Here, the truth that definitions do not include existence is used as a reason for believing that something can satisfy the definition of being an accident while not exhibiting the mode of existence that characterises accidents.

Which, of course, makes the answer no answer at all. Aquinas writes correctly that definitions do not include existence (by defining a flying saucer, I do not claim that there are any); but that does not stop definitions from saying what must be the case *if there exist samples of what is being defined* (otherwise, I could suppose that there might be flying saucers, but flying saucers that were not flying saucers at all). Once more, talk of divine power is not to the point: the point of the objection was to challenge appeals to omnipotence on the grounds that intelligibility is more basic; and intelligibility has simply not been shewn here.

But there is, needless to say, one way in which all objections like this can be overcome – the reification that we have seen run through what Aquinas writes of the eucharistic conversion. Take accidents as products of 'dissection', and their preservation can be effected by divine power. As Aquinas puts it, God is the first cause of both substance and accident; the accident was preserved in existence by its substance as by its own cause; so the first cause can still preserve it when the substance has been removed; just as the first cause can produce the effects of other natural causes without those causes – as when it formed the body of Christ in the Virgin's womb (*ST* 3.77.1). This analogy with the incarnation embodies the weaknesses of appeals to omnipotence. We are given supposed components of reality, and invited to agree that God can deal with them in ways we cannot, much as he can effect miracles we cannot. But the invitation blurs the thing that really matters: we are not dealing with components to begin with; distinctions are not dissections, unintelligiblity cannot be bought off by power. A semblance of content has been given to the doctrine of transubstantiation, but no more than a semblance. There is *discohaerentia terminorum*. The terms and distinctions being put together are themselves legitimate, but their putting together is not. Things fall apart, the centre cannot hold.

'But why on earth should they not fall apart? You began by pointing out that Aquinas does not claim to classify transubstantiation within the terms he uses of natural changes. You even directed attention to the qualifying phrases he interposes in his text. But if the eucharistic conversion is acknowledged by him to be unique, what else can his language do but give way? Is not his eucharistic employment of it a piece of rule-breaking that is creative? A *discohaerentia terminorum* if you like, but one that points to what language cannot seize? And is not this "pointing" the permanent contribution of what Aquinas wrote? All that long recitation of what he says of natural change; that even longer recitation of its eucharistic extension, and of the paradoxes that attend it – is this any more than pedantry pushing at a door which is already open? Is it not unfair to pretend that the content of eucharistic belief is tied down to the categories of an obsolete philosophy of nature? After all, who thinks now in terms of substantial forms and prime matter? What counts, surely, is that we profess our belief in what is and has been believed – that Christ is truly present in the Eucharist, although the appearances are of bread and wine, and that the reality of what we receive is our Risen Lord? Is not this our abiding belief, and does not the permanently valuable element in tradition testify to it, an element that is not constricted by the formulations of another age?'

More than one reader, I suspect, has found questions of that sort presenting themselves ever more insistently over the last two sections. Such readers can now be of good cheer: in a way, all the rest of the book will be preoccupied with the questions that have just been rehearsed. Preoccupied, that is, with unravelling their multiple complexities. For it is not that questions like those make no sense, the trouble is that they make all too many senses. Indeed, they go beyond eucharistic topics, and so the answers I offer will have to go beyond them as well in the chapters which follow. For the present, I make a general claim that will be filled out in the sequel: the terms in which these questions have been put are labels for problems, not solutions. The general effect of the questions is one of a refreshingly sane recall to common sense and inherited belief, away from the idiosyncrasies of recondite medieval speculations. That effect, I submit, is illusory; things are just not so simple. The terms in the questions and the claims made in them must be open to scrutiny just as much as the technicalities to which they take exception. They have, if I may so put it, to work their passage. Which means that there is no short cut to an evaluation and analysis of such claims; we need contexts that are specific enough to force us into trying to see just what the generalities of the claims and questions amount to in practice. Which means that an answer to the questions cannot be brief.

My answer begins in the next section, and takes a form that some may find puzzling: I discuss matters raised during a debate on transubstantiation in the 1950s. The topic may seem a venture into the antiquarian, and I concede that the debate is commonly regarded as the last in the line of such discussions, where both sides not only accepted Trent's decree but wrote within the scholastic tradition. (Indeed, as we shall see, it is regarded by some as the *reductio ad absurdum* of that tradition.) But I have myself long regarded the debate as of unusual interest, and in the next section I notice the general course it took and reflect on some positions adopted by the disputants. To do this will begin to bring out the point made in the preceding paragraph – that the seeming common sense which would dismiss formulae and objections to them in favour of a generic and enduring content of belief is no more than seeming; it is in fact a refusal to face a problem that will present itself to us ever more as the book goes on: the problem of belief and time.

Because examining the debate will lead us further, will lead us in fact to review topics already discussed. I noticed the difference between the distinctions drawn by Aquinas about change, and the investigation of change by physical science as we know it. The relation between the two will turn out to be complex, and to need elucidating in terms of specific examples. And so, after the analysis of the debate itself in the next section, I go in the fifth to earlier medieval sources about the Eucharist, and to other texts of Aquinas himself, in order to see more of what were his concerns and interests, and so to see more of what his terms meant. Then in the sixth section I go to scholastic texts that are later. They come from the seventeenth century, when the scholastic tradition in which Aquinas wrote was under attack, and science as we know it was beginning. To examine those texts, written by authors inside that tradition, will further elucidate how what Aquinas wrote stands with respect to what we ourselves ask nowadays about the nature of things, and with respect to what is asked by those who claim to be his followers.

So the three sections that follow move through the debate itself, then to what preceded Aquinas, and then to what came later. The journey is not brief, and the reader may need convincing that it is worth the time. The best reason I can offer is that making the journey will oblige us to deal in concrete and specific terms with the relation between past and present beliefs; and that this relation lies at the heart of what this book is about.

4 A DEBATE ON TRANSUBSTANTIATION

The debate was between Filippo Selvaggi of the Gregorian University at Rome, and Carlo Colombo of the Pontifical Faculty of Theology at Milan.[7] It was conducted – at the cost of some prolixity – with conspicuous fairness by each side, and in its course covered more topics than those I select here. I do not attempt to disguise my sympathies in what follows, but my purpose is less to take sides than to notice the nature of the differences that emerged – differences over the placing of transubstantiation with respect to modern science, and over the placing of modern science with respect to the scholastic concept of substance.

The occasion of the debate was an article in 1949 by Selvaggi, in which he raised and offered an answer to a question that must also have been presenting itself to readers. Whatever be thought of the eucharistic employment by Aquinas of Aristotelian distinctions, surely the distinctions themselves are no more than a museum-piece? Modern science as we know it began with a conscious rejection of the scholastic tradition in the seventeenth century; it has gone from strength to strength by the deployment of the very mathematical and experimental techniques which distinguish it from the scholasticism that preceded it. What is there left for the distinctions between matter

---

[7] I considered this debate in greater detail in FitzPatrick 1987b, but neither there nor here do I follow its fortunes beyond 1957. Gutwenger 1961 gives further information and references. Colombo ended as Archbishop of Milan, a cardinal, and something called 'Personal Theologian' to Paul VI. I wish I knew more about this post than its Firbankian title. Back in the days of Pius XII it was held by a kindly, rather ramshackle old Irish Dominican called Michael Browne; nobody seems to hold it today.

and form and the rest to *do*, outside a eucharistic setting? Questions of this sort have had to be asked ever since the neo-scholastic revival of the last century, and Selvaggi is well aware of their necessity. The answer he offers is on the general lines of that given by his colleague Pieter Hoenen. That is, he claims that distinctions like those between substance and accident, or between matter and form, are not only compatible with physics and chemistry, but are demanded by them. They are needed because the findings of modern science call for something more in their explanations than extension and motion – the categories of the 'mechanical philosophy' associated with Descartes, which in the seventeenth century was the apparently triumphant adversary of the scholastic tradition inherited from the middle ages. The supposed clarity of that mechanical philosophy, with its desire to explain all phenomena in terms of extension and movement, is no more than specious, because science now calls for justice to be done to notions like unity in things, and unity that is more than a simple aggregation. The notion of substance, inherited by Aquinas from Aristotle as a principle of unity which allows at the same time a potential multiplicity, is both compatible with and called for by what science has discovered. For example, the heterogeneity of the atom does not exclude it from being a substance in the scholastic sense, for accidental heterogeneity can go with substantial unity. And that there is such unity in the atom is shewn by the genuine novelty of the behaviour of particles inside the atom compared with their behaviour outside it (Selvaggi 1949: 28–33).

But, he goes on, retaining the scholastic terms as a complement to modern science demands that, if we consider transubstantiation, we take seriously the findings of science. Aquinas wrote of the conversion of 'the whole substance of the bread' and treated bread as if it were a substance in the sense that, say, a living creature is – an object exhibiting a unity in itself irreducible to the independently observable qualities of its constituents. But by the standards of modern science (and it is science to which we go here, not philosophy), bread is no more than an artificial compound of ingredients, and its difference in taste and texture from them does not justify us in attributing to it a substantial unity. It is rather the components of the conglomerate called bread that are substances – atoms, molecules, micro-crystals and the rest – and so it is to these that we must apply the Council of Trent's claim that 'the whole substance of the bread' is converted into the substance of the body of Christ. It is these atoms and the rest that cease to exist, leaving only their accidents – extension, mass, electric charges and the rest – and leave in consequence all the effects of these accidents, namely the totality of phenomena open to direct experience (Selvaggi 1949: 39–43). Transubstantiation is therefore not a physical change, in the sense that it cannot be 'operatively defined', it is not open to investigation by any physical procedures. But it is a physical change in the sense that its starting-point (the substances that compose the bread) and the end-point (the substance of Christ's body) are physical realities (43–4).

It was to this talk of 'physical realities' that Colombo took exception in 1955, and to Selvaggi's identification of substance with the particles of modern science. 'Substance', 'accident' and the rest are, he contends, metaphysical concepts, not part of what physics deals with. Substance is not to be identified with any reality open to physical experience, nor does the eucharistic change affect the physical reality of the bread, the object of modern science; it touches realities that are beyond (*al di là*) anything physically attainable, realities that are strictly metaphysical (Colombo 1955: 120–1). Selvaggi's approach, while dogmatically orthodox, ties theology too closely to the variations that attend upon science (Colombo 1955: 96, 116–17).

Selvaggi was understandably perplexed at placing just where the disagreement lay, given that both he and Colombo accepted Trent's decree, and were agreed that the eucharistic conversion, though objective, was beyond experience. He will in consequence allow Colombo's claim that the 'physical reality' of the bread does not change, if the term be used to mean perceptual or instrumental data. But he submits that so using it is unfortunate, as it suggests that physical science is concerned only with phenomena. But it is not; physical science is an intellectual and experimental activity concerned with understanding things as they are (Selvaggi 1956: 17f.). As he wrote in his first article, our direct natural judgment, by which we gather the data of experience and pronounce upon the nature of things, is aimed at the concrete reality of substance and accidents. Material substance is operatively definable by its properties, and we do know it – it is an object of physics (1949: 26–7). The physical reality of the bread is that with which common sense, science and metaphysics are alike concerned; and if science has told us more about bread than was known when Trent met, its findings should be accepted (1956: 20–3).

Colombo sharpened the difference in the second article by distinguishing 'physics' in our own time from 'physics' for Aristotle. Physics for Aristotle (and here Colombo has in mind things like Aquinas' account of change described in the second section) sought to shew the ontological, real causes of real phenomena; whereas physics in our time is concerned with bodies only to the extent that they are subject to measure and experiment. All its claims are in the phenomenal order, and this includes its talk of atoms, molecules and the rest. Substance cannot be identified with these particles of modern physical science, because they all lie in the accidental order. The ultimate substantial reality of bodies is unknowable physically; it is knowable – to a limited extent – only by metaphysical reasoning, and of the metaphysical order physics has nothing to say. But it is in this order that the eucharistic conversion takes place: the particles of physics lie in the accidental order, and so are not changed thereby (Colombo 1956 : 263–6, 277).

In the last item of the exchange that I consider, Selvaggi gives references to Aquinas to support his own view that substance and accidents are alike incomplete, and must not be thought of as independent realities (Selvaggi 1957: 503–6). Substance is known by an intellectual judgment working upon sensible properties. Modern physics is more than organised sense-experience. It makes its judgments, in terms of its mathematically expressed theories, upon the whole material reality, substance and accidents alike. To relegate it to the order of the accidental, as Colombo does, is to do it no more justice than do empiricism and positivism (512–14).

So much for an outline of what concerns us in the debate: why do I claim it to be of such interest? The course of the chapters that follow will, I hope, shew that the two disputants, whatever be thought of their respective merits, exhibit attitudes that touch far more than simply the theme of transubstantiation. Here and now, I consider what each has to say of this theme, and suggest something of its wider consequences. And I go first to Colombo.

My first comment is that, whatever we think of Colombo's relegation of physical science to the accidental order, this view of substance is, as a piece of *Realpolitik* in eucharistic theology, eminently well chosen. We can see why if we set it beside what Selvaggi claims. Selvaggi refuses to remove substance from the concern of physics, or to consider it as if it were an impalpable kernel beneath the shell of accidents: the judgment of the intellect about a substance is a

judgment working upon sensible properties (Selvaggi 1957: 513–14).
Unfortunately, it is the philosophical coherence of this position that
makes it recalcitrant to employment in eucharistic theology. Indeed,
Selvaggi is in a position similar to that which we saw occupied by
Aquinas, whose distinctions drawn to elucidate natural change called
for abuse and violence doing to them before they could be turned into
the dissections we found in the *Summa*. Colombo, on the other hand,
is at his ease with eucharistic theology from the start, for he has
removed the notion of substance from anything which experience
and investigation can discover about things, and so has isolated it
from its original setting of change and continuity. The convenience of
such an account for eucharistic theology is undeniable. It seems to let
the talk of substance there pre-empt all distinctions we might want to
make between how things appear and what they really are – pre-
empt them in the sense that substance now appears as something
independent of this or that philosophical system, appears as
something to which our own distinctions, whatever they may be, are
obliged to bear witness. And so the talk of substance in Trent's decree
is apparently emancipated from any dependence upon medieval
patterns of thought, and imposes itself upon any thought at all. A
writer of an earlier generation, in what is still a standard account of
the decree at Trent, takes this view. Trent's terms, he says,

must be understood only in the light of the *philosophia perennis* ... a philosophy
that needs no studying to be understood, which stands apart from all
philosophical systems, or which rather must underlie all such systems, for
without it they would be no more than outrages on common sense.
(Godefroy 1924: cols. 1348–9)

It is only to be expected that Colombo should write in the same
remarkable way:

In short, Trent employs the term 'substance' in a wider sense than that
which is peculiar to Aristotelico-scholastic philosophy. If it does speak of
'the whole substance' of the bread and wine, and does so speak with
reference to ... [the scholastic account of change], it does this only so as to
express the revealed truth of a total conversion in an exact way according to
concepts of the time about the composition of bodies. (Colombo 1955: 95)

But it is precisely this apparent loosening of Trent's decree from the
scholastic tradition that is responsible for what I have called the pre-
empting of any distinctions we might make. For Godefroy, Trent

commits us only to a 'perennial philosophy'. For Colombo, the use of 'substance' in the decree is wider than that of the scholastic tradition. But it is the very *breadth* and *timelessness* of this interpretation that make Trent's talk of substance and appearances take on an inevitability. Appearance and reality; constancy amid variation; unity in diversity; meaning and its embodiment: these are contrasts and distinctions which run through so much of human reflexion on the world. And they now seem to have been subsumed by transubstantiation, because divine power there actually puts asunder what we have distinguished.

So we should not be surprised that Colombo, while wanting to keep Trent's teaching distinct from scholastic speculations (see the text just quoted; and see in the same article pp. 110–12, 119–22), ends by making the distinction between creed and philosophy mean very little. For him, the pronouncement of Trent presupposes a real distinction between the 'substance' that does change and the 'appearances' that do not; it is a doctrine '*proxima fidei*' (bordering on the faith) that these appearances are objective, not just subjective; and it is '*theologice certum*' (theologically certain) that 'appearances' (*species*) in the decree is to be understood in the sense of 'accidents' in scholastic philosophy (Colombo 1956: 278–9; the Latin phrases indicate various degrees of mandatoriness, details do not matter at this point). We seem to have boarded a tram that has no stops on its route. By keeping apart physics and substance in his theological speculations, Colombo lets modern science and scholastic meta-physics go their separate ways. But he then promptly awards himself, as scholastic theologians so often do, a philosophical degree *ad eundem* as he elaborates his theory of substance; he gives to the terms used in Trent a meaning that is apparently wider than their scholastic sense; but he ends by making the scholastic tradition seem inevitable. It is as if Trent's decree had vindicated Aristotle's *Metaphysics*.

It is, as I said, all excellent *Realpolitik*. But it is very little else. The various contrasts and distinctions that were supposed to lead us ineluctably to transubstantiation – appearance *versus* reality, and the rest – do nothing of the kind, the ineluctability is no more than a consequence of our not making those contrasts 'work their passage', of not insisting that their range and significance be discussed in specific terms.

Let the complexities hidden in the phrase 'appearance and reality' serve as a caution about the use of other distinctions we might want to draw. The contrast can obviously make good sense, but the sense has to be filled out from the context, we cannot build on the distinction as if it made one obvious and plain sense when taken in isolation. We draw the distinction to take account of error ('the box *looked* heavy but *really* wasn't'), of progress in knowledge ('water *really* consists of two isotopes'), of ideological claims ('what *looks* like benevolence *really* only prolongs an unjust society'). We can make the distinction record unexpected gaps between data and verdict – fools' gold *is not* gold, although it *looks* like it, vaporised gold *is* although it *does not*. We can retain the distinction even when the gap has become second nature (*really* straight sticks *look* bent in water). The distinction can also recall the range of variation in common things compatible with their being what we call them – water remains water, whether hot or cold. The distinction can even serve to bring out the gap between the vagueness of data and the sharpness of what they enable us to say – the significance of a diagram goes beyond the quirks of the chalk-marks on the blackboard. No good purpose is served by lumping all such distinctions together without qualification; to do so tempts us almost irresistibly to conceive of 'reality' as a kind of privileged super-appearance, accessible only by metaphysical re-flexion, and able to be the seat of divine action in the Eucharist. 'Gold as such', 'water as such', 'the real stick', 'the meaning of the diagram' – these are not entities to be set beside vaporised or solid gold, cold or hot water, apparent sticks or marks made with chalk. Nor of course are they to be identified with them either: it is the 'they' and 'them' that are the trouble. But it is just this trouble that comes when appearance is set against reality in so specious a way. Take the distinctions seriously, place them in the particular settings in which they can be legitimately drawn, and they give no warrant whatever for drawing the conclusion useful for this view of the Eucharist – that there might be appearances that are appearances of nothing, phenomena with no reality, accidents without a substance. There is nothing ineluctable about such a conclusion – drawing it is of a piece with the procedure blamed in the preceding section, namely *reifying* the terms of the distinctions we have drawn and turning distinguishing into dissecting.

Which is all that Colombo is doing, only his move is given a plausibility through his separation of substance from anything that can ever be reached by judgment based on experience – and in particular through his claim that the systematic judgments of science have nothing to do with substance, but are entirely in the order of accidents. But his claim reveals his confusion. What is so general a distinction intended to convey about the scope and limitations of physical science? Physical science has devised mathematically and experimentally linked theories to account for the behaviour of things, and shews its power and its limits in observation, in prediction and in practical application. Presumably it will go further along the road it has travelled, with achievements and blunders in the future to match those it has encountered in the past. When Colombo claims that whatever is achieved by science in this way – however powerful the claim and however resistant to falsification – never gets beyond the order of accidents, what more on earth does he want? What is supposed to be lacking to scientific procedure as opposed to metaphysics? What is his *al di là* al di *of*? What inability have we here more than an inability to catch the horizon?

But I repeat my admission that what Colombo writes is excellent *Realpolitik*; and the excellence of the manoeuvre is going to shew itself in other contexts. By *insulating* his concept of substance from all else, Colombo is able to make of it an inaccessible region where nothing need be considered save the divine power which effects the eucharistic conversion. Such a process of insulation is attractive in itself – it seems to promise release from the limitation of time and context in what we claim, and to be a pledge that our claim is invulnerable. The promise and pledge I regard as deceptive, but we are going to meet them time and again.

So much for the present for Colombo's position, I turn to Selvaggi's. I noticed that his concept of substance, because of its philosophical coherence, lacks the adaptability of Colombo's to eucharistic employment. To take up the word I have just used, it has not been subjected to insulation, and the physical science of our own day is not cut off from it. And this difference over 'insulation' is something that we shall meet again, and in more than one setting. What reservations I do have about Selvaggi's position naturally do not touch this concern of his for modern science. I can best express them in two questions. What *content* is there to his claim that the scholastic account of change we have met is needed as a complement to modern science? And what meaning should be attached here to *complement*? I take the two questions in turn.

The first is simple enough. Let us grant that modern science does need more than the laws of classical mechanics, and does make more of notions like unity than did the 'mechanical philosophy' which had poured scorn on the medieval tradition. How much *content* is provided by the distinction we saw Aquinas draw in his account of change? How, for example, are we supposed to decide that the unity of this or that entity (an atom, a molecule, a crystal, etc.) is substantial or not? The difficulty is more than one of technique. When physics acknowledges that particles outside an atom behave differently from those inside, the acknowledgment is made in a mathematical and experimental setting wholly subsequent to the medieval schoolmen. How far can distinctions drawn within a broadly Aristotelian tradition (a tradition with living things for its paradigm of unity) be transferred to so alien a context?

This first stage in my reservations has touched the weight of the contribution which scholastic distinctions could make to modern science. But it has also touched the feasibility of transferring terminology from one setting to another. Of such transference I shall have more to say, and the second question in which I express my reservations will help us to see just what difficulties the transference can harbour. This second stage concerns the fittingness of talking here in terms of *complement*, and I begin it with what may seem a frivolous example. We have seen that Selvaggi holds on scientific grounds that bread is not a substance – that is, he believes physical science shews that the unity produced by the operations of kneading and baking is not of a profound order. It is not, he says, for philosophy to pronounce on the substantiality of things, but science; and science makes bread to be no more than a mixture of distinct ingredients. Now, curiously enough, Aquinas raises the very same question. He asks whether the substantial form of the bread remains after the consecration, and of course his answer is that it does not (see above, pp. 12–13). But an objection he puts to the conclusion is that *there is no substantial form in the bread to begin with*. That is, the accidents remain after the consecration; but bread is an artefact; and so its form is an accident; and so its form remains (*ST* 3.75.6 obj. 1). Now see the answer he offers:

It is not impossible for artefacts to have forms that are substantial, not accidental: for example, it is possible to produce frogs and snakes artificially. A form like that is not produced by the specific power of art, but by the power of natural principles. That is how art produces the substantial form of bread – by the power of the fire that cooks the material composed of flour and water. (*ST* 3.75.6 ad 1)

Aquinas writes of frogs and snakes presumably with the Egyptian soothsayers of the book of Exodus in mind, but the data he offers matter less than that he thought the whole question one that he could himself answer – unlike Selvaggi, who makes the substantiality of bread be for the scientist to determine, not the philosopher. And if it be thought unfair to adduce a biblical example, then other texts in Aquinas tell the same story. For the moment, here is one: he denied that alchemical gold was real gold, on the grounds that the substantial form of gold can be induced into the matter only by the heat of the sun (*per calorem Solis*), not by fire (in 2 *Sent*. dist. 7 q. 3 art. 1 ad 5; Aquinas 1929: 196).[8] Is this a philosopher turning aside to pronounce on physical science? Or are the philosophical distinctions traced by Selvaggi in Aquinas only interludes in writings primarily concerned with the constitution of things? Or what? After all, our second section gave us enough and to spare of what Aquinas wrote about matter and form, why should he not write about frogs and alchemy too? If so, how are the two themes linked in what he wrote? Do his concerns match those of Selvaggi, who claims to share his philosophical opinions?

The questions demand that we look more closely at what Aquinas wrote and at its setting. And this we shall do in the next section.

5   AQUINAS: LIGHT FROM WHAT PRECEDED

An apparently trivial difference between Selvaggi and Aquinas came to our notice at the end of the last section – it concerned the 'substantiality' of bread. But the difference touched the beliefs of Aquinas, it touched what he regarded as falling within the intellectual discipline he practised. We saw earlier what Selvaggi thought of distinctions like that drawn by Aquinas between matter and form – for him, they complement the findings of modern science. But the difference we have just noticed demands that we look again at the distinctions. We have already seen how Aquinas applies them to the Eucharist; we need now to examine some texts, both from earlier authors and from Aquinas himself, that will let us see more of them

---

[8] Given this belief about the sun's heat engendering gold, and given that the Polish unit of currency is the Złoty, which is Polish for 'gold', Saint Malachy has proved as successful in his prophecy for this papacy (*De calore solis*) as he was for the month's duration of the last (*De medietate lunae*). Let us hope he will be equally on the mark for the Next-in-Line (*Gloria olivae*, which we might freely render as 'Glory of the Olive-branch'). We could certainly do with one.

in practice, and to see more of the preoccupations and claims of
eucharistic speculation in the middle ages. All that will occupy us
throughout the present section. Then in the next section we shall see
more texts, but this time from authors later than Aquinas, authors
who wrote when science as we know it was beginning and the
scholastic tradition was under attack. In both sections, we shall be
concerned with 'placing' what we have seen Aquinas write – with
placing it in a setting that both has its position in time and is also part
of a wider setting protracted through time. All we have encountered
so far – the decree at Trent, the speculations of Aquinas, their
eucharistic application, and the disagreements between Selvaggi and
Colombo – have their respective places in time. The consequences of
this I shall try to bring out in the specific examples I offer in this
section and the next. The lessons we can learn from them will be
needed throughout the rest of the book.

And so to earlier medieval writings on the Eucharist – evidently a
vast topic. It is with gratitude that I acknowledge the debt which all
investigations owe to the scholars who have revealed the range of
eucharistic practice and speculation over those centuries. Here and
now it is the achievement of the German scholar Hans Jorissen to
which I am especially indebted. His monograph (Jorissen 1965)
considers the development of the doctrine of transubstantiation from
the early middle ages to the beginning of the great age of the
scholastics – his first author (after a preliminary discussion of earlier
debates) is Alan of Lille (+1202) and his last is Alexander of Hales
(+1245), whose *Summa* provided the model for the form used by
Aquinas. Not only is the book remarkable for its judicious clarity, it
prints much source-material, of which a sizeable amount is otherwise
accessible only in manuscript. Although I cannot share all Jorissen's
evaluations of his authors, or indeed of Roman Catholicism, I stress
that the few texts I discuss from his book give no more than a hint of
the range of its contents. My purpose in choosing those I do is simply
to convey a sense of how eucharistic speculation was then conducted
– what analogies it used, whence it derived its terms and what it
thought relevant to its conclusions. I do not want to convey an
impression of learning that would mislead, so any text I know only
from Jorissen's book I cite by 'J' and his page number. To all others
I refer in the usual way.

I first notice that earlier writers shared with Aquinas the belief that
omnipotence can take the place of intelligibility, and that 'matter',

'form' and so on are so many objects for the exercise of God's power. Baldwin of Ford (Archbishop of Canterbury 1184–91; died at the siege of Acre) writes in his *De Sacramento Altaris* (before 1180) that 'Jesus is served by every form and matter, by every appearance and substance' (J 20). We should not of course read into Baldwin's vocabulary all the Aristotelian associations of the terminology used later by Aquinas. Indeed, Baldwin (he was a Cistercian) represents the more contemplative school of theology associated with the cloister rather than with the universities. But Baldwin also claims, along with what has just been cited, that it is not enough to believe in the truth of what Christ said at the Last Supper, we must understand what he meant. All that eludes us is the manner of its accomplishment (*ratio modi*). Once again, a reading of distinctions as dissections is presumed to make sense: omnipotence can do the rest. And the same invocation of omnipotence is made about 1205 in the *Summa Caelestis Philosophiae* of Robert Courson (eventually a cardinal: Jorissen might have added that he is an alleged collateral ancestor of Lord Curzon). Courson puts the objection that if all perceptible properties of bread remain in the consecrated host – colour, taste, nutritive power and the rest – then surely the host is still bread? To this objection (which is well put, and to which I shall be returning in the next chapter) he replies simply by invoking wonders that outstrip the order of nature, such as the giving of sight to the blind and the virginal conception of Christ (J 118–20). We have, of course, already encountered this appeal to omnipotence in Aquinas himself, and commented on its lameness.

But we find more than appeals to omnipotence. We find texts which speak against the isolation of the eucharistic conversion in some order set apart from other changes. There are examples and to spare: perhaps the range of analogies offered to elucidate the eucharistic conversion will convey an effective first impression. We are offered by various authors the Egyptian magicians' rods into serpents, the water into wine at Cana, Lot's wife into a pillar of salt and hay into glass (J 75f., 87, 123 etc.; the last of these changes is not miraculous, whatever some modern authors cited by Jorissen may think – my colleague D. M. Knight tells me that, because hay contains silica, burnt haystacks leave beads of glass). A further analogy, if that be the word, is found in a source not given by Jorissen, the *Rationale Divinorum Officiorum* (*c.* 1165) of John Belethus. Justifying the practice of having the words of consecration said inaudibly, John offers a cautionary tale, and incidentally provides an early use of the verb 'transubstantiate'. In days of yore, it seems, the words used to be said aloud, and some shepherds once repeated them in the fields over some bread (their 'bait', presumably). And at once the food was transformed 'and perhaps transubstantiated, if I may so speak, into the body of Christ'; the shepherds naturally being all struck dead in the process (202 ML 52). Seeing how all these analogies depict a range of natural and miraculous transformations, the Eucharist does not concern some order of being to which the rest are alien. Other pieces of argument from the same time have the same effect. For the author of a *Summa de Sacramentis* (*c.* 1170), just as God created matter in the beginning without qualities, so he can preserve a quality without any subject (J 79–80). For Peter Cantor in his own *Summa de Sacramentis* (*c.* 1195), natural change means that the form or essence changes, while the subject (*ypostasis*) remains, whereas in the Eucharist the *ypostasis* changes while the form remains (J 87). Whatever meaning all this has, it is at least opposed to any claim for a total difference in order between the two kinds of change, and to talking in terms of some 'insulated' substance.

From these analogies I pass to another theme in these earlier sources – the consequences drawn from the belief that there is no subject to the qualities of a consecrated host. First, what of the subsequent fate of the host, when it is broken and eaten? The answers offered, like the analogies, are couched in terms that are (to use a distinction that I hope is beginning to strike the reader as unsuited to these speculations) physical rather than philosophical. A *Sententiae Divinitatis* of about 1145 holds that what remains after the consecration has no reality whatsoever. It can be said to 'inhere' in Christ, but only in the sense that the appearance of a stranger inhered in him on the road to Emmaus; it could be said to inhere in the air at the spot where the consecrated host appears to be (here the writer is repeating an opinion of Abelard, +1142); but it has no reality, so that the breaking of the host at Mass is no more actual than the apparent breaking of a stick immersed in water (J 78; we shall find that the analogy with Emmaus will prove popular in the seventeenth century). As for the substance of the bread, this was deemed by some to have been dissolved into its elements. One who held this view (J 27) was Roland Bandinelli (later Pope Alexander III, 1159–81; vainly tried to curb the fanaticism of Becket). That Bandinelli should have thought in terms of resolution is interesting, because he is generally credited with the invention of the word *transsubstantiatio* (about 1150 – J 7 unfortunately prints this as 1250). We can notice at once how the introduction of a word does not guarantee identity in its subsequent uses. We can also notice that some supported that opinion in a way just as 'physical' – they offered an example of another dissolution into elements, namely the star of the Magi (J 29).

But the main consequence of denying that any subject survived the consecration was the problem it raised for nutrition by the host – after all, mirages may be perceived, but they can hardly nourish. Alan of Lille gives more than one opinion in his *De Fide Catholica* (*c.* 1190), when considering the case of the hungry church-mouse who gnaws his way into the vessel where the consecrated hosts are kept. (The example was perennially popular, and we shall meet it later on in Aquinas – does it cast a dim religious light on conditions in medieval churches?). One view is that the mouse only *appears* to eat (might this be a remote ancestor of 'poor as a church-mouse'?). Another view, preferred by Alan, is that with the matter and substantial form of the bread gone, the nourishment must be miraculous, but – see yet again how the eucharistic conversion is set beside natural, physical activities – we should not marvel at the miracle, because do not some peoples live off the smell of apples, and is it not possible to get drunk simply by smelling wine (J 93)? Another writer goes to the same analogy, but this time to prove the opposite. This is Peter Cantor again, for whom not only do the colour, texture and so on of the bread (*panis*) survive its consecration, but also – untranslatably, I fear – its *panitas*. And, since *panitas* survives, admittedly by a miracle, we need no further miracle to account for the power of the host to nourish; and the apple-smellers – Indians in fact – appear once more, only this time against a miracle rather than for one (J 93). As if this were not enough, a third writer offers what we might rashly call an *experimentum crucis*: William of Durham, writing about 1230, claimed that someone had once tried to nourish himself on the consecrated elements, but in vain. Only he thinks that the experiment is not decisive, since their nutritive power might on this occasion have been miraculously suspended (J 153).

I have lingered on all this nonsense because I think it illustrates so happily the setting in which earlier medieval writers discussed the eucharistic conversion. They 'placed' it in a physical although miraculous setting, not in an order of substance insulated from all else. At the same time, they exhibited their incapacity to develop the concepts of experiment and rational conjecture – concepts that we use, consciously or unconsciously, when we talk of physical changes and of their investigation. The concerns of these authors do not match either 'philosophy' or 'science' as we use the terms. With that in mind, we can turn to some more texts of Aquinas. My earlier objections to what he wrote about the eucharistic conversion will shew that I am not now going to credit him with having brought all these earlier speculations to a happy conclusion (more or less, this is what Jorissen himself seems to hold). What I can say is that the account we have found so far in texts of Aquinas can at least be read as achieving more *economically* what was the aim of the texts we have just examined. We saw how Aquinas takes the terminology of the Aristotelian tradition and gives it an initial distortion and reification for eucharistic purposes. Given that, the rest follows (if that be the verb) readily enough, he does not need the picturesqueness of his predecessors. But there is still more to be said, because Aquinas himself had more to say; and we must set other texts of his beside those we examined earlier.

It will be recalled that the distinction between matter and form, originally elucidated with reference to moulding the plasticine, was then extended to changes like burning the plasticine, where we end up, not just with a different shape, but with a different kind of thing (pp. 5–10). I suggest that the texts of Aquinas we are now going to see will oblige us to distinguish more sharply between these two uses of the distinction. The original use is not a *rival* to what our own physical science would say about the moulding of the plasticine. The distinction between matter and form there does not in any way *compete* with the mathematical and experimental procedures by which we investigate the effects of rotatory pressure. Thus, when Aquinas writes that the form is 'educed from the potentiality of the matter', he is not suggesting an origin for the new shape that could be an alternative to explanation in terms of pressure. His terminology is simply part of his warning against abusing the distinction between matter and form and treating them as if they were things. What he writes at this first stage can indeed be said to complement physical science, even if only modestly. It cannot be said to compete with it.

But when the distinction between matter and form is extended to cover the profounder sorts of change – 'generation and corruption' we saw Aquinas call them – then we find him taking the distinction he draws as more like a specific account of such changes, an account which could compete with others. Already, when introducing this extended use of the distinction, I pointed out that it could be taken – even though by a logically dubious step – as a claim for some primary and indefinitely malleable 'stuff', and I noticed the use by Aquinas in this sense of the expression *materia prima*, prime matter. But there are texts where his use of this phrase is not what we should call 'philosophical' at all. He writes in his Commentary on Aristotle's *Metaphysics* that the *materia prima* of one bodily humour differs from that of another, but that both of them come from a prior principle which is *materia prima* – this time in our stricter sense. He claims that all things subject to generation and corruption have one prime matter in common – but he then makes the exception that earthly things need not have it in common with the heavenly bodies. They were, of course, believed to be incorruptible in Aquinas' day, but the reason he offers for the absence of a common prime matter is that the respective proper matters of things earthly and heavenly are so different (VIII 4; 1729–30). It is not difficult to see how what we first met as an abstract extension of the difference between matter and form has here for Aquinas empirical associations. And a question he puts in the same *lectio* of the Commentary reinforces this conclusion. Since matter is potentially either of the extremes which can qualify it, should not water be just as potentially vinegar as wine? Not so, he answers; vinegar is a corruption of wine, and water is related to vinegar only indirectly, through wine (VIII 4: 1748–9). The change between wine and vinegar is in one direction only; for vinegar to be changed into wine, there would have to be a *resolutio ad materiam primam* (1752–3). I would render this Latin as 'a getting back to basics', since that preserves the view of Aquinas here: form and matter are seen as contributing to an understanding of how things specifically behave; they are not simply what we ourselves see as a philosophical framework into which any change may be fitted. So it is not surprising that when Aquinas adapts this terminology for eucharistic purposes, he preserves its links with the particularities of physical change. Thus, a specific, physical analogy is used to elucidate the effect of mixing water (which is a substance) with consecrated wine (which is only an accident, the wine's substance having been converted into the substance of the blood of Christ). How can such a mixture be possible, he asks, given the difference in category of what are being mixed? By there being two measures of unity, he answers – one of quantitative continuity, the other of the mode of existence;

just as, he goes on, a body made up of two metals is quantitatively one, but is not one as far as specific natures are concerned (*ST* 3.77.8 ad 2).

Not only physical analogies, but the very processes and consequences of physical change find their way into what Aquinas writes of the Eucharist. He asks about the water that is mixed with the wine *before* the consecration. It cannot stay unaltered (nothing must be in the chalice but Christ); it is not transformed into the water that flowed from his side on Calvary (that would call for a separate consecration); it seems best to say that it is converted into wine, and then the wine into the blood of Christ (*ST* 3.74.8). Elsewhere, when he rejects Abelard's opinion that the appearances of the bread are in the *air* on the spot, two of his reasons are physical. First, air cannot take on such appearances; and secondly, the appearances in question are not where any air is, in fact air is moved away when the host is moved (*ST* 3.77.1). He also rejects, and for just as physical a reason, another opinion we met: that the substance of the bread is resolved into its original matter. Such a process, he replies, would have to terminate in the four elements, it cannot end in prime matter without any form whatever, because prime matter cannot so exist. What then if it terminated in the four elements? That will not do either. Nothing but Christ may be under the sacramental species; so the elements would have to be moved out; and if this did happen it would be a perceptible process (*ST* 3.75.3). Once more, whatever we think of an argument like this, its placing of eucharistic speculation does not lie in moving from 'science' to 'philosophy' or 'metaphysics', as Colombo would have us believe.

A last text from Aquinas shews affinities with the accounts of nutrition we have found in Alan of Lille and in Peter Cantor. Aquinas does indeed shew his usual good sense in incidental remarks here. He dismisses the analogy with the Indians smelling apples as 'perceptibly wrong' – such activity would be no more than a temporary palliative, it could not repair bodily wastage (*ST* 3.77.6). But there are questions he considers here to which he offers just as 'physical' answers as they did. What if the host is burned, and so produces ashes; or decays and so (as was then believed) produces worms? What is to be the subject of the change here? It cannot be the body of Christ, for that is incorruptible, so some said that the surrounding air supplies the matter: that corrupts, and worms or ashes are thereby generated. Once more, it is objections of a physical character that Aquinas raises to this answer. First, corruption calls for preliminary changes, but the air near the host does not exhibit any; secondly, air is not by its nature the kind of thing from which ashes or worms can be produced; and thirdly, were a great many hosts to be burned or to corrupt, the production of so much solid material (worms or ashes) would call for a great and eminently perceptible thickening of the air. He goes on to say that solid containers of the Eucharist cannot provide the required matter either – corruption of the host can take place without their being altered in any way (*ST* 3.77.5).[9]

'Was Aquinas doing science or philosophy?' should by now, I hope, seem a question essentially flawed with ambiguity – not in the sense that we lack sufficient evidence, but in the sense that the distinction has come to seem ever more alien to the interests and concerns in what he writes. He exhibits a power vastly superior to that shewn in the earlier texts we have seen, and yet what we felt of them we feel of him – distinguishing philosophy from science in the way we do is something that belongs to our time, not to his.

And it is this feeling that leads us naturally to the topic of the next section. As I said when introducing this section, the position of Aquinas needs illuminating by being set in its place in a temporally extended process. Part of this we have now done, by going to texts of earlier authors and to further texts of Aquinas, with the results we have seen. But if our distinction between science and philosophy seems alien to him, this is in its turn due to the fact that the temporally extended process is one to which we ourselves belong. Between us and the setting in which Aquinas wrote lies the growth of what we now mean by science, with its systematic use of theory, mathematised wherever possible, and of controlled experiment. It is the seventeenth century that is associated with the origins of the new sciences, and it is to seventeenth-century texts that we shall go in the

---

[9] Readers may be curious to know what answer Aquinas himself gives. He calls the problem a difficult one, suggests several solutions, and offers his own tentatively: the dimensive quantity of the bread and wine is given by the consecration the power to become the subject of further generation and corruption (*ST* 3.77.5). My only comment is that, if all this ingenuity be so, we have the somewhat eerie result that there are, scattered through the world, the products of past corruptions of consecrated material, apparently substantial but really accidental; that any further corruption of these will leave them accidental; and so that the general category of things is, slowly but surely, slipping from Substance to Accident. It is a speculation worthy of Jorge Luis Borges, and I was delighted to find I had been eloquently anticipated as long ago as 1704 in framing it, by the Cartesian philosopher Sylvain Régis (Régis 1704, Book III, chap. 4: 327).

next section. My aim will be modest – to see something of how the scholastic tradition was then attacked, and how it was defended. Attack and defence alike will shew us more of what that tradition was then judged to be, specifically with reference to the terms and distinctions we have seen Aquinas use about change.

Readers who have found the details of this section tedious, or who are at least puzzled at their relevance to the theme of this chapter, must continue their endurance in the section that follows – there are still more details to be encountered as we examine, in specific instances, the relation between present and past beliefs. The terms we found in Trent's decree, and in the *Summa* of Aquinas, have been given repeated approval in theological contexts. What does it mean to use them now, when the setting of our knowledge of the world has changed so much? These are not antiquarian questions, nor are we concerned only with illuminating what Aquinas wrote by earlier and later witness. We are concerned with the whole relationship between past and present. And that is something we shall have to face ever more as the book goes on.

6 AQUINAS: LIGHT FROM WHAT FOLLOWED

'Why does opium induce sleep?' 'Because it has a dormitive power.' The medical candidate in the uproarious *finale* of Molière's *Le Malade Imaginaire* wins applause for this answer, which has passed into the folklore of philosophy. And deservedly so, because the joke was of a piece with so much that was said in the seventeenth century, deservedly or undeservedly, against the older ways of thought. The candidate was congratulated by the jury for his eloquence, he is the *novus doctor qui tam bene parlat*, but the innovators thought that that was the trouble: they wanted more than words. For Legrand, a populariser of Descartes' philosophy, the scholastics' talk of substantial forms is as vacuous as saying that fire is fire and water water; what can scholastic appeals to substantial forms as to 'inward principles' contribute to understanding an astronomical phenomenon like the phases of Venus (IV 7; Legrand 1694: 102)?

We know by this time how scholastic philosophers of our own time would answer such an objection, whether talking with Selvaggi of their discipline as complementary to science, or talking of it with Colombo as going beyond science to the level of substance. The present section, by examining particular examples of the debate in the seventeenth century, will let us see more clearly what such recent moves involve.

And we note first how, in the face of such attacks, seventeenth-century scholastics took neither of those courses, but stood their ground and charged their opponents with themselves leaving things unexplained.[10] Eustachius a Sancto Paulo, author of a popular *Summa Philosophiae* (he was a French monk, but his book saw an edition in Cromwellian Cambridge in 1649), gives the argument for matter that can be found in Aquinas. Nothing can come from nothing; so when, for instance, fire turns into air, the air must come from something pre-existent, which remains in it when it has come to be; and this is prime matter, an incomplete substance capable of assuming all forms ('De principiis', Quaest. II; Eustachius 1649: 120). As for substantial forms, the *Metaphysica Scholastica* (1675) of William Ayleworth (he taught at the Jesuit College in Liège) argues against the Cartesians' exclusion of them in favour of a uniform matter distinguished only by shape and motion: how, on this hypothesis, can the unity and constancy in things be explained, or their material cohesion and the regularity in their behaviour (Tract. I, Disp. III, Cap. II, nn. 17–21)? See how an argument like Ayleworth's appeals to the actual behaviour of physical objects, while what is put forward by Eustachius offers a pattern of reasoning that he claims to apply to any change at all. We are going to find that this two-fold interpretation of the scholastic tradition repeatedly appears in seventeenth-century debates over what had been inherited from the middle ages.

A first example is found in the disagreement over what was called 'the reality of accidental forms'. Quite apart from the eucharistic associations of the phrase, we can see two senses in it. There is the *logical* sense – for a quality to be real, it does not have to be like some substance, which adheres to or is applied to another substance. Elucidating what 'reality' means for qualities is a genuine philo-sophical problem, but it is not the same as the problem raised by the *physical* sense of the phrase: are there namely properties irreducible to extension and movement, or to the simple putting together of components (*compositio elementorum*)? Some specimens then offered by

---

[10] The topics here are too complex for justice to be done to them in the few pages that follow. The points I make can be found in the texts I cite; obviously, others can as well. I have gone into greater detail in FitzPatrick 1987a, and hope to return to the themes elsewhere.

scholastics of real qualities in this physical sense are picturesque, such
as those provided by the zealous Thomist Goudin – the capacity of
jasper to staunch blood and of jade to ease neuralgia (Goudin 1692,
III 3, *De generatione et corruptione*; the argument for which these
examples are adduced is at 165f.). Another specimen touches a
widely shared preoccupation of the time, namely the persistence in
movement of projectiles (Lagrange 1675, c. x: 146. The general thesis
that 'pushes and pulls' are not enough is argued in his Introduction).

Mixtures provided a second example. The scholastic tradition had
demanded a substantial form for them, and those who favoured the
newer ways declared the form to be idle – a putting together of the
mixture's components (*compositio elementorum*) was enough. But now
see how this 'philosophical' objection has a physical side. For
Duhamel, in his work that claimed agreement between old and new
(*De consensu veteris et novae philosophiae* II 2 §9), the scholastic position
entails that mixtures be homogeneous, which they are not –
'anything can be disintegrated by chemistry' (Duhamel 1681: 638).

The last example I offer of this 'two-fold' interpretation of the
scholastic tradition comes again from Eustachius a Sancto Paulo, and
it concerns the origin of forms. We saw in the second section how
Aquinas deals with this. We must not apply phrases to forms that *reify*
them, turn them into things. If we do, we shall fall into puzzles like
'where do forms come from?' and have to offer quaint answers like
'they are lurking in the matter' (pp. 6–8). We have seen how
Eustachius uses the argument for prime matter in a way that
resembles what we found in Aquinas, and in the same work he too
denies as Aquinas does the *latitatio formarum*, the lurking of forms in
the matter. But now notice what form his argument against *latitatio*
takes. Did it obtain, he writes, we should be able to feel the fire in
wood before igniting it – the 'lurking' form would be perceptible
(Eustachius 1649: 124). We have passed from the point of logic that
forms cannot be treated as if they were things, to an argument
involving physical evidence. Once more, the scholastic tradition has
proved open to this two-fold interpretation.

I can best give what I think is the reason for this by distinguishing
between *formulations* and *recipes*, and I explain the distinction by
means of a simple mathematical example. We associate with Euclid
– not that it is from Euclid – the definition of a straight line as the
shortest distance between two points. This is a *formulation*, it tells us
what condition has to be satisified if a line drawn is to be deemed

straight. But how are we to draw such a line? That question calls for a *recipe*, and we may answer in terms of rulers or plumb-lines or – better – in terms of some geometrical construction, not itself involving any straight line, which produces movement in a straight line by one of its components. The distinction, which some will recognise as Aristotelian in origin, is important to preserve. If I confuse a formulation with a recipe, I may go on to take the formulation as a *privileged* recipe, a recipe guaranteeing success: after all, a ruler may fail to be straight but how could the Euclidean definition be wrong?[11]

We shall find that the distinction will be useful more than once in what follows. Here and now, it can enable us to put a question about the later scholastic authors we have just been citing. Why did they choose so often to conduct the debate with the newer opinions in terms of recipes – in terms involving how things behave and why they do so – when they might have confined themselves to terms of formulations? That is, why did they not write as we have seen Colombo write, and take their tradition as a piece of philosophy pertaining to the metaphysical order, which did not compete with the specific claims of the newer physical science? What we have seen so far, both of the earlier medieval thinkers and of these later scholastics, may make us uneasy about this way of putting the question. Our uneasiness is well-founded; our examples have made us aware that the disciplinary boundaries of one age are not those of another. To give a name to what this awareness concerns, I go to a dialogue of Plato. There, the question is put whether Socrates can be said to have changed if the young Theaetetus (pronounced more or less 'Thee-eat-eaters'), who was previously shorter than he, should have grown up and have now become taller. The peculiarity of the change here is not the point, what matters is that 'the Theaetetus Effect' is a useful label for something which has been with us in this chapter and which will go with us in the chapters that follow: the fact

---

[11] The mistake may seem too crude to be a danger. In fact it occurs more often than we might expect. Thus, Newman's 'Illative Sense', by which we draw conclusions in concrete, particular reasoning, is defined by him as 'right judgment in ratiocination'. Which, of course, imports success into the definition: if we judge wrongly, we cannot have been using our Illative Sense. A *formulation* has been taken as a *recipe*; for more, see FitzPatrick 1991b. Readers who have encountered concepts like *Verstehen* and *Nacherlebnis* in writings within the hermeneutical tradition might like to consider how far the mistake occurs there. I add that I chose the mathematical illustration in the hope that some will consult for themselves the modern reprint Kempe 1953, which sets out with delightful clarity the achievements of Peaucellier and others, and shews how working models for drawing straight lines can be constructed.

that what we have inherited from the past is modified in retrospect by what we do in the present and by the distinctions we draw there. I want now to trace the Theaetetus Effect in what we have been investigating so far. To encounter it in these specific examples will prepare us for recurrences of it later on. And I go first – well aware of the over-simplifying I shall have to impose – to the texts we have seen of the later scholastics.

Those who followed the scholastic tradition in the seventeenth century were confronted by a mass, unprecedented in its quantity, of new questions and of answers offered to them. The questions and the answers alike took for granted both ordered experiment and the application of mathematical techniques to the understanding of the world. The techniques and the experiments were used to devise concepts in which the world might be understood, and to answering specific questions about how things happen. It is not surprising that those scholastics took the tradition to which they belonged as itself providing recipes for an account of the nature of things, or that they held their tradition to do justice to phenomena of unity and stability in a way that a purely 'mechanical' account could not. They took their tradition as they did because of the Theaetetus Effect of the new discoveries. But their so taking it was not mere caprice; the tradition was already open to such an interpretation. Recall what we saw of the distinctions drawn by Aquinas in connexion with change. They can be taken as an analysis which does not˙ compete with physical explanations of this or that process in the world. But we have seen too how those distinctions can also be taken – and are so taken at times by Aquinas – as specific and physical accounts of changes in terms of matter and form (pp. 5–9, 34–6). I wrote earlier that the question 'was Aquinas doing philosophy or science?' was turning out, as the examples mounted up, to be ill-framed. But we should not express this by describing his activity as if he – and others – were hesitating between the two disciplines, or confusing one with the other. We, in our later place in the development of knowledge, can look back and can draw distinctions he could not. We acknowledge the Theaetetus Effect of what has happened since; we see him and others from a setting which has changed since they wrote what they did.

That is why we can notice things in medieval practice which we can now see as encouraging this two-fold interpretation of the tradition. Thus, we notice the ease with which the step can be taken from 'matter' to 'prime matter' (pp. 8–9). We notice the widespread lack then of an ordered practice of experiment and theory in investigating the nature of things, and the far greater facility of medieval Latin for forming abstract nouns than for expressing explanations of concrete facts and events.[12] And we notice the temptation to reify distinctions drawn, and so to make components out of what is distinguished. This abuse we met in the eucharistic application of the distinctions; but the texts we have seen since shew that the abuse was not altogether a surprise. Given that abuse, the seventeenth-century interpretation of the tradition in terms of recipes was all too natural. By providing recipes in terms of form and matter and so on, the tradition could apparently compete with the newer accounts that were being proposed. At the same time, the terms used in the scholastic recipes retained enough of their origin to seem deeper and more privileged than anything which the new sciences might discover. Formulation taken as recipe seems to depict a process guaranteed to compete successfully.

And competition mattered then. By claiming a privileged place for the distinctions, scholastic writers were giving house-room to a terminology they regarded as bound up with their religion. Just so, attacks on the scholastic tradition were seen as undermining the expression of eucharistic belief, which had used the terminology of that tradition, and used it even in the solemn declarations of the Council of Trent. It is not surprising that more than one seventeenth-century writer finds fault with the innovators for this reason. Lagrange, whom we have already met, blames the Cartesians in his Introduction for destroying 'the ordinary philosophy, which theologians have in a manner consecrated by their use', while the Carmelite friar Augustinus a Virgine Maria writes in the preface to his *Philosophiae Aristotelicae-Thomisticae Cursus* (1664) that the rules of his Order demand that its members 'follow Aristotelian principles to the extent that the Catholic Faith allows'. This line of argument may not be surprising, but as an example of the Theaetetus Effect it is undoubtedly amusing. Four hundred years earlier, medieval popes and bishops had been doling out, in pyrotechnically furious Latin,

---

[12] The untranslatable *panitas* of Peter Cantor that we met in the previous section occurred in a eucharistic context. But Peter (like others) uses such abstract nouns in settings that are not eucharistic at all. The change from hay (*fenum*) to glass (*vitrum*) is described by him at J 78 as matter putting aside *fenitas* and assuming *vitritas*. Such patterns of language, inherited by later scholastics, invited them to take what they wrote as offering recipes rather than formulations. The medical candidate in Molière's play was not without precedent in the kind of answer he offered.

condemnations of those who *followed* Aristotle. For Gregory IX on this in 1228, see DS 824; for a general account of suspicion of Aristotle, see the sources cited in footnote 2; I suspect that the passage quoted by Augustinus from the Carmelite rule was originally designed to *limit* adhesion to Aristotle, not to encourage it. Once more, the nature of an inheritance is shaped by what has since befallen the legatees; the Theaetetus Effect is present here too.

But the Theaetetus Effect is also present in what the scholastics themselves came by degrees to make of the tradition they had inherited. The growth of the new sciences had altered the balance of the range of topics open for investigation, and indeed altered the notion of what investigation involved. The tradition itself had in it a great deal of assertions that increasingly embarrassed – we can recall Aquinas on frogs and snakes or on the heavenly bodies, or what other scholastic sources had to say about the star of the Magi, church-mice, jade, jasper and the rest. Even commendable things in the tradition, such as its insistence on the inadequacy of purely 'mechanical' explanations, mattered ever less as the years went by and the new sciences themselves became ever more detailed in their investigations, leaving behind generalities like 'mechanical' or 'extension and motion'. What was left for the scholastic tradition to *do*?

We have seen two answers to the question, in the debate between Selvaggi and Colombo. Colombo's demotion of physical science to the order of the accidental, and his removal of the order of substance away from 'physical reality' can now be placed in the development of the scholastic tradition. What he claims is in some way like the responses made by the seventeenth-century scholastics to the beginnings of modern science. I have suggested that those responses treated the scholastic distinctions as recipes, and indeed as privileged recipes; and Colombo retains the privilege when he contrasts the status of physical science with that of metaphysics. But the progress made in science over the centuries has in its turn exercised here the Theaetetus Effect: Colombo's privileged status for metaphysics, and his 'insulated' notion of substance, may be eucharistically convenient, but the convenience is purchased at the cost of content; there are no claims made by him of a specific character about change. But I repeat my earlier admission that, in terms of theological *Realpolitik*, his account of the eucharistic conversion can be attractive. Insulation is attractive, so is privileged status – as we shall be finding later, in other contexts.

As for Selvaggi, I have deliberately confined myself to topics immediately concerned with my own purposes here. I stand by my opinion that his claim for the scholastic distinctions as a complement to physical science is much more exiguous than it looks; but his wide knowledge of science and interest in it have yielded much more than that. What distinguishes him from Colombo here points to the profound difference between them, and it is the difference that makes him for me so much more interesting than his adversary: he takes seriously the consequences of the passage of time. He does not attempt to withdraw from time the philosophical tradition to which he belongs, but tries to let what has come later play its part with what has gone before. I wrote earlier that his notion of substance, precisely because it was more philosophically acceptable than Colombo's, was recalcitrant to eucharistic employment (p. 24). He does not seek to remove it from the whole activity in which intellect and experience try to discover what the world is like, and he takes seriously the development of the activity. It is this 'openness' of his concerns that I admire, despite all our further disagreements, both philosophical and eucharistic. One of the themes in what lies ahead is that openness is essential in these matters, if only because there is so strong a temptation to remove what is highly valued from any outside interference.

If I have to find fault with him, it is for something he writes in Selvaggi 1954, in the course of a useful paper on the relation between physics and philosophy: for him there, the chief fault of the medieval scholastics lay in 'thinking they were doing physics when they were really doing natural philosophy' (201). I concede that this is a natural thing for him to write – he accepts the philosophical contribution of the scholastic analysis of change, while regarding much of the medieval account of the world as obsolete. But I submit that his phrase can mislead. It reads all too much like a description of this sort: 'Tom thought he was drinking claret when he was really drinking burgundy.' A claim like that can be made by a speaker to an audience that also distinguishes the two, and where Tom himself would draw the distinction as well but has on this occasion fallen into a confusion. And that, we have seen, is just the kind of thing that cannot be said about those who made the medieval distinctions and used the medieval terminology. 'What they were doing' is a description that we spell out the way we do because we distinguish the way we do. We cannot reasonably talk as if medieval writers were getting confused between two topics of investigation separately possible for them. We make the judgments we do on them because of – among other things – the Theaetetus Effect of what has intervened. Development in thought brings with it a new appraisal of the past, and can allow distinctions to be drawn that were not drawn before. I have made this point repeatedly, but now make it again – it too we shall meet in later chapters.

7 SOME CONCLUSIONS AND QUESTIONS

It is possible – just – that some readers may recall a passage quoted earlier (p. 24) from a standard account of Trent's decree on the Eucharist. To understand the decree, the passage claimed, all that was needed philosophically was the

philosophia perennis... a philosophy that needs no studying to be understood, which stands apart from all philosophical systems.

I have a great deal further to go in what I want to say of the Eucharist, but as the first chapter draws to an end I hope that readers will agree with me that the way forward is not going to lie through comforting verbiage of that sort. This chapter has begun to face the problem of time for understanding. We began with the decree at Trent. We saw that, whatever else needs saying, the decree resembles the text of Aquinas in the *Summa*. We went to the setting of his text, and saw that it uses terms with a systematic origin. We saw that the system was concerned with natural change, and we examined the system. The eucharistic employment of it I alleged to be an abuse, and an abuse that ends by combining terms from the system in a way that makes no sense. But then the system itself was given another review, in the setting of a debate over the placing of the eucharistic conversion with respect to 'physical reality'. And the debate obliged us to go back over the system, and to examine more of the historical setting of its terms and distinctions. I had rejected the opinion in the debate that would set the system, as 'philosophy', at a deeper level than the discoveries of 'physical science'. But we now saw that the system straddled the present boundary line between those disciplines, and that therefore its terms have what in our perspective is an ambiguity. I developed the general point of the effect of later thoughts upon earlier, and gave specific examples of it from the defences of the older system when it was under attack. If there be anything in all this, and in the other analyses I have offered, then there is simply nothing in the suggestion that we may, when dealing with the past stages of belief, have recourse to a *philosophia perennis*, a philosophy that needs no study for its acquisition and, because perennial, is not involved in the problems of the relationship between present and past. Nothing as facile as that is going to be right – this chapter should have taught us that much. True enough, any move which seeks to insulate what we value, both from time and from all other disturbances, may seem more comfortable than the acceptance of time and what goes with it; but the chapter should also have taught us that the comfort will be no more than specious.

Now that we have reached the end of the first chapter, we can notice something more about it. Although it started with Trent's decree on the eucharistic presence, and went on to find fault with the account from which the decree borrowed its phraseology, the range of its concerns has been more than eucharistic. This greater range will be found in the chapters that follow. Thinking more about our topic will necessarily lead us back to questions like those about the present and the past, which in this chapter we have begun to encounter.

If my submissions in this chapter have anything to them, then the doctrine of transubstantiation is no more than muddle, and the appearance of content it possesses comes from a misuse of scholastic terminology, the kind of misuse to which that terminology has turned out to be naturally vulnerable. But if this be so, it leads to more questions, not answered so far but needing to be looked at. One group of questions touches the decree at Trent. Can this be extricated from the terminology we have investigated and found wanting? I noted earlier a suggestion that the collapse of the terminology in the account of transubstantiation might be accepted as a piece of 'creative rule-breaking', pointing towards what cannot be caught in words. Is there anything in the suggestion, and might it provide a way of escape for a revaluation of Trent's decree? The decree, moreover – like so much else in the Church – lies back in the past, and much has been made so far of the retroactive effect of present beliefs upon what used to be believed: can this 'Theaetetus Effect' be exercised on things like the decree at Trent?

Another group of questions touches something that I hope has surprised some readers by its absence up to now. Whatever else the Eucharist is, it is a *rite* of some kind; and yet there has been no word on ritual so far. What place had ritual in the account I have been attacking? We shall see that the answer complements the criticisms of this chapter, and we shall then have to see what link there could be between ritual and other accounts offered of the Eucharist. And ritual will lead us in a multitude of directions: we shall not be short of subject-matter.

But the present chapter has one last lesson for the chapters that follow. The lesson is that there is no escaping into some privileged area which can exclude encountered awkwardness. Godefroy's claim for the sufficiency of a 'perennial philosophy' was cited a second time when we had finished the long journey through a variety of texts. Its second citation was meant to make its insufficiency apparent, but the whole structure of the chapter itself, and not only the material quoted in it, illustrates the insufficiency. It is not possible to devise a form of expression in which we can comment on the temporal limitations of our inheritance, without ourselves being temporally limited in turn and open to comment in the same way. The course of the chapter shewed as much, when things that had been set down received a new cast from what was added in later pages. The vocabulary of Trent's decree led us to the *Summa*, and the vocabulary there led us to distinctions drawn in a context outside theology. When their theological employment was blamed, it looked as if we had a piece of philosophy maltreated for theological ends; but then the nature of what this 'philosophy' was turned out to be more complicated, while later polemic with newer ways of thought gave the medieval tradition at times a cast it had lacked. And this new cast, we saw, could lead in different directions, as the debate between Selvaggi and Colombo itself bore witness. No stage in this succession was immune to modification by what succeeded it. There was no escaping the process by which an inheritance is modified in its transmission. Let that thought end this chapter.

CHAPTER 2

Against transignification

8 PRESENT DISCONTENTS

The place of Aquinas in theological speculation has been a special one. He is part of an intellectual tradition that has been a distinguishing mark of the Church of Rome; he has been regarded as the most eminent representative of that tradition; phraseology like his can be seen in the formulation of eucharistic belief at the Council of Trent; and generations of clergy have been, directly or indirectly, instructed in terms of his thoughts, not just in eucharistic matters but in the whole range of Catholic belief. Devoting the first chapter to what Aquinas wrote within the scholastic tradition about the eucharistic presence was no more than justice.

Still more needs to be said about Aquinas, but the present chapter must with equal justice turn to other themes. The many changes in the Roman Church over the last quarter of a century have included change in the place there of scholasticism and of Aquinas himself. The debates at the Second Vatican Council, the growth in discussions with Christians of other traditions, and above all the changes in public worship, are only some of the things that have both encouraged and been encouraged by newer thoughts about the Eucharist. In the previous chapter I expressed my dissent from the older tradition of eucharistic speculation. I have a good deal more still to say of that tradition, because I regard its implications as being more than eucharistic. But now I want to examine the newer style of speculation, because I think that here too the lessons to be learned go beyond the particular theme with which the writings are concerned.

Many of these writings are in Dutch, although there is available in English an excellent account of them in Schillebeeckx's book on the Eucharist, of which the original appeared in 1967 and the English version in 1968. As I shall be expressing some disagreements with

49

what he writes there – and even more with earlier opinions of his on the topic – I should like to set down here at the outset my admiration for his book, and my pleased astonishment at the amount of material he has fitted into so small a compass. In a little over a hundred and twenty pages, he gives us a brief but welcome account and evaluation of the debates and decrees at Trent concerning the eucharistic presence; an outline of the growth of the newer opinions and a survey of them; his own substantial contribution towards an expression of eucharistic belief in newer terms; and, in the light of that, an appraisal of his contemporaries' suggestions. Over and above all this, he gives copious references to original sources for recent opinions, references that were among the starting-points for the investigations I have made for myself. In fact, the one thing Schillebeeckx does not do is the thing which, given the size of his book, he cannot be expected to do – provide quotations from the recent authors liberal enough to give the 'feel' and direction of what they have been writing. But few of their texts have been translated, as far as I can tell; the newer opinions are in consequence notorious among us rather than well known. The notoriety is easily summed up. The opinions have a habit – Holland; they have a distinctive vocabulary – 'transfinalisation' and 'transignification'; they have a philosophical background of their own – rejection of the scholastic tradition and a preference for something called 'phenomenology'; their proponents indulge in disconcerting comparisons – for one writer, the Eucharist is supposed to be like tea-and-a-biscuit; they do scant justice to the mandatory nature of the decrees of the Council of Trent; and, ever since Pius XII's encyclical *Humani Generis* in 1950, papal and curial utterances have been directed against them.[1]

---

[1] I have worked directly from texts – largely in Dutch, with some in French and in German – where the newer accounts are given. The generous footnotes in Schillebeeckx's book provided a starting-point in my quest for material, and I renew here my thanks to the librarians who gave me access to it. Once again, there is much more to the authors I have translated than the themes in the extracts I provide; and there are many more sources I have read than those I have translated. Further references and citations (in the original) can be found in an author we shall meet later, Wohlmuth 1975. For earlier disagreements among scholastic philosophers during this century, J. T. Clark 1951 is copious and useful. Filograssi 1954 is – as one would expect – a charming retrospect upon philosophy and theology at the Collegio Romano (Gregorian University) in days gone by. Schillebeeckx's own book I translate and cite as usual, but add in square brackets the corresponding page number of its English edition. From what Schillebeeckx writes, it seems clear that words like 'transignification' go back further than what is available in print – he writes that he encountered them when studying in France (presumably at Le Saulchoir) just after the Second World War (Schillebeeckx 1967: 84 [1968: 108]).

That is why, in the first four sections of this chapter, I provide a fairly extensive range of texts from these authors, in order that they may speak for themselves; and I hope this will prove of some interest, whatever be thought of the appraisal I shall be offering. This range of texts I follow in two more sections with a selection of texts from Schillebeeckx himself. In one section I notice two principles in what he writes, principles which I think are valuable but ambiguous; in the other I state the reservations which he expresses about the views of these contemporaries of his that I have translated.

More questions are raised by the texts than I can examine in this chapter, but I begin my critique of them in its last two sections. What my critique is – and what further problems it points to – I shall leave for the moment; my present concern is to let the reader have a good sample of what the newer authors have written, of what Schillebeeckx sees as the right path here, and of what he himself makes of the authors. Needless to say, there is much more to them than what the extracts present; I have made my choice with my own concerns in mind.

For the rest of the present section, I give texts which exhibit some of the dissatisfaction felt with the older style of eucharistic theology; I turn in the next to texts where the philosophical setting of the newer authors can be seen; and in the third and fourth, I consider the eucharistic application of the philosophical concepts they employ. And so first to present discontents.

My first text (I number them to make reference easier) is taken from the French theologian de Baciocchi, one of the first to broach the new ideas.[2] I put it first because it contains, not his own exposition, but his humorous comment on a view that by this time should be familiar:

1. Last of all, let us keep transubstantiation apart from an imaginative solution with which it is quite often confused, and which the Church has never either approved or condemned. The solution lies in imagining that the bread and the wine have a kind of external film, made up of their perceptible and scientific properties; and that they also have a mysterious kernel, unknowable in itself, a pure '*en-soi*', which is called 'substance' in rather the same sense as Locke used the word. Cut the bread to get at this mysterious

---

[2] *Clarum et venerabile nomen.* I cannot but believe that this theologian is a kinsman of the de Baciocchi who once held the post of Napoleon III's *maître de menus plaisirs* (did ever an adjective do scanter justice?). Readers of the Goncourt diaries (24 September 1866) will recall how the equally copious Victor Emmanuel II arrived in Paris, hot for the chase, and gave the memorable command: '*un fiacre, et Bacciochi!*'

'*en-soi*', and you are thwarted – the film of the perceptible properties at once redeploys itself over the two halves. The epithet 'metaphysical' is bestowed by way of adornment on this occult reality, and by this means its curious properties cease to perplex. Given all that, it is easy to picture the eucharistic change. While the external film on the bread and the wine stays in its place, God miraculously expels the metaphysical kernel – which is reduced to falling back into nothingness – and puts in its place the kernel of the body and blood of Christ. It is Christ who thus prevents the inflated skin from collapsing and supports the accidents of bread and wine, so taking the place of what has been expelled. The believer encounters him dressed in these borrowed robes, but his faith allows him to recognise him there; the unbeliever is punished for his incredulity by remaining deprived of sight. But we have slipped unawares from the order of faith into the order of conjuring, nor is it given to everyone to imagine things so, in the present state of the sciences. All that has nothing to do with transubstantiation. (de Baciocchi 1959: 157–8)

I direct the reader's attention to argumentative techniques here that we shall be coming across in other places. The 'pictorial' version is distinguished by de Baciocchi from transubstantiation and is utterly set apart from it; the Church is distanced from the pictorial account; and the concept of substance involved in the pictorial account is associated with Locke. Claims are being made here substantial enough to call for evidence. So we should notice at this point that no attribution is made of the pictorial account to any scholastic (save that the introduction of 'metaphysical' may well point at Colombo), and no attempt made to spell out what distinguishes it from transubstantiation. It is enough here to notice this unfinished business.

When I gave an account of the debate between Selvaggi and Colombo, I expressed sympathy for the former's approach, despite my dissent from what he had to say about transubstantiation. But much less sympathy is shewn him in the next extract, from the Flemish theologian Vanneste, writing about the same time as de Baciocchi. For him, the whole attempt to accommodate scholastic speculations to the discoveries of modern science is misconceived and slightly comic. As we saw for ourselves in the previous chapter, Selvaggi denies that the bread and wine for consecration are, philosophically speaking, substances. They are rather aggregates; what is 'substantial' is the molecular, atomic and sub-atomic particles, and it is these that cease to exist, being converted into the body and blood of Christ, leaving only their qualities (p. 21).

Vanneste, reprobating 'physicalist' accounts of transubstantiation, prints a lengthy extract from Selvaggi 1949 in this sense – prints it as an exhibit rather than as a topic for discussion, for he excuses himself in a footnote from turning it into Flemish. He then comments:

2. Such a physicalist representation of the religious events of the consecration seems indefensible. Some might retort that this is the only way in which the old teaching can be translated into modern terms. (Vanneste 1956: 324)

But, while reprobating these attempts, Vanneste admits that the medieval account was designed to place the eucharistic mystery in a setting which was, for that time, intellectually respectable:

3. By asserting on the one hand that the substance of the bread is wholly changed into the body of Christ, it [transubstantiation] holds clearly and plainly what is the essence of eucharistic belief – that the Eucharist *is Christ himself and nothing else.* On the other hand, it does not take up the claim that what is perceived by the testimony of the senses is no more than semblance. On the contrary, the *species* [appearances] really remain; but they remain precisely in as much as they are the accidents, and do not constitute the specific 'value', the substance. (330)

Indeed, he goes there further in his admissions – the scholastic account has been all too successful:

4. In concrete terms, it was the theory of transubstantiation, as built up in the great age of scholasticism, that enjoyed a definitive success. It has therefore often been virtually identified with the dogma by many authors since then. The fact that this view imposed itself almost without rivals explains why publications in this field are very rare. (322)

In consequence, any novelty here will have to be of a radical kind – and Vanneste explains how radical he thinks it should be:

5. It is no part of our intention to serve up a kind of modern *réchauffée* of the theory of transubstantiation. What we have in mind is to shew how such adaptation generally leads down the wrong road ... we shall try to confront this exhausted theology with the data of faith itself ... we hope to convince the reader that such a return to the faith itself is the only thing that can emancipate modern eucharistic theology from the puzzles – insoluble for many – that go with its involvement with what is termed an antiquated philosophy. (324)

Once more, we have unfinished business. Vanneste's wish to confront the scholastic theory with 'the data of faith itself' is stated but not elaborated – we are not told how the data are to be identified, and we are not told what form the confrontation is supposed to take.

The last group of texts in this section comes from the German theologian Gutwenger, and it expresses in a more general way the unease felt with the older account by those who favour something newer. Gutwenger doubts whether Selvaggi's talk of substance in terms of fundamental particles goes to the heart of the problem here:

6. Offer a cosmological elucidation of transubstantiation while taking account of modern physics, and you must then set about drawing the distinction between substance and accident, only now in the fundamental components of matter. And you will end up with making assertions similar to those of traditional theology. (Gutwenger 1966: 187)

Not only are we driven back to what the scholastics said, we have made no progress towards resolving the puzzles they have bequeathed to us here, Gutwenger continues:

7. Besides, the cosmological elucidation of the eucharistic change is laden with difficulties to which no convincing answer can be given. To accept on the one hand that by the consecration the substance of the bread ceases to be, and on the other hand that – in the sense of the Councils of Constance and of Trent – the accidents persist without a subject, is to be faced with a paradox that offers no route of escape. A length has to be here, but nothing that is long; a roundness, but nothing that is round... The accidents have to be expressed as if they were abstract nouns... A cosmological elucidation of the eucharistic change leads to conceptual difficulties that are either taken seriously, or put aside by an appeal to mystery and to the omnipotence of God. (187–8)

For Gutwenger, these difficulties point to a deeper deficiency in the whole scholastic approach to the eucharistic presence. He contends – and we shall see that he is not alone in his contention – that the philosophical background to scholastic theories of transubstantiation is not 'personal' enough here:

8. Aristotle took his categories of basic concepts principally from the inorganic order. As a result, when his philosophy is applied to the mystery of the Eucharist, there must always be something stolidly material about the application. For Aristotle, the personal order was to a great extent a closed book. (195)

If our first chapter taught us anything, it will have made us cautious about using words like 'cosmological', and about describing eucharistic theology as 'Aristotelian'. But Gutwenger's complaint does fairly represent a theme in many recent writers, so we must now see what they wish to put in place of this 'cosmological' approach, and so something of their own philosophical background.

9 A PHILOSOPHICAL TRADITION

I introduce the theme of this section with some texts from the Dutch theologian Schoonenberg, who has written at some length on the notion of *presence*. For him as for Gutwenger, the cosmological approach of the scholastics cannot now satisfy; and for him, we do now possess a philosophically adequate notion of presence that can be put to eucharistic employment. It is *personal* presence that Schoonenberg holds to be the best starting-point for an account of the eucharistic presence – not spatial presence, which he regards as having been the starting-point chosen by the scholastics.[3] Spatial presence is not the most profound form of presence, although our imagination may tempt us to think that it is:

9. Presence is not in the first place the contiguity of, say, water in a glass, a dog in its kennel, a corpse in its coffin, our body in a chair. We can call these 'spatial presence', which is the lowest form of presence. Presence in the fullest sense is that between persons, personal presence, synonymous with interpersonal communion. Where this breaks down between human beings, spatial proximity is sensed rather as an absence... Personal presence can also grow ever more. A beloved person can come closer to me during spatial proximity and also during spatial absence. (Schoonenberg 1964a: 333)

Personal presence goes deeper than spatial presence, and is more subtle and demanding. Spatial presence is essentially local:

10. Spatial presence lies, not only in contiguity in space, at a particular point thereof, at a place; it lies at the same time in being in a spatial manner in space, and in a local manner at a particular place. (1964b: 402)

Personal presence is not tied down in this way, nor is it as automatic. Just as contiguity does not guarantee it, so neither does communication as such between persons. We need more than the simple imparting of information, we need some kind of utterance or witness that reveals the speaker for what he is:

11. Personal presence consists, then, not in the communicating of factual information, but in the communicating of the person himself, of the insights into life that have irrevocably shaped his spirit, and – most of all – of the relations to life that have been his means for building up what has the

---

[3] I mention here once for all that Dutch resembles German in having two words for 'presence', *tegenwoordigheid* and *aanwezigheid*. It is the former that is favoured by our authors for personal presence, and where the variation was otherwise untranslatable I have kept 'presence' for that, reserving words like 'contiguity' for a presence that is no more than spatial. The context usually decides the matter, and Schoonenberg himself admits that the linguistic usage in philosophy is rather artificial (1964b: 397–8).

deepest significance in him... It is important to notice here that this personal presence comes about through what is deepest in our capabilities. It does not come about through fantasy, day-dreaming, or hallucinations. (404)

And Schoonenberg acknowledges the philosophical tradition which makes much of this notion:

12. In the personalist philosophy of Gabriel Marcel, '*presence*' has an almost mystical ring, as '*Anwesenheit*' has for Heidegger. (397)

Some readers will already have discerned the style of philosophy that informs these remarks of Schoonenberg on personal presence. I complement his remarks with some other texts that shew the same style: they are from the Dutch theologian Smits, and they concern the rôle of *the body* in communication. Smits holds that we have emancipated ourselves from a pattern of thought which was dualistic, which opposed soul to body as two separate entities. Dualism, he contends, touched the older accounts of the eucharistic presence, but dualism is astray from the start, and it needs correcting by an approach

13. in which the body is no longer set over against the soul, but is the soul itself in its outwardness. When I laugh, that is not a signal which denotes some kernel in me, the soul, which is happy. When I laugh, my soul is happy thereby; better still, the happiness of the soul is nowhere else than in the laughter, and is not intelligible apart from this outwardness. My body is not a window onto my soul, but is the soul itself in its outwardness... When I laugh, someone else does not have to make a leap, and to reason from the laughing face to the happy soul. In the laugh itself, he grasps without reasoning the spirit that is there and nowhere else. So the body is no longer a *signal* or *empty sign*, but above all an expression of spirit, a sign that is full. (Smits 1965: 23/5, col. 2, my italics)

This unity in the significance of what I do is found even when I communicate by means of some object. Smits writes in the article I have just cited:

14. While I am playing the violin I feel myself one with the instrument; in it, better than in my own body, I can express and live out the feelings that reign in me and that I wish others to share. The listeners perceive my feelings only in the sounds of my violin – there, and nowhere else, is immediate contact made between us. Not only my body but my violin too is felt by me to be identical with me, and not alien to me. (cols. 2–3)

In another of his articles Schoonenberg expresses his agreement with Smits, and observes as Smits did that the communication which goes with personal presence can be by deed as well as by word. But Schoonenberg singles out one kind of deed as deserving the special notice that he and others accord it. The deed is *giving*:

15. One special gesture is giving. By giving, I have handed over something from my own sphere, something of myself, and I make it pass over into the sphere of the person I love. What I give is no longer merely a thing, a purchase, or a means of nutriment. Such a function is now wholly taken up into the Reality-as-Gift, into the Reality-as-Sign, of my self-giving to the other. That is why a gift, more than any other gesture, makes the giver live with and in the other, in the receiver. The most intimate contact that there is between human beings is simultaneously a gesture and a gift. (Schoonenberg 1965: 49)

From this passage, let us keep in mind what Schoonenberg has written about the 'Reality-as-Sign' which an object acquires when it becomes a gift – we shall be meeting it again.

Some readers, as I said, will already have recognised the philosophical tradition within which texts from Schoonenberg and from Smits have been written. It is phenomenology, with its cognate tradition of existentialism, and no fair account of the recent opinions can ignore it. But phenomenology is, even by philosophical standards, heavy going in its more technical elaborations; it is not homogeneous among those who claim to follow its methods; and the newer authors we are meeting exhibit rather than acknowledge their dependence on it.[4] For our purposes, I need to express as simply as I can some beliefs associated with this philosophical tradition, beliefs that have shaped the newer approaches to the Eucharist. Fortunately, those beliefs are also found, although in a very different idiom, in a tradition where philosophically minded readers of this book are likely to feel more at home. So I can best make the points I need to make by noticing something that both traditions have set themselves against. And that is the style of philosophy associated, in a very general way, with Descartes in the seventeenth century.

For Descartes and the Cartesian tradition, the philosopher must seek an unshakeable point in knowledge, an element proof against all scepticism, and that element is to be found in the self-awareness of the individual thinker, an awareness of thought that goes beyond any

---

[4] A good survey of the phenomenological movement is in Spiegelberg 1970; on Husserl himself, its founder, D. Bell 1990 is admirably shrewd and informative. In the main text I have deliberately confined myself to what is of immediate concern to our topic, and deliberately refrained from embarking on the complexities which attend on this tradition in philosophy. The references I have given in this note will reveal them soon enough.

doubts concerning the external world, the reliability of memory or the existence of the thinker's body. From this citadel of security, cautious forays can be made into what purports to be a world of objects, among which are other rational beings. The Cartesian style of philosophising took many forms, and its rejection in our own century has also been varied; but the rejection can be seen in traditions as apparently distinct as phenomenology, pragmatism and the later writings of Wittgenstein. For these traditions there is no absolute starting-point, we must rather get back to what Wittgenstein calls 'the rough ground', a life shared with others in the material setting within which we act and think: the *Lebenswelt* or 'life-world', as it is called in the phenomenological tradition. Only within that setting can meaning be sought, only there can gestures and words be interpreted and answered. 'Meaning' is not something only accidentally linked to shared expectations and activities – removed from them, it loses the life it had. 'Thought' is not some essentially private activity, of which visible behaviour is no more than the outward sign. The Cartesian divorce between matter and spirit, between the orders of extension and of thought, needs mending; shared activity between human beings is not something in which inferences have to be made from gestures to meanings and thoughts, as if meanings and thoughts were of another, inner order, private to each individual. Inference is simply not in place here, nor is the body a window onto the soul.

Observations of the sort will be familiar to some readers, who will be aware of my brutal oversimplifyings in them, but all readers will have detected in this summary a position akin to what we have found in Schoonenberg and in Smits. Further texts can strengthen the link. The stress laid in phenomenology upon the *Lebenswelt*, the shared human world where alone meaning and communication can exist, finds an echo in what Schoonenberg writes about how the eucharistic presence needs to be 'placed'. We must, in his view, start with the community of persons who worship:

16. The eucharistic celebration begins with a *praesentia realis*, a real presence of the Lord *among us*, and its aim is to make this presence more inward. And this takes place in the signs of the word and the bread and the wine. It is only as a function of this making more inward of Christ's presence that we can speak of his presence under signs of the consecrated bread.

The latter presence is called *praesentia realis*, 'real presence', and rightly so. But not rightly when it alone is so called, or so called as the primary example. As de Lubac well put it, the presence is '*réelle parce que réalisante*' [real because making real]. It is a presence that actualises; one could almost say an emanating, a transitive presence; a presence that is an invitation. It is forever proceeding from the Lord into his assembled community. The host is always the bread over which there has been recited in the Lord's name the consecratory and hallowing canon, with the words of institution at its heart. (Schoonenberg 1964a: 334)

In consequence, the specifically eucharistic presence needs to be subordinated to the presence of Christ in the community:

17. For us, what is more important than the presence of Christ under the *species* is the whole presence of the Lord in his Church, namely as she celebrates the Eucharist. It is just when we gauge the richness of this presence in the community that we grasp there the significance of the presence under the *species*... [The eucharistic presence] is not the focal point of it all, but rather a subordinate element. As we have already indicated, the presence in the community is more important. (1964b: 396)

These texts from Schoonenberg can be complemented by some from Smits. Like Schoonenberg, he attaches a particular significance to the gesture of giving, and reflects at some length upon a special kind of gift, the ceremonial offering of food and drink: in fact what he writes here includes the notorious 'tea-and-a-biscuit' passage. Earlier, in (13) and (14), we saw Smits denying dualism and stressing the embodiment of ourselves in a gesture. What he has to say about the gift of food and drink exhibits the same themes, but we can now see them in the light of what we have seen about the claims bound up with phenomenology. Notice first the denial of dualism in the gift:

18. I must not speak of the tea as a sign that points outside itself to the housewife's hospitable feelings, she being somewhere else: the tea is not a signal. No, the tea is the incarnate welcome, which I perceive in a single intuitive grasp. The sign is the incarnation of what is signified: in all the tea is embodied all the housewife's welcome, making one indissoluble whole. (Smits 1964b: 9/4, col. 3)

And as there is no cleft between an outward gift and an inward feeling, but rather one incarnate unity, so the proffered food and drink undergo a change:

19. But as soon as the tea and biscuit are employed as gifts, they are changed. They have become signs of friendship. Even when I can no longer see any trace of the tea or the biscuit, and they no longer have for me any significance as food and drink, I can still highly value them, as an expression of welcome. (col. 2)

The change goes with the way in which, more than in any words, welcome is embodied in gifts. It is so embodied as to make the gifts a bodily extension of the one who welcomes, an extension that raises to a new order what is given – and here we find Smits in the same article writing in terms that resemble what we saw Schoonenberg write in (15) about 'Reality-as-Sign':

20. The housewife might of course have expressed her welcome in words only, but she feels that things cannot stop there … she prefers to fill out the defect by these gifts … These gifts constitute an extended bodiliness, a kind of mystical body … Food and drink take over the rôle of the body itself, the welcome becomes tangible in the gifts. What I could originally call no more than a snack and a drink, in the material and biological sense of the expression, I can no longer indicate by the word 'snack', because its activity is no longer part of a relationship that is biological; it is part of one that is personal. (col. 2)

Just as Smits has applied his earlier remarks about dualism and incarnation to the ceremonial presentation of food and drink, so Schoonenberg takes up what he has said about giving and about Reality-as-Sign, but now deliberately introduces a eucharistic term. When gifts are made,

21. they have a new and deeper reality – the sign-reality that communicates personal presence. We very nearly ought to say that they are transubstantiated. (Schoonenberg 1964b: 407)

So the term 'transubstantiated' at least is employed by Schoonenberg, but his use of it elsewhere reminds us that he is not writing within the scholastic tradition. He compares views like those he and Smits hold with the scholastic accounts, and places the novelty of the newer opinions in their explicit appeal to the concept of personal presence:

22. There is something new in what is said by Fr Luchesius [i.e. Smits] and by myself, and in related expositions … its explicit invocation of a new dimension – that of the existence of a person along with other persons. The presence under the appearances is now seen as belonging to the order of personal presence; and transubstantiation is seen as a change of meaning, whereby the bread acquires an irrevocable significance in the relationship between Christ and ourselves. (1965: 49)

At this point, it might be thought that the position adopted in the newer accounts of the eucharistic presence is plain enough. We are to look for meaning and significance in the *Lebenswelt*, in shared human life; it is in the communal activities and interests of human beings that the world we know is known and constituted, so that our descriptions and our patterns of action are mutually dependent. So speaks phenomenology, so speak other philosophical traditions and so apparently speak the newer accounts of the eucharistic presence. To stress the human and communal setting of the eucharistic rite is a natural result of the influence of the phenomenological tradition. Another result is the stress upon 'embodiment' in gesture, and especially in the gesture of giving; a third is the stress upon the change in reality-as-sign when gifts are made. But do not the texts that exhibit these emphases also exhibit an inadequate view of the eucharistic presence, a reduction of it to the community's action, and to the use the community makes in faith and in love of gestures and signs? I think it is fair to say that the reputation of the newer accounts is something like that. If so, the reputation has been too easily reached. The newer accounts do undoubtedly stress these things, but the authors of them want to stress a great deal more. And to that we must now turn.

10 BEYOND PHILOSOPHY

It was Schoonenberg who provided us with the most elaborate account of personal presence, and it was from Schoonenberg that was taken the last of the quotations at the end of the preceding section – quotations that suggested a reduction of the eucharistic presence to purely human terms. So it seems fitting that the present section should open with some texts by the same author that explicitly deny any such reduction. In an article where he surveyed the observations he had made about the different forms of presence, he added a caution:

23. When we tried just now to fill out our considerations of spatial and personal presence, our object was not to effect a deduction of the eucharistic presence as a possibility, or to fit it neatly into the distinctions we had drawn. As we have already stated, this presence of Christ is first and foremost something unexpected, and revelation alone, interpreted by the Church, can bring us to acquaintance with it. However, we do have to interpret this revelation afresh for theological and catechetical purposes; and perhaps the considerations I have been offering will help us here. (Schoonenberg 1959b: 321)

He may have used the analogy with personal presence during spatial absence, but in another article he explicitly denies that what he has written can be applied without qualification to the presence of Christ:

24. The absent friend is present for me above all because I love him; Christ is above all present because he bears me in mind. The presence of the friend is active, but at the same time heavily dependent on my own activity; but the Lord is rather he who actively makes himself present. (1959a: 155)

But it is not only Schoonenberg who writes in this way. De Baciocchi introduces a theme of which we shall be seeing a good deal later on, what we might call the salvific and ritual setting of the Eucharist:

25. The relation of the Last Supper to the redemptive act corresponds to the relation between the first Passover and the Exodus from Egypt; in each, there is established a memorial, both institutional and religious, of salvation... In each, the memorial does more than summon up a memory. God himself intervenes, with his almighty power to save, in the assembly's own time, because of a commitment that goes with his command that they should repeat afresh the commemorative signs. And so intervening, he gives that which he makes the assembled faithful express by what they do. (de Baciocchi 1959: 139)

Indeed, it is in the whole setting of Christ's action in the Incarnation and Redemption that the Eucharist must be seen, and Smits recalls that the words used by Christ instituting the Eucharist were uttered in a tradition that was Semitic, and that they should be construed within that tradition:

26. 'Body' for them is the whole person, but in its bodily manifestation: what we are concerned with is the person of Jesus, who is about to suffer. 'Blood' for them is the whole person, but seen as living, because the blood is the life of the whole human being. For a Jew, no covenant is thinkable without a bloody sacrifice; so the presence of the word 'covenant' points to the Lord's passion. The same thing is said twice, according to the rules of Semitic parallelism; in each case are concerned with the person of Jesus, who says 'this is myself, who am to suffer for you'. (Smits 1964b: 9/4, col. 1)

The Eucharist is to be seen in a communal setting, but the setting is the shared life of Christians. To this the shared *Lebenswelt* of the phenomenological tradition offers no more than an analogy, because the life shared here is the life bestowed by Christ upon the Church: that is why Schoonenberg writes in (16) and (17) that the real eucharistic presence of Christ must be set within the real presence of Christ in the Church that is his body. He does indeed write there in terms of personal presence, but he makes clear the special nature of the presence in the context of the Church:

27. What matters is that the salvific presence of Christ... This personal presence... means being a member of Christ, being a fellow-member with others; it means the reality of the Church, because the Lord lives in the Church as in his body. This presence of the life of Christ in us and in each one is real, it is no poetic fantasy or figurative language. It too is a *praesentia realis*, even prescinding from the part played by the Eucharist here. And it is in within this presence of Christ – with, for, among and in us – that are situated the eucharistic celebration and the presence in the signs of bread and wine. (Schoonenberg 1965: 48)

In other words, when Schoonenberg subordinates the specifically eucharistic presence to Christ's presence in the community of believers, it is a matter for him of placing the power of Christ, not of eliminating it:

28. By Christ's eucharistic presence we do not mean in the first instance his presence under the eucharistic species; we mean *his presence in the community that is celebrating the Eucharist*. That is where we assemble, to hear his word and to shew forth his death in the holy meal. The Lord is then among us, even though no consecrated hosts are there in the place. (Schoonenberg 1964a: 334)

And we shall in due course meet other texts of this kind, in Aquinas.

I would confirm by yet another group of texts this insistence by the newer authors on the primacy of divine power in the Eucharist. These further texts touch a theme which will be met in later chapters, so here we can simply note its presence in what they write. The theme is one we have come to take for granted of late in the Roman Church: that the Christ who is present among us is our glorified and Risen Lord. Schoonenberg makes this part of his contentions about personal presence:

29. Even during the earthly life of Jesus, his spatial propinquity was never of importance for those who believed in him, apart from his personal presence. Now that the Lord is glorified, spatial propinquity has been transcended, and the Lord is present wherever hearts believe in him, whenever two or more are gathered together in his name. (334)

It is in this Easter setting that our authors approach the eucharistic presence, with the help of concepts we have encountered such as 'personal presence', 'Reality-as-Gift' and 'embodiment'. If Christ leaves his disciples, it is for their good; 'absence' here no longer plays the part or has the sense it has in ordinary personal relationships:

30. When we are dealing with human beings, spatial absence can threaten and even do away with personal presence – 'out of sight, out of mind'. [The Dutch is literally 'out of eye, out of heart'.] For Christ, on the contrary, the absence is a guarantee that personal presence will endure and be enriched: 'it is good for you that I go away'. (1959a: 154)

When we speak of the Eucharist in terms of sign and of gift, we must do so with the glorified status of Christ as our setting:

31. The farewell uttered by Jesus at the Last Supper took the form of a promise that they would see him again. Here as elsewhere, the God-Man has not done away with what is human, but brought it to fulfilment. Next to the desire to purify himself from spatial proximity by means of absence... there is a desire for the embodiment and incarnation of personal presence, but for an embodiment that is more transparent to the person, is more of a sign (1964b: 409)

So the Eucharist is in the deepest sense a union with the glorified Christ, beyond the reach of any human power or adequate language:

32. The holy Eucharist is the *self*-giving of Christ to the highest degree among all the sacraments, and is in the deepest way a union with him. Every human gift, in the union it effects between giver and receiver, is only a shadow of Christ's union with us; and so the actualising presence of the human giver in the human gift is only a remote indication of the actualising presence of the Lord's Body in the eucharistic gift and food. (414)

Once more I remind the reader that we shall be returning to this theme of the Risen Christ. I now conclude this section with two texts that concern his self-giving in the Eucharist.

Each celebration of the Eucharist ritually presents this greatest giving, and we see that de Baciocchi suggests, in a way similar to what Smits wrote in (26), how the rite presents it:

33. St Paul puts us on our guard against the temptation to take the body and blood as primarily two physical components of the man Jesus. In fact, the duality pertains to the liturgical order more than to the biological. The body, shared among us, exemplifies the communion-sacrifice; the blood, poured out, exemplifies the threefold sacrifice: covenant, passover and expiation. (de Baciocchi 1959: 144)

It was in texts by Smits himself like (14) and (18) to (20) that we found these concepts of 'embodiment' and 'giving' most elaborated. We can now notice how, for him also, the setting of the incarnation, death and resurrection is the way in which these concepts, human in origin, can be applied to what Christ did at the Last Supper; but we can also notice how the application brings out what sets the gesture of Christ apart from all else:

34. On the night before he suffered, the Son of God, truly made man, took bread and wine and made them extend the possibilities of expression in his own bodiliness. But in this way bread and wine were not only an embodiment of human inwardness; in this unique case, they embodied divine inwardness as well. (Smits 1965: 23/5, col. 3)

So here, as in the other texts of this section, philosophical background is held not to be enough. The place of Christ and the whole setting of salvation are what make the eucharistic presence unique. And we can now pass to seeing how this uniqueness is spelled out.

II AND SO TO TRANSUBSTANTIATION

So it is Christ, the Word of God and our Risen Lord, who is at the centre of all these accounts of the eucharistic presence, and who makes that presence more than any human giving or signification could achieve. But it is precisely this lordship of Christ that has provided our authors with their new ways of representing tran- substantiation, and it is with these new ways that the present section is concerned. Two of them, de Baciocchi and Vanneste, offer similar accounts here, and it is convenient to begin with a text that expresses their general thesis:

35. By his word and his human actions, the Word made flesh *tells* us the deep meaning and final destination of the things that are; sometimes, by his human expression, he even *gives* them this meaning and this destina- tion... The Risen Christ reigns over all things... It falls to him to give each creature its name and to change that name if he thinks fit. When he changes a name, he transforms what is denoted by it – we can all remember the examples of Abraham and Peter. So things *are* purely and simply what they are for Jesus Christ. (de Baciocchi 1955: 576)

To see how de Baciocchi wants these claims to be taken, we must go a little further afield.

In 1955 there appeared a book to do with the eucharistic presence, *Ceci est mon corps*. The 'realistic' tone of its theses made all the deeper impression because its author, F. J. Leenhardt, was a Swiss Prot- estant theologian. The book was given a sympathetic if discriminating review by Vanneste (1957), who also cites it with respect in the article we have already met (1956), and it is from Vanneste and de Baciocchi that I have gathered themes from Leenhardt, themes

which have affected what these two authors have written. Leenhardt,
we learn from Vanneste, not only stresses the reality of the presence,
he is even prepared to accept the term 'transubstantiation', but with
a proviso:

36. We must be careful not to take Christ's words 'This is my body' as
Greeks would. Greek ways of speech are logical, and try to express things as
they are. Hebrew ways of speech, on the contrary, do not look upon things
in the world for what they are, but for what they are called to be; they refer
them to their purpose. When Jesus Christ took bread and gave it, saying
'This is my body', the declaration must not be taken in a logical sense, as if
it expressed brute reality: logically speaking, the bread is bread. But it is a
Hebrew who is speaking. The bread is referred to a purpose that is
transcendent; the bread is what it becomes with respect to this ultimate
reference. (Vanneste 1957: 270)

This claim made here is part of a more general claim about the
purpose of things and the will of Christ:

37. In what sense should we speak of a transubstantiation? If the substance
of things is what they are as instruments in the hands of God ... if substance
is what things are with respect to the purpose that God assigns to them, then
faith will here admit that this bread, with respect to what Jesus Christ wills
in this case, has no longer the same substance, because of the new purpose
assigned it. The word 'transubstantiation' expresses this change, without
pretending to offer an explanation of it. (270–1)

For Vanneste, the moral is that the scholastics have elaborated the
concept of substance in a way that we might call too *secular* for the
eucharistic context:

38. When scholasticism set about making this concept of substance more
precise, it was not wholly successful in arriving at the genuine sense of the
concept. That is, instead of deepening the concept purely in terms of its
religious significance, it remained – usually remained, at all events – on the
ordinary philosophical and rational plane. (1956: 332)

A better way is to let the notion of what things are be a matter of their
fundamental religious significance in the eyes of Christ and of the
Father. Do that, and first things are put first:

39. When Christ says of this bread that it is his body, he expresses the
fundamental religious significance of it. In other words, the bread, in his eyes
and in those of the Father, is no longer bread, but simply his own adorable
body. And so it is that – to use F. Leenhardt's apt phrase – Christ's word is
a creating word, a word that makes things be what he wants them to be. This
is no merely human naming of the bread – something like 'this bread

reminds you of my body'. Things are what God wants them to be. If to our eyes bread is still there, we can only say this: we see it thus only at the level of our human experience, which does not penetrate to the divine and uniquely true vision. (332)

This appeal to the place of Christ and to his will is developed by de Baciocchi. But now let us notice that part of the development lies in drawing conclusions about human knowledge from eucharistic assertions:

40. If the christology of the letter to the Colossians is sound, if Christ really is the keystone of the universe, then the one absolute point of view on things is that from which Christ sees and judges them. Things are purely and simply what they are for Christ, because the mind of Christ is the absolute norm of our own minds, just as his existence is the absolute norm of our own existence. Perceptible properties, physical and chemical properties, have a significance that is no more than relative. (de Baciocchi 1959: 151)

We shall see in a moment that Vanneste draws similar conclusions, and we shall have to see later on what can be made of them. De Baciocchi goes further in the next text, and introduces an *holistic* consideration – it is the place a thing has in the whole of creation that determines what it is:

41. If I define what is by its empirical properties only, I shall see [in the Eucharist] nothing more than an extrinsic change. But if I define it by its place in the totality of things, by the totality of its properties and relations, and take account while doing so of the hierarchy of those properties and relations, then the reality of the bread is changed. What remains is relative and accidental in character.

In the last analysis, it is a matter of one's scale of values. Is or is not the world in the first place made by Christ and made for him? If it is, then the lordship of Christ and its application in the Eucharist cannot be an extrinsic or accidental relation for anything. (156)

For de Baciocchi it is this central place of Christ, the Word of God, that makes transubstantiation unique to him in the Eucharist. But notice once more that this claim goes with a claim about human knowledge:

42. Christ alone can transubstantiate, for he alone – in his being as God-Man, and in his liberty as Lord – is the centre of reference for every created existence... An object exists only as an element, only as this or that element of the universe. What is the most determining factor in this its cosmic situation? The sum total of its empirical properties? No: it is the relation the object bears to Christ, who is the universal point of coherence and of unity,

and Lord of every calling. It is true that the relation things bear to Christ is modified by changes in the function they exercise with respect to humanity, and that this change comes, *as a general rule*, from change in their empirical properties. For all that, at least the sacramental order provides an exception: it introduces fundamental changes in function, linked with changes in significance, while empirical properties as such persist. (160)

And in a similar text from another article, he combines his appeal to the lordship of Christ with the notion of giving that we found in Smits and in Schoonenberg:

43. If scientists, by rational interpretations of experience, could give the final word about things, there could be no question of transubstantiation. But if this final word belongs exclusively to the creating Word expressed humanly in Jesus Christ, it is difficult to escape the conclusion. Jesus declares that he gives his body: in doing so, he makes to exist *now* as his body what had originally been created by him as bread... (1955: 577)

Yet again, we can notice the claim made about human knowledge.

Similar claims are made by Vanneste, but they are expressed somewhat differently and need a little introduction. We have already seen in (38) and (39) how he regards scholastic theology as insufficiently religious in its elaboration of the notion of substance, and holds that we should rather concentrate upon the will and creative word of Christ. His opinion shews itself in a comment he makes upon someone we encountered in the first chapter – Godefroy, who made the remarkable claim that 'substance' in Trent's decrees has no technical connotations, but belongs rather to a 'perennial philosophy' which needs no study to be understood (see the passage at pp. 24–5). Given Vanneste's lack of sympathy for the scholastic tradition, it is not surprising that he should shew some sympathy for another piece by Godefroy, where the concept of substance is supposedly emancipated from that tradition by being stated within this mysterious *philosophia perennis*, and so stated as being 'nothing more than what common sense sees in it':

44. C'est-à-dire ce fond insaissable de tout, que la science n'atteint pas...que les sens ne perçoivent pas et que cependant la raison nous dit exister en toutes choses, comme point d'attache et raison dernière des phénomènes...la réalité en tant qu'elle se distingue des apparences. (Godefroy 1924: col. 1349)[5]

---

[5] I have left this passage in French because I cannot translate it into English without robbing it of even the appearance of making sense. Having cited it, I shall be able to refer the reader to it later in the chapter.

Vanneste's only reservation about this extraordinary passage is that Godefroy does not go far enough. He comments:

45. That naturally sounds very attractive, and it sets the dogma of transubstantiation free from all Aristotelianism. Fundamentally, however, Godefroy is committing the very fault for which we have been reproaching the Aristotelians. He is still looking for a structure or distinction within reality itself, so as to be able to say that the bread is Christ and yet still seems to be bread. (Vanneste 1956: 333–4)

And it is just such an approach that Vanneste finds wrong. He proceeds to give what he thinks is the right way:

46. But it is not a matter of a change in reality seen simply in itself. It is not '*les apparences*' that remain while what is deeper goes away. The whole creature goes away, but remains for our secular experience. (334)

So it is in terms of the central role of Christ and of his creative word that both de Baciocchi and Vanneste elaborate their account of the eucharistic presence; and it is in those terms that each of them accepts the word 'transubstantiation'. In (42) de Baciocchi explicitly links the word with the unique place of Christ, while in (37) Vanneste makes the word express – without explaining – the fundamental change of purpose in the Eucharist.

We have also seen that both Smits and Schoonenberg make Christ's action in the Eucharist go beyond any simple application of the philosophical concepts they employ. I now give texts which will shew how, for these authors as well, it is the unique place of Christ that extends what they have been saying to the acceptance of the word 'transubstantiation'. And I go first to Smits.

The analysis offered by Smits of gesture and communication stressed the *embodiment* of feelings and thoughts in a way that was opposed to any dualism. To go to his example of laughter in (13), there is no leap to be made, no reasoning from outer laughter to an inner world. To think that there might be is to confuse a *signal* or *empty sign* (where what is signified is remote) with a *full sign*, the laughter that is an embodiment of my happiness. We have already seen in (34) how he applies the notion of embodiment to Christ's action at the Last Supper – an embodiment of divine as well as of human inwardness. I now give the continuation of that text, in which Smits makes the unique place of Christ into the reason for transubstantiation:

47. Transubstantiation begins precisely when God's Son expresses the inwardness of God for us, and does so not just in his humanity but in the signs of human intersubjectivity as well. In Christianity, there is but one fundamental mystery: the Son of God became man even to the death of the cross, in order to send us his Spirit. The real presence of Christ is the consequence of that, it is not a self-contained miracle. (Smits 1965: 23/5, col. 3)

In writing of our own celebration of the Eucharist, Smits takes up the 'tea-and-a-biscuit' example we saw in (18) to (20), but makes it clear that this is a starting-point, not a reductive description. He writes, after giving the example:

48. What takes place when the Lord expresses for us his love in the offering of bread and wine? In as much as he is truly man, there takes place what took place in our example.

He incarnates there his human love. The bread and wine express his inwardness in a way that surpasses its expression in language. In bread and wine, the Lord expresses without reserve the gift of himself. What is signified is in the sign, and forms a unity with it. (1964b: 9/5, col. 1)

But, he goes on, more needs to be said if we are to speak of transubstantiation:

49. Yet this is not yet transubstantiation. The Lord is ever more than a human being. As the Son of God, he expresses for us in his humanity the 'concerns' of God himself for us. Jesus thus expresses, not only what concerns us in his own human inwardness, but what concerns us in the inwardness of God. In the gifts, there is incarnate not only the love of a man, but the love of the God-Man. God's love becomes 'testable'. Once more, I have no need for deduction here, there is no leap for me to make from the gifts (seen as signs that are signals) to what is outside them. No, the gesture is consummated in the sign; the sign is the incarnate love of the God-Man. (col. 1)

Notice in this text the insistence that we are dealing here with signs, not signals, dealing with gifts that embody the giver, not refer to him as to something else. Smits stresses the point in another article. He gives a similar account of the embodiment, and once more invokes Christ's place to make this gift of himself be transubstantiation:

50. At that moment, he extends into the bread the expression of his own bodiliness. The bread will now function along with Christ's own bodiliness. It becomes, along with Christ's own body, an expression of what concerns me in the Lord as man – that he now wishes to give himself to me in and through this bread. And so the bread is never Christ's body as taken in itself,

but always as taken in hand by the Lord and handed out by the Lord ... The mystery begins for faith at the point where the bread is taken in hand by Christ as man, and is handed out to me as an expression of self-giving – and expressing not just the self-giving of a man, but that of the Son of God himself. All this truly human action is 'taken up' by the Son of God. We have an *unio hypostatica* [that is, the union in the Incarnation], whereby this humanity becomes an expression of divinity. And we have a transubstantiation, whereby this human gift becomes an expression of divine self-giving. (1964a: 342)

But having given this text, Smits considers the charge that what he is suggesting is a poorer notion of the eucharistic presence than what the scholastics proposed, with their talk of the conversion of one substance into another beneath the accidents. And he counters the charge by the distinction between signs and signals. To think in terms of signals does indeed demand that (if we are to preserve Catholic belief) we do hold to this conversion of substances. But we should not now think in such terms:

51. This new conception is indeed an impoverishment, if in this way we do not succeed in grasping a sign except as a signal that indicates something outside itself... A Catholic who cannot understand signs except as signals would be surrendering the whole point of the dogma if he no longer accepted the change of substances under the appearances of bread. But as soon as we manage to approach the mystery in quite another way – approach it as a sign that does not indicate anything outside itself, but indicates something in itself, with which it is identical – as soon as we do that, then the possibility arises of a deeper understanding and a more apt formulation. In such a case, we are again thinking more Semitically. (343)

Some texts from Schoonenberg speak to the same effect. We saw at (15) how he made that which is given acquire a 'Reality-as-Sign' and 'Reality-as-Gift'. Indeed, we saw at (21) that he even takes and associates the word 'transubstantiated' with giving. But now, writing of the Eucharist itself, he wants to apply the word in its proper sense. Once more, he starts from the concept of giving and of sign, although this is only a starting-point:

52. In the Holy Eucharist, bread and wine have wholly become the gift of Christ. They are not just taken up into an action that emphasises words, and so not essentially changed when the sacramental action has run its course. The bread and wine are essentially changed, are transubstantiated as a gift, but on the level of the God-Man. Jesus Christ, in whom dwelleth the fullness of the Godhead bodily and truly (Coloss. i, 19), gives himself to us in this gift, in this food. (Schoonenberg 1965: 50)

Once more, it is the unique status of Christ that sets this giving apart from all others. And just as unique for him is the use by Christ of *signs* here, the signs of his unique self-giving. Transubstantiation lies in this use of signs – in transignification – but the use is one that Christ alone can achieve:

53. This actualising presence comes about in that bread and wine *become signs*... And so by this consecration Christ is not 'brought out of heaven' in a spatial sense, and even less is there any physical or chemical change in the bread and wine. What happens is a change of sign. Transubstantiation is a transfinalisation or transignification, but then in the depth that Christ alone reaches, in his most real self-giving. Bread and wine, accompanied by the word, become the signs that actualise this deepest self-giving. (1964a: 335)

We have now spent four sections on newer accounts of the eucharistic presence, and several themes have emerged – the philosophical background of some of the concepts employed, the stress laid upon the uniqueness of their application to the Eucharist, the place of the Risen Lord, and the ways in which our authors respectively reach the formula expressing the eucharistic presence as transubstantiation. I said at the start of the chapter that I wanted to offer a selection of texts liberal enough to give the 'feel' of what was being written in these accounts, and I hope I have by now succeeded. But the texts were given for another purpose as well: they provide material for considerations that will be part of what follows in the book. With the texts – and with others, yet to be given – I shall be concerned in later chapters also. In the present chapter I shall begin my appraisal of them. It is an appraisal which does not touch all the questions that might be raised about the newer opinions. It is also an appraisal whose general direction does not match what is commonly said of the opinions. I move towards this appraisal by considering the account offered by Schillebeeckx in his book, and the reservations he expresses about his contemporaries. As we shall see, what he writes raises matters that point beyond the present chapter to what is yet to come.

12   A CONTEMPORARY'S PRINCIPLES

I have already praised Schillebeeckx's book for the amount of material it contains, and of this material I am concerned only with what touches my theme. As we might expect, he has much in common with the new authors we have been examining: he too writes in the phenomenological tradition, and he too is dissatisfied with the 'cosmological' approach of the scholastics to the eucharistic presence. Again like his contemporaries, he insists that no philosophical scheme can do justice to the Eucharist, and that we must put our consideration of it into the whole redemptive context, with our Risen Lord at the centre. My purpose in this section is not to dwell on these resemblances but to suggest that what Schillebeeckx writes allows two principles to be discerned in it. The two principles will turn out to be decisive, both for the account he offers and for the reservations he expresses about the newer opinions. One of the two principles is ontological – that is, concerned with what is: I call it the principle of the Givenness of Reality. The other is epistemological – that is, concerned with what we know: I call it the principle of the Humanness of Perception.[6] In this section, I illustrate the two principles themselves with a selection of texts, and in the next I give further texts, to shew how Schillebeeckx makes use of them in what he writes of his contemporaries. It is only when I begin my appraisal of what we have seen that I shall claim to detect an ambiguity in both.

I begin with the Givenness of Reality. It amounts to a 'placing' of the whole *Lebenswelt*, the human world we constitute by our activities and intentions. The principle claims that this human world both manifests and conceals a reality we can never wholly grasp, so that our knowledge of it pertains to the category of sign, with the revelation of God as what is signified. A section of Schillebeeckx's book is concerned with shewing that 'reality is not of man's devising' (1967: 100f. [1968: 126f.]). It is from this section that I have taken texts, and the first of them touches the revelation in things:

54. For the believer, things are not only what they are in themselves, not only what human beings come to know of them in the course of the plans they make in this world for their lives here. Things are also, each in the measure of its own being, a revelation of God. (101 [127])

The deeper significance of reality is more than personal persuasion of believers, but accepting the significance does not mean that we set no store by what we can perceive in the world around us:

[6] I have called these two themes 'principles' and set them apart from the others because of the rôle they play in Schillebeeckx's thought here. He himself refers to the first of them as a principle at 100 [126]. What I call the second comes later in his book, where he asks about reality and what appears of it, and says that the topic demands a 'placing' of human perception, 116 [145].

55. By the salvific will of God that creates, things *are* – in what they are –
values for salvation, and a revelation of God, disclosing and at the same time
veiling him. And they are all this metaphysically, in a realistic sense, not just
in the thoughts of believers…we can say that the whole material world
already possesses a pervading quasi-sacramental significance. This Christian
vision and idea of creation does not devalue matter, but correctly estimates
it in its most profound sense. (101 [128])

And so Schillebeeckx comes to the notion that reality is *given* to us,
and that, being so given, will never be wholly within our grasp:

56. Man indeed is by nature an interpreter, and is enlightened in some
measure by truth in its capacity as manifestation. But the sense he gives is
governed by a reality that is first of all God's (the priority here is
metaphysical, not temporal), and only then man's. That is why reality is a
mystery, the form of God's revelation that both discloses and veils, and that
is why the deepest reality of persons and things always escapes us…the
explicit content in what we know points towards the mystery that ever
escapes and is ahead of us. (101–2 [128–9])

Our knowledge exists, then, within a reality that is its foundation,
and yet which is a mystery that the knowledge cannot wholly grasp.
From this, Schillebeeckx draws his conclusions about the involvement
of human knowledge with *signs*, signs of a reality which is a mystery,
the mystery of the presence of God:

57. In consequence, all our explicit contents of consciousness do no more
than point towards the mystery; we know reality only in signs. Even the
content of our perceptions of bread and wine is only a sign of a reality that
escapes us – and this quite apart from any eucharistic context…The basic
property of making-sense-for-me is accorded by reality itself, a reality which
in its origin is not *mine*, but is rather bestowed upon me so that I can make
sense of it. (102 [129])

But if our knowledge of reality partakes of the nature of a *sign*, we
must go on to admit the limitations imposed upon all our human
activities of giving meaning – all those activities that exist in and go
on to make up the *Lebenswelt*, the 'life-world' of which philosophy
speaks:

58. On the basis of this fundamental intelligibility-for-me, I can proceed to
establish all manner of meanings, determining what things shall in particular
mean for me, on the ground of what they themselves are. I cannot set about
this just as I please, because I am tied to the reality that there is. Within this
given reality, I *establish* a human world, and incessantly modify the human
sense of it. But only its human sense – its deepest sense, its metaphysical
sense, lies beyond human grasp or intervention. (102–3 [129–30])

So much for the Givenness of Reality. I turn to texts that concern the Humanness of Perception.

The principle is, as I see it, partly a claim about the dependence of perceptual data upon the perceiver, partly a claim about the *human* unity that covers all our varieties of knowledge, and partly an evocation of what Schillebeeckx has already claimed in the principle of the Givenness of Reality. First, for the human unity of what we do – the humanness of perception, in fact:

59. Purely sensory perception is not to be found in human beings: they see, hear, touch and taste in a *human* way, and so render human both what is perceived and the perception itself. (116 [146])

Now we have already seen how the first principle claims that all our activity of giving human sense to things takes place within a reality that is bestowed upon us and not of our own devising. Perception in consequence, since it is human, is caught up into this activity:

60. So perception – along with its content – is elevated above its own sensory relativeness, and is borne along with the spiritual aiming at reality. (116–17 [146])

It is the phrase 'sensory relativeness' here that we should notice, for it introduces the next theme in the second principle – the status of what we perceive of reality:

61. Perception in human beings – it is of these alone that we speak – has its own quite distinctive *unity*. The unity is that which joins a spiritual act (an act namely of positive openness to reality) with what is perceived by the senses. Sensory apprehension as such (what is perceived and the perception itself) can in consequence be called neither objective nor subjective, and it can be interpreted neither realistically nor idealistically. What is perceived does not stand apart from the perceiving subject. It is not independent of the surrounding world and its summonings, and so is not a mere state of consciousness; but just as little is it independent of the reaction of a subject, and so it is no objective qualification of reality. (116 [145])

But if the perceiving subject so touches human perception, we must not conclude that perception is to be relegated to an inferior status. On the contrary, it is on human perception itself that we depend for our approach to the mystery of the reality that has been given us (see how the two principles come together). Our knowledge of reality in terms of signs, of which Schillebeeckx wrote in (57), is set within perception, and there is no other starting-point for us. He writes:

62. Without these further references of (humanly qualified) sensory perception, there can be for the human spirit no drawing near to the mystery of the reality that for ever eludes it. In this sense, all our human consciousness lies *in* human perception, not behind it, above it, or beneath it. (117 [146])

And this refusal to separate human consciousness from perception has immediate eucharistic consequences. Traditionally, *perception* of accidents has been separated from the *understanding* which, enlightened by faith, acknowledges the substance of Christ's body beneath the accidents. Schillebeeckx, by stressing the Humanness of Perception, removes from the start what made the distinction between substance and accidents seem of use here:

63. The sensory contents that we acquire by living contact with our surroundings (in our case, with bread and wine) cannot be regarded as an objective qualification of reality. That is why it is impossible to call them accidents, objective properties of a 'substance' existing at a deeper level. In our opinion, the distinction between substance and accidents, when taken in its Aristotelian sense, can be of no help if we are trying to elucidate the dogma of transubstantiation. (117 [146–7])

Schillebeeckx now fills out the consequences of what he has claimed for human perception. Its dependence upon the kind of beings we are calls for a distinction between the real and the phenomenal – between what is and what appears:

64. How reality *appears* is determined by the human condition – by our sensory powers, our ability to conceptualise, and our particular relationship with things. A consequence of this is that there is a certain distinction between reality itself and what is phenomenal. True enough, reality does not lie behind the phenomena, it is reality itself that appears to us. But what does appear is, precisely as such, also coloured by the complex way in which we approach reality, a complexity that is due to our own complex mode of existence. (118 [147])

And now this distinction between phenomena and reality brings us back to what the first principle claimed – reality ever eludes our grasp, our knowledge lies in *signs*:

65. That there is a certain distinction between phenomena and reality goes back to the inadequacy of our knowledge of reality. In this sense, what appears – the phenomenal – is a *sign* of reality; it signifies reality. In this context 'the phenomenal' includes not only what pertains to the senses, but everything in reality itself that is *expressed* there, or specifically appears to us; everything that does not adequately match what it is that is being expressed – reality as a mystery. (118 [148])

So much for texts that embody the two principles I claim to discern in what Schillebeeckx writes, and we can notice how the two have come together in what has just been cited. My own comments on the principles must wait for the general appraisal I shall offer of all we have seen so far in this chapter. Meanwhile, I pass in the next section to seeing what use Schillebeeckx makes of them, in particular with respect to the reservations he expresses about what his contemporaries have written.

13   THAT CONTEMPORARY'S RESERVATIONS

I began the previous section by noticing some things which Schillebeeckx has in common with the other recent authors. Now that we have seen something of the two principles I discern in what he writes, we can link the resemblances to the principles. Thus, he writes as did his contemporaries about changes in significance:

66. Something can be essentially changed without its physical or biological make-up being changed. In relationships between persons, bread acquires a sense quite other than the sense it has for the physicist or the metaphysician, for example. Bread, while remaining physically what it was, can be taken up into an order of significance other than the purely biological. The bread then *is* other than it was, because its determinate relationship to man plays its part in determining the reality about which we are speaking. (104 [131])

These changes Schillebeeckx places in the context of the Givenness of Reality:

67. In the natural order itself, human life does in fact involve persisting 'transignifications'; man *humanises* the world. And such changes of sense intervene more deeply than purely physical changes, for the latter are situated at a lower level, a level that in this sense is less real. Bestowing sense is more than a psychic intentionality; there is an essential relationship between bread (the object) and human giving of sense (the subject); and the relation obtains inside the *mystery* of reality, within which the world is bestowed upon us, and we are bestowed upon ourselves. (104 [131])

The two sides to transignification – its reality and its placing – yield a conclusion that is just as general:

68. It is precisely in the humanised world that the change of sense is accomplished, and the change is substantial in that world. (104 [131–2])

But it is the same principle of the Givenness of Reality that also underlies Schillebeeckx's refusal to identify transubstantiation with transignification:

69. Suppose that reality…cannot be traced back to a human bestowal of sense, but only to God's creative gift. Suppose on the other hand it to be evident – both from Trent's dogmatic decrees and from the whole of tradition – that the Church's sense of the faith has urged in the strict sense the *reality* of what is eucharistically present. Supposing all that, it is obvious to a Catholic theologian that eucharistic transignification is not identical with transubstantiation, but is intrinsically connected with it. (119 [148–9])

Just so, it is this principle that prompts his dissatisfaction with at least some ways in which the views of his contemporaries could be read:

70. I cannot personally be finally satisfied with a *purely* phenomenological interpretation without metaphysical density. Reality is not of man's contriving: in this sense, realism is essential to Christian belief. (121 [150–1])

Having seen this much of the employment of the first principle, we must now see how Schillebeeckx employs the second – the Human-ness of Perception – in what he writes of transubstantiation and transignification.

I start with a text that serves to sum up the link between the two principles:

71. Prompted too by sensory apprehension, human beings open themselves to the mystery of reality. They open themselves to the metaphysical actuality that is bestowed as a preliminary for the ontological sense of man, for his *logos* [rational power], which *makes manifest* that which is, and by so doing *establishes meaning*. (117 [147])

Some readers may think that the text also serves to sum up the obscurity which dogs writing in the phenomenological tradition, but the drift of it is plain enough – our givings of meaning presuppose a reality that is bestowed upon us; and it is to this 'reality', this 'mystery', this 'metaphysical actuality' that we begin to open ourselves in perception itself. But now Schillebeeckx goes further. Since reality is so given, any thinking about the things of God must take account of the fact:

72. All theological reflexion has at its heart the dogma of creation, together with the metaphysical realism that follows from it. Any human giving of sense is preceded by the reality of creation. Human beings can bestow sense and so make a *human* world only within this given mystery, and only by building on the intangible but mysterious gift that is 'God's world'. (117–18 [147])

Once more, the two principles have come together – the human world lies within the mystery of what is given.

It is from these claims that Schillebeeckx draws specifically eucharistic conclusions. The first conclusion touches appearance and reality:

73. It is precisely in the Eucharist that the distinction obtrudes itself between reality and this reality as it appears (the phenomenal). Usually we pay no heed to this distinction, and in our practical lives this does no harm. It is reflexion that brings it out; and in the Eucharist we are so to speak forced up against it. *That which* is manifest as bread and wine for our experience *is* the manifest 'body of the Lord', manifest as sacramental food. (119 [149])

From this first conclusion follows another – transubstantiation and transignification are closely linked but not identical:

74. In the Eucharist there is an unbreakable link between transubstantiation (*conversio entis* [a change in reality]; 'what *is* the reality that is present?' – 'Christ's body') and transignification (a new giving of sense or sign-value). However, they *cannot* be identified *without qualification*. Sense is actively bestowed by the Church, and by the individual believer along with her, a bestowal that comes from belief. But that bestowal is effected within the mystery of grace, the mystery of the really present 'body of the Lord', given by God and attained by the movement of faith towards reality. (120 [149–50])

It can be seen that these eucharistic conclusions are of a piece with the general pattern displayed by the two principles – primacy must be given to bestowed reality, and our own givings of sense must take that reality for granted, they can never wholly grasp it.

But just as much of the pattern are the further conclusions Schillebeeckx draws in eucharistic theology, conclusions in which he spells out his reservations about views of the kinds that we have been meeting. First of all, to talk in terms of signs *presupposes* the reality of the Lord's presence, it cannot *replace* it:

75. The bread and the wine are really *signs*, a specifically sacramental form of appearance of the Lord who is already really and personally present for us. If this be denied or left out of account, the reality of the eucharistic presence is threatened. (110 [138])

He comments too on analogies with human hospitality (this must be what we saw Smits write in (18) to (20) about the tea-and-a-biscuit). They cannot, he claims, do justice to the kind of reality that goes with the Eucharist:

76. The transubstantiation that is implied by this context plainly calls for a very definite degree of reality: that of the celebration of a meal, exercised in a religious activity with symbols, in a rite that both *asks for* and *bestows life*, a rite that is a memorial of the offering of life, 'the Lord's death'. The bread and the wine that are involved in this are not simply a hospitable offering made on the occasion of a visit. (108 [136])

Schillebeeckx then considers the position we found in texts like (15) and (18) from Schoonenberg and Smits, texts which speak of the presence of the giver in the gift:

77. Transubstantiation does not mean that Christ, living in the Church, gives *something* when establishing this new meaning, gives an embodied token of love, in the way that we experience the giving hand and above all the giving heart in every significant present, and so end with an experience of the giver himself. The relationship here goes far deeper than that. What is bestowed is the giver himself, and in a way that makes the phenomenology of 'self-giving *in* the gift' fall radically short. (110 [138-9])

Nor will he allow the gap to be bridged in the way we saw attempted in (47) to (53) by Smits and Schoonenberg – by an appeal to the unique status of Christ:

78. 'This is my body, my blood' – that is not just a 'gift-of-self-in-what-is-bestowed', not even in a sense that is deepened because the giver here is Christ, the personal revelation of the Father. No, *nothing* is bestowed upon us in the Eucharist *other* than *Christ himself*. It is this that the sacramental forms of bread and wine signify while making present: it is not a gift that points towards Christ who bestows himself therein, it is Christ himself in giving, personal presence. (110 [139])

And so it is that Schillebeeckx comes to place transignification itself – he places it within the context of a presupposed reality that makes possible our givings of sense. It is reality that must come first:

79. The significance of the phenomenal forms of bread and wine is changed *because*, by the power of the creating Spirit, the reality is changed to which the phenomena refer. (119 [149])

Once this priority is conceded, he continues, we can then also concede the reality of transignification:

80. This transignification of the phenomenal deeply affects those who believe. The new significance of the forms of bread and wine lies in that believers actively give a rôle to the phenomenal as they direct themselves and open themselves to *that which* is really appearing – the 'body of the Lord' in the form of sacramental nourishment. (120 [149])

A passage near the end of his book can serve as a summary of the reservations he expresses:

81. In my reinterpretation of the datum of the Council of Trent, I can never make do with an appeal simply to a human *giving of sense*, even when this is situated within belief. A transignification of that sort naturally has its place in the Eucharist, but it is supported and summoned further by the creative activity of the Holy Spirit, the Spirit of Christ, sent by the Father. (121 [151])

Such are the reservations that Schillebeeckx expresses about the opinions of his contemporaries. The reservations, I have tried to shew, are applications of two general principles to be discerned in his book. As for the opinions, we have seen them in some variety and at some length in earlier sections. Those recent authors were allowed their own words in the statement of what they hold, and Schillebeeckx has been allowed his in what he had to say of them. But now that all have had their say, we must go further. What are we to think of it all – of all this newer family of opinions? Schillebeeckx himself has certainly expressed reservations, but it is obvious that he has a great deal in common with the others. What is this newer style worth?

14 A LACK OF NOVELTY

Whatever it is worth, it is a style to which many readers will have grown accustomed. The philosophical background and the vocabulary of the newer authors may have sounded strange to some, but there are at least some preoccupations of the authors that can hardly have sounded strange at all. The changes in worship in the Church of Rome, and the changes there in emphases (and in reticences) in preaching and instruction, are matters we have yet to consider. But we can say by now that the awarenesses and priorities shewn by the newer authors are not alien to the present state of the Christian tradition to which they belong. The *style*, if I may so put it, of the newer writings is not unfamiliar, given all else that has been happening in the Church of Rome; there is a sense in which the writings represent, not tentative suggestions, but a going concern.

I have given what I think is a liberal selection of material from the new authors, and to this I have added texts from Schillebeeckx's book in which I discern two principles, principles which underlie his own account of the Eucharist, and his appraisal of what his contem-

poraries have suggested. Some readers may have found the appraisal
somewhat harsh – that he is not taking sufficient account of the
insistence we saw in the texts that no philosophical tradition can do
justice to the eucharistic presence, that it is a mystery which has at its
centre the Risen Lord, the Word of God made flesh for us. Those
readers will, I hope, not be unduly disappointed if I decline to
adjudicate the matter. My concern is different. I have given the texts
at the length I have because I think that all the authors – and this
includes Schillebeeckx – exhibit, amid a great deal of what is good,
an ambiguity which is both deep-seated and of central importance to
the theme of this book. The ambiguity, I shall suggest, leads here to
confusions that resemble the confusions we met in the first chapter. In
other words, my objection to the newer opinions is not that
transignification evacuates the Eucharist of mystery, or does not do
justice to what is claimed by transubstantiation. My objection is
rather that the newer opinions are no more than seemingly new; that
they are really of a piece with what we found Aquinas writing about
transubstantiation in the first chapter, and so are in just as bad a
plight.

The thesis may strike the reader as eccentric, and will need spelling
out. I begin to spell it out here, and adduce in its support some texts
we have already met from de Baciocchi and Vanneste. I then pass in
the next section to seeing what support my thesis can get from the two
principles I claimed to discern in Schillebeeckx's book. And in the
final section of this chapter – leaving Schoonenberg and Smits and
other texts for later consideration – I point to the unexpected and
unwanted destination which older and newer opinions turn out to
have in common.

The series of quotations in this chapter began with passages from
two authors, de Baciocchi and Vanneste, who made merry at the
expense of older speculations. The former ridiculed the picture of a
'film' of accidents round a 'kernel' of substance (1), whilst in (2) to
(5) the latter exhibited, without even translating, a lengthy quotation
from Selvaggi, before dismissing such 'physicalist' attempts as
misconceived. It is only poetic justice that we should begin once more
with these two authors.

Let us start with Vanneste and recall other texts already given
from him. In (37) to (39), we read that substance is what things are
with respect to the purpose God assigns them; that the scholastic
account of substance took insufficient account of religious signifi-

cance; and that it is this significance of the bread which the words of Christ express. We are not to look as the scholastics did, Vanneste writes, for some structure in the bread, so as to allow its appearance to remain; it is rather the whole creature that goes, but remains for our secular experience: see (45) and (46).

We are surely entitled to be puzzled at what this final clause could possibly mean. The rejection of the scholastics' 'structure' in the bread has been achieved at the cost of what looks like either a flat contradiction or some kind of illusion. Perhaps 'illusion' is not the word – there is a passage in Evelyn Waugh's *Brideshead Revisited* which is nearer what I have in mind. A character there is being instructed in Roman Catholicism, and is asked by his teacher what he would think if the pope said it was going to rain and it didn't. He answers that 'it would be sort of raining spiritually, only we were too sinful to see it'. Does Vanneste make any better sense? One critic of Vanneste's pertinently asked how the creature can still remain for our secular experience if it all goes (Schelfout 1960: 307). Vanneste himself defends his account by urging an analogy with the older view: just as the scholastics distinguished substance from accidents, so he will himself distinguish between what something is for God and what it is for man. The former is what is more profound, since it is God who gives the final significance of things, this final *en-soi*, this ultimate noumenon, or whatever name for it one's preferences suggest; it presupposes no particular philosophy (Vanneste 1956: 334–5). But what does he achieve through this move, except an embarrassing resemblance to the scholasticism he rejected? We saw in chapter 1 how the reification of philosophical distinctions turned Aristotle's speculations into a kind of dissection of the bread, and allowed transubstantiation to be conceived as an admittedly miraculous reshuffling of the products of this dissection. We also saw that the confusion in this shewed itself in the appeal made to *divine power* for the accomplishing of the reshuffle, when what we needed was attention to the *intelligibility* of what was being proposed for the exercise of that power. But what else is Vanneste offering in his supposedly novel account? He makes the assignment of purpose by God into the norm of what things are, but makes it in such a way as to allow this assignment to be changed while 'secular experience' – the norm for our own saying what things are – remains unaltered. In other words, divine power is invoked, when it is the intelligibility of what is being said that needs attention. Indeed, Vanneste himself

seems aware of the resemblance of what he writes to the appeal made
by the older writers. He puts an objection to his talk of the whole
creature's going but remaining for our secular experience, and puts it
on the ground of intelligibility – God cannot do anything which is
intrinsically contradictory. His reply points to the analogous difficulty faced by the scholastics:

82. Indeed God cannot bring about a contradiction. Yet none of the
scholastics will have the audacity to claim that it is easy to shew that the
separation of accidents and substance is not a metaphysical contradiction.
(Vanneste 1956: 334)

The point is well taken, but shews no more than what I have been
contending: that Vanneste and the scholastics are in the same plight.
It is only natural that he should also talk in terms of a contrast
between what secular experience tells us and what is the noumenon
or *en-soi* or ultimate substance in the Eucharist – we are simply being
presented with the 'dissection' offered in the older view. His denial of
a 'structure' in reality has been to no purpose; we have heard it all
before; if Vanneste began by smiling at Selvaggi, he ends by writing
like Colombo.

As for de Baciocchi, we saw that he gave a spirited account of how
transubstantiation gets pictured in terms of an 'external film' of
properties and a 'metaphysical' kernel of substance. We noticed that
he insisted there upon keeping this 'imaginative solution' apart from
transubstantiation itself, but that he did not explicitly attribute the
solution to anyone, or explain its relationship to what, for example,
Aquinas wrote. We can now notice that his own positive account does
not furnish an explanation either, because he ends with the very
separation between properties and substance that he began by
repudiating, and ends with it through the kind of move made by
Vanneste. Things are, de Baciocchi contends, simply what they are
for Christ (35); they exist only as elements in the universe, in which
he is the point of unity and coherence (42); to him belongs the final
word about things (43), for his is the one absolute point of view on
them (40). All of which is no more than what we found in Vanneste
and found in the scholastics: divine omnipotence is made to do duty
for the intelligibility of how words are being put together. Equally
familiar is the way in which de Baciocchi separates appearance from
reality. The sacramental order, he writes, provides an exception to
the rule that changes in the function of things for us come from

change in their empirical properties (42). In that order, the significance of physical and chemical properties is no more than the relative and accidental: see (40) and (41). Indeed, what follows that last text is even more emphatic:

83. If then Christ gives himself in giving bread and wine as signs of this gift, the secular functions and the physical and chemical properties of the bread and wine no longer offer direct information about the true reality of those things, but only about subordinate qualifications of them. (de Baciocchi 1959: 151)

If we are not back with the film and the kernel, where are we? There, the unbeliever encounters Christ in the borrowed robes of the accidents of bread and wine, and is 'punished for his incredulity by remaining deprived of sight'. Here, in de Baciocchi's own account:

84. If the rationalist gives an absolute sense to the experience he has rationally interpreted, he is doing something hard to avoid doing, but he is mistaken for all that. The believer can hold the perceptual and scientific aspects of reality to be relative, because what is Absolute gives itself to him in the person of Christ, and by Christ's word assigns each thing its true place in the universe, its definitive reality. (de Baciocchi 1959: 151)

So we have found in de Baciocchi what we found in Vanneste – an initial amusement at some scholastic writers is no guarantee against ultimate agreement with them. 'Metaphysical kernel', I suggested, may well have been a gesture at Colombo. But it is Colombo who laughs last.

I shall turn in the next section to what I have seen as two principles in Schillebeeckx's book, and these will demand a lengthier examination. By way of conclusion to the present section, and by way of introduction to the next, we might recall something we found in the previous chapter, when examining the disagreement between Colombo and Selvaggi. To the extent that the concept of substance is philosophically sound, it is recalcitrant to being used in eucharistic speculation; to the extent that it is 'insulated' from all else, it is all too readily adapted to this employment. This inverse variation we are going to encounter in what Schillebeeckx – and not only Schillebeeckx – writes about reality and perception.

15   AN AMBIGUITY OF PRINCIPLES

We saw at (54) to (65) some texts from Schillebeeckx's book in which
I claimed to discern two principles – the Givenness of Reality and the
Humanness of Perception. We then saw at (66) to (81) the principles
at work in the reservations he expressed about the newer opinions. I
contended in the previous section that the newer opinions are not
new at all, that they share the confusions we had met earlier in the
scholastics. In this section I take up Schillebeeckx's principles again
and claim to find in them an ambiguity: I claim that they can be read
as wisdom, but that they can also be taken as leading back to the
confusions found in the older tradition – yet again, new here is but
old writ large. But this openness of the principles to abuse does not
rob them of their value; and so one theme in what follows is the
nature of the way in which the abuse can take place. I begin with the
first principle.

The principle of the Givenness of Reality can indeed be read as
expressing what is not only good sense but good sense badly needed.
That there is always more to be explored is a platitude worth stating,
because it can so easily be obscured by considerations of immediate
profit, or by those shapings and concentrations of attention that
make habit for each one of us so good a servant and so bad a master.
And that the reality we explore is not an artefact of our own devising,
but something to be respected for its own patterns and nature, is an
even more valuable platitude, a platitude that is in our own time
being rediscovered – not too tardily, let us hope. But if this first
principle is grounded in what life ought to be, its eucharistic
employment is just as fitting. By reminding us that our own bestowals
of significance are never what is most profound, the principle can
guide us in rightly approaching what goes beyond our own bestowing
in the Eucharist – the meal that is more than a meal, the Passover
transcending all that the Passover ever meant. If we are so guided,
then our celebration will in its turn furnish a goal and a paradigm for
how we should treat the Earth that has provided us with the material
objects for our celebration. Our 'thanksgiving' will extend to that
too, and the very transcendence of the Eucharist over what is no more
than earthly will make its significance for what is earthly all the
greater.

This theme will claim our attention later on, and for the present we
should notice rather how the wisdom in Schillebeeckx's first principle

finds expression in contexts that are not technically theological at all. Reality there is seen – seen in privileged moments – as bestowed upon us, as offering depths unsuspected, do we but have an open eye. Readers are likely to have their own examples in mind, I simply recall favourites of my own. There is D. H. Lawrence, writing in the opening chapter of *The Rainbow* about Tom Brangwen thinking of the prospect of marrying and of what marriage will bring:

85. But during the long February nights with the ewes in labour, looking out from the shelter into the flashing stars, he knew he did not belong to himself. He must admit that he was only fragmentary, something incomplete and subject. There were the stars in the dark heaven, travelling... (Lawrence 1958: 40)

There is Blake, in words from 'Auguries of Innocence' that some will already have by heart:

86. To see a World in a Grain of Sand
    And a Heaven in a Wild Flower,
    Hold Infinity in the palm of your hand
    And Eternity in an hour.

There is Blake again, warning us this time against the dangers of not seeking such acquaintance with the things that are:

87. Now I a fourfold vision see,
    And a fourfold vision is given to me;
    'Tis fourfold in my supreme delight
    And threefold in soft Beulah's night
    And twofold Always. May God us keep
    From single Vision and Newton's sleep!

And there is Newman, at the end of a life's labours concerning the things of God and their right expression: and he chooses for his epitaph *ex umbris et imaginibus in veritatem* – 'out of shadows and images into the truth'. Reality is indeed bestowed upon us, it does indeed go beyond what we ourselves shall ever wholly grasp, and to think otherwise is indeed to suffer from single vision. An author frequently cited in this chapter can sum up the matter: 'l'être est inépuisable à la connaissance humaine' (de Baciocchi 1955: 576) – human knowledge can never get to the end of reality.

But if there is wisdom in the first principle, there can be confusion as well, and the confusion is present in other texts from de Baciocchi, those cited or recalled near the end of the last section. The central place in reality which he allots to the Risen Christ goes, we saw, with a claim that physical and empirical properties have a significance which is no more than relative or accidental. I charged him with slipping back into the kind of position taken up by Colombo. I now submit that the values I praised in Schillebeeckx's first principle have changed here into an isolation of substance from what we can discern with our senses and understanding. The 'insulation', as I called it, we first encountered in Colombo; it is philosophical muddle, not an insight into the Givenness of Reality.

And if de Baciocchi slips from insight to muddle, he is not alone in doing so. The three authors from whom I have just been offering wise sayings can, in their own ways, lapse into foolishness. Lawrence could write in *Fantasia of the Unconscious* egregious folly about the very kind of thing he wrote of in *The Rainbow* as an epiphany of the reality that is given. In *The Rainbow* it was the stars; here it is the moon, but to very different effect:

88. And the moon is some strange coagulation of substance such as salt, phosphorus, soda. It certainly isn't a snowy cold world, like a world of our own gone cold. Nonsense. It is a globe of dynamic substance like radium or phosphorus, coagulated upon a certain vivid pole of energy, which pole of energy is directly polarized with our earth, in opposition with the sun. (Lawrence 1961: 152)

Blake puts 'Newton' in a context that associates it with single vision, and he may well be using the name there symbolically or 'prophetically'. But the name is the name of a man, and so carries historical claims; and not all those who value Blake's warnings will accept that the claims are just. We shall be seeing more of Newman, and I need for the moment do no more than state what I have argued in FitzPatrick 1969 and 1991b: that his sensitivity to the imperfections of all formulae made him unsure when dealing with propositions of a straightforward and factual character, and made him purblind to the purely secular claims of education. Each of these authors shews an admirable awareness of the Givenness of Reality, and yet each is capable of offering a distortion of its truth, just as de Baciocchi's insight in a eucharistic setting is distorted into an error. But if the principle seems open to ambiguity in what we are to make of it, how can we draw the line here between use and abuse?

We must draw it, I suggest, by insisting that the insights expressed in the principle *cumulate* knowledge that is homely and workaday, they do not *compete* with it. To think that the insights do compete is to think that they should in some way *replace* what is workaday and negate it. I give the mistake a name – 'the Fallacy of Replacement' – and I do so because we shall be meeting it a good deal as the book goes on. In this section, I first shew how the distinction between cumulation and competition keeps use apart from abuse in Lawrence, Newman and Blake, and I then apply the distinction to what Schillebeeckx himself has written.

When insight cumulates but does not compete, both workaday knowledge and privileged insight can be allowed full force. Tom Brangwen's skill with the ewes is a real skill and they are really his ewes; and neither skill nor ownership is denied by his moments of clearer vision, even though the vision shews him a far wider scene, and puts into a far wider context his skill and his ownership. Newman's abiding acknowledgment that we move amid shadows and images could not and certainly did not release him from the hard work of evaluating what was to be said here and now of things human and divine. And Blake's warning against a philistinism that will accept no categories except those of scientific utility does not and cannot deny that the grain of sand and the wild flower have to be really there – were they not, we could not glimpse what he invites us to glimpse in a golden moment. But life is not all golden moments. We do also know what grains of sand are in the humble but genuine sense of being able to distinguish them from sugar, and (if we have the skill) of being able to measure their silicon content. No moment, however golden, can negate this knowledge, however much it reveals its incompleteness. That some uses of language are humble and limited does not rob them of their (equally humble and limited) criteria for being right or wrong.

On the other hand, when insight is held to compete rather than to cumulate, confusion follows. Lawrence's picture of Tom Brangwen engaged in the night-labours of lambing-time, and thinking under the stars of his own life and its meaning, is memorable. But when Lawrence allows his vision to let him play the armchair-astronomer, he forgets (among other things) that the study of the heavenly bodies is as exigent in its own way as the craft of a shepherd. Just as Blake's use of 'Newton' in his poem – however symbolically justified – obscures the simple fact that, if the heavenly bodies are to be studied, those who study them will need mathematics. And just as Newman, when he spells out in his *Grammar of Assent* the all-pervading rôle of personal insight and intuition in human knowledge, fails to do justice to simple and public pieces of evidence that all intuition, however personal, must respect. But, having said all that, I must say something else. I took my texts from those three authors precisely because all three, whatever mistakes they do make, possess a palpably valuable grasp of truths that are precious. The Fallacy of Replacement is a fallacy; but it is seldom far from an acknowledgment of things that matter. Such is life. We know in part, and we prophesy in part – another truth that we shall be meeting again.[7]

I pass from ambiguities in those three authors to the ambiguity in what Schillebeeckx himself makes of the Givenness of Reality. We have already seen the wisdom that is enshrined in his first principle, we must now consider how for him too the Fallacy of Replacement

[7] In this footnote, I complement the main text with references and examples. The two citations from Blake in (86) and (87) come respectively from 'Auguries of Innocence' and from a letter to Thomas Butts: they are to be found in Blake 1939 at 118 and 861–2. Blake's reference to Newton in (87) can be complemented by his symbolic portrait, where Newton is shewn ignoring the starry heaven in favour of a geometrical diagram he has drawn on the ground. The picture is deservedly celebrated, but it also illustrates with unhappy felicity what I have called the Fallacy of Replacement. Why should a grasp of the mathematics of the heavens be inimical to wonder at the sky at night (if there is Blake, there is also Dante)? The suggestion of Newton's absorption is even odder – if Newton had not been so great a mathematician, he would have been more renowned than he is as an observer and 'mechanic' of superlative dexterity and keenness.

Lawrence's claims about the moon go with the Fallacy too, and with the evaluation of science we have met so often in these pages. In the Foreword to that book, he speaks of 'the science which proceeds in terms of life and is established on data of living experience and of such intuition', whereas 'Our objective science of modern knowledge concerns itself only with phenomena, and with phenomena as regarded in their cause-and-effect relationship' (Lawrence 1961: 6). Elsewhere he goes even further along the same road. To Aldous Huxley he dismissed evidence in favour of evolution by saying that evidence meant nothing to him, as he did not 'feel it here' – 'here' being his solar plexus (Huxley 1937: 336).

Passages from Newman of the sort I have in mind can be found in his *Grammar of Assent*. He pursues there the general theme that reasoning in concrete matters cannot be reduced to formalities of logic, because it calls at each stage for particular acts of intuitive estimation. The contention hesitates between the platitudinous and the more than debatable. He offers as an example a debate over a proposed emendation to Shakespeare in the light of an old copy that had been discovered some years before – must not controversy give way here to a photographing on the mind of the sum-total of argument (Newman 1887: 271–7)? All other considerations apart, the said 'old copy' was nothing more than one of Payne Collier's impudent forgeries; the unmasking of his fraud called for no mental photography, but only for the detection of pencil-marks below the ink in the supposed annotations; and the unmasking had taken place over ten years before Newman was writing. Intuition cannot replace evidence. But neither can it replace admissions of failure: in a note on the passage added in a later edition, Newman writes only that he has been told that 'the verdict of critics has been unfavourable' to the annotated copy. Perhaps the remark will at least illustrate my contention earlier that Newman was not at his ease in statements of an uncomplicatedly factual kind. I point out here that I have examined the *Apologia* in FitzPatrick 1969, the *Grammar of Assent* in FitzPatrick 1978, and both in FitzPatrick 1991b; to these items I shall be referring later. I also point out here, as I have pointed out elsewhere, that I was given no chance myself to correct the proofs of FitzPatrick 1978, and that their proofreading exhibits marks of a painful mixture of myopia and illiteracy.

turns wisdom into confusion. We can best approach this by seeing what he makes of his second principle – the Humanness of Perception.

Although that principle is more 'professionally philosophical' than the first, it does enshrine claims of a more general character, and the claims are worth making. In the texts we saw from (59) to (64), Schillebeeckx insists that all our perception is distinctively human and that it is all caught up into the general human movement towards reality – a reality which, as his first principle reminded us, is initially bestowed and not of our own devising. Perception, because it is human perception, is indispensable for this movement – without it, 'there can be for the human spirit no drawing near the mystery of the reality that for ever escapes it'. When the second principle says all this, it excludes from the start any *isolation* of what is distinctively human and open to divine grace. It warns us against thinking of the Givenness of Reality as disclosing itself to us in a way that is insulated and cut off from the whole array of our perceptions of the world in which we live. The warning is more than salutary – there can be no justice done to eucharistic or to any other ritual if the perceptual order is irrelevant to what we saw Schillebeeckx call 'the spiritual aiming at reality' (60); and any quest that regards what is perceived as unimportant will end in disaster. Schillebeeckx's second principle enshrines a truth that we need to value and to keep in mind.

It is when the second principle is taken as making claims about the status of human knowledge that caution is needed. It can indeed be read here too as good sense. 'What is perceived does not stand apart from the perceiving subject' (61); 'what does appear is, precisely as such, also coloured by the complex way in which we approach reality' (64): claims like those point to the dependence of what is perceived upon the perceiver, and they rightly point to it. But the claims appear with claims of a different sort, claims that 'sensory apprehension...can...be called neither objective nor subjective...it is not an objective qualification of reality' (61); and that our sensory contacts with reality cannot therefore 'be called accidents, objective properties of a substance existing at a deeper level' (63). Quite apart from the use of depth-imagery for substance, I am uneasy about this second kind of claim. What makes me uneasy is what makes me uneasy over more than one theological employment of philosophical distinctions – the employment brusquely over-simplifies matters that cannot be robbed of their complexity without distortion. Philosophers draw distinctions where practical life can dispense with them, and philosophers devise words for those distinctions, words that others may for their purposes safely ignore. But if others do choose to adopt philosophical distinctions and words, they must be quite clear as to what they are doing, under penalty of falling into the very confusions which made philosophers draw their distinctions in the first place.

And this is just what has happened here. If 'objective' and 'subjective' are to mean anything, they cannot be used as briskly as Schillebeeckx uses them. I do not want to linger on the point, because I have already drawn attention to it when (and notice when) objecting in chapter 1 to Colombo's account of the distinction between substance and accidents, and to his account of the status of physical science. I simply ask the reader to consider briefly how *varied* are the problems to do with human knowledge. Think, for example, of how we learn and develop as we live – live in fact in the *Lebenswelt*, the 'life-world' of which the phenomenological tradition speaks. We grow into that world by what we learn, perceive and say; by the mistakes and successes that go with our activity; by our increasing familiarity with criteria for descriptive words and with how to apply – and how to withdraw – the criteria. We learn to say that the paper really is white although it looks red, a more complicated judgment than saying that pillar-boxes are red or that snow is white. We learn – in a very elaborate and rarely articulated way – to pass from a range of fragmentary and fleeting evidence to quite stable verdicts as to what things are. Those who spend time on such matters know that the first step to a right understanding of them is a refusal to impose procrustean alternatives like 'objective' and 'subjective'. And the refusal is all the more necessary when we turn to the extension of the *Lebenswelt* into the concepts and vocabulary of physical science. Here, the classification of things that we reach is more powerful, but is also removed from what we habitually perceive, and our ordinary vocabulary of colours does not play the part that it did when we were talking about paper and pillar-boxes. The extension into physical science means that there can now be a new looseness of fit, between what science tells us about the structure of things, and what descriptions we should give of them in words learned in familiar contexts. To go back to an example used earlier, we accept that fools' gold looks like gold but is not, while vaporised gold does not look like it but is. And so on – I do not want to labour the examples further, and I return to examining Schillebeeckx's use here of 'objective' and 'subjective'.

There would be less harm in it if he did not lean so much on the distinction. But he does so lean – indeed, he has to. Consider the stages in which he moves from this oversimplification of the Humanness of Perception to a distortion of the truth contained in the Givenness of Reality. He begins sensibly, claiming that what appears is also 'coloured by the complex way in which we approach reality' (64). But in that same text he infers from this colouring that 'there is a certain distinction to be drawn between reality itself and what is phenomenal', and here any agreement should be hesitant, if only because we can hardly be clear as to what it is we are supposed to be agreeing with. Is it the distinction between what the white paper under the red light looks like and what colour it really is? Or is it rather the distinction between the appearance of the vaporised gold (terrifying, I should think) and what we have been taught about gold's atomic structure?[8] Or what? Our unease ought not to be diminished by words we also find there: 'True enough, reality does not lie behind the phenomena, it is reality itself that appears to us.' Theologians may be better behaved, but when philosophers give such reassurances we know that they mean to do more or less the opposite of what they say. And so it turns out here, for in the very next text we find that the reason for the distinction between phenomena and reality is 'the inadequacy of our knowledge of reality' (65). Which sounds like an explanation of why iron pyrites is called 'fools' gold', and in such an explanation the distinction makes good sense. But the distinction as Schillebeeckx draws it cannot mean anything as sensible as that. It is too sweeping, as the same text goes on to shew: 'In this context "the phenomenal" includes not only what pertains to the senses, but everything in reality itself that is *expressed* there, or actually appears to us.' And now we have got back to what is dismally familiar. The white paper under the red light, the pillar-box at noonday, the fools' gold and the vaporised gold are all lumped together under 'the phenomenal', and contrasted with 'reality'. The multitude of distinctions that can be drawn is collapsed into a

---

[8] Some readers will recognise the 'vaporised gold' from the interesting analyses offered by philosophers like Kripke and Putnam in matters to do with evidence, descriptions and 'natural kinds'. I add my personal opinion that similar distinctions can be drawn in moral and historical matters. I shall be noticing them again later.

contrast that is just the contrast Colombo drew between his inaccessible substance and everything else.

But now notice that Schillebeeckx adds for good measure to all this the vocabulary of 'sign'. Still in (65), he writes: 'In this sense, what appears – the phenomenal – is a *sign of* reality; it signifies reality.' And we can see why he added the word when, at the end of that text, he sums up his position by counting under the phenomenal 'everything that does not adequately match what is being expressed – reality as a mystery'. That final step completes the justification of my submission about Schillebeeckx. The 'mystery' in reality – so well expressed by him earlier – is now conceived in terms of a negation of ordinary knowledge, which is relegated to the order of 'the phenomenal'. An acknowledgment of the inexhaustible and divinely bestowed character of reality has been touched by the Fallacy of Replacement. From an over-simplification of the Humanness of Perception, Schillebeeckx has proceeded to a treatment of the Givenness of Reality that makes it deny and replace what we reach by ordinary cognitive means. That principle, which we found to be ambiguous in Lawrence, Blake and Newman, turns out to be ambiguous in Schillebeeckx too. If we read it aright, it justly points to the mystery that does indeed lie at the heart of things. But if we read the first principle as it has been read here – if we juxtapose it with an abuse of the second principle that isolates reality from appearance – then we are left with nothing more than the confusion I have blamed so often. And what we then present as mystery is no more than muddle.

That Schillebeeckx is able to adapt what he has written to eucharistic employment is of course undeniable. Indeed, he does what we saw de Baciocchi do in (40) to (43) – he draws conclusions about human knowledge from eucharistic assertions. In (73) he contends that the Eucharist itself forces us to accept the distinction between reality and the phenomenal, a distinction which we usually ignore, but ignore without harm to our practical lives. But this text does no more than provide yet another example of what I have called 'inverse variation' in eucharistic theology (p. 85) – the smoother the adaptation, the worse the philosophy. Take 'appearance and reality' in any way that makes sense, and it will not so adapt. 'Practical life', with all due respect to Schillebeeckx, sets great store by distinguishing appearance from reality, and would soon be in a pretty plight if it did not. Philosophical speculation, as we have seen, devises a multiplicity of related distinctions to cope with a multiplicity of related problems – problems touching things like inner structures, the relation of perceptual to scientific vocabulary, error and language. But these distinctions are various and delicate, and Schillebeeckx's vocabulary here is too brusque to do more than reflect, in terms of the theory of knowledge, a view of substance that resembles Colombo's account – a *terra incognita* beyond any possible appearance. Having mentioned Colombo, I look back to (58), one of the texts in which Schillebeeckx stated the Givenness of Reality, and I notice its vocabulary. After saying that within the given reality we establish a human world and modify its human sense, he added a limitation: 'But only in its human sense – its deepest sense, its *metaphysical* sense, lies beyond human grasp or intervention.' I made no comment when first giving this text, so I allow myself here an italicisation of what now reads so ominously. And if it seems unfair to fasten on one word, another text altogether puts the matter beyond cavil.

The text, Trooster 1963, is some years earlier than Schillebeeckx's book, and I shall be suggesting in a later chapter that there occurred in the interval a change in his opinions. But this part of the earlier source offers what I take to be also offered in texts I have cited from the book; and so I set it here beside those texts. Trooster's article is a paper by a Catholic theologian on recent developments in eucharistic theology among Lutherans and Calvinists, followed by a discussion in which both Protestants and Catholics took part. Of the writers we have met here, Schoonenberg and Schillebeeckx were present, and the later portion of the discussion was in great measure a putting of questions to Schillebeeckx. I have more to say of what is in Trooster, but give here two exchanges between Schillebeeckx and his interlocutors. He himself remarks at one point:

89. Physically nothing is changed at the consecration. After the consecration, what is physically bread has become a *signum substantiale* [a substantial sign] of Christ's body. What we have is a *conversio metaphysica* [a metaphysical change], which is accomplished inside the order of symbolic activity. (Trooster 1963: 134)

That we do have more than a verbal echo of what we found Colombo asserting is clear from the exchanges that follow:

90. SCHILLEBEECKX: Physically nothing changes, but everything changes ontically...
VAN LEEUWEN: Can I say that after the consecration there is bread there for my experience?

SCHILLEBEECKX: No; in as much as sense-experience never reaches reality.

VAN LEEUWEN: That remark of yours I cannot defend against physicists.

SCHILLEBEECKX: Physicists get to one aspect only of the reality that is present after the consecration. (134)

The protest of Schillebeeckx's interlocutor is understandable, and of a piece with my own complaints against Colombo. But let us not forget that the principles I have discerned in Schillebeeckx's book can be taken in ways that are not touched by the Fallacy, are often so taken by him, and that so taken are precious and indispensable.

16 A STRANGENESS OF DESTINATION

I have tried to shew that the new can be less new than it looks. There need be nothing blameworthy in the lack of novelty, but it can suggest that profitable dissent here calls for a new start. In the next chapter I shall start explaining what I think this start should be. Here and now I prepare the way by contending that older and newer sources are not only similar, they lead to similar and unwanted consequences. Old and new are similarly amiss, and shew it by the destination they have in common.

When introducing Schillebeeckx's principle of the Givenness of Reality, I went outside the range of the works already considered, and offered quotations from other writers which I thought embodied the principle. Although I went on to claim confusions in the same authors, I insisted that the confusions did not touch the wisdom of what else the authors wrote – indeed, the confusions themselves testified to the insights of those who fell into them. One of the authors was Newman, and I offer here a text of his to do with transubstantiation, a text that in my opinion illustrates forcibly how his abiding and precious insight – an insight into the transitoriness of this world and the imperfection of the words used of it – lends itself to the kind of distortion we have met, time and again, in both older and newer sources. In the part of the *Apologia* where he offered in 1864 his 'General answer to Mr Kingsley', he writes thus of transubstantiation:

91. It is difficult, impossible to imagine, I grant – but how is it difficult to believe? Yet Macaulay thought it so difficult to believe, that he had need of a believer in it of talents as eminent as Sir Thomas More, before he could

bring himself to conceive that the Catholics of an enlightened age could resist 'the overwhelming force of the argument against it'…But for myself, I cannot indéed prove it, I cannot tell *how* it is; but I say, 'Why should not it be? What's to hinder it? What do I know of substance or matter? just as much as the greatest philosophers, and that is nothing at all' – so much is this the case, that there is a rising school of philosophy now, which considers phenomena to constitute the whole of our knowledge in physics. The Catholic doctrine leaves phenomena alone. It does not say that the phenomena go; on the contrary, it says that they remain: nor does it say that the same phenomena are in several places at once. It deals with what no one on earth knows anything about, the material substances themselves. (Ward 1913: 332–3)

The text has the merit of apparent force, that much all can admit. The similarity of what Newman writes of physical science to Colombo's view of physics needs no comment, and the similarity of what he writes about 'substance or matter' to the confused version of the Givenness of Reality needs comment just as little. What does deserve a mention is the effect exercised by Newman's text, when he shelters transubstantiation from possible objections by removing material substances from the order of knowledge. He leaves his reader feeling much as Alice felt after reading 'Jabberwocky'. 'Somehow it seems to fill my head with ideas – only I don't exactly know what they are!' Which is, of course, the trouble. Newman's admission 'I cannot tell *how* it is' deflects attention from the question he ought to be asking. It is not the '*how* it is' that matters, it is the coherence of the 'it' itself. Considerations of power have yet again usurped the rôle of considerations about intelligibility, and I must once more make the complaint I have made against old and new alike.

But I admit – I could hardly not admit – that some do not so complain. For them, the distinction between substance and accident, in Colombo's and Newman's sense, is intelligible and indeed is reinforced by the doctrine of transubstantiation. Of how such a view might be defended F. Clark gives a clear exposition, in an article where both Colombo and Newman are cited and approved:

92. Within the order of corporeal ontological reality, we must distinguish between the empirical level of phenomena and the metempirical level of ultimate substance, which we can conceive but cannot imagine. We are led to affirm the existence of this metempirical reality not only by the common reflection of mankind and all sane philosophy, which acknowledges that the flux of empirical phenomena cannot be identical with the abiding reality of things, but also theologically, in as much as this is necessarily implied in the

eucharistic doctrine of the church and the further explanations of the magisterium. It is at this level of metempirical ontological reality, yet still within the corporeal order, that we must place the ontological change that occurs in the eucharistic consecration. (F. Clark, 1967: 40)

I notice and respect the honest avowal here that theological exigencies help to support a philosophical position, and I wish the honesty were more common – I take the text of Schillebeeckx to be making the same avowal, when he writes that the Eucharist forces us up against the distinction between the real and the phenomenal (see his (73), and see my remarks at p. 94. But, while acknowledging the honesty of the two authors, I have to point out that they are on a very slippery slope, as another quotation, from quite another source, will shew us:

93. Thus it becomes evident that the real table, if there is one, is not the same as what we immediately experience by sight or touch or hearing. The real table, if there is one, is not *immediately* known to us at all... Thus what we directly see and feel is merely 'appearance', which we believe to be a sign of some 'reality' behind.

That, of course, is Bertrand Russell talking about the table at which he is writing the first chapter of *The Problems of Philosophy* (Russell 1943: 16 and 23–4). So (i) Russell's 'real table' lies beyond what we perceive, indeed beyond anything we immediately know at all; and (ii) our belief is that the 'appearance' is a sign of some 'reality' behind it. Put 'substance' for 'real table' in the first clause, and we have Colombo; put 'phenomena' for 'appearance' in the second, and we have Schillebeeckx; and other appropriate substitutions will bring us back to Clark. But unfortunately we do have something else in the text – a doubt as to whether there is a real table at all. And even a slight acquaintance with Russell's works will shew just how far he was prepared to take doubts of that sort. If writers like Colombo, Schillebeeckx and Clark do not want to follow him, ought they not to look again at the distinctions they have drawn, supposedly in the service of eucharistic belief? The distinctions have an air of giving pride of place to substance. They succeed only in making it a *roi fainéant*, and in proposing a view of things that comes uncomfortably close to the variations on phenomenalism in Russell's philosophical speculations.

That the supposed exigencies of eucharistic theology should push theologians towards phenomenalism is something I confess to finding amusing, but I do not find the tendency altogether strange – phenomenalism, the reduction of things to their appearances, is perennially attractive to the devout. I wrote earlier that distortions of the wisdom in the Givenness of Reality do not destroy the wisdom of the principle itself, and my point here is the same: there are ways in which phenomenalism can, even in its errors, respond to the instincts of those who are strongly aware that we have here no abiding city, that the fashion of this world passeth away, that *alles Vergängliche ist nur ein Gleichnis* – all that doth pass away is but a parable. To such people, any work of the understanding in human terms will seem only provisional, and any description it offers will sound imperfect – what can truly be said, they feel, except that beyond appearances there lies that which, in itself all-important, we can at present know by faith only, and not by sight?

I hope that by this stage in the book I shall not be suspected of believing in phenomenalism myself. My aim here is simply to shew its attraction, an attraction that comes from other sources than philosophical muddle, even though such muddle is inseparable from it. Indeed, I am prepared to go yet further in my expression of sympathy. The distortions in phenomenalism, because they separate as they do reality from appearance, can have worthwhile consequences for religious belief. They can serve to stress the irreducibility of sacraments to human life and activity (the 'unknown' behind appearances will do that). They can remind us of the lameness in any account of things like the eucharistic presence (how can language seize what lies beyond knowledge?). Most of all, perhaps, their devaluing of 'human' assertions can enforce the moral we drew at the end of the first chapter – that there is no 'sticking-place' in religious belief, no fixed point at which we may take our stand and then go on to judge the belief as from some neutral position.

But saying and admitting all that does not mean that I have ceased to regard phenomenalism as a mistake. I have not; I regard it as a philosophical confusion that will prove a very awkward consequence for eucharistic belief to have. The confusion starts, we have seen, when the wisdom in Schillebeeckx's two principles is touched by the Fallacy of Replacement, by the mistake of supposing that truths from an exalted and privileged source replace and cancel knowledge that is more workaday, instead of cumulating it. We have seen the Fallacy in action when the gradations and varieties of human knowledge are all lumped together as 'the phenomenal' and contradistinguished from a mysterious 'reality'. And we have seen, time and again, what follows from the Fallacy – ordinary words are denied their force in the name of something higher, intelligibility gives way to power, and we talk with Newman of not knowing '*how* it is', when we ought to be talking with Aquinas about *discohaerentia terminorum*, the failure of terms to hang together. But still more follows, and we must now see what it is.

In the first chapter, we encountered a remarkable claim by Godefroy that no technical philosophy but only a *philosophia perennis* is needed to understand Trent's terms about the eucharistic presence, and we saw that Colombo makes a similar assertion (p. 24). We have met similar claims since. Godefroy himself (in a passage that defied translation) gave in (44) an account of substance in terms of what he called common sense and was given in (45) some commendation by Vanneste, who had himself proposed to emancipate eucharistic theology from Aristotle and confront it with the data of faith (5). And we have seen in the present section F. Clark's claim that 'all sane philosophy' makes the distinction demanded by Trent's decree (92). I have given reasons for thinking that such talk of a 'perennial philosophy' is no more than a weakness for perennial confusions. But now I can say something more. There is indeed a *philosophia perennis* underlying all the eucharistic theories we have examined, but I suspect that it is not the kind of philosophy those authors had in mind. The *philosophia perennis* I discern there – and it is unquestionably perennial, whatever else it fails to be – is scepticism. Scepticism is the unwelcome destination to which tend both the old and the newer theories.

How do I know that this penny will fall to the ground when I let go of it? There are contexts (we can imagine some scientific fun-fair) in which that question could be given a limited and definite sense, and so provided with a corresponding answer. But the distinguishing mark of doubts that are philosophically sceptical is that they are without limitations or definiteness; they disallow from the start any evidence that might be offered to close the gap which the sceptic is lamenting. It is not difficult to imagine a sceptic visiting a chocolate factory and objecting to calling its products 'chocolate'. 'How do I know it's chocolate? It looks like chocolate, tastes like chocolate, passes the tests for chocolate, I concede – but all that is just a matter of physical science, of sense-impressions, just a relative verdict, just empirical data, just subjective. In the context of total reality, at the deepest level, ontologically, objectively, metaphysically, metempiri-cally, substantially, it could be something else.' No further evidence will help here. Any tour of chocolate factories we organised, any further chemical analysis we offered, would be disallowed as irrelevant, as being on the wrong side of the gap. And 'gap', of course, is the trouble. As far as a sceptic can be refuted at all, he cannot be refuted on his own terms – it is his very formulation of the problem that must be questioned. The force of his position comes from a crude presentation of the distinction between appearance and reality, evidence and verdict, behaviour and thought, in order to affect a divorce between them. The efforts of his adversaries to mend the divorce distract their attention from noticing how badly he drew the distinction to begin with. His doubts lie at the threshold, and it is there that they must be dissolved.

We have encountered repeatedly a distinction between appearance and reality drawn in such a way as to share the defects of what the sceptic says here. My examination of the distinction in the different forms it takes has had to be lengthy, precisely because – just as happens in scepticism – it is the initial drawing of the distinction that causes the subsequent trouble. The phenomenalism to which the eucharistic accounts lend themselves comes from this initial mistake, and it will not be hard to shew that these accounts have sceptical implications. We can do so by considering the time-honoured eucharistic formula that the host 'looks like bread, tastes like bread, but is not'.

The formula in its eucharistic setting has in common with sceptical doubt the property of resembling our doubts that are not sceptical, while standing apart from them in the way it excludes from the start whatever might be offered towards a solution. There are, of course, other settings, in which the formula could make reasonable sense. Suppose we were confronted with something that had all the appearance and taste and nutritive effects of bread, but were told that it was in fact made from some chemicals devised by the men of science. How should we describe it? Probably, at all events until the substitute became well known, we should refuse to call it bread, because our criteria include origin as well as appearance. At the same time, the appearances and effects are there, so we should perhaps end by calling it 'bread' with some alienating adjective like 'imitation' or 'artificial' prefixed to the noun. 'It looks like bread, and tastes like it' we should say; 'but it is not, it is only artificial bread.' And our denial would be based on what we regard as a necessary condition for being bread – being made from flour. 'We regard', I say, because there is no suggestion here of any elaborate analysis of food. Learning to recognise bread is not a matter of acquiring precise standards, but simply of getting to know when certain rather vague but practically manageable criteria have been fulfilled. Quite apart from hypotheses about ingenious substitutes, it is easy to imagine situations where we should not know whether to call something bread or not, and where our inability would not be a matter of ignorance, but a matter of the indefiniteness of the criteria we have learned to use. They work well enough most of the time; but they may well leave some cases undecidable. In the hypothetical case I mentioned, what decision was eventually made would not be predictable on purely semantic grounds. Thus, it might be that the majority would not be at a loss when confronted with our bread-substitute. Conditioned by other alienating adjectives like 'wrapped' or 'sliced', they might un-hesitatingly class the new arrival as bread. Nothing of philosophical importance would hang by such pieces of linguistic behaviour, nor is there anything untouchable about the usage by which some farinaceous foods are at present called bread and some are not.[9] What matters is that we do have here and now rough but workable standards by which we come to call something 'bread'. That does matter, because it robs the phrase 'looks like bread...but is not' of meaning in a eucharistic setting.

For what meaning could the phrase have, now that the context has gone in which the bread-substitute was encountered? No theologian will claim that subsequent investigations of the sort might decide that the consecrated host is not, despite appearances, bread. The conversion, he will admit, lies beyond any traceable process. But the trouble with such an admission, in old and new theology alike, is that it directs our attention away from the real problem. And it does so in a way I have complained at so often that it is with hesitation I go back to the charge here: the admission makes us think in terms of a

---

[9] If the statement seems unreasonable, consider the eucharistic wafers of the Latin Church. They are, or so we are told, made from wheaten flour, but if it were not for venerable custom who would think of calling them 'bread'? I take occasion to refer here to a lesser-known text of Aquinas, in which he asks about the proper material for the eucharistic bread (*ST* 3.74.3). Rye would count (Aquinas thought that it sprang up when wheat was sown in bad soil). Barley would not, as its origin is different. Moral theologians of yesteryear waxed eloquent on these topics. But McHugh 1961 shews what variety of opinion has existed, and indicates that Christ may have used barley-bread at the Last Supper. *Nous avons changé tout cela.*

miraculous and imperceptible transformation, when we ought to be thinking in terms of what words mean; it makes power do duty for intelligibility. To say that something *only looks* like bread is to commit oneself to saying that not all the criteria for being bread are satisfied: and, whether true or not, such an assertion at least makes sense. But to say that something *only looks* like bread and at the same time to say that *no* criterion for being bread is absent, makes no sense. It is simultaneously making an assertion and removing the context which gives the assertion meaning. Theological phenomenalism here rejects the setting of investigation and correction that alone can give sense to distinctions between how things look and what they are. Having rejected the setting, it can no longer accommodate any real link between appearance and reality. We cannot venture beyond what is phenomenal, all else is hazard. The gap is unbridgeable; the theology that claims to open us to transubstantiation opens us in fact to anything we fancy.

Scepticism is not a comfortable posture if only because – as a sceptic once admitted – 'you cannot be a philosopher all the time'. That is why sceptical drives are usually tempered by an appeal to something deemed even stronger than doubt. Hume admits in his *Treatise* (1 iv 7) that cheerful conversation and a game of backgammon make his speculations seem ridiculous in retrospect. Newman in an Oxford sermon prefers the Being and Providence of God as an antidote, and postpones questions about the substantial truth of the senses to another world (Newman 1843: 348f.). For Descartes, the clarity and distinctness of ideas, along with the 'Cogito', resisted the essay in doubting which he had set himself. Later on in the seventeenth century, some philosophers found interaction between objects an enigma. So they invoked divine power, and made creatures only the *occasions* of their effects, not the *causes*. We have seen an echo of this 'Occasionalism' in what de Baciocchi wrote about the lordship of Christ in (40) to (43), and in Vanneste's talk in (36) to (39) of Christ's word making things be what he wants them to be. We might call it 'Semantic Occasionalism', an occasionalism of *meaning*, an invocation of divine power as the standard of what words mean. But, of course, the occasionalism is not found only in those two authors, it is here whenever an appeal is made to omnipotence instead of to intelligibility. Or, which is what the appeal rests on, whenever the Fallacy of Replacement touches eucharistic speculation. The appeal links the meaning of words with criteria that are loftier than the criteria we normally use; in doing so, it negates these humbler criteria, even though the conditions for their use are present; it makes the two kinds of criteria *compete*, and decides in favour of what is more exalted. Which is precisely why the Fallacy of Replacement causes the trouble. It is not a matter of denying revelation the last word, or indeed (if we wish to speak so) of denying Christ the first word. It is a matter of letting simple and unpretentious words mean what they do mean.

The text from Newman at (91) attributed to Macaulay the view that the example of Thomas More's belief in transubstantiation was needed to persuade him that Catholics of an enlightened age could resist 'the overwhelming force of the argument against it' (the source is in fact Macaulay's essay of 1840 on von Ranke's *History of the Popes*). So it is worth ending the texts in this chapter with an anecdote about Macaulay which shews him distinguishing between divine power and intelligibility in just the way I have been arguing they should be distinguished. The reminiscence comes from Lord Carlisle, and is to be found in the eleventh chapter of G. O. Trevelyan's biography of his uncle:

94. Macaulay argued very forcibly against Hobhouse and Charles Greville for the difference between the evidence of Christ's miracles and of transubstantiation. To put them on a level, Lazarus ought to have remained inanimate, colourless, and decomposing in the grave, while we should be called upon to believe that he had at the word of Christ become alive. (Trevelyan 1908: 480)

I have now spent two chapters expressing my disagreement with older and newer accounts of the eucharistic presence, and the disagreement has led to my charge that older and newer are far closer than they are usually held to be. They have in common a divorce between appearance and reality. The divorce is prompted by a desire to preserve what is precious, but for all that it is incoherent and leads to the sceptical conclusions we have encountered. Much remains to be said of older and newer accounts, but I recall here the admission made earlier in the section about the Fallacy of Replacement: a fallacy it is, but it is never far from an acknowledgment of things that matter (pp. 89–90). The Fallacy is an abuse of the supremely important insight into the divinely bestowed and inexhaustible character of reality, into the quasi-sacramental significance it already possesses, into the limits of all our own contrivings and describings, and into the transcendence of what the Eucharist bestows. I am submitting that we need a new start in the matter, but a claim to absolute novelty here would be – among other things – comically pretentious. In giving my own proposals, I shall be glad to use such insights, and all else I find valuable in older and newer accounts. And my own proposals will labour under the difficulties that attend upon every account, new or old. Any eucharistic theology is concerning itself with a mystery which can never be satisfactorily articulated in human speech – which is why any eucharistic theology lays itself open to objections which its proponents will not be able to answer as they should like.

I have given more than one warning that what I have to offer cannot be briefly put, because things are not as straightforward as they seem. Things here are not straightforward, and so the journey we now undertake cannot be brisk either. I am aware that it will lead through topics which seem at first sight only vaguely connected with our theme. And so I state here in broad outline what course the journey ahead will take; we shall find that what we have seen so far will have its part to play there.

In the next chapter, 'History and language', I take up once more our theme of present and past. We saw how the vocabulary and distinctions used by Aquinas do not match our own, and that the difference has developed because of what lies between his time and ours. It is this temporal spread of thought about the eucharistic presence that the next chapter explores, and the demands which it makes. The temporal spread necessarily touches the language of speculation. I shall claim that language itself has forces and tendencies that can lead us in unwelcome directions; and I shall also claim that the newer authors do not recognise sufficiently the demands of a language that is spread over time and inherited by them. We shall meet in this third chapter a wider form of the Fallacy of Replacement – a form that muffles the need we have to face just what our past is and just what our present is to make of it. Reflexions on these themes will touch what is to be said of the eucharistic presence, but they will also touch the tradition itself within which the speculations take place.

But 'speculations' here is not an altogether happy word, because the Eucharist is not a matter of speculation, it is a ritual. And so in the fourth chapter, 'Signs and disguises', I spell out where I think both older and newer accounts have gone astray – for all their merits, neither takes the eucharistic ritual in ritual terms. And because neither does, each is treating the Eucharist in what amounts to the category of disguise. That category has attractions here, but the replacing of disguises by signs is indispensable for a better account. But the replacement itself has consequences for the relations between present and past. The older account of the eucharistic presence, hallowed by time and resembling in its vocabulary what was decreed by Trent, turns out to be a more mixed business: there are darknesses in it, and we tend to forget them. So novelty here is not just a falling away from what was whole and satisfactory. Once more, things prove less straightforward than they looked.

The fifth chapter I call 'Eucharist proclamation', and in it I try to offer an account of the eucharistic presence that builds on what has been argued in the preceding chapters. The 'Givenness of Reality', which I praised in Schillebeeckx's book, I take up again; but I note in the reality which is given a darkness and inadequacy that are the starting-point for the 'Way of Ritual', as I call it. This way moves from the darkness, through rituals that promise release from it, and moves through these successive stages towards what surpasses our language and understanding. Once more, what I submit has consequences for the relationship between past and present. The 'Way of Ritual' itself has darknesses in it, and their place and nature need investigating. Moreover, since I have tried to write of the eucharistic ritual in ritual terms, so I consider the changes there have been in the pattern of worship in the Roman Church. The older rite of the Mass I compare with the older account in terms of transubstantiation. And I examine an array of techniques by which an awkward past can be accommodated to the present – and I draw the moral that accommodation cannot be enough.

But accommodation is only to be expected when past and present involve beliefs deeply held within a tradition that is revered. And so it is that the sixth and final chapter, '*Corpus mysticum*', extends the conclusions reached to the Church – the temporally extended community and tradition within which the ritual of the Eucharist has been and is celebrated. It is notorious that the Roman Church has, over the last quarter of a century and more, been subject to tensions and unhappinesses that remain unresolved. It will be my submission that their nature, and a way towards overcoming them, can be seen in terms of the rite of the Eucharist; just as the rite can point to what that Church might have to contribute to the world we share – the reality which is given to us.

But broad outlines are one thing, the journey itself is another. The journey calls for a search into concrete particularities. We are to *look*, not to say how it *must* be. And we start by looking in the next chapter at what touches history and language.

CHAPTER 3

History and language

17 RETURN TO A FALLACY

'A little too miraculous': so, one Sunday in September 1966, a preacher described the story of the raising to life of the widow's son at Nain – it had formed the Gospel of the Mass. The French writer Julien Green recorded in his *Journal* the congregation's calm acceptance of the description, his own astonishment ('what then of the raising of Lazarus? Of Easter Day?'), and his feeling that the incident represented so much that had become amiss with the Church in recent years (Green 1977: 406).[1] I submit that Green's anecdote recalls the Fallacy of Replacement, but now in a wider setting. In this setting the Fallacy raises wider questions, and will eventually lead us to consider the tensions that exist in the Church of Rome today. I begin my submissions by offering some observations upon narratives of the miraculous.

Miracle stories of their very nature combine the unusual with the workaday. If there were nothing out of the ordinary in them, they would not be concerned with the marvellous; but if that marvellous did not shew itself in human and homely settings, it would not be recognised as marvellous in the first place. The double-sidedness of these narratives has been further complicated by what biblical criticism declares about the structure of all the gospel texts – the

---

[1] Julien Green (born in 1900) is of American origin, although he writes in French and lives in France. His *Journal* (Green 1977) repays reading on almost every page – I have just come across one day's entry which gives perceptive accounts both of Lawrence's *The White Peacock*, and of the electrical force emanating from the virginity of a golden-haired blue-eyed future monk (29 May 1971). Green's remarks on Roman Catholicism in our day will be cited more than once in this book, and I venture the prophecy that ecclesiastical historians will find him a rich primary source. His *Journal* exhibits him as burdened (not unwillingly, I suspect) with a whole Jack Ketch of hang-ups, but also as capable of dry amusement at life's little absurdities – such as finding odious Claudel's *Positions et Propositions* classified by a bookseller under Erotica (20 September 1966).

shaping of them for doctrinal purposes, the use in them of imagery from earlier parts of the Bible and above all their having been composed among people who did not share our notions of investigation and explanation. And so it is often said that this complexity of formation makes it at times difficult or impossible to discern just what does lie behind the narratives we possess. But another and stronger claim is sometimes made. We are told that to ask 'whether it all really happened' is to miss the point of the stories, and even to put a question that makes no sense. Many readers will have come across the claim in one form or another; I go to an example in *The Times* for Easter Monday 1988. The writer claims there that our civilisation has a general presumption in favour of the scientific world-view, and says that the view is found among participants on both sides of the debate about the Empty Tomb, so that the controversy was conducted in those terms:

it was between those for whom it was a 'scientific fact' that the tomb was deserted, and those for whom it was a 'scientific fact' that it was not. Such is the suffocating embrace of scientific materialism in modern culture, that anyone who asserted that the rival propositions are neither true nor false nor even interesting was likely to be ruled out of court. (Longley 1988)

I do not pretend to seize the writer's purpose here as much as I should like. But I can use his remarks in order to introduce my contention that we have here once again, this time in what I would call a wider setting, the Fallacy of Replacement.

There are of course cases where to ask 'did it really happen?' shews we have wholly missed the point of what we have read (think of narratives in Victorian arithmetic books about workmen boring holes in baths). But not all cases are as extreme as that. Suppose someone reads *Gulliver's Travels* and then asks whether it all really happened. He would have to be enlightened as to what Swift's book *was*. But the enlightenment would not and could not involve telling him that questions like 'is there really a country where wrens are as big as our turkeys?' cannot be put.[2] They can be put, and they can be given an

---

[2] I have gone to *Gulliver's Travels* for my example because just such a question was once put to a former pupil of mine when she was reading the book with a class of children. Her explanation of Swift's purpose in writing about Lilliput and Brobdingnag met with a disconcerting response – he should not write what was not true. What makes the anecdote more interesting is that the pupils were girls in a remote backwater of Nigeria: I confess that I have ever since been a trifle sceptical over talk of 'primitive mentalities'. It is worth adding

answer, even though our answer will not be negative in the simple way our answer is to a question like 'are the Alps as high as the Himalayas?' Our answer will not be *all* that we want to say, and we shall regard what more we do say as seizing what matters most. That does not prevent our having to give an answer to the original question.

This general contention I now apply to the specific case raised in *The Times*. I insist that, whatever we mean by 'scientific world-view', the narratives of the resurrection have been read in Christian Churches from early days, and that the narratives have been taken there – rightly or wrongly – as claiming that those who went to the tomb found it empty of the body, and went on to find that the emptiness was not caused by someone's having gone in and removed the corpse. That the resurrection means far more than this, I naturally do not deny; but I do insist that 'Was the tomb empty?' is a question that can both be put and be given an answer, whether 'Yes', 'No', or 'I do not know'. Longley's phrase 'scientific fact' only obfuscates what matters – a proposition is being stated that is homely as well as wonderful, and the wonder must not be allowed to cancel the homeliness. What is simple is not *replaced* by what is more exalted. Though our humbler claims are seen as part of something far higher and greater, that does not prevent us from making them.

Which, of course, brings us back to the Fallacy of Replacement. I used the term to describe what happens when the insight I discerned in Schillebeeckx's principles slips into a negation of ordinary judgments and into a demotion of physical knowledge to the order of appearances (pp. 88ff.). We have now met something similar, but this time in a biblical setting: what is wondrous is seen as cancelling the homely, and as forbidding homely words to have their homely meanings. I have claimed that the Fallacy now raises wider questions and leads us towards later topics. I spell out my claim by noticing how the biblical example points to two themes we have already met and are going to meet ever more as the book goes on: the first is what I have called 'insulation', the second is the relationship between present and past. I say something of each in turn.

Insulation we first met when examining the debate between Colombo and Selvaggi. The very convenience of Colombo's substance for the Eucharist was a danger signal, and the reality of the danger was shewn by the scepticism implicit in the divorce there between

that the same pupils exhibited horror and revulsion at the final voyage, that to the Houyhnhnms and Yahoos. How pleased Swift would have been!

appearance and reality. It was Selvaggi's 'open' concept of substance that, precisely because of its coherent link with the whole process of coming to understand the world, proved recalcitrant to abuse for eucharistic employment. But the convenience of Colombo's notion was deceptive: its eucharistic employment simply encouraged a distortion of philosophical distinctions into unintelligible dissections, and fenced off a mysterious 'metaphysical order' from whatever physical investigations might reveal: insulation yielded only grotesques. It fared no better in Godefroy's contention that Trent's formulae call for nothing more than a mysterious *philosophia perennis* – the said perennial philosophy ended by producing untranslatable gibberish in what it claimed about substance (pp. 24, 68). In each case, insulation seemed to put a defensive wall round what was valued; in each case, the insulation imposed led to nothing more than fantasies. Openness, not insulation, was what was needed. The concept of substance makes sense if it is set within the attempts we make to understand the nature of things in a changing world; language makes sense if it is allowed its place in the whole array of words, actions and associations, an array that we inherit, develop and pass on in our turn. Openness will not yield the ease that insulation offers; but neither will it yield the grotesques that insulation ends by delivering.

That is why rejecting insulation in favour of openness necessarily involves taking seriously the second theme – the relation between present and past. Of that too we have already seen something. We have met examples of the way in which what belongs to and is written in one age is part of a temporally extended process, and examples of how, by what I have called 'the Theaetetus Effect', later things affect our encounter with what came earlier. Thus, what Aquinas wrote about the eucharistic presence was elucidated by earlier and later texts, while the writings of recent authors were set beside those in the scholastic tradition, and unexpected resemblances were seen. To reject insulation is to open oneself to the consequences of language and of time: that is why, yet again, to choose 'openness' is to face the prospect of discomfort.

But there is more than discomfort to be faced. We should not be surprised at the manifestations of what I have called 'insulation'. Insulation is put at the service of what is valued, whether this be the eucharistic presence or the status of narratives in the gospels. It seems to provide them with a fence against awkwardness, and to render them inaccessible to attack. The manoeuvre is a mistake, but it is an understandable one. To admit the validity of the question 'did such-and-such in the narrative really happen?' can be just as awkward as admitting the validity of the question how far a long-established tradition of eucharistic speculation makes sense. That is why we are going to find in what follows a variety of attempts to insulate what is valued.

In this chapter I want to spell out more of what is involved in insulation and in its rejection. I first consider the charge that insulation, with its separation of appearance from reality, simply has to be accepted in eucharistic theology: and I counter the charge by claiming that to accept it is to involve ourselves in muddles of our own making. My claim I support in the next section by an example from Aquinas, which will touch both insulation and the relation of present and past. The example will touch insulation, in that a phrase Aquinas uses drives him back to just the kind of dissection and reification for which I blamed him in the first chapter, and drives him back because of terminology and distinctions he uses. Language, in other words, cannot be insulated by us, it has implications and associations with powers of their own. But the example will also touch the relationship between present and past – when, in the section after that, we turn from Aquinas himself to what recent writers have made of the phrase and of similar terminology used by him. I have called this chapter 'History and language': its general moral will be that the temporal spread of human activity must be faced; that language is part of the heritage developed over time; and that, if we are to think aright, neither language nor any other part of the heritage can be simply ignored. And so in the final section I go to Schillebeeckx for what I think is an example of the ignoring.

First then for the charge that eucharistic belief obliges us to admit the kind of divorce between appearance and reality that goes with insulation. I complained in the last chapter against the divorce in what Schillebeeckx wrote, and I do not repeat my strictures here – I simply repeat my admission that there is much value in the principles he invokes. De Baciocchi also writes good sense, as well as falling into similar mistakes. For him, the mystery in reality is inexhaustible, as it is for Schillebeeckx (p. 87). For him also, substance is that which exists as grasped by the intelligence, and perceptual data do not conceal it but invite the understanding to closer acquaintance (de Baciocchi 1955: 576). But he describes accidents there as what is 'made manifest at the level of sensory *and scientific* experience', where the phrase I have italicised relegates science to the order of the accidental. So it is no surprise to find him writing of the Eucharist:

Our senses are not deceived. At the level at which our senses attain reality, nothing is changed in the bread and wine. (de Baciocchi 1959: 149)

Or, putting things less kindly, our senses are in no worse a position when confronted with the Eucharist than when confronted with anything else. Mystery is once more reduced to muddle, and we are back with Colombo and his inaccessible substance.

Vanneste, we saw, follows Leenhardt in allotting a decisive rôle to Christ's word, and sees that word as replacing what we have learned of things in an ordinary way: see (36) and (39). But he offers no argument for construing Christ's word as a denial in this sense, and there is just as unargued a preference for 'replacement' by Schoonenberg and Smits. For Schoonenberg in (52), bread and wine are 'not just taken up into an action that emphasises what is said' (I cite the phrase because we are going to meet it again in the next chapter), they are transubstantiated as the gift in which Christ gives us himself. Giving plays the same part for Smits: 'the Lord does not want to give bread and wine, but himself wholly' (1964b: 9/4, cols. 1 and 2). No argument is offered by either author for the validity of the *exclusive alternative* which he puts before us; it is in these unargued alternatives that each commits the Fallacy of Replacement; and it is the Fallacy which, in my submission, lies at the base of the phenomenalism I have been opposing in eucharistic theologies, new and old.

Which confronts me with the charge that phenomenalism simply must be accepted in eucharistic theology. I have taken up a position in which I find fault with older and newer opinions alike, charging them with incoherence and with a divorce of appearance from reality. But is not my common charge a proof of an insight common to old and new? What kind of new start can there be left for me to offer? It is all very well complaining at phenomenalism, but do we not need something of the sort if we are to preserve the eucharistic presence? Christ is not perceived in the Eucharist, and yet either he is there or he is not: in my talk of a new start, am I not condemned by this alternative to either a lack of novelty or a lack of orthodoxy?

One of my persistent themes is going to be that questions of the sort have not been clearly put. Whether we talk in scholastic terms of substance and accidents, or with de Baciocchi and Vanneste in terms of Christ's ultimate word or with Schoonenberg and Smits in terms of a total giving, we do indeed appear to be offering a proposition about the presence of Christ that can be simply affirmed or denied. One reason for the length of this book is that I do not think that any such propositions are in fact being offered. In my view, all we are being offered by old or by new is confusion, and confusions resist a straightforward response, whether it be positive or negative. To give my reasons, and to explain what I have to suggest instead, is something that cannot be briskly done. My first step, as I promised, will be to consider a phrase in Aquinas, how it fares with him (better, perhaps, how he fares with it), and how it is treated by later authors.

18 A PHRASE AND ITS FORCE

The phrase is *per modum substantiae* – by way of substance – and we met it in the first chapter. Aquinas asks how Christ can be equally present in large or small consecrated hosts. He replies that he is present *per modum substantiae*, and so questions of dimensionality do not arise: human nature is present as much in a short as in a tall man; large and small portions of air are equally air (pp. 15–16). I gave my reasons there for thinking that Aquinas is confusing a predicate like 'being human' with the predicate 'being Christ', but here I go further. The language of Aquinas when he uses the phrase drives him in the very direction from which the phrase was meant to keep him away.

When introducing the phrase in the *Summa Theologiae*, Aquinas draws a distinction between presence in the Eucharist 'by the power of the sacrament' (*vi sacramenti*) and presence 'by real concomitance' (*ex reali concomitantia*). The former is the presence of that into which the substance of the bread is directly converted by the sacrament – namely the substance of Christ's body. The latter is the presence of what is really conjoined with that substance (*ST* 3.76.1). And Christ's dimensions are not present by the power of the sacrament, as is his substance; they are present only by their real concomitance with his substance. And so Christ's presence is not by way of quantity but by way of substance – *per modum substantiae* (*ST* 3.76.1 ad 3; 4).

Aquinas offers no further elucidation of what he has just claimed for the dimensions of Christ, so I turn to the vocabulary he employs, and italicise what goes against the grain of what he is trying to suggest. The 'specific totality' of a substance, he writes, *is contained* just as much in a small as in a large quantity…and so the whole substance of Christ *is contained* in the sacrament after the consecration, just as the substance of the bread *was contained* there before the consecration (*ST* 3.76.1 ad 3). Argument goes one way, the associations of 'is contained' (*continetur*) go another. Which is what happens again when he contrasts 'presence by way of dimensions' with 'presence by way of substance': in the former, the dimensive quantity of something is *under* the dimensive quantity of a place; in the latter, we have presence in the way that substance is *under* its dimensions (*ST* 3.76.3). One and the same preposition (the Latin *sub*) holds together what Aquinas is trying to keep apart. Later in the same question, presence *per modum substantiae* is elucidated without more ado in terms of containment: it is 'the way in which substance *is contained* by its dimensions' (*ST* 3.76.5). And the same Article continues in the same vein, when Aquinas denies that the substance of Christ is present as in a place: the substance of bread was not *under* its dimensions as in a place; but the substance of Christ *succeeds* the substance of the bread; so the substance of Christ is not there as in a place either. The denial made by Aquinas is couched in terms that go with just what he wants to deny.[3]

A final text from this Article of the *Summa Theologiae* will lead us naturally in the next section to what later writers have made of *per modum substantiae* and of allied phrases in the scholastic account. Aquinas puts the difficulty that the bread itself is present as in a place, is present *localiter*; but the dimensions of the bread remain when the bread's substance is converted into the substance of Christ's body; why then should not Christ's body be present also 'as in a place'? The answer offered is that the *bread's* substance, though not under its dimensions as in a place, was the *subject* of the bread's dimensions; so the bread was related to (*comparabatur*) where it was by means of *its own* dimensions; and so it was there *localiter*, as in a place. But the substance of Christ is not the subject of the bread's dimensions; so the substance of Christ is related to that place by means of dimensions *that are not its own*; and all that excludes any *location* of Christ's body in the Eucharist (*ST* 3.76.5). The answer, unfortunately, suggests all too strongly that one substance is replaced by another, and that

---

[3] For all that, it is worth noticing that here Aquinas offers one of those qualifying phrases that can be so easily missed (see footnote 5 to chapter 1). He recapitulates his general position as a claim 'that the body of Christ is not in this sacrament according to the manner pertaining to dimensive quantity, but [my italics] *rather* according to the matter of substance' (*ST* 3.76.5), where the usual *per modum substantiae* has given way to *magis secundum modum substantiae*. Notice too a qualifier in a text already referred to – Christ's dimensions are present 'by concomitance and [my italics] *as it were* (*quasi*) by coincidence' (*ST* 3.76.4 ad 1).

the second substance escapes location only because the dimensions it is under are not its own. It escapes only because it is dressed 'in borrowed robes'.

Those words from Act I of *Macbeth* I used in the second chapter, in the first of the texts I translated there from recent authors. They expressed de Baciocchi's *vêtement d'emprunt* in his humorous description of 'an imaginative solution with which transubstantiation is often confused'. As we come to consider how he and others treat the scholastic account, we need to bear in mind what examining *per modum substantiae* has taught us. The use of the phrase by Aquinas occurs in the context of the whole adaptation he makes of terminology, Aristotelian in origin, to do with substance and accidents. Whatever be the merits of the adaptation, it does provide the setting for the contentions that Aquinas makes here. The specific purpose of his contentions is to emancipate the eucharistic presence from dimensionality, and I have submitted that the purpose is not attained, that the words used speak against it. But, once more, the failure occurs in the setting of the eucharistic adaptation of the distinction between substance and accident, it is not some isolated lack of success. We know by now what part the wider setting plays: the eucharistic adaptation goes with a *reification* of the terms – goes with a turning of distinctions into dissections. And so we have the moral I said we could draw from the phrase *per modum substantiae*: language cannot be insulated from the implications and associations it possesses. But what we have seen enables us to draw another moral – that we must take seriously the relation between past and present. The scholastic speculations have their own setting, and that setting is of a particular time and has its own distinctive patterns. Just as we noticed in the first chapter that the claims made by Aquinas about the Eucharist seemed to straddle the disciplinary boundaries we draw ourselves, so we must respect the distinctive 'placing' of the terminology which we have found in his speculations. With all this in mind, let us see how the terminology has fared among recent authors.

19 PHRASES AND THEIR FORTUNES

I referred to de Baciocchi towards the end of the last section, and I begin this section by noticing the *purpose* of what he wrote in the text I mentioned there. His humorous description of 'an imaginative solution' of the eucharistic presence was meant to keep such a solution apart from transubstantiation – 'all that has nothing to do with transubstantiation'. But it was also meant to keep the solution apart from what has been laid down by the Church – the solution is 'quite often confused' with transubstantiation, but the Church has never 'either approved or condemned' it. Neither contention now looks plausible. In the first chapter we saw that distinctions drawn elsewhere by Aquinas have to be abused in eucharistic speculation if they are to yield the results he seeks; that the abuse has just those 'imaginative' consequences de Baciocchi reprobates; while the preceding section has shewn that the very steps Aquinas takes to avoid 'dimensionality' drive him back towards it. But we have also seen that the Council of Trent has used terminology similar to that of Aquinas; and we know that the scholastic tradition in eucharistic theology was shared by those who assembled at Trent, just as it was part of the formation of generations of clergy in the Church of Rome. Just as we cannot dismiss the 'imaginative' associations of the scholastics here, so we cannot deny the place of scholasticism in what the Church has been. I have insisted that we must take seriously the relation between past and present. To take the relation seriously involves facing just what it is that lies in our past – and I submit that de Baciocchi's historical insouciance shews he is not facing it.

But this insouciance is found in other authors, and touches the scholastic method itself. Gutwenger, we saw at (8) in the second chapter, found fault with the application to the Eucharist of Aristotelian categories – there will always be 'something stolidly material' about it. But in the very article from which I took that quotation, he also claims that our use today of the notion of substance should take as its starting-point the experience we have of ourselves as something persisting – although such a notion of substance, having its origin in the spirit, will be at best only analogously applicable to the material world (Gutwenger 1966: 186). I am not concerned with the rights and wrongs of these two notions of substance, but with what Gutwenger hopes to achieve by replacing one of them by the other. He can of course obtain thereby a *verbal* coincidence with what the scholastics held, but he needs to prove that he can obtain anything more. And of proof, or of a hint of the necessity for proof, he gives no sign.[4]

---

[4] I cannot resist the temptation to compound all this confusion. Schelfout, in a critique of Vanneste that we met at p. 83, takes a diametrically opposed view about substance to Gutwenger's: for him, it is in living beings that the distinction between substance and

Just as little of a sign is given in what Vanneste writes of the scholastic tradition. In (38) in the second chapter, he charged the tradition with staying on the philosophical plane in its notion of substance, instead of deepening the concept in religious terms. But he attributes to the great scholastics a better way. They

> take Aristotelian categories as their starting-point, but they do not omit to correct them fundamentally. So fundamentally that a central element in Aristotelianism falls away; in that system, no change is possible without at least the prime matter remaining. (Vanneste 1956: 328)

After what we have seen of how Aristotelian terms are used by the scholastics, 'correct them fundamentally' seems a strange description. Stranger still is the example offered of the correction. Whatever be thought of the body of distinctions used by Aristotle in his account of change, his terms do have definite parts to play there, and I submitted in the first chapter that the denial by Aquinas of any 'subject' to the eucharistic conversion is at the root of the incoherence in what he writes (pp. 12ff.). But for Vanneste, 'falls away' seems an appropriate phrase here – it is as if some built-in curb on a machine had dropped off; the force and connexion in Aristotle's terms are represented as a limitation which theologians remove. You had as well speak of curing the inability of squares to be circular.

Vanneste has more to say, and I shall return to it. I pass now to seeing how the terminology of the scholastics fares with Schoonenberg, who offers an explicit consideration of the phrase *per modum substantiae*. As we saw in the second chapter, Schoonenberg's own account is in terms of personal presence and of giving. He claims correctly that scholastic theology used *per [modum] substantiae* to emancipate the eucharistic presence from dimensionality (1959b: 321–2),[5] and of the phrase he writes that it:

> sums up all that theology's dialectic which seeks emancipation from spatial proximity, and the securing of Christ's presence in the species. The formula

accidents seems at first sight *less* acceptable (Schelfout 1960: 311–12). Who shall decide when Schoolmen disagree? However, Schelfout claims that the thomistic distinction is part of the *philosophia perennis*, that Trent's account can easily be given a clear and correct significance for the man in the street (297), and – who would have guessed? – that physical science does not attain to the order of substance (314–15). So I suppose that settles it.

[5] I have put *modum* into square brackets because Schoonenberg writes '*medium*' ('means') instead. Since he goes on to suggest a complementary formula *per modum cibi* ('in the manner of food'), I take it that '*medium*' is only a slip of the pen. Aquinas, as far as I know, does not

is true, it is masterly, but it needs complementing by one that seeks to give a description starting from personal presence. For this, we can find no better formula than 'presence in the way of food', *praesentia per modum cibi*. This may look disappointing, because all the scholastic dialectic of the first formula is no longer to be traced in it. (Schoonenberg 1959b: 322–3)

What I find disappointing here is not the absence of 'scholastic dialectic' in the formula Schoonenberg proposes, but the absence of any criticism of that dialectic. If personal presence is to be a complement to the dialectic, then – should there be anything whatever in my critique of *per modum substantiae* – we need to be much clearer than we are as to just what is supposed to be being complemented. Once more, a knowledge of the past is essential to a grasp of what the present needs. Historical insouciance is, once more, not enough.

Nor do we get help from other texts of Schoonenberg. He describes the intention we should read into Trent's decree: an opposition to 'any sign regarded simply as a thing, and separated from inter-personal relationships' (1965: 50). Perhaps we should so read it; but Schoonenberg has explicitly stated, in an article already cited, that the scholastics preferred to think in 'cosmological and general ontological' categories, and that their presences went with an age in which concepts to do with personal relationships were not developed (1959b: 321–2). How then are we to justify a reading of Trent in terms involving those relationships? Once again we are faced with historical insouciance. Phrases from the past are kept, but their presence is held to dispense us from seeing just what our past has been, and so just what the phrases involve.

use the phrase *per medium substantiae*. I take the occasion to notice another slip, in his footnote to 1959b: 324, which compares the phrase *illocaliter in loco* (non-locally in a place) with Aquinas, *ST* 3.76.5. Aquinas did not write that phrase there. What he did write, we saw at p. 115: that Christ is not in this sacrament as in a place, and that his substance is related to (*comparatur*) the place by means of the bread's dimensions that survive the conversion of the bread's substance. I notice these things because they might give Schoonenberg's opponents an excuse for not trying to grasp the points he is making, even though they themselves unconsciously make similar adjustments to texts. For instance, when Schoonenberg (1965: 50) reports the Council of Trent as declaring that Christ's body 'is present under the appearances of bread and wine *vere, realiter et substantialiter* [truly, really and substantially]', his report is identical with what so many scholastic expositions have reported. But in fact that is not what Trent said. Trent spoke of Christ being truly, really and substantially *contained under* the appearances (Sess. XIII, Can. 1, DS 1651 and Cap. 1, DS 1636; 'contained in' is also found, in Can. 3, DS 1653). The phenomenon of unconscious adaptation we shall be meeting again.

But we cannot be so dispensed, if we are to be aware of what we now hold, and of what place it has in the temporally extended tradition to which we belong. Without this awareness, we shall be thinking in the way to be found in another text of Schoonenberg, where he has asked how far the recent views are *other* than what has been held in the past. He answers by setting bounds to the otherness:

Not in a way other than the dogma of Trent, which remains fully operative as a condemnation of an *empty* symbolism; nor in a way other than thomistic theology, at all events in as much as this means to exclude any spatial presence or physical change; but certainly other than what is suggested – sometimes even by theologians – in popular expositions. (Schoonenberg 1965: 49)

And now, unfortunately, we find ourselves in much the same position we saw de Baciocchi in, with his talk of 'borrowed robes', 'mysterious kernel' and 'inflated skin'. His phrases were part of an amused dismissal of what was held to be no more than a piece of picturesqueness; they turned out to be part of what can legitimately be read into texts of Aquinas. We have something similar here. *Per modum substantiae*, we saw, has embarrassingly spatial connotations. Schoonenberg retains the expression, but relegates what embarrasses to the status of 'popular expositions'. That description has been all too over-worked in eucharistic discussion; it, and other things in what Schoonenberg writes, are not dissolutions of problems, they are pieces of unfinished business. And the business includes a consideration of why *per modum substantiae* was retained by recent authors in the first place.

We know from the second chapter that Schoonenberg aligns his own views with those of Smits, and we shall find in Smits too an example of historical insouciance. He begins, we saw in (13), (14), (18), with a denial of any divorce between sign and signified; rather, the former is an incarnation of the latter. He goes on, we saw in (47) to (51), to write in terms of the incarnation of human love in the Eucharist, but of a love that is the love of God made man. But he asks in another article whether the word 'transubstantiation' should still be applied to the account he has offered:

Is it not confusing to keep to this word? People always associate its use with the scholastics' endeavour to make more precise the data of faith; they will gradually come to discover that the flag no longer covers the cargo. (Smits 1965: 23/6, col. 2)[6]

By way of answer, he recalls that he has reported (in that article) three expositions of the eucharistic presence: the sensualistic, the physical and the scholastic. The first of these (it will be the gross formula imposed in 1059 on Berengarius, of which more later) makes our reception of the Eucharist, an apparent biting into bread, be a real biting into Christ's body. The second (could he be thinking of Selvaggi?) lets survive the physically perceptible appearances (the electric charges etc.), while letting depart the imperceptible kernel (the atoms, electrons, etc.). The third allows to survive the quantity and quality of the bread, and has them supported by the substance of Christ's body. Each of these accounts, he goes on, is orthodox, although each of them gives a different meaning to 'substance' and so to 'transubstantiation':

All these attempts at precision have this much in common – substance means the reality, and what we are faced with is a real change, not one that is symbolic or spiritual. That is exactly why 'transubstantiation' is so suitable for our exposition. In our account too we are concerned with the same datum of faith – a real change, a genuine transubstantiation. It would be unfair to take the word in only one of these more precise senses, and then attach it to the dogma of transubstantiation. The Church does not demand that, nor may the theologian. (Smits 1965: 23/6, col. 2)

The counterattack is vigorous, whatever we think of the accuracy with which the three views are stated. But the very way in which Smits formulates his question and answer shews how much is still in the dark.

He writes that people associate the word 'transubstantiation' with the scholastics. They surely associate it with much more: they associate it with the decree at Trent, where terminology of the scholastics is to be found; they associate it with centuries of theological and catechetical training; and (if they know anything more than the word) they associate it with the whole body of terms and distinctions we have investigated. More is at stake than the survival of a word. But Smits also writes in the text that 'transubstantiation' in Trent's

---

[6] My 'the flag no longer covers the cargo' literally renders the *de vlag de lading niet meer dekt* of Smits. My Dutch dictionary, however, renders the phrase as 'more cry than wool', and perhaps some readers will prefer this. In his *Dictionary of Phrase and Fable*, s.v. 'wool', Brewer will give them some, not very helpful, information.

decree allows the orthodoxy of the scholastic account, of the formula imposed on Berengarius and of an account that might sound to some like Selvaggi's. I am not concerned with the truth of this claim but with its content. Selvaggi wrote four centuries after Trent, in the setting of a widely different knowledge of the nature of things; Berengarius had to accept a formula five centuries before Trent (at a time when the term 'transubstantiation' had not yet been introduced): how can Smits, without argument or explanation, make the claim he does? If time and its effects are to be deemed of no moment, we need to be told why. I have given the title 'Phrases and their fortunes' to this section, and it is *phrases* that are the trouble – the recent authors seem content to preserve them without more ado. There was 'transubstantiation' for de Baciocchi, but with a repudiation of the content we saw it possess; 'substance' for Gutwenger, but with two quite different origins for the notion deemed interchangeable; 'substance' again for Vanneste, but with abuses described as corrections; '*per modum substantiae*' for Schoonenberg, but not subjected to criticism and indeed juxtaposed with talk of personal relationships; and now 'transubstantiation' for Smits, but (to use his metaphor) as a flag that can cover many cargoes. Phrases so taken cannot be enough: to treat them as isolated objects is indeed to insulate them; and the insulation goes with a disregard for the force and connexions in language, and for the relationship between past and present.

But in the text just given, Smits claimed something else: the three accounts he mentions have in common 'that substance means the reality and that what we are faced with is a real change, not one that is symbolic or spiritual'. To see what this claim amounts to demands that we first see why it is made, and I can best begin what I have to say here by noticing a claim made by another recent author. This is Trooster, who introduced the dialogue between Schillebeeckx and others we met in the last chapter (we shall be returning to it). In his part of the article, Trooster has this to say about Trent's eucharistic teaching:

I should like to state first that the reality which Trent formulated in the expressions 'transubstantiation', 'fittingly and appropriately', and 'most suitably'... must be accepted without more ado as truth of faith. The witness of tradition here is too strong and too univocal, the affirmation of it by the teaching Church is too plain, to admit of doubts here. Should preaching be unable to make anything of the mystery, it can remain silent. But it may not raise doubts over belief in this mysterious reality. (Trooster 1963: 129)

At first sight, that is the style that I have known Italians call *molto monsignore*. At second sight, however, the claim has undergone a sea-change. Theological reflexion on the mystery, he goes on to write, has ended in a blind alley, the categories of substance and accidents seem inappropriate for bread and wine, and the traditional teaching about the eucharistic presence has isolated it as a 'cosmological miracle' (129). After rehearsing several recent attempts to rethink the matter, he expresses his own preferences for a reformulation in terms of the phenomenal and the noumenal, and says that if we do so talk 'we have simply paraphrased the teaching of Trent' (130–1).

I hope it is not necessary by now for me to point to the oddities in all this – 'the reality formulated by Trent' is set beyond all legitimate doubt, although the tradition from which Trent borrowed its formulae is deemed profitless, while the Kantian distinction between phenomenal and noumenal is regarded as a 'paraphrase' of what was expressed by Trent in scholastic terms, two centuries before Kant was born. This is indeed historical insouciance. But notice how it is complemented by something else – a belief that what Trent taught imposes itself on us, even though couched in ways that call for refashioning. And it is this mixed feeling towards the past that we can find in the other recent authors. We can find it forcefully expressed by Vanneste in texts we met in the second chapter. He disclaimed there in (5) any wish to serve up a *rechauffée* of transubstantiation, and expressed his intention of confronting with the data of faith 'an exhausted theology'. He claims elsewhere that no particular philosophy of nature is demanded by eucharistic doctrine, only the belief that man is not the ultimate bestower of meaning for the bread, and that the ultimate substance does not lie there. For him, all that the real doctrine of transubstantiation deals with is this ultimate substance of things, 'this ultimate "en-soi", this ultimate "noumenon", or whatever other name be given it' (Vanneste 1956: 335). Vanneste's profession of indifference to speculation here brings into the open what I have called a 'mixed feeling' over the past in all the recent authors we have examined. The Council of Trent is accepted, but the associations of the terminology it uses make this or that author uneasy; Aquinas is venerated as a great thinker, but this style of thinking is seen as alien to our present condition; the presence of Christ is believed in, but the sources for approaching it are not those that earlier thinkers would use. The recent authors do indeed exhibit what I have called historical insouciance – but they exhibit it towards a past that is for them *both revered and unsatisfactory*. I have italicised the phrase because this tension in attitude is something that we shall be meeting time and again in what follows – and indeed, given the nature and setting of theological speculation, we could hardly avoid meeting it. But as we meet the tension, we shall time and again meet an attempt to shew that the tension does not exist. We met the attempt when our authors treated inherited phrases as if they were detachable from their settings. We met it again when Vanneste suggested that he can in some way leave the controverted areas of speculation for an immediate access to the truth about which there is controversy. Just as his aim was to confront the scholastic theories of the eucharistic presence 'with the data of faith itself', so now he wishes to detach the 'real doctrine of transubstantiation' from any particular philosophy of nature – so much so that, as long as we admit that the ultimate substance of the bread does not lie in the meaning man bestows, we may call it the *en-soi*, the *noumenon*, or anything else we please.

But the suggestion is not capable of resolving the tension between the present and a revered but unsatisfactory past – it is no more capable of doing so than what we have seen the other authors write. Vanneste is not speculatively neutral in what he writes, when he claims that we may call this ultimate substance the *en-soi*, the *noumenon*, or what we will. Indeed we may, as long as we see nothing odd in juxtaposing without comment terms from the scholastics, Heidegger (Hegel?) and Kant. But that is not speculative neutrality or philosophical innocence, it is a refusal in the present to take account of the past. No expression, formal or informal, stands wholly outside the temporal spread of language, stands as it were in a timeless, neutral setting to which a retreat can be made from speculative elaboration. Retreats can naturally be made to what is less speculative, but where these retreats terminate is just as much of its own time and place as where they began. And this limiting by time will be especially true of technical and systematic terms, which make up a more strongly connected structure with other elements. Vanneste's position here is no more speculatively innocent than his description of eucharistic theology as correcting Aristotle's distinctions. Phrases like his 'ultimate substance' do not and cannot stand apart from speculation, we have seen all too much of such phrases to think they might. Just so, when Smits writes that three accounts of the eucharistic presence have in common 'that substance means the reality, and that what we are faced with is a real change, not one that is symbolic or spiritual' (see p. 121), he is not standing apart from speculation either. What he writes is a claim that is itself part of the temporally extended tradition of speculation, not a comment thereon made from a neutral standpoint and couched in a neutral vocabulary.

To seek such a standpoint is understandable, given that we revere a past that fails to satisfy – we feel we could attain thereby something outside time, and could give it timeless expression as the satisfying heart, or essence, or something, of what we revere. But this is no more than trying to insulate language, and so trying to ignore the relation of past to present. Whatever we say will carry in itself implications (perhaps unsuspected by its users), will possess associations and links with other things – whether they be other ways of thought and insight, half-forgotten disputes, or dormant fallacies. Whatever we write is part of a whole tradition of speculation, and we do no good to ourselves or to the tradition by thinking that time does not matter, or by pretending that conflicts can be resolved by a retreat to what stands apart from any tradition at all.

I have traced in recent authors what I have called 'historical insouciance', and have offered an account of why it can prove attractive. But there is one author whom I have not cited in this section, and that is Schillebeeckx. I turn to the opinions he offers in the dialogue (Trooster 1963) we have already met. An examination of them will form the next section, and the chapter will then end with some general reflexions on what it has taught us.

20 PAINTING ONESELF INTO A CORNER

The discussion I have in mind took place some years before the publication of Schillebeeckx's book, and I do not claim that his views remained unchanged in the interval – indeed, in my opinion he shews in the book a greater awareness of the historical limitations in the formation of Trent's decrees (see 17–20 [25–9], and notice at 79 [102] a reference to renewed reflexions on the whole topic). But, as we might expect, Schillebeeckx gives forceful expression in this earlier writing to what his views were then – views which go even further than the texts we examined in the preceding section, and are worth examining for their own sake.

Schillebeeckx rightly objects to what Trooster himself writes of the phenomenal and noumenal: the contrast strikes him as Kantian. But, having said this, he goes on to deny that Trent's text can be called scholastic:

The *substantia panis* [the substance of bread] is definitively the reality I confront. I may not appeal to Thomas or to Aristotle for the Council of Trent's concept of substance. It is the dogmatic definition that must make clear what substance is for Trent. (Trooster 1963: 134, col. 2)

Which, of course, brings us round again to the idea that we can retreat from speculation and argument to some neutral ground – only this time it is the conciliar decree that is surrounded by a *cordon sanitaire*. The idea of such retreats, I have submitted, is no more than an illusion, but I am not thereby suggesting that we should 'appeal to Thomas or to Aristotle'. Indeed, after all that I have said about the way Aquinas is obliged here to abuse Aristotelian distinctions, I think it ominous that the two names should have been linked by Schillebeeckx in the first place. All I am suggesting is what I have pointed out so often before. The council's decree was drawn up (how could it not have been?) by those who had been for the most part trained in the scholastic tradition. The council's purpose certainly deserves investigation, and cannot simply be read off from the terms employed. But the council did have to use words in the decree that embodied its purpose, and we do know the tradition within which those words are used.

Schillebeeckx's claim that Trent should be detached from scholasticism may seem unlikely, but the next text I give goes further. Elsewhere in the discussion, he gave his opinion that the bread changes to a *signum substantiale*, a substantial sign: see (89) in the second chapter. To his use of *substantiale* here an objection was put and an answer offered:

VAN LEEUWEN: I fear that the term 'substance' will arouse misunderstanding. The term is almost inevitably associated with typically scholastic patterns of thought.
SCHILLEBEECKX: I have no objection to the term 'substance'. I should find it objectionable only if people were to think of it according to the scholastic relation between substance and accident. In my opinion, real objections can be raised against this distinction, on the ground that

should the substance change, the accidents change as well. Even in the case of the Eucharist, I should want to say that substance and accidents alike change. (Trooster 1963: 135, col. 1)

This is even odder than the last text. There we were told that the sense of Trent's term 'substance' must be construed without reference to Aquinas or to Aristotle, and I expressed my puzzlement at the isolation this imposed upon the council. But now we are told that the term 'substance' may be used as long as we do *not* use it in the sense the scholastics did; and so presumably our reading of Trent's decree must not only prescind from scholasticism, it must be positively opposed to it. Could detachment from the demands of time go further?

But just how far Schillebeeckx was prepared to take this detachment can be seen from what he made of the scholastic phrase *per modum substantiae* with which we have been concerned so much in this chapter. He intervened himself when two other participants in the discussion were talking about it, and his comment was:

the formula '*per modum substantiae*' is often misunderstood. All it means is that he is present, and that he is so in an unusual way. What we are concerned with here is a '*praesentia spiritualis*' sive '*non per locationem*' ['a spiritual presence', or 'not in the manner of being located in a place']. (134, col. 2)

But the phrase simply cannot be explained away in this fashion. 'Unusual' is not enough, nor indeed is 'spiritual' (or anything else in the Latin, none of which I have come across in Aquinas). *Per modum substantiae* does what it does – leads to the confusion it leads to, I should want to say – precisely because it is more than a generic claim. It goes with the way eucharistic speculation treats the distinction between substance and accidents, and it goes with the concept of transubstantiation; it is meant to solve problems to do with the dimensions of the host; it rests (I have claimed) upon confusing specific with individual identity; it ends (I have also claimed) with importing the very spatialisation it was devised to keep out. No matter whether my charges are founded or unfounded, the sense and the use of the phrase lie in its specifically scholastic associations. What can be left if it is regarded as detachable from them? How can words survive such treatment?

The last quotation I have to offer suggests that they do not survive. I introduce the text and let it speak for itself before passing any comment.

It may be recalled from the second chapter that Schillebeeckx drew in (90) a distinction between the 'physical' and the 'ontic': physically, nothing changes in the Eucharist, while ontically everything does. At that point in the second chapter, I made my own objections to this, but the difficulty put to Schillebeeckx in the discussion was differently expressed – will not the unacceptable side of the scholastics' distinction recur in what Schillebeeckx himself has written? I give the question, and his answer:

SCHARFF: Is there no danger that the same mistake will be made concerning the relation between 'physical' and 'ontic' as was made concerning the relation between substance and accident?

SCHILLEBEECKX: The danger is there. I use the term 'physical' so as not to let· [the Latin] *'species'* blur itself into [the Dutch] *'schijn'* [semblance]. The word *'schijn'* is just as wrong as the [Dutch] word *'gedaante'*. I should want to say: the bread remains, but not the bread-reality. (135, col. 1)

We have seen enough, both in the second chapter and in the present, of how Schillebeeckx in his book wants phrases like 'the bread-reality' to be taken. What concerns me here is something more disturbing – his remarks in this earlier text on the Latin word *species*. The remarks demand that I now say something about translation.

It is often noted that when the Council of Trent spoke of the eucharistic conversion, it used the word *species* rather than *accidentia* to describe what persists of the bread and wine after the conversion. What is noted much less often is that *species* already had a standard use in scholastic theology. Aquinas, for example, uses *species sacramentales* – the sacramental *species*; *species panis et vini* – the *species* of bread and wine; and *sub utraque specie* – under each *species* (*ST* 3.76 and 3.77). Just so, the canon at Trent which asserts the suitability of calling the eucharistic conversion 'transubstantiation' also speaks of 'the *species* alone of bread and wine remaining' (Can.2; DS 1652), and the next canon claims that the whole Christ is contained 'under either *species*' (Can.3; DS 1653). How are we to translate the word? A dictionary of late Latin (I went to Maigne d'Arnis, s.v.) will give a splendid range of meanings for *species*, from bribes offered to a judge, via evening collations on fast-days (whence *épices*), to medical potions. But the meaning here is at first sight plain enough. *Species* has its philosophical sense, and goes with *forma* – an object belongs to such and such a *species* (see how the word has survived!) because its *forma* is such and such. From this connexion with *forma*, *species* became a term in eucharistic contexts for 'form' in the sense of 'what can be perceived'. Trent so used it, and so did Aquinas. For him (see e.g. *ST* 3.77.3) the word interchanges with the *formae accidentales*, the accidental forms, of the bread and wine. How then should we render *species* here? We should do what we do when any technical term is to be translated – make some convention and abide by it. English sometimes uses 'appearances': Christ is present 'under the appearances of bread and wine', said the old Catechism. But in *sub utraque specie* and related phrases, it has been the custom to use 'kind': Christ is present 'under either kind alone' the old Catechism asserted with Trent, against those who justifiably blamed the Roman Church for maiming its eucharistic rite. 'Kind' here is as in 'natural kind', a natural sort or species. Receive, in other words, nothing but the host, and you still receive the whole Christ.

On the rendering of *species* into Dutch I naturally speak with a good deal less assurance, but it is not difficult to gather that the usual word is (in the plural) *gedaanten*. Schillebeeckx's very complaint shews it is common, Trooster cites the 'fully traditional description of the mystery of the *realis praesentia* [real presence]' as 'the real presence of Christ under the *gedaanten* of bread and wine' (Trooster 1963: 126), and a small and ancient Flemish prayer book I possess addresses Christ as 'hidden beneath these adorable *gedaanten*'. 'Shape, form, figure' says my dictionary, and renders *onder beiderlei gedaanten* as 'in both kinds'. Why then was Schillebeeckx complaining?

His complaint is both understandable and unacceptable. I wrote two paragraphs back that the meaning of *species* here is at first sight plain enough; the trouble is, of course, that at second sight it is not plain in the least. If what I have said about scholastic speculation concerning the eucharistic presence has anything to it, then there is *no* version of *species* that will stand examination, because the whole account suffers from *discohaerentia terminorum*, its terms simply fall apart. *Species* has to be an appearance – but it has to be an appearance of nothing. The host must look like bread, while not being it – but the whole setting for 'looking like but not being' has gone, and we are back in the chocolate factory with our sceptic. What rendering of *species* here *could* be coherent? When Schillebeeckx condemned the version *schijn*, the drift of his condemnation was that *schijn* and *gedaante* alike suggest deception, or a divorce between appearance and reality. But, as I have done my best to shew in this chapter and the second, Schillebeeckx in his book distinguishes between 'pheno-

mena' and 'reality' in a way that is not essentially different, and ends
where Colombo stands in what he says of the physical sciences. Of all
this we have seen enough and to spare, what we need to see here is the
extreme awkwardness of the corner into which Schillebeeckx has
painted himself. He begins by saying that we should keep the notion
of substance in Trent's decree independent of what the scholastic
tradition makes of that notion – which leaves the decree itself in
isolation. He then contends that we can talk of Trent's decree in
terms of substance and accidents only if we do *not* make of them what
the scholastics did – which turns the independence of Trent from
scholasticism into divorce, and leaves his own formulations isolated
from a venerable tradition of speculation. He goes on to reject *gedaante*
as a translation of *species* – which isolates what he writes from the
whole traditionally employed vernacular rendering of what the
council decreed. I have contended that the term *species* goes with a
confusion from the start, but even those who can still find sense in
what Schillebeeckx said of 'bread' and 'bread-reality' in this
conversation will have to admit that the sense has become a very
lonely one.

We have come back to where we have come back so often. Whether
we like it or not, we belong to a continuing tradition. Just as we
cannot isolate the content of a decree from all speculative connotations, so we cannot isolate what we ourselves are now saying, and
imagine that, by successively discarding this and that formula, we
can reach a position whose very apartness exempts it from the
limitations of all other accounts. To put it bluntly, if Trent used
species, Trent used a word already endowed with connotations, and
used it for a purpose. Time spent in finding an 'unadulterated'
translation of the word would be better spent in seeing what the
word's connotations are, and in seeing whether the council's purpose
made sense. And whatever our verdict may be, it will have to be
expressed in words that are themselves just as much open to similar
appraisal. An imperfect past is appraised by an imperfect present.
There is no leaving the arena.

This chapter has looked back on what has gone before. It has
reflected on the divorce between appearance and reality which is
common to older and newer eucharistic theologies, and which makes
them converge in confusion. The confusion, I have submitted,
excludes both a simple affirmation and a simple denial of what older

and newer claim. A longer journey is needed if the confusion is to be dissipated in favour of something better.

And because the journey has begun in this chapter, what we have seen in it also points forward to what lies ahead. We began with one man's unhappiness over the treatment of inherited biblical narratives long taken as straightforwardly factual. His unhappiness touched both the Church and the Bible, and we shall be seeing much of both these forms. The chapter went on to consider one way in which the unhappiness can be masked – the denial that straightforward questions of fact can be put in such biblical contexts. I saw in this the emergence of the Fallacy of Replacement we have met in the previous chapter – everyday matters were deemed to be replaced and cancelled by what was marvellous. But the Fallacy had now taken on a wider import – it touched the whole relation of present to past in a religious setting; and we are going to be concerned with that relation as it is found in the Church of Rome, both with respect to eucharistic theology and with respect to that Church itself.

One contention in this chapter has been that we must respect history and language: that we must not attempt to *insulate* either, but rather accept an openness in them that will expose us to tensions and awkwardness. I took a specific example – the phrase *per modum substantiae* – to illustrate the impossibility of insulating language: the force of the words Aquinas used drove him back to the very 'dimensionality' he wanted to avoid. But the subsequent fortunes of the phrase, and of similar expressions, shewed the impossibility of insulating the past too, if we are to do justice to what we now are and to what we have been. The 'historical insouciance' exhibited by newer authors either treated inherited phrases in isolation from the setting which gave them what meaning they had, or made a succession of denials of the inheritance, which left what was being claimed in a disconcerting isolation.

Throughout the chapter, the need to accept awkwardness and tension has been urged. Our religious past proves revered but unsatisfactory, and so gives rise to the attempts to accommodate our past to what we should like it to have been. The attempts offer a comfort that is not to be had. We need to face our past, not to muffle it; but the facing is of an imperfect past by a present that is imperfect as well.

But if all that be so; if we must take account of all these cautions which the successive sections of this chapter have provided – whither should we now turn, if a new start is to be made? I ended my criticism of Schillebeeckx by saying that we cannot leave the arena. Where then should I stand in it? The next chapter will begin to shew, and will start by examining a notable characteristic of recent eucharistic theory and practice.

CHAPTER 4

Signs and disguises

21 AN ACQUISITION AND ITS DANGER

A mark of all Christian Churches today in the West is a revived awareness of the resurrection, and the recent authors we have considered shew this awareness in a eucharistic setting. We saw in the second chapter how de Baciocchi stresses the link between Passover and Eucharist (25). Smits points out the essential unity of the mystery of faith – the obedience of Christ even to the death of the cross in order to send us his Spirit (47). For Schoonenberg, reflexion on the Eucharist must begin with the Risen Lord's presence in the community (16). Schillebeeckx would like even greater stress laid upon this presence in eucharistic theology (1967: 109–10 [1968: 138, where for 'much greater' read 'even more strongly' – Schillebeeckx has *nog sterker*]).

This revived awareness is obviously not a clean break with the past, but the recent authors are only a few among many examples of the real change in emphasis there has been. I set down my own joy at the change, and shall be drawing out consequences of it in the next chapter. Here and now I must set down my unease at how the resurrection is being used in some texts from these authors. I can best describe my unease by going back to a distinction drawn in the first chapter between formulations and recipes (pp. 40–1). I drew the distinction there in a setting that was complex, but the distinction itself is not recondite: a formulation expresses what is to be achieved, a recipe offers ways of achieving it. And it is my contention that the distinction is not always preserved in the recent writings on our topic: that, in their eagerness to do justice to the resurrection in what they write of the Eucharist, some authors fall into treating it as a *recipe* for the eucharistic presence.

In this section I want to give examples of the confusion and to ·

133

reflect on them. My first submission will be that the authors appeal
to the risen state of Christ in a way that resembles the appeal by
Aquinas to presence *per modum substantiae*; and that their appeal ends
where his ended – a move made to escape 'dimensionality' leads only
to its reinforcement. My second submission will be that, just as old
and new have come together yet again, so they share the apparent
attractions of talking of the eucharistic presence in terms of disguise.
My third submission recalls what we have seen throughout our
journey – that 'disguise' here is incoherent – and suggests that the
incoherence points to a better way. We shall, to go to the title of the
chapter, have to pass to signs from disguises. That still lies ahead, but
this section contains a final submission, and this will matter for what
I want to offer myself: it concerns language and its limitations in
these matters. In the preceding chapter, I wrote that we cannot
'insulate' language, attractive though the idea may be. I shall
develop the thought as the present section goes on.

Schoonenberg makes the most elaborate appeal to the risen state of
Christ, so I shall take what he writes as my starting-point. We saw in
the second chapter that he stresses the superiority of personal over
local presence, and moves on in terms of personal presence to a
specifically eucharistic setting. It is in the context of Christ's presence
– a real 'personal' presence in the community – that the eucharistic
celebration must be understood: see (27) and (28). In one text,
already given at (29), he sums up his position:

Even during the earthly life of Jesus, his spatial propinquity was never of
importance for those who believed in him, apart from his personal presence.
Now that the Lord is glorified, spatial propinquity has been transcended,
and the Lord is present wherever hearts believe in him, whenever two or
more are gathered together in his name. (Schoonenberg 1964a: 334)

Other texts elaborate the consequences. Personal presence goes with
deeds as well as words, and the gesture of *giving* is pre-eminent, for it
makes the giver live in the receiver, and what is given has its original
function (purchase, food and so on) quite taken up into the Reality-
as-Gift, the Reality-as-Sign, the action of self-giving by the donor: see
(15). When spatial proximity is taken up into personal presence,
bodies and things become *signs* of persons. When this is done,

A bodily movement becomes a gesture; a sound becomes a word; hearing
becomes listening; looking becomes gazing. (1959b: 318).

Schoonenberg writes elsewhere that in a happy marriage of long standing, a simple gesture of affection can communicate a great deal more than prolonged intimacy could in its early days. The body in this way

becomes ever more emancipated from the status of being simply a thing, simply near-by in space, simply an object; it becomes ever more a sign of fellowship; it becomes ever more a body in the fullest sense of the word, and thereby a promise or foreshadowing of the glorified body in the age that is to come. (1964b: 409)

But Schoonenberg then points to what he holds to be limitations to personal presence in this life. He writes:

the whole body never really enters that of another, nor is the body as a totality both the expression and the instrument of personal fellowship. (1959b: 325–6)

In personal presence, as he puts it in the same article, 'the absence ceases that is due to the apartness of material bodies'. That is to say, personal presence can take up material contact and make it an expression of itself; and in this way 'the external apartness of [two] realities is abolished without the one being devoured by the other and its independence annihilated'. But in this present life the overcoming of apartness can never be complete. Bounds are set by the fact that creatures are limited, and by the fact that 'our bodies (and things in general) cannot yet function wholly as signs of this personal presence' (317). It is in the risen body that these bounds are overcome. The risen body 'will have been released from all limitations of being an object [*zakelijkheid*, matching the German *Sachlichkeit*], just as it will have been released from mortality and from all that follows from it' (320). In the future life, these limitations will have gone. 'Not only will God be "all in all", but each self will be able to exist for and in all others' (317). And from these claims about the risen life, Schoonenberg moves to his invocation of it as a recipe in eucharistic theology. In the present life, he writes, it is only in the Eucharist that the body can become, as we have seen him put it, 'both the expression and instrument of personal presence'. In the Eucharist, the limit is crossed that the union in marriage approaches but never reaches. Here,

the body is present wholly as the gift of a person; personal presence is expressed and communicated, not just in a gesture or in part of the body, but in all the body. (325–6)

I have more texts of Schoonenberg to cite, and the comments I have
to make will occupy us both in this and in the next section. I begin
here with some of the reservations I feel.

The first is a reservation I have expressed in earlier chapters: what
worries me is not claims made about mysteries we do not understand,
it is claims made about ordinary things we do understand, claims
made that try to contradict what is not mysterious at all. For what
sense can we give to the way Schoonenberg talks of overcoming
limitations here? In this life, he states, we remain ultimately outside
each other in our bodies, and bodily contact is only partial – 'the
whole body never really enters that of another'. But who on earth
wants it to? What limitation is this? Human beings have been
acquainted with the growth and decay of personal presence from
time immemorial. There have been times when absence has made the
heart grow fonder, and times when it has not. There have been
occasions when sexual relationships have yielded less than they
promised, and so prompted remarks such that love is but the contact
of two skins. There are, repeatedly, occasions when (braving all
category-mistakes) we wish we could get inside someone else's mind
and see how he or she works. None of this provides any support, or
even any content, for the suggestion that our bodies cannot function
wholly as signs because they as yet cannot emulate the risen body,
when each self will be able to exist 'in and for all others'. An appeal
to the limitations of personal presence makes sense if the limitations
are those which life and experience shew to be real. But an appeal to
the limitations based upon the absence of some mysterious dissolution
of boundaries makes no sense. Schoonenberg makes the appeal
because of his eucharistic concerns, but the appeal is no better for
that. He is confusing significance and permeation. He writes of the
Eucharist, as we saw in the second chapter, in terms of a new
significance bestowed by Christ's self-giving; this new significance he
now attempts to explain as some kind of total, all-pervasive and
interpenetrating presence, unattainable in this life, achieved by the
Risen Christ in the Eucharist, and promised to us all in the life to
come. Which is, of course, to make Christ's risen state into a *recipe* for
his eucharistic presence.

I have claimed to detect a confusion between significance and
permeation in what Schoonenberg writes. I now notice the part
played in the confusion by language, and I take up here the reflexions
on language I offered in the preceding chapter. There, I pointed to

the forces implicit in language, and to how the forces can work even against the will of those who use language. Here, I point to the dangers that go with those forces if language undergoes *prolongation*, and I first explain the term. There is an old saying that often gets applied to theological writing – *omnis comparatio claudicat*, 'every comparison limps'. Which is true enough, but hardly seizes the real trouble. The real trouble – we met it in the last chapter – is that comparisons and images and vocabulary have a life and direction of their own. The more we prolong their use, the greater the danger is that their own life and direction will dominate what we say or write, however sincerely we may protest that they do not. The phrase *omnis comparatio claudicat* should be complemented by another: *claudicat tamen progreditur*, 'limp it may, it still moves on'.[1] Schoonenberg is writing of the presence of the Risen Christ among believers, and rightly takes it as the starting-point for an account of the eucharistic presence. We saw texts of his in the second chapter to this effect, such as (16), (17) and (27), and I express again my agreement with them. But to my agreement I must add a warning. When we speak of the presence of the Risen Christ among us, we are confronting what exceeds our grasp. We are on a journey without maps. We have no notion of what the risen state is like, we have no bearings when it comes to talk of glorified bodies or of the life of the Lord who dieth now no more. We cannot talk sense about, if I may so put it, the physiology or topography of what is yet to be revealed. Since we cannot, we cannot attempt to make of the risen state a means – a 'recipe', as I have called it – for achieving the eucharistic presence. And the trouble with 'prolongation' here, with letting vocabulary and images have their way, is that it tempts us to think that we can.

True enough, Schoonenberg insists that we have to do with a mystery, that the analogy of human giving is grossly imperfect, that there can be no 'deducing' by us of the eucharistic presence: see (23), (24), (32). Admirably put; but the trouble with prolongation is that it turns these acknowledgments of incapacity into something else. Not content with acknowledging in the face of a mystery that they are

---

[1] I note here, for the benefit of readers interested in such things, that I am aware of the dangers of images and implicit comparisons in regions of discourse other than religious. My warnings in the last chapter, against attempts to escape from language into some neutral area, can be given in other settings as well. It is a difference of degree, but (with due respect to some recent advocates of the irrational) the history of religion shews that the difference is a very real one.

lost, theologians insist upon giving the precise bearings of where the losing took place. They wish to pass from a legitimate acknowledgment of a mystery to a 'placing' of the mystery that exhibits just what it is, and how (admittedly in a mysterious way) it works. The wish has shewn itself repeatedly in the sources we have examined. For the scholastics, philosophical distinctions were turned into dissections, and so constituted a kind of invisible machinery for divine power to effect transubstantiation. For recent authors, a new significance was held to displace significance that was everyday, appearance was divorced from reality, and terms were wrenched from the setting that had given them sense. Old and new alike acknowledge the mystery in the Eucharist; but old and new alike have prolonged language, have ended by situating the mystery in how something concealed is to be made to work. Old and new alike are talking in terms of recipes; Schoonenberg's appeal to the risen state of Christ is but one example among others.

I insisted in the preceding chapter that we cannot insulate language, but I conceded that refusing to insulate condemns us to a lack of comfort. The lack of comfort is to be found here too, if we refuse to prolong our language and so refuse to talk in terms of recipes. Prolongation can be the prolonging of something good – that is part of its attraction – and there is much in what Schoonenberg writes that is good. I have no wish to deny the special place of giving in human relationships (although Schoonenberg is curiously reticent about *receiving*, which is just as special and sometimes more difficult). Nor do I deny the special and demanding character of personal presence, nor its embodiment in human actions and humanly used objects, nor that a long-shared fellowship can give such actions and objects a personal significance and a richness of content for those concerned, and in a way that eludes the grasp of others. All this I readily admit, and I value the account Schoonenberg has offered in the items of his I have read, even though I think the account might have been briefer.[2] The trouble lies in prolongation. It is by the prolonging of language like this, by regarding the risen state as open to survey by us, that Schoonenberg confuses significance with

---

[2] And the titles less confusing. The Dutch word associated with personal presence is *tegenwoordigheid*. The articles of Schoonenberg I have used translate as 'The *tegenwoordigheid* of Christ', 'A retrospect: spatial, personal and eucharistic *tegenwoordigheid*', 'Eucharistic *tegenwoordigheid*', '*Tegenwoordigheid*' (preceded by an editorial introduction 'Christ's *tegenwoordigheid* for us'), and 'Eucharistic *tegenwoordigheid* once again'. I was half-disappointed not to find 'Son of *tegenwoordigheid*'.

permeation, and achieves what he wants by an appeal to the risen body's *adaptability* (I can think of no better word). But talk in terms of recipes can undoubtedly comfort – it seems to offer something by which we can 'place' what lies beyond our grasp. Just so, to reject such talk must be more than a matter of simply acknowledging a mystery. We find such an acknowledgment in Gutwenger, who also makes an appeal to the risen state of Christ. He adds to his appeal what is meant as a caution:

The nature of the risen body is in great measure cut off from us, which is why it is impossible to enumerate its properties in a way that is both clear and devoid of gaps. (Gutwenger 1966: 191)

But those words are the reverse of cautious: they invite us to think about the risen state as a Victorian man of science might have thought about the constitution of the atom – unknown, but a possible extension for his discipline, were only further information available. Rejecting prolongation must mean more than that. At the back of my warnings against invoking the resurrection as a recipe lay the wider acknowledgment that we lack the capacity to pronounce on the risen life. But the acknowledgment is not one that we can adequately state – if we could, we should be able to 'place' the mystery; which is just what we cannot do. We face the unavoidable paradoxes that the incapacity of language here extends even to the drawing of boundaries to its incapacity, and that an acknowledgment of the limits of language goes with a need to use language in making the acknowledgment. We cannot stand outside language and comment upon its shortcomings. I made the point in the preceding chapter, but such warnings cannot be given once for all. They need repeating, because even what is recognised as an abuse can still provide a recurrent problem. To resist prolongation is to resist something that comes all too naturally, for language with its images and comparisons tends to take on a life of its own. Resistance means breaking off what invites continuation, means petering out, means accepting lame silences. The discomfort can be real enough.

But there is more still to the discomfort. I wrote in the last chapter that to reject insulation is to commit oneself to taking seriously the relationship between past and present. Prolonging language in the way I have described amounts to insulating it – amounts to letting its images and propensities grow in isolation. And so a refusal to prolong implies a refusal to insulate, and this in its turn calls for an appraisal by us of what insulations and prolongations have taken place in the past that is ours. And, here as elsewhere, the past can disconcert. I offer an example from it here which will do so. Schoonenberg writes of the risen life with caution, but things have not always been so. Let us see what Aquinas writes about it in the *Summa Theologiae.*

Christ spent in Hell the time between Good Friday afternoon and Easter Day (*ST* 3.52.4), visited in a manner the damned, for their confutation and confusion (*ST* 3.52.6 ad 1), bestowed the life of glory upon the waiting saints of the Old Testament (*ST* 3.52.5), but left in Hell the children who had died too young to have faith in him (*ST* 3.52.7). On Easter Day he rose from the dead – and all the blood he had shed took part in the resurrection too, any relics of it now displayed in churches are only of blood that flowed from pictures of him (*ST* 3.54.3 ad 3). After the resurrection, his bodily whereabouts are unknown during those times when he was not appearing to his disciples (*ST* 3.55.3. ad 2; the *Summa* published in 1948 by Marietti reports in its commentary medieval views that he may have been staying with Our Lady, or with the Old Testament saints I mentioned above). His ascension, of which the starting-point was a movement upwards from the earth (*ST* 3.55.2 ad 2), was fitting because earth is the region for generation and corruption, while the heavenly region is not (*ST* 3.57.1; Aquinas is here following Aristotle and making the planets and stars be unchanging and incorrupt). By his human nature Christ is in a place and is subject to motion (*ST* 3.57.2). To rise upwards is against the nature of a human body in its present state, but a glorified body is wholly subject to the spirit (*ST* 3.57.3 ad 2), even though Christ's motion in his ascension was not instantaneous, but with the velocity decided by God (*ST* 3.57.3 ad 3). To move from one point to another involves passing through what is in between; and so Christ's ascension entailed his passing through each of the heavens (*ST* 3.57.4 obj 2; details of the heavens in *ST* 1.68.4); but he was able by divine power to penetrate them, just as he had emerged from the closed womb of his mother, and had passed through the closed doors of the room where the disciples were assembled (*ST* 3.57.4 ad 2). The cloud that received him from their sight when he ascended was a sign of his divinity, it did not provide a vehicle for him as he went upwards (*ST* 3.57.4 ad 3).

The texts prompt reflexions to which I shall be returning as the book goes on, and the first of them touches the embarrassing *confidence* of the stuff. Why are we embarrassed by it? Perhaps the best answer is that, for a multitude of reasons, human beings have lost their speculative innocence. A study of biblical language and of its setting; an awareness of history and myth; the strained and special character of religious discourse more practically acknowledged; the growth of topics where plainer questions can be put and plainer answers obtained; a greater knowledge of how the world works; a vision of what cruelty can inflict in the name of fanaticism – these are some of the causes that, directly or indirectly, have touched our ways of religious thought, and so made what Aquinas writes here seem so very far off. And this *distance* of ourselves from such things in our religious past will also be a theme for later reflexions.

In this section I have considered the confusion which arises when the risen state of Christ is regarded as a recipe for his eucharistic presence. The confusion is between significance and permeation, and is due to the prolonging of the language we are using. To refuse prolongation brings discomfort, and part of the discomfort lies in an awareness that past and present can be distant here. Now one element in the past is the appeal made by Aquinas to presence *per modum substantiae*, and I took the appeal in the last chapter as an example of how the force of language can work against those who use it. I am now going to set the appeal made by Aquinas beside the appeal we have seen Schoonenberg make in this section. Once more, old and new will be seen to come together in similar confusions; but now the nature of the confusions can point to something better.

22 THE HUMBLER CREATION

Aquinas made the appeal he did to presence *per modum substantiae* in order to emancipate the Eucharist from dimensional connotations. Schoonenberg makes his appeal to the risen state of Christ for the same purpose. He suggests that the eucharistic presence should be approached in terms of personal presence, but that the limits of personal presence as we know it are overcome in the Eucharist – boundaries are no longer set by bodies, we have a presence that I called 'all-pervasive and interpenetrating'. I now point out that a likeness has beem claimed for the two appeals. In the last section, a quotation was given from Gutwenger about our knowledge of the risen state. The same article shews why Gutwenger is writing of the risen body – the Eucharist involves no dimensional contact by Christ (*contactus quantitativus*), his manner of existence there is inextended and

his presence is as of spiritual things (1966: 191). Vanneste is even
more explicit – and, incidentally, pleasingly exhibits the historical
insouciance for which I blamed him earlier:

It should consequently be noted that describing the presence of Christ as
being *per modum substantiae* is perhaps in the last analysis not so very far from
what the presence of the pneumatic Christ must be. For this phrase *per
modum substantiae* indicates a way of existence that has put off all the
limitations and dependences that go with ordinary natural substances,
because of their relations with various accidents. (1956: 330)

With difficulty I resisted the temptation to italicise here the example
of insouciance in 'perhaps in the last analysis not so very far from'.
It can be said for Vanneste that he aims at what Aquinas aimed at
– an emancipation from dimensional associations – but if my submissions about the two appeals are well founded, then old and new
have yet again come together in confusion. The appeal made by
Aquinas drives him back by its very language towards the 'dimensionality' he wants to avoid; the appeal made by Schoonenberg
speaks vacuously of limits to personal presence, and ends by
presenting significance in terms of a permeation that makes no sense.
I have charged him with prolonging language, and so with treating
the resurrection as a recipe for the eucharistic presence. In other
words, Schoonenberg is thinking as the older authors did, thinking in
terms of some occult mechanism. And so I see in what he writes
something we have been seeing all along – the presentation of a
mystery in terms of concealment.

I try to spell out just what this concealment is by recalling what we
have seen so often of the Fallacy of Replacement. It lies, we know, in
making what is exalted replace what is humble. The former is held to
compete with the latter, and to win the victory in the competition. We
know well enough what follows – a divorce between appearance and
reality, a demotion of physical knowledge, and all the rest. But now
we need to notice how the victory is disastrous for the victor; how the
very notions of competition and replacement lead us whither we
would not go. And the reason is simple.

The most fundamental kind of presence – not thereby the most
important, but bound up with any presence that we can understand
– is presence in a workaday, spatio-temporal manner: cats on mats,
tea in cups, people in chairs, shops on corners, and in general what we
might call 'the humbler creation'. Schoonenberg legitimately insists

upon the greater depths in personal presence, but it is just as true that personal presence takes spatial presence for granted in its origins and in its development. Intimacy between two persons leads to closeness in ways that transcend what can be expressed in spatial terms. But the two grow together in the shared adventures and discoveries of life, in reflexion on what they have shared, and in things given and received. And adventures, discoveries and gifts alike presuppose the simple locations and stabilities that help to give sense to our gestures, purpose to our actions and content to what we say. It is not a matter of reducing all other concepts of presence to spatial proximity. That suggestion is foolish, and indeed physical science itself in this century has been shewing what unsuspected complications and paradoxes lie in the notions of place and time that we take for granted. The initial simplicities, if I may so call them, are certainly not the only realities. But they are the starting-point for all else, whether it be investigations into the nature of things, personal relationships, or the love and worship of God. However wonderful the journey may be, we must not forget that it needs this starting-point. Thus, the personal presence of Jesus to the disciples would never have come to be without a setting – an ordinary, spatio-temporally limited setting – in which they and he walked and talked together in Galilee. We cannot do without the humbler creation. Spatial, everyday proximity is, as Schoonenberg rightly insists, only part of the story. But there would be no story at all without it.

Competition with presence as fundamental as this means that what is supposed to replace it must be fitted into the category of what it is supposed to be replacing. I am in no way claiming that exalted forms of presence are reducible to things like spatial proximity. They are not; but once we make those forms into *competitors* with what is present in the most basic way of all, we treat them as *alternatives* to it. And so the competition takes spatial presence for granted, and asks only which of the alternatives is to be so present.

What we have here is not distinctively theological, the history of philosophy offers notorious instances: dualistic accounts of mind make it sound like an elusive body, and Plato's Forms seem to behave all too like the objects they are supposed to transcend. But the course of this book has been full of examples. We started with the 'reification' of distinctions by Aquinas, and its treatment of them as dissections – as so many components present in this basic spatial way. And we continued in the newer authors, with their setting apart of appearance from reality in ways by now familiar. Old and new alike, by unsaying what is yielded by evidence in the most basic, spatial, order of presence, are condemned to conceive of the eucharistic presence in just that spatial order – and condemned to endure all the paradoxes which go with so conceiving it.

At the root of the paradoxes lies the nature of the concealment which old and new have in common. We have seen that the dimensionality, supposedly eliminated, manages to return even by the attempts at its elimination, and we have seen why it manages to return – dimensionality goes with the most basic presence of all for human knowledge, and what is exalted is being wrongly displayed here as if it competed with and replaced what is present in this basic way. So there is nothing left for what is exalted except concealment – it cannot be perceived, while what it is supposed to replace is perfectly perceptible. And that, of course, is what makes the concealment so very odd. A text from Aquinas not so far met can recall the kind of things we have seen from the first chapter onwards. He is denying the charge that, because we judge of substance by its accidents, the Eucharist must be held to involve deception:

In this sacrament there is no deception. The accidents are evaluated by the senses. The intellect, whose specific object is substance (Aristotle, *De Anima* III [6]), is preserved by faith from deception. (*ST* 3.75.5 ad 2)

Take 'substance' and 'accidents' as Aquinas uses them outside a eucharistic context, and we can indeed make sense of the claim that the intellect's specific object is substance. We distinguish between descriptions in perceptual terms and verdicts like 'this is copper', 'that is a Red Admiral'; we acknowledge that fools' gold looks like gold but is not, and that vaporised gold does not look like gold but is. But none of these truths helps in the eucharistic context Aquinas has in mind. Here, every conceivable perceptual datum for something's being bread must be allowed without bread being there. Here, we have no disguise that can be removed. Here, concealment is of a reality inaccessible behind appearance. Here, we are back with our sceptic in the chocolate factory. In other words, the concealment we have is no ordinary concealment, it is the concealment that goes with scepticism. And we saw that the newer accounts end with the same kind of concealment, in their demotion of what investigation can learn of reality, and in their divorce of appearance from reality by the Fallacy of Replacement. Old and new converge in concealment, but the converging of the twain is only in confusion. I have more than once referred to the carefree way in which de Baciocchi keeps apart transubstantiation from 'an imaginative solution' where substances are interchanged beneath 'an inflated skin' of accidents. It should be clear by now that however we may judge the historical insouciance he displays, it is only the grotesque picture he offers that gives transubstantiation whatever appearance of content it has. Defenders of transubstantiation vehemently claim that concepts like substance cannot be understood in terms of what is pictorial. And they are quite right – which is why concepts like substance cannot, when properly grasped, serve eucharistic purposes; they need to be 'pictorialised' if they are to work. I have given reasons for holding that the newer opinions are not novel, but converge with what is older in the theme of disguise and concealment associated with scepticism. The same reasons, I submit, demand that we do not try to keep apart the older account from what sounds less respectable. It is what is not respectable that keeps the older account in business. Transubstantiation is bankrupt; it makes ends meet only by living off the immoral earnings of its disowned relation.

Back in the first chapter, after stating objections to the scholastic account, I interposed a protest from an imagined reader in favour of simply accepting the presence of Christ in the Eucharist and leaving it at that. My comment then was that things are not so simple and the choices not so straightforward, and by this time it should be clearer why I made the comment. But I admit that the paradoxes on which I have dwelt do have an attraction. Whatever faults a spatial presentation has, it does seem to offer alternatives between which we can legitimately choose, a proposition which we can plainly affirm or deny. The appearance is deceptive, but it is there. The proposition will be couched in terms of what I have called disguise and concealment. And where is the concealment to be effected, if not in or behind (or some other preposition) that which is being replaced? And the very notion of concealment has a further attraction, for it pleasingly suggests access being granted to privileged spectators, suggests a view behind the scenes as to how things work. I have dwelt at what may seem excessive length on the convergence of old and new, and on their convergence in confusions. But I do not deny that the very confusions have their attractions – indeed, the attractions are for me the surest symptom of where old and new have gone wrong. I want to break the mould of concealment, but I repeat my earlier admission that to claim absolute novelty in a topic like ours would be ridiculous. And so I end this section by asking what other attractions can be found in old and new alike – attractions not so evident, but providing a better starting-point. And I answer by recalling what I wrote of Schillebeeckx in the second chapter, and have returned to since: his talk in terms of phenomenalism and of demoting physical evidence is an abuse, but it is an abuse of something good. To acknowledge the mystery in things is indeed good, as Schillebeeckx does in writing of the 'Givenness of Reality', where he makes things in themselves possess already a 'quasi-sacramental' significance. He is in this way proposing an openness to God, he is exhibiting a willingness to undertake a journey. He and others may commit the Fallacy of Replacement; but that Fallacy (like the scholastic account in terms of transubstantiation) can bear witness to a reality not of our own devising, can exhibit the defects of any 'single vision' that sees no further than our own needs and powers. The witness, I have argued, is distorted; but it is still borne. Might it not be possible to let the witness be borne with less distortion? The next section will begin the search for a way.

23   OUT OF CONCEALMENT

I have contended that there are good things to be found in the attitudes which have led old and new to the themes of concealment and disguise. One was the principle invoked by Schillebeeckx that I called 'the Givenness of Reality': an acknowledgment that the world in which we live and act manifests a reality not of our own devising, so that in the very setting of life itself we have the beginning of a quest. But although I have commended the attitude that prompted the Fallacy of Replacement, of which so much has been said, I have insisted that it is still a Fallacy, and that the similar confusions in old and new are still confusions. And so I am asking whether we might not hold to the intuitions that prompted things like the Fallacy of Replacement, while not denying plain words their plain meaning and so lapsing into phenomenalism. If we try to do these things, whither shall we be led?

Schillebeeckx uses the phrase 'disclosing and at the same time veiling' when speaking of reality as a form of divine revelation, and claims that we know this reality only in *signs*; earthly things have a function as signs because the whole material world has 'a pervading quasi-sacramental significance': see (57) and (55). After those texts he goes on to invoke the principle of the 'Humanness of Perception'. This principle makes a proper acknowledgment of the part played by perception in our coming to know the human world. Its abuse amounts to a confinement of human knowledge to the order of appearances, and we have seen how the vocabulary he employs lends itself all too easily to the phenomenalistic account of knowledge we know he gives: see (59) to (65). Suppose we hold back from making this step with him. We shall still stress the mystery of reality, and his phrase 'disclosing and at the same time veiling' we shall take as a description of the invitation to set out on the journey, on the quest. 'Disclosing' we shall take as referring to the way in which our experiences in the world can be clues to or manifestations of what is deepest. 'Veiling' will then be fairly used, because the clues are not obvious – it is easy to have the experience but miss the meaning – and the journey to which we are invited is a long one, on which we learn as we go. We shall not take the phrase as if something clear enough in itself were being covered up at intervals and then displayed; we have rather a process in which more is seen by degrees, in which significance is grasped that was not grasped before, in which we have an experience and this time do not miss the meaning, and so are led on to see further meanings in what we experience later. In concealment by disguise, we know what we want from the start, and have only to penetrate the method of the disguising. But here we are moving out of concealment: we have clues in this 'veiling' and must learn to grasp what it is they point to. And we shall say that our capacity to learn develops as the journey goes on.

Alles Vergängliche – ist nur ein Gleichnis; 'all that doth pass away – is but a parable'. I quoted Goethe's lines in the second chapter, when stating why the Fallacy of Replacement is perennially attractive. For those sensitive to the limited and ultimately mortal nature of all our namings and contrivings, the replacement of humble words by words more glorious may seem almost inevitable. I notice how readily words like 'parable' and 'sign' can be taken in a way that goes with the Fallacy: they can be used to relegate human knowledge to an order that is denied by the revelation of what is more exalted. Schillebeeckx, as we know, develops such a notion of sign by appealing to the Humanness of Perception. Our human perception, he contends, is where lies our approach to the mystery of reality, but our sensory contacts cannot be regarded as objective qualifications of reality; and so there is a distinction between reality itself and the phenomenal order; and the phenomenal is a *sign* of reality (pp. 76, 94). I have already expressed my disagreement with all this, and mention it here only to notice the double use Schillebeeckx makes of 'sign'. On the one hand, the word points to the claim he makes in his principle of the Givenness of Reality as I have been recalling it – and for this I have used the word 'clue'. On the other hand, the word goes with a distinction between reality and appearance that proves only too adaptable to Schillebeeckx's account of the eucharistic presence; and here I may fairly used the word 'disguise'. 'Sign' is not a word we can treat as if it had one meaning only. We must try to keep alive and yet keep in check a supremely important intuition: that a mystery confronts us, and that we have signs – clues – on the quest that is our response to it. The intuition can fade – the world is too much with us. But the intuition can also be confused with debatable positions in the theory of knowledge; and should it undergo that confusion, signs will become disguises to be penetrated instead of clues to be followed up. So much is easily said. But given the nature of the world, and the nature of those who are invited to read the signs and the parables there, we should not be surprised when the vocabulary of disguise seems more vivid than talk of clues, and when what is exalted is taken as replacing what is humble, instead of being discerned through it – in a word, when 'sign' passes from the first of Schillebeeckx's senses to the second. And when it so passes, we have the confusions we have noticed so often in the recent authors. To put it in terms of what we saw Schoonenberg write, the orders of significance and permeation are confused, and a disguised, permeating presence is seen as total significance. And in my submission that is the whole trouble, because signs as clues and signs as disguises are simply different; just as in my submission the keeping of the two apart is the first step towards a better account of the Eucharist.

'You have been in Afghanistan, I perceive.' Dr Watson was puzzled as to how Sherlock Holmes could perceive it, and only later on in *A Study in Scarlet* learned how Holmes had noticed that he was a medical type with a military air (and hence an army doctor), had his face darkened by a sojourn in the tropics (the darkness was not natural, since his wrists were fair), and had been injured (an arm was stiff). Where else in the tropics but Afghanistan could he have been wounded? The clues were there, but the clues could be said to conceal something (which is why Holmes at times expresses annoyance when Watson, on having clues explained to him, exclaims that it is all perfectly simple). But such a concealment is not at all the concealment that goes with disguise. With disguise, what needs to be seen is not the *significance* of what is there, but its *misleadingness*. Holmes, when counterfeiting a fever in 'The dying detective', would not allow Watson to draw near him for fear that his deception would be exposed; here indeed, precisely because there was disguise, what appeared to be there and what was really there were rivals, and competed for assent. But there was no rivalry or competition between Watson's appearance and his having taken part in the Afghan War; it would be absurd to offer the two as alternatives for belief.

Signs in the sense of clues may well be deceptive, in the sense that a sign may signify more than one thing. Holmes takes Watson to have come from a hot climate because of his darkened complexion. His inference would have been unsound if Watson had (admittedly at the expense of an anachronism) been using a sun-lamp, and the craft of writing detective fiction includes the art of getting readers to recall and to forget this plurality of significances at appropriate moments. But in no sense does the plurality mean that because Watson has been in Afghanistan, his complexion is not really bronzed at all, but only disguises his military service there. Signs in this sense and disguises are simply different, and the problems they present are just as different. Faced with an 'x' written on a torn-off scrap of paper, I may wonder whether it means a kiss, an illiterate's signature, the preamble to a bishop's signature, a mathematical or logical symbol, or the rejection of an answer submitted for evaluation. These several interpretations compete for assent, and we may or may not be able to make a decision in the matter. But there is no competition between the 'x' itself and the significance we attach to it, nor does the 'x' disguise any of its significances. For instance, if we end by taking the 'x' to be the marking of an answer as wrong, then the sign expresses the marker's verdict – but it does not disguise the verdict, as 'well tried' might. Nor, because of the significance the 'x' has, may we cease to call it an 'x', as we should if closer scrutiny revealed that the ink had run and the sign was really a 'y'.

The preceding section had for its title 'The humbler creation', and contained my arguments against letting exalted predicates in eucharistic matters compete for assent with what is present in a straightforward, spatial way. Once more, signs shew their difference from disguises: far from competing with the humbler creation, signs demand that it be acknowledged and respected for what it is. The mark on the scrap of paper allows of more than one interpretation, and perhaps I can reach no choice among them. But there could be no talk of interpreting the scrap of paper at all if the 'x' were written so minutely as to be imperceptible; or were written in sympathetic ink; or were forever changing its shape, like bonfire-smoke on a windy day. If Sherlock Holmes is to follow up clues about Dr Watson, Watson must not be forever changing his appearance. What is humbler is indeed humbler, but it is also indispensable. To think that its denial and replacement are possible is to adopt the pattern of disguise, while at the same time taking away whatever gives sense and content to the notion of being disguised. If we think in terms of signs, we shall not fall into this muddle. Precisely because they are not disguises, signs do not follow the pattern of competition and replacement, they do not end by denying what is the setting for the sense they have. Which is why signs, and not disguises, are the path to the eucharistic presence.

'You have been in the Netherlands, I perceive.' One reason why I have spelt out the recent views at such length is the reputation they have for minimising or reducing or failing to do justice to the eucharistic presence. I hope I have shewn at least that there is more to what the recent authors write than their reputation suggests. But I willingly admit that reputations are rarely redeemed by argument. The recent sources are not easily accessible, and many will have simply come across at second hand the analogies of tea-and-a-biscuit, bricks re-used to build a house, a cloth that is a flag, and the rest: if so, they may not have felt surprised at protests from Rome, from Schillebeeckx, and from others that 'transignification' is not of itself an adequate expression of eucharistic belief. At the same time, if anything in this book has seemed reasonable, what am I to suggest instead? To go by the protests, transignification falls short of a transformation in the order of imperceptible reality. But we know by now that objections of that sort are not as straightforward as they look, because we have seen all too much of the dubious path they invite us to tread: a path where we end by making a claim whose only apparent content comes from a picture that we cannot take seriously. Worse, this destination lies in wait – if my contentions have anything to them – for newer as much as for older writers; I have submitted that there is a fundamental lack of novelty in what is more recent. But if this be so, can talk in terms of signs still be a path to the eucharistic presence?

It can be. But much more needs to be said of the path, and I begin to say it in the next section.

24 *RITUS SERVANDUS*

The last section ended on a note of unease. Does not my very insistence upon the difference between signs and disguises point to the source of the uneasiness? We seem condemned to think in terms of marks on paper or gestures of hospitality – are they not a little too obvious? And if we think instead of signs that it takes Sherlock Holmes to spot, are we not giving an importance to sheer difficulty that it does not deserve? Is what he does essentially different from taking a door's squeak as a sign that its hinges need oiling? Can signs really do all that we want them to do here? I acknowledge the unease and I make it the starting-point for my claims in this section. There is a clear expression of it in Trooster's article, where he is criticising adversely an account he attributes to de Baciocchi. He writes:

Others have attempted to plumb the mystery further by way of a 'transfinalisation' [here a footnote refers to Vanneste 1956 and to de Baciocchi 1959]. But in my opinion it has not been made clear up to now that a transfinalisation of the sort really includes a 'transubstantiation'. J. de Baciocchi has very honestly brought out by means of an example the principal difficulty in this attempt, an attempt he himself seeks to formulate: when I use a saucer as an ash-tray, the saucer does not become an ash-tray! At the very least it has to be shewn that in the Eucharist we have to do with a transfinalisation *that is permanent*. De Baciocchi can do so only by an appeal to the doctrine of transubstantiation; which means that he is presupposing what he wants to shew by means of transfinalisation. (Trooster 1963: 129–30)[3]

The accuracy of this claim about de Baciocchi does not concern me, but its content does: that those who intend to explain in the new way have to end by following the old. So let us recall the general direction of de Baciocchi's account. Christ's is the one absolute point of view,

---

[3] It is hardly for me to complain at a Dutch-speaker's Dutch, but 'saucer' in what I have just translated from Trooster, while it expresses his '*schoteltje*', does not match what de Baciocchi actually wrote. As we shall see, he wrote '*dessous de bouteille*', which is not 'saucer' but 'coaster'. How *that* goes into Dutch, I have no idea. Perhaps they do not use them in Holland (an examination of interiors in Dutch paintings failed to find any), and Trooster had to make do with a saucer.

and empirical properties have no more than a relative significance:
(42) and (43). In the last analysis, he claims, it is a matter of one's
scale of values: to think that the eucharistic change might be
regarded as true for believers but not true for others is to make the
scientific view-point the final arbiter:

> We could well imagine a rationalist saying to us: 'You really want this bread
> to be for you the body of Christ? It's an odd idea but it's your business after
> all. You can of course use the bread as a religious symbol without making
> any change in it. I myself on occasions use a coaster as an ash-tray, without
> making any change in it.' (de Baciocchi 1959: 150)

De Baciocchi comments that the believer is aware of this point of
view, but regards it as relative; what for him is the last word on things
is the value given to them by Christ (150–1).

I hope that at least some readers have felt the juxtaposition of ash-
trays with the Eucharist to be even odder than Christian belief in it,
but let us see what else de Baciocchi has to say. Later in the same
article, he returns to the example and claims that the eucharistic
change deserves the name of transubstantiation. The name first
excludes any change of the kind that chemists study – at that level,
nothing changes in the Eucharist. Just as much excluded is

> an extrinsic or purely relative change, as in the example of the coaster that
> is now an ash-tray. That object is in no way affected in its own reality [*son être
> même*], all that changes is the use made of it. We make use of a capacity that
> was already present though not exploited; and the use does not abolish the
> bottle-supporting aptitude of what is now 'an ash-tray'. (155)

Christ's gift, he goes on, falls under neither of these, it is rather

> a radical newness with respect to the original reality of the bread and the
> wine; it puts an end to their former availability for secular use. (155)

Once more, I hope I am not alone in feeling the extreme oddness of
locating the eucharistic change by keeping it apart from the Scylla of
chemistry and the Charybdis of ash-trays. Once more, however, let
us go with de Baciocchi and see the rest of what he claims. Christ's
action is a giving, he writes, an action *whose object is the thing itself*. The
employment of the coaster is different:

> The function of being an ash-tray is based simply upon a certain *way of
> existence* [*manière d'être*], a way common to many things – ordinary ash-trays,
> saucers [my footnote about Trooster's '*schoteltje*' had a point], shells, lids of
> tins etc. The sacramental function presupposes that the object employed is
> bread or wine, but it is not based primarily upon the empirical properties of

bread and wine. It comes from the fact that such a piece of bread or such an amount of wine is in a certain fashion *given* by Christ to the Church. What gets given is not a way of existing, but *something that exists* [*un être*]. Whereas we employ as an ash-tray a hollow, non-inflammable object of a certain size – and what object provides such a hollow is in the last analysis of little moment. (156)

I have long held that the crucial points in an argument shew themselves in its footnotes and parentheses. The citation I have just given has a footnote, to which I shall soon return. First – having marvelled, I hope, at the elaboration of the example – let us turn to the third and last position which transubstantiation excludes for de Baciocchi:

It also excludes an intermediate position, for which the eucharistic bread would *remain* bread and become *in addition* the body of Christ: from one point of view it would be bread; from another, the body of Christ. Such a duality makes … [no sense] when we are concerned with what itself exists, with basic ontological unity. *Either* bread remains bread *or* it becomes the body of Christ. To assert consubstantiation (for that is what we have here) is to claim that the bread is the body of Christ. But, by the rules of formal logic, propositions with two singular terms are convertible; therefore, if the original statement is true, so is the proposition that the body of Christ is the bread; and if it is this bread, *it is bread*. The absurdity of this inevitable consequence obliges us to deny its basis. One and the same object can be simultaneously both coaster and ash-tray, because we are dealing here with accidental and compatible properties. When we come to the very being of things, it is just as difficult to admit consubstantiation in the Eucharist as to think of a lion that would also be a fir tree, taking each expression in its strict sense. The Principle of Identity stands in the way. (156–7)

I readily admit that, if we are to talk in these terms, I cannot think of a lion that is also a fir tree. Nor, for good measure, can I think of a lion that passes every conceivable test for being a fir tree, but is still a lion because its substance has replaced the fir tree's substance under the inflated skin of the tree's accidents – and de Baciocchi would presumably welcome my admission. I admit another incapacity, and here de Baciocchi would presumably be less enthusiastic: I cannot think either that what is a fir tree in the order of empirical properties might, by Christ's final and absolute word, be declared to be a lion. But I am not concerned here with judging between the different incoherences we have met so often. I have in mind something that goes far deeper. I am concerned with one vast missing of the point.

De Baciocchi exhibits in his example the believer and the

unbeliever as at odds over what is to be given pride of place: the word of Christ, or the declarations of science based on empirical and practical properties. But the one thing we never hear about in all this is the one thing we ought to be hearing about: that the Eucharist is a *ritual*, an inherited form of words and actions. Not only do we hear nothing of ritual, we are encouraged to think it does not matter, as the footnote I omitted will now shew. In the main text, de Baciocchi was contrasting the use of the coaster (where its properties of being hollow and being non-inflammable prompted the new employment) with the 'sacramental function' in the Eucharist (which 'is not based primarily upon the empirical properties of bread and wine'). At this point comes the footnote:

The function, however, is not independent of the empirical properties: the nutritive properties of bread and wine are taken for granted by the use that is to be made of Christ's gift. (155, fn. 1)

Belated, understandable and still inadequate qualification! Anxious to set the Eucharist apart from coasters used as ash-trays, de Baciocchi stresses the potentiality of the former utensil for being employed as the latter, and correspondingly diminishes the link between the presence of Christ and the perceptible activity and material of the Eucharist. True, he does write that the sacramental function presupposes the properties of bread and wine, but – so the main text would suggest – it is the giving by Christ to the Church that matters, the properties of what is given do not. Understandable indeed it is that de Baciocchi should here insert a qualifying footnote, for otherwise this giving (like the 'final word' of Christ to which he appeals) would remain detached from any concrete embodiment in ritual at all. For the main text, the Eucharist is placed in the categories of gift and speech, and ritual has only an extrinsic and accidental link with it. A footnote was certainly needed, but the qualification it provides is still inadequate. He writes there that the nutritive properties are 'taken for granted in the use to be made of Christ's gift'. It is as if the gift were made; and then our use of it were subsequently guided by what the gift was. The giving is allotted an isolated and independent place, it is not linked with the specific activity of what Christ did at the Last Supper and of what is still done in the celebration of the Eucharist.

A further text confirms this diagnosis. The bread and wine, he writes, were gifts of God for maintaining *temporal* life and cohesion among mankind, with at the same time all that they imply concerning invitations to union with God and aptitudes for this. Christ's word, leaving the empirical content of these gifts unaltered, totally changes their social and religious destination. From now on, this bread and this wine will no longer serve to nourish or to refresh the body – save in an accessory fashion, and to a negligible degree. They will be signs and instruments of Christ's gift... (149–50)

Notice the tension running through what de Baciocchi has written here. He starts with the point made by Schillebeeckx in his principle of the Givenness of Reality, but he then contrasts the original state of the gifts with their eucharistic employment. Here their rôle is to be signs of Christ's gift, their natural functions of nourishing are now negligible and accessory. The link is weakened as before between what is used in the ritual and the use made of it there. Christ's act of giving is isolated from what is given, and becomes an almost disembodied donation. Ritual has nothing essentially to do with the matter.

We have come back here to what we have met so many times already, the cancellation and denial of our starting-point in the name of what we are said to have reached from it. What we must now come to see is how the Fallacy of Replacement is opposed to ritual as well, precisely because ritual needs the very things that the Fallacy denies. The Fallacy weakens the link between Christ's act of giving and the original, natural properties of what he gives. And if we go back to the text about the ash-tray that started our thoughts in this section, we shall see just how profound the opposition to ritual is. For, outside Bedlam or a theological essay, who would institute a comparison between the Eucharist and the improvising of an ash-tray? I can imagine an unbeliever accusing Christians of cannibalism in what they say about the Eucharist – indeed, by the end of this chapter I hope to have shewn that the accusation has more to it than Christians like to think – but the comparison between eucharistic ritual and the depositing of ash where once we deposited a bottle is a lunacy that calls for more drastic treatment. Of course, I am not denying that someone might (just might) offer the analogy; the question is, what response should the believer give?

According to de Baciocchi, believer and unbeliever are disagreeing about a 'scale of values'. The ultimate norm for what things are – is it to be provided by empirical properties or by the person of Christ? I set aside for the moment my objection that the alternative is unreal, and note that de Baciocchi presents the believer as competing with the unbeliever in *naming* things. To Christ it falls to name, so the believer says, to change names, and to transform thereby those whose names he has changed – Abraham and Peter are adduced as examples in (35). The unbeliever, of course, will not accept this norm; and that is where the two are at odds. Such is de Baciocchi's claim: why do I think it is a missing of the point?

If a believer and an unbeliever are talking about what divides them, then indeed it is more than likely that their respective scales of values will prove to be different, and that their disagreements will naturally touch the Eucharist. Nor is it probable that their conversation will end with their dissent over it being terminated. But to depict their disagreement as being over what is to be the ultimate standard for the naming of things is to miss the point of what the Eucharist *is*. The Eucharist is a rite, a ceremony; it is simply not about ultimate norms for reality and for naming. De Baciocchi is exhibiting a blindness here just as great in its own way as what he deplores in his imaginary unbeliever. By this time, of course, we know what a position like de Baciocchi's amounts to: he is transposing into norms for naming and reality the move made by the scholastics in terms of substance and accidents. That position, in its older and newer forms alike, I have rejected as vacuous confusion; what we now need to grasp is that it is also a missing of the point at issue in the Eucharist. Putting things as simply as possible, we can say that de Baciocchi's unbeliever does not need talking to about norms for naming things, he needs to be shewn by the believer what ritual is, and what the eucharistic ritual is really like. He may at the end of it remain unmoved; probably will, if you prefer; but at least the endeavour will have been directed to what divides the two of them, and not to something extraneous.

What then would be involved in exhibiting the Eucharist as ritual? We can begin to see by recalling other texts of de Baciocchi already given, for he shews there a perceptive awareness of ritual and of what goes with it. Thus, he is at pains to place the Eucharist in the setting of the Passover, and sees in each the institution of a rite that is a memorial and yet more than a memorial; and he writes good sense concerning the 'double' character of the eucharistic elements (bread and wine), elucidating them in terms of different rituals in the inheritance from the Old Testament – 'the duality is not so much biological as liturgical': see (25) and (33). And he offers elsewhere a useful corrective to the speculations about 'resurrection as recipe' that we met earlier in this chapter – what matters, he writes, is not to know how a glorified body can be in many places, but how the bread and wine become signs of Christ's gift of himself (1959: 148). When he writes things of that kind, he is not only pointing to what matters, he is exhibiting the pattern of exposition found in other recent authors. I hope to be able to incorporate in the next chapter a good deal of what we have read in these authors, and I gladly acknowledge the debt I owe them. For all that, the tension is there when de Baciocchi moves from talking of the Eucharist as a rite to construing what is ritual in alien terms – as a naming by Christ and as an abstractly considered giving by him. The tension is bound to occur in any author who combines an awareness of ritual with a persistence in the Fallacy of Replacement, and so I complement what we have seen in de Baciocchi with what can be seen in two others, Gutwenger and Schoonenberg. We shall in this way get nearer to the course we must take in the next chapter.

Gutwenger exhibits a positive attitude to ritual when he acknowledges what de Baciocchi called the 'implications' of the bread and wine for our relationship with God. Natural food has of itself a suitability for symbolising a supernatural and grace-bestowing food. Indeed, did the world lack such symbolic capacity, discourse about the things of God would be impossible (Gutwenger 1966; 196). All of which makes excellent sense, but makes all the more incongruous a remark in the paragraph preceding it, that the Lord removes the bread from the secular order and makes it into a symbol of his self-giving presence, so that the bread no longer has the significance (*Sinn*) of natural nourishment, the content of its significance being now wholly comprised in being a symbol of the Risen Lord's spiritual presence. From acknowledging the implicit openness in food to expressing the things of God, Gutwenger has passed to talking in terms of the replacement of one significance by another, and of the relegation of natural nourishment to another order altogether. But something more appears when Gutwenger explains, earlier on the same page, how he thinks a eucharistic account in terms of changed significance should proceed. Such a change indicates a change in essence or reality (*Wesensverwandlung*), and an example is provided – a house may be pulled down and its bricks used again to build a bridge: without any loss or abolition of matter, a change in essence has been affected, by a change in purpose. The defects of *that* for elucidating ritual can, I think, be best put in the words J. L. Thomas used to his friend George V, when the monarch asked him why he disliked Balmoral: 'It's a bloody dull 'ouse, Sir.' Ritual may be strange, humdrum, botched or enchanting, but it is not like recycling house-bricks. Gutwenger, of course, admits there the banality of his example, and proposes it simply with the intention of convincing his readers that change in significance can be a change in essence without loss of matter (Gutwenger 1966: 196). He wants to convince them of this because he is dissatisfied with the older account of the eucharistic change in terms of the conversion of the whole substance of the bread. I am even more dissatisfied with the older account, but I do not think that the way out lies simply through analysing significance, any more than I think it lies simply through de Baciocchi's debate over ultimate destinations and namings. Just as neither author confronts head-on the confusions that lie in transubstantiation, so neither suggests anything sufficiently tied to what the Eucharist actually is: a *rite*. Once that tie is loosened, anything can be brought in. We should not be surprised that oddities like ashtrays and bricks should turn up in what the two authors propose.

Ritual is not reducible to the theory of knowledge or of naming, ritual is not reducible to changes in purpose, ritual cannot be elucidated in terms of differences in the practical employment of material. But neither can ritual be considered as needing to be eked out by something else, and here what Schoonenberg writes repays examination. He too does justice in some texts to the Eucharist as ritual, insisting on its being placed in the setting of the worshipping community, and on its being construed in terms of Christ's presence there in believers: see (16) and (28). But he also allots the primacy to the notion of giving (15), and the notion becomes isolated from its specifically ritual context in the Eucharist. Indeed, he links giving with transubstantiation in (21) even before he begins with the Eucharist. Just so, the institution of the Eucharist is elucidated in (31) in terms of the notion of presence – as a purification from spatial proximity and a desire for an embodiment more transparent of the person. Once more, it is not the content of all this that worries me, it is its apparent detachment from a ritual that we know Christ carried out, and with which our present eucharistic ritual is linked. Recall the text we saw at (52), where Schoonenberg begins his application to the Eucharist of what he has said about giving: the bread and wine have wholly become the gift of Christ. He now goes on:

They are not just taken up into an action that emphasises words, and so not essentially changed when the sacramental action has run its course. The bread and wine are essentially changed... (Schoonenberg 1965: 50)

I have italicised what worries me. Schoonenberg wants the elements to be essentially changed, and regards as inadequate for this that they should be 'just taken up into action that emphasises words'. That would not do, for it would not produce a change that endured after the action. More is needed, and the text continues by saying what it is:

The bread and wine are essentially changed, are transubstantiated as the gift, but at the level of the God-Man. Jesus Christ, in whom dwelleth the fullness of the Godhead bodily and truly (Coloss. i 19) gives himself to us in this gift, in this food. (50)

Schoonenberg's contrast does no justice to ritual. Ritual is not simply an 'action that emphasises words', it must be approached on its own terms, and we must not assume that we need to import something extraneous to ritual if we are to get what we want. Schoonenberg makes just such an assumption. For him, ritual is 'an action that emphasises words', and so has its effects limited to its own duration. He has therefore to import the factor of giving, Christ's self-giving, to ensure a permanent change, and – as the text shews – the giving he imports has nothing essentially bound up with ritual at all, it is the 'disembodied donation' I found in de Baciocchi (p. 155). There, I qualified my phrase with an 'almost', and of course I do the same here; it would indeed be unfair to contend that either author effects a complete break between giving and ritual. But I do contend that neither de Baciocchi nor Schoonenberg links giving with ritual as it needs to be linked. Schoonenberg's appeal to 'resurrection as recipe' is simply another example of the need he feels to eke out ritual with something else. His search for such a recipe goes with his separation of giving from what is essentially a ritual. He wants what he offers to achieve what the scholastics' transubstantiation did, while expressing what he offers inside the newer categories of personal presence, giving and significance. Invoking the resurrection seems to remove all bodily barriers and so seems to let significance and permeation come together; newer and older styles can both be satisfied. If my contentions have anything to them, the satisfaction is illusory. New and old indeed converge – that we have seen time and again. But, just as we have seen them converge in confusion and in a divorce of appearance from reality, so now we see that they also converge in failing to do justice to the ritual character of the Eucharist.

But for some readers an unease may remain, the unease which I noticed at the start of this section. Will not the removal of disguise and concealment make us lose something, and condemn us to an account that is too open and obvious for comfort? Can signs here bear the burden that is to be put upon them? I have spoken of ritual, but can ritual fare any better? We saw that Smits makes much of the ritual of a hospitable offering of food and drink in what he writes of the Eucharist; but his account has become – rightly or wrongly – notorious as an example of alleged inadequacy here. A full answer to these questions must wait for the next chapter, but there are things to say about them in this, both here and in the next section. And I begin what I have to say by suggesting that there are two causes for the unease that need to be noticed before we do anything else. One is (as we have already seen) the *vividness* of the accounts I have been opposing; but the other is (yet again) the rôle of *time* in these matters.

I wrote earlier that older and newer accounts alike were condemned to the very 'dimensionalising' of the presence of Christ that they were anxious to avoid. But I went on to add that this unwanted destination gave an apparent vividness and definiteness to what the accounts claimed, for the simple reason that spatial presence is the most basic form of presence known to us (pp. 142ff). So it is here. We may have rejected the picture that goes with the dimensionalising, but the picture can still have power, can still apparently allow a straightforward question to be put: 'is Christ beneath the appearances or is he not?' We have seen much of this vividness. But we have also seen something of time, and are going to see a good deal more; and it is this factor of time which also contributes to the uneasiness to which I have referred, and so needs to be mentioned here as well.

Perhaps I can best put what I have in mind by saying that the older accounts are more *venerable* than the newer. First, more venerable in their tone and demeanour, being expressed, if I may so put it, in a grave and metaphysical fashion. Eucharistic theology, the scholastics claim, moves here in the order of substance, where only the intellect can cope; pictures belong to the imagination, and so have nothing to do with the case; all we need is the perennial philosophy (and here

Godefroy's untranslatable gibberish from (44) can be invoked);
objections like mine are vulgar missings of the point. And so on; the
manoeuvre lies in attaching deterrent labels to whatever might lead
to awkward questions, and readers can by now decide for themselves
what they think of it. But the older accounts are more venerable not
just in this sense, but by having time on their side. Whatever may be
said against the scholastic account of the eucharistic presence, it does
have the advantage of seniority over anything that can now be
suggested, and the further advantage of having terminology resembling what is in a Council's decrees on the subject. If the
scholastic account is no more than confusion, it is a long-established
confusion, and the Inquisition's complaints we met at the start of the
first chapter should at all events not surprise us. The recent authors
– because they are recent – have to take up their stance with respect
to 'a past that is for them both revered and unsatisfactory' (I used the
phrase in the last chapter and it will be recurring ever more
frequently). The scholastic account has apparently no such stance to
adopt, and that is its strength. There is no muffling of the clarity it
apparently possesses, even if we judge that clarity to be spurious. And
there lies the force of being venerable: I have rejected old and new
alike, what am I to do? Can talk in terms of ritual provide anything
more than surface-ornament to what has taken so deep root for so
long? Must I not end by having to appeal to something deeper? We
saw at the start of this chapter how Schoonenberg allots the rôle of
'recipe' to the risen state of Christ. And we saw in the second chapter
how Schillebeeckx, while accepting the vocabulary of transignification, adds that it has to be seen in the setting of a transubstantiation,
and that the former needs the 'metaphysical density' of the latter to
be acceptable; that, in brief, 'the significance of the phenomenal
forms of bread and wine is changed, *because*... the reality is changed
to which the phenomena refer': see (69), (70), (79). Do not both
those authors encourage us to think from the start that, whatever I
succeed in doing by means of ritual, I shall have in the end to invoke
something else, something resembling the older tradition, under pain
of not doing justice to the theme I have undertaken?

The older account interpreted eucharistic ritual in terms of natural
philosophy. The newer accounts interpret eucharistic ritual in terms
of human relationships and activities like presence, giving and
naming. I am trying to interpret eucharistic ritual in terms of ritual.
There, in three sentences, is the thesis of this book. But in no sense

does it mean I can give the topic of ritual short shrift: the reverse is the case. Ritual does not lend itself to being talked about as picturing does, because ritual is primarily what is celebrated.[4] And not only is ritual celebrated rather than discussed; discussions of it must range far and wide, because ritual can never be 'detached' from natural things. Ever since the first chapter, the attraction of a concept of substance like Colombo's has proved real, precisely because of its splendid isolation, and a similar attraction is present in the divorce between appearance and reality found in the newer authors. If I am to offer an account in terms of ritual, I cannot provide anything so seductive. My account will have to be long, and must embrace many things.

I have raised two difficulties: the supposed inadequacy of an account in terms of ritual, unless it be filled out with something like the scholastic account; and the venerable status of that account. I begin to deal with both difficulties together, in the final section of this chapter. I have yet to consider what Aquinas has to say about ritual, and to draw conclusions from what he does say. Some of the conclusions must wait for the next chapter, but some we shall now see in the section to come. In it, we shall have to ask just what it is that has acquired the favoured and venerable status commonly associated with the older tradition. Yet again, things will turn out to be less simple than they seem.

25 THE SHADOW OF THE PAST

Back in the first chapter, texts from Aquinas and from earlier medieval writers were examined. The examination shewed that the later application of words like 'philosophical' or 'metaphysical' to his eucharistic speculations and terminology is misleading, because disciplinary boundaries were not then what they are now, and the style of what Aquinas writes about the eucharistic conversion brings him closer to what we should call natural science. Of the examples I then chose, I recall one here: Aquinas' preference for the view that the water mixed with the wine in the chalice is itself first transformed into wine, and then transubstantiated into the blood of Christ

---

[4] I have allowed myself a small pun in this section's title, to bring out the point. *Ritus Servandus* – 'Ritual to be followed' – was the title of a eucharistic service-book of yesteryear. The phrase can serve to sum up what I am proposing.

(p. 36). I go now to another text in Aquinas to do with the water, and this text will set the tone for what is to follow. Must water be mixed with the wine? Aquinas says it should be, and one of his reasons is that it signifies the union of Christian people with Christ (*ST* 3.74.6), and so the sharing in this sacrament by the faithful. But he also says that the sacrament lies in the consecration of the matter, the use by the faithful is not essential to the sacrament but something subsequent to it. So, since that is what the admixture of water signifies, the addition cannot be essential to the sacrament's validity (*ST* 3.74.7). We need not accept the inferences Aquinas makes from symbolism to obligation, or from symbolism to non-essentiality, in order to see that he does place the Eucharist in an act of consecration, and not in any communal sharing in a rite.

The placing can be confirmed by the answer he gives to a standard medieval problem: would it be possible for a priest to consecrate all the bread in a market-place or all the wine in a cellar? Some writers (Bonaventure was one) denied the possibility on the grounds that such an action would have no relation to use by the faithful. Aquinas does not accept the opinion – 'it does not seem to be true' – because the determining factor is what the sacrament's purpose is, and that purpose is the use by the faithful (*ST* 3.74.2). Which looks at first sight open to ritual, but not at second sight. The number of the faithful, he adds, cannot be reckoned from those who are actually present – otherwise a priest in a small parish could not consecrate many hosts – so it must be reckoned absolutely; that is, as an indefinite number; and so a limit cannot be set to the amount of matter consecrated. In other words, an abstract consideration of possible numbers takes precedence over treating the Eucharist in its concrete reality, a celebration in which determinate people are to a greater or lesser degree taking part.

It is interesting to notice that Aquinas does set some bounds to the amount of matter when he deals with the question in his earlier *Commentary on the Sentences*. Here he denies that the priest could consecrate all the bread there is in a city or in a market-place. But once again, the appearance of greater openness to ritual is illusory. The bounds are not set by the demands of ritual or celebration but by grammar. Since the formula of consecration employs the demonstrative pronoun ('this' in 'This is my body'), it shews that what is to be consecrated must be in the presence of the priest – a priest could not, while staying at home, consecrate bread put upon the altar (in

4 *Sent.*, dist. 11, q.2, art. 1, qu.la 3, ad 1; 463/168). The mere entertaining of the bizarre and disconcerting hypothesis about the stay-at-home priest embodies the drift of the whole answer. What we have is not so much a ritual or a celebration as a transformation to be duly effected on matter duly present.

His *Commentary on the Sentences* also gives the answer to a question already met in the first chapter (p. 33): if a mouse breaks in and eats the consecrated particles, does he receive the body of Christ? Those like Bonaventure who gave a negative answer did so on the grounds that, once in the mouse's stomach, the species of the bread can no longer be directed to human use; and, since the body of Christ is present only in as much as it is so directed, its presence then ceases. Aquinas denies the presupposition of the argument – since the species do not immediately pass away on being swallowed, they could still be extracted from the mouse's stomach and appropriately used. This gruesome hypothesis is followed by the repetition of his claim that the Eucharist lies in 'the consecration of the matter'; and so, while the mouse cannot receive the sacrament in this sense that we can, it does receive 'that beneath which is the body of Christ' (In 4 *Sent.* dist. 9, art 2, qu.la 3, with its objections and replies: 367/40, 370/60f.).[5] What Aquinas writes here has moved further away from any link with eucharistic ritual or religious activity.

And in another early text he moves yet further away. The text comes at a point where he is offering what is essentially the account we already know of presence *per modum substantiae*. He asks on what ground can we attribute this multiple presence to Christ's body, and puts a series of objections. Because it is a body? But that would mean that every body could have such a presence. Because it is a glorified body? But that would mean that, *a fortiori*, angels would have it. Because he is the Son of God? But the divinity of Christ does not place him outside the limits of his own body. The answer he offers starts in a way familiar to us from what he wrote in the *Summa*: he writes of

---

[5] Although Aquinas does not draw the conclusion, the mouse will drift from substance towards accident, in the way we met in footnote 9 to chapter 1. A novel by Robert Musil had for its title what translates as *The Man Without Qualities*: our poor mouse is doomed to be nothing but qualities.

   The differences between Aquinas and Bonaventure here were the starting-point for Montcheuil 1939, reprinted in the memorial volume Montcheuil 1946 (he was shot by the Gestapo). He rightly brings out the differences, and rightly disagrees with the attempts of the editors of Bonaventure's works to minimise them (Montcheuil 1939: 359). He might have added that the attempts were made under pressure from Leo XIII, who was averse to any differences from Aquinas at any time.

presence *per modum substantiae*. But the text then goes on disconcertingly:

And the same [i.e. multiple presence] would be attributed to the body of a stone, if God in a similar fashion were to convert the substance of bread into a stone. As there is no doubt that he could. (In 4 *Sent*. dist. 10, art 1, obj. 8 and ad 8; 403/7; 406/24)

'Convert the substance' means, of course, 'transubstantiate' (see the account at pp. 11–12). So transubstantiation has now been wholly detached from any eucharistic setting whatsoever: it is a mysterious change that does occur there, but could occur elsewhere too. Whatever words we want to use about it, they had better pertain to things like alchemy rather than to things like ritual. Or indeed to things like religion either.

The sharing by the faithful in a rite has been subordinated to the achieving of a transformation. Aquinas investigates in the *Summa* the *forma* of the Eucharist, the formula by which the sacrament is effected. In other sacraments, the form implies a use of matter (water in Baptism, and so on), but the form of the Eucharist implies only the consecration of the matter by transubstantiation (*ST* 3.78.1). From this he infers that 'This is my body' alone is the form. 'Take, eat' is not essential, because that connotes 'the use of the consecrated matter', and this is not essential, but pertains to 'a certain completion' (*quandam perfectionem*) of the sacrament (*ST* 3.78.1 ad 1 and ad 2). The very phrases 'use of consecrated matter' and 'a certain completion' express all too well the meagre awareness shewn here of the Eucharist as a shared rite, but the *Commentary on the Sentences* is even more meagre. There, the Eucharist is contrasted with a Sacrament like Baptism, where an external action is to be performed; in the Eucharist, completed in the consecration of the matter, 'the minister has no action to perform beyond the pronouncing of the words, just as in any other sanctification of matter' (In 4 *Sent*. dist. 8, q.2, art. 1, qu.la 3; 331/151). Action here is as absent as ritual is: it is a *verbal* business that we have to deal with.

Which is why, if taken as concerned with the use of words, what Aquinas writes will appeal to those who have similar interests themselves. For example, he asks why, if the Eucharist is essentially the effecting of a transformation, we should not rather use the subjunctive in its form and say 'Let this be my body' (*ST* 3.78.2 ad 2). He answers that the power of God operates here sacramentally, that is, 'according to the force of significance' (*secundum vim significationis*). Sacramental forms signify in the way forms produced by human activity (*formae artificiales*) signify – they signify the effect as completed (the builder's aim, we might say, is the *completed* house, not the *construction* of it). So the sacramental form should exhibit the final result of the consecration, by using the present indicative (*ST* 3.78.2 and ad 2). Again, and even more impressively, he asks whether the sacramental forms are *true*, and answers by comparing them with an operation of the practical intellect, which terminates in making something. Other propositions have only a significative power, their job is to state how things are. But sacramental forms do not presuppose the truth of what they say, they bring it about (*ST* 3.78.5; there is still more to the Article, and readers who have been thinking in terms of 'performatives' will find that Aquinas even uses *virtus factiva* – 'effective power'). Here indeed we do not feel in a strange land.

Unfortunately, we do not have to leave the question to find the countryside alien once more. Aquinas puts the difficulty that the form should include what Christ used. But we read in the Gospel that he *blessed* and broke the bread, saying 'Take, eat, etc.' So should we ourselves not use this blessing too as the form (*ST* 3.78.1 obj. 1)? Before going further, let us notice that Aquinas shews good sense in the answer he finally offers – the participle 'saying' can be taken so that we mean 'while he blessed and broke and gave to his disciples, he said "Take, eat..."'. What disconcerts me is the list of opinions he feels obliged to pass under review and reject. Christ wordlessly consecrated, and then uttered the words for us to imitate (wrong, because 'blessed' connotes words). Or Christ consecrated by words unknown to us (wrong, because we are supposed to narrate now what was done then). Or Christ first used the form silently, to consecrate; and then aloud, to instruct (wrong, because the priest would not be uttering the *consecratory* words of Christ). Or the Evangelists do not keep to the original order, which is that Christ took bread, blessed it by saying 'this is my body', and then broke and distributed it (not necessary, for 'saying' can be taken in the way already noticed). Certainly, Aquinas argues perceptively against all these, but what he feels is amiss with them lies in the order of language and of transformations. There is not a word by him on their total missing of the point, not a word to call them back to the *rite* that the Eucharist actually is.

The chapter that follows will have other texts of Aquinas to consider – including, indeed, the question in the *Summa* entitled 'On the rite of the Eucharist'. The texts I present here I have chosen because of the suggestion considered near the end of the last section – that an account in terms of ritual, whatever its merits, will need 'filling out' with the solidity and density of the tradition in which Aquinas wrote. The texts examined so far in this section will, I hope, have shewn that the solidity and density are not what they seemed at first sight: what we have is rather a blindness to ritual and an occult transformation only tenuously connected with a shared celebration. Just as describing the eucharistic account of Aquinas as 'metaphysical' or 'philosophical' had to give way to a more complicated and alien description, once we got down in the first chapter to the details of what he and others actually wrote, so it is here. I suspect that 'solid' and 'dense' are no longer quite the words we should pick – or, if they are, it is because we now mean something less complimentary by them than what is meant by those who invoke the scholastic tradition against recent proposals. An examination of what Aquinas actually wrote shews that the usual invocation of the scholastic tradition has to be selective. Some texts in the tradition speak in terms of a transformation that has no essential link with worship whatever.

But texts still more alien now present themselves, and these too are part of what Aquinas wrote. Here, I submit, we shall have to say that alchemy gives way to anatomy, and the reason for the title of this section – 'the shadow of the past' – will become clearer. Let us start with a text connected with the notion of presence *per modum substantiae*. Aquinas asks in *ST* 3.76.7 whether Christ can be *seen* in the Eucharist, and answers that he cannot. Two reasons offered we have already met: vision demands appearances, and the appearances here are of bread; Christ is present *per modum substantiae*, and substance is grasped by the intellect alone. But the same Article has two more texts. The first expresses bluntly the disguise and dimensionality with which I have charged the scholastics: one way the sacramental appearances impede our vision of Christ is that they act as a covering does – just as we are impeded from seeing something shrouded in a bodily veil (*ST* 3.76.7 ad 1). But in the second text I find the *prolongation* I have mentioned. It leads to novelties that will prove unwelcome.

In this second text, Aquinas makes an exception for Christ himself in the matter of ocular vision. Christ's eyes cannot see his substantial mode of existence in the Eucharist (that is the achievement of his intellect), but he still does see himself in the Eucharist *because his eyes are themselves under the sacramental appearances* (*ST* 3.76.7 ad 2). I have italicised here what I find disconcertingly novel. Presence *per modum substantiae* raises problems that are abstract, such as the persistence of 'dimensionality'; the confusion between signs and disguises can be discussed in equally abstract terms; even the insensitivity to ritual is dull and regrettable rather than positively offensive. But here we have something more, in this appeal to the presence of Christ's eyes under the appearances. We have a 'recipe' for what Christ does that goes with what I have to call a dissection and anatomising of his presence. (Aquinas in fact writes not 'eyes' but 'eye' (*oculus*), which I find even more offensive). The words put together are pictorial if they are anything at all, and the picture is not pleasant. Unfortunately, more is to come. We must see some other texts.

The Eucharist uses both bread and wine, and the words of Christ are spoken over first one and then the other. De Baciocchi rightly pointed to the duality as pertaining to the order of liturgy rather than of biology, and suggested cultic actions in the Old Testament as an indication of where the significance lies: (33), (25). What has Aquinas to say?

He uses a distinction we saw him draw when he was talking of presence *per modum substantiae*. The substance of Christ's body is present 'by the power of the sacrament': it is that into which the sacramental conversion takes place. But his dimensions are present 'by real concomitance': they are really conjoined with what is present in the former way (*ST* 3.76.1; see pp. 114–15). Aquinas now uses this distinction to elucidate the twofold consecration in the Eucharist. In the host the body of Christ is present 'by the power of the sacrament', while his blood, soul and divinity are present 'by real concomitance' – they go with his body in reality. Just so, in the chalice it is his blood that is present 'by the power of the sacrament', his body and the rest are present by real concomitance (*ST* 3.76.2). In my judgment, an abstract distinction has become a means of dissection. And if my judgment seems unfair, another reply made by Aquinas earlier in the same question will shew that it is not.

In the sixth chapter of John's Gospel, Christ says that his flesh and his blood are true food and drink. So, by his words, flesh (*caro*) and blood (*sanguis*) are present in the Eucharist. But there are other parts of the body that do not fall under either heading – muscles, bones and so on. So they are not present? Aquinas replies that muscles and bones are indeed present in the host, and by the power of the sacrament, because our Lord used 'flesh' to stand for all the body, since we live off the flesh of animals rather than off their bones and other things of the sort (*ST* 3.76.1 obj. 2 and ad 2). Quite. But let me sharpen the point by going to the slightly different reply to the same enquiry given by him in the *Commentary on the Sentences*. Once again, 'flesh' is said to be used because it is the primary instance of what is eaten – but now the reminder is added that bones and other things do have some relationship with eating, because Avicenna tells us that some animals live off them (In 4 *Sent.* dist. 10, art. 2, qu.la 2, obj. 1 and ad 1; 407/28, 410/41). I find the precision endearing as well as dotty, but surely it arouses associations that are grotesque and offensive.

And just as many are aroused by a text in the very next article in the *Summa* – the Article in which we saw the two kinds of presence distinguished. Suppose that 'flesh' be taken, as was suggested, to include parts of the body like bones and muscles. If it be so taken, why should it not be taken to include blood as well, which is also a part of the body? And if so, why should a separate consecration of the wine be necessary? The reply given is that it was the blood alone which was separated from the body during the passion, and it is of the passion that the Eucharist is a memorial (*ST* 3.76.2 obj. 2 and ad 2). Not only is Aquinas here wholly in the order of transformations and wholly outside the order of ritual – contrast the passage with what authors like de Baciocchi have to say! – but he is speculating over physiology. And the way he speculates echoes what we read earlier in the chapter, when his quaint list of details about the resurrection included the fate of Christ's blood then. But quaintness has now given place to something darker. Assertions are being prolonged, and to the very verge of queasiness. And a final group of texts will surely take us over the verge.

I have, at considerable length, accused both the scholastics and recent authors of talking in terms of disguise and concealment. What I have not yet offered is scholastic texts to do with the *reason* for disguise, texts which ask *why there should be the appearances of bread and wine at all*. The question I have italicised, because we have to make some effort to see how it can be asked – what possible alternative is being considered by the questioner? Aquinas asks it at *ST* 3.75.5. Two things concern us here: the reason he gives for asking why there should be the appearances of bread; and the answer he gives to the question he has put. In my opinion, the reason he gives for putting the question is in a different order to the answer he offers, and I will accordingly give question and answer separate consideration.

The very idea of asking why there should be appearances of bread is indeed odd, but the reason Aquinas offers for asking it does point to a weakness in the whole plan of approaching the Eucharist in terms of disguise. We make judgments about substance, he says, by means of accidents – is it right that we should be deceived in the sacrament of truth? And if faith, though above reason, does not contradict reason, and if reason takes its start from the senses, is it not unfitting that there should be this contrariety between faith and the senses (*ST* 3.75.5 objs 2, 3)? I am not claiming that the objections here shew Aquinas moving towards another approach to the eucharistic presence, an approach in which signs are not confused with disguises. But I do claim that his objections point to an awkwardness he felt in the juxtaposition of the Eucharist with what does, at least at first sight, look like deception. And I think that the awkwardness he felt was not forgotten by later writers of another cast of mind.[6]

So much for the reason he gives for putting the question. What now of his answer? I had better let him speak for himself:

It is reasonable that divine providence should bring it about [that all the accidents of bread and wine remain after the consecration]. First, since it is not usual for human beings, but horrible, to eat a man's flesh and drink his blood, the flesh and blood of Christ are given to us to consume under the appearances of what are used more frequently by mankind, namely bread and wine. Secondly, lest unbelievers should mock at this sacrament, were we to eat our Lord under his own appearances. Thirdly, that our reception of the Lord's body and blood, being invisible, should add to the merit of our faith. (*ST* 3.75.5)

The corresponding passage in the *Commentary on the Sentences* has distinctive material which I shall consider in the next chapter, but some items there can be set beside this text from the *Summa*. Aquinas

---

[6] I notice here once again an author mentioned in the first chapter, the Cartesian Sylvain Régis. His eucharistic polemics lie outside the present work, but I can at least set to his credit a very forceful presentation of the difficulties of disguise in the Eucharist. If we depend on human testimony for the transmission of religious belief over the centuries, and if this testimony relies ultimately on the senses, how can we have articles of eucharistic belief that contravene the senses? (Book II, chap. 4; Régis 1704: 282). Some readers may find with me a foreshadowing here of Hume's argument against miracles. More could be said, but it is enough here to have mentioned the matter.

refers in it to the *Littera* (that is, to the text of Peter Lombard himself) for one reason for the disguise, and then adds a reason of his own. I first give the reason in Peter's own text, and then the reason added by Aquinas:

Christ gave his flesh and blood to be received under another species, for three reasons... [For the merit of faith]... Again, lest the mind should abhor what the eye would see, since it is not our practice to eat raw flesh and blood. Since then it is not right to chew Christ (*vorari dentibus*), he entrusted flesh and blood to us in a mystery. Thirdly, lest religion be insulted by unbelievers. (4 *Sent*. dist. 11; 430/8)

The reason Aquinas himself adds is not given in the *Summa*. It runs thus:

The use of this sacrament lies in eating... But eating calls for the division of food, brought about by mastication. But no division could be made in the true body of Christ, which is glorified. So there had to be at all events some other appearances, of which the breaking might be made. (In 4 *Sent*. dist. 11, q. 1, art. 1, qua.la 2; 434/19)

And this passage we can fill out with another from the same quaestiuncula. The difficulty is put that our faith in the Eucharist demands that we believe the body of Christ to be eaten there without being damaged; so it would not be horrifying to receive his body, no matter what appearances were there. The reply made is that it would indeed not be horrifying because of revulsion (*ex abominatione*), but it would be because of reverence (*ex devotione*). (In 4 *Sent*. dist. 11, q. 1, art. 1, qu.la 2, obj. 3 and ad 3; 434/17, 437/35.)

Let me begin what I have to say about all this by making it clear that Aquinas never taught that the body of Christ was in any way damaged or broken in the Eucharist. Aquinas is the reputed author of the medieval sequence *Lauda Sion*, and we can go to it for a brief summary of his position:

> *Nulla rei fit scissura,*
> *Signi tantum fit fractura*

More or less:

> What is real there is not broken,
> Breaking is but of the token.

Indeed, in his *Commentary on the Sentences* he puts the objection that readers may well have already been putting themselves – eating human flesh connotes bestial cruelty and lack of respect to whoever is eaten. He replies that the accusation would indeed be warranted if the body of Christ were eaten as bodily food is – torn and comminuted by the teeth. But this does not happen in sacramental eating (In 4 *Sent.* dist. 10, art. 1, obj. 1 and ad 1; 402/7, 404/14).

Aquinas wrote that, and we must not forget he did. The trouble lies once more in *prolongation*: words and images have a life and direction of their own, and can lead us, despite our protests, into areas we do not want to enter. I gave the warning originally about recent appeals in eucharistic theology to the risen state of Christ. I submit that it can be given even more urgently about the way Aquinas has prolonged notions to do with eating and drinking. We saw at the beginning of this section that the essence of the Eucharist is placed by him in 'the consecration of the matter', which is introduced in a way that has only a tenuous connexion with ritual, and turns out in one text to have no necessary link with religion at all. It is rather the categories of transformation – I used the word 'alchemy' – that seem most suited to what he writes. But alchemy is not all; further texts have more to do with dissection and anatomising. Distinctions which, whatever their value, were at least used in abstract settings, are now employed in some quasi-physiological speculations – flesh, blood, muscles, bones, Avicenna and the rest – that move us still further away from ritual, and arouse in us pictures that are unseemly and repellent. And now, in the question he puts as to *why* there should be appearances, the whole confusion I have been blaming between sign and disguise comes back, but comes back in a new and virulent form. The appearances are camouflage, dictated by consideration to us and diplomacy towards unbelievers. But what is being camouflaged here if it is not cannibalism?

Nulla rei fit scissura, signi tantum fit fractura. Precisely – but the real trouble lies before that, lies in how the *res* and the *signum* – the reality and the sign – have been construed by Aquinas. If 'sign' be taken as he has taken 'accidents' or 'appearances' time and again – that is, taken in the sense of disguise – then no repetition of the *Lauda Sion* will be enough for us to escape the destination for which we are bound. Aquinas does, as we have seen, explicitly deny damage to the body of Christ. He denies that his glorified body can be damaged; indeed, he raises in his phrase 'sacramental eating' a theme that must be examined in the next chapter. But for all that, he still makes the appearances into a merciful dispensation of Providence, and can still envisage the mockery of unbelievers if we were to 'eat Our Lord under his own appearances'. What this means, in terms of what the unbelievers would see, is not elaborated, we have only the statement that a glorified body could not be chewed.

If we want details – I hope we do not – the text of Peter Lombard (who seems to think that raw flesh and blood would be involved) shews less inhibition, but least inhibited of all is what we read in a writer senior to Peter, Alger of Liège (+1132). In his *De Sacramentis Corporis et Sanguinis Domini* (Lib II, cap. 3; 180 ML 817–18), Alger rehearses the argument, already old then, which we have found in Peter and in Aquinas, but with a *brio* quite his own. The appearances have to be there, because for men to eat men is regarded as a horrible crime; moreover, it is healthier (*salubrius*) for us to eat Christ in a sacrament than without one. For we cannot receive him dead, as he is immortal; so we should have to receive him alive. Alive as he was before the Crucifixion? But who could swallow down (*deglutire*) a thirty-year-old man? Glorified then? But human beings could not bear the glory. So, by hiding his body in the sacrament, he spares us the inconveniences (*incommoditates*) of horror and splendour alike.

I submit that two things have been achieved in this section. The first is that a substantial gap has been filled in my account of the views of Aquinas on the eucharistic presence. The filling has been disconcerting. We have seen again the natural philosophy we met in the first chapter, and the speculations about presence *per modum substantiae* we met in the third. But we have now seen them used in accounts of what the rite of the Eucharist involves. The embarrassment produced by the account means that yet again the whole scholastic approach has been called into question – but this time not just on abstract grounds like incoherence or confusion. This time, the grounds concern its remoteness from ritual of any sort; and – this has to be said – they concern its fittingness and morality. I have exhibited what I have called 'the shadow of the past'.

And in exhibiting this shadow, I have achieved the second thing. At the end of the preceding section, I had expressed in some questions the unease that has been felt at the newer approaches. Whatever those authors write about the eucharistic presence, will it not need filling out with something in the spirit of the scholastic exposition? Must not the depth and solidity in what Aquinas writes (elements which resemble what is in Trent's decree) be a necessary foundation for it? Must not dissent here imply inadequacy? The questions were first directed at the newer approaches, from which I had expressed my own dissent. But I had myself been talking in terms of signs, and had expressed my intention to elucidate the eucharistic ritual in terms of ritual. Are then the questions not directed to me as well? Indeed they are, but I submit that what we have found in this section gives an answer to them. I have still to give my own account, and when I do it may well fail to satisfy the reader – indeed, one of my contentions is going to be that 'satisfy' is just what such accounts should not do. But I now submit that my account cannot be excluded from the start simply because I reject transubstantiation and charge Aquinas with incoherence. We have now seen something of the shadow of the past, and are to see much more. 'Transubstantiation' and 'Aquinas' have been and are words of power, because they are associated with what has venerable status in the Roman Church. But a scrutiny of their setting reveals a medley of opinions, some of which are grotesque, and some of which I defy any reader not to find revolting. True enough, I fancy that few of my readers, even those acquainted with standard passages in Aquinas about transubstantiation, have ever heard of them. But that was my point in bringing out the texts I have cited: a point important for this section and important for what follows.

The point can be put very simply: we distinguish in our practice between 'Aquinas' and Aquinas. The former is the word of power and status; but it denotes a filtered and domesticated version of what was actually written by the latter, not all of which lives on in memory and speculation. The chronicle of *faits divers* about the resurrection, and the physiological speculations, are just as remote from us as are the things we have met in Peter Lombard and in Alger. What has made them so? We have seen something of the relations between past and present – clearly, we shall have to see a good deal more, and not just in a eucharistic context; time is part and parcel of what we make of things. These are topics that lie ahead, just as there lies ahead the exposition of my own approach in terms of ritual. I shall not be claiming anything exhaustive for it, and I can well imagine readers finding it to be defective. Such is life; we know in part and we prophesy in part. Only, please – so did those who went before us.

CHAPTER 5

Eucharistic proclamation

26 ACQUISITIONS AND AGENDA

I have claimed that older and newer accounts alike of the eucharistic presence divorce appearance from reality. I have claimed that something else is needed, but that no account can ignore the historical setting of inherited language, or the forces and tendencies that language harbours. And I have claimed that we need to pass from talk in terms of disguises to talk in terms of signs, if we are not to fall back into the confusions common to all the accounts we have met.

These claims I have made in succession over the four preceding chapters, but the sequence has been offset by other themes running through all we have seen so far. The themes are going to occupy us in what follows, so I set them down here, grouping them under three headings.

1. *Ritual and belief.* I gave a Latin title to one of the sections in the preceding chapter. *Ritus servandus*, 'Ritual to be followed', expressed my dissatisfaction with the accounts I had been examining – neither older nor newer did justice to the Eucharist as a shared and inherited ritual. The scholastic texts of the first chapter used a quasi-physical terminology, and its remoteness from ritual appeared again in the curious speculations at the end of the fourth chapter. The more recent texts given in the second chapter used categories of naming and giving that seemed only accidentally linked with the ritual they were meant to elucidate; and the fourth chapter once more shewed where this approach could lead.

My own intention, I claimed, was to elucidate ritual in terms of ritual, but I warned that an approach of this sort to the Eucharist cannot offer the appearance of a comforting definiteness which is provided by accounts – older or newer – in terms of disguise. Ritual itself is not primarily linguistic; language itself contains forces we may not welcome; language is inadequate even to drawing bounds to its inadequacy: we are, as I put it, condemned to an uncomfortable posture if we approach the topic in the way I have suggested. The lack of comfort will become yet more evident in what follows. I shall be able to use good things from older and newer sources alike in what I have to offer; but the balance I must try to hold is not and cannot be easy.

2. *The Present and the Past.* I insisted in the third chapter that we must not refuse to acknowledge the temporal spread of the tradition within which statements have been made about the Eucharist. But just such an acknowledgment had been made from the outset of the book. The scholastic tradition proved complex on closer examination, disciplinary boundaries were seen to change as time elapsed, and by the 'Theaetetus Effect' what we make of the past is shaped by what we do in the present. As for the newer authors, they are writing within a tradition where the past is for them, as I put it, 'both revered and unsatisfactory'. The tension between present and past we are going to meet in several forms, both by seeing how mixed the past here is, and by seeing something of how the mixture is treated in the present. But this theme of 'Present and Past' will also concern us in contexts wider than eucharistic, as the last of the three themes will shew.

3. *Corpus mysticum.* That is, 'mystical body'. I have chosen this phrase – indeed, have made it the title of the final chapter – because of the two meanings it has had. Up to about 1050 AD, the phrases *corpus Christi* ('the body of Christ') or *dominicum corpus* ('the Lord's body') meant the Church, while the Eucharist was described as *corpus mysticum* ('the mystical body'), and those who shared in it were said to receive *sacramentum dominici corporis* ('the sacrament of the Lord's body'). Then usage began to change: eventually the adjective *mysticum* was dropped for the Eucharist, and the term *corpus mysticum* became a way of referring to the unity of the faithful in Christ. The details of the shift can be seen in Lubac 1949, which has deservedly become a classic. And so the phrase can serve to name the third theme I mention: the link between what I am claiming about the eucharistic presence and what I am claiming about the Church. Once more, the link has been there from the start. I have made charges and to spare against the doctrine of transubstantiation, but I am obliged to admit that it has been regarded as a test case for membership of the Church of Rome – which is why I began the first chapter with Ruskin's

gaucheries on the subject towards a French girl, and with the Royal Declaration against it. Both my preoccupation with past and present, and my concern for the relation between ritual and belief, have been exhibited in the setting of the inherited life of the Roman Church. What am I to make – what have I already made – of that setting? The scholastic tradition we met in the first chapter has played a dominant part in the setting, whether in the use by Trent of phrases and concepts to be found in Aquinas, or in the activities of preaching and instruction there. But we have come to see just how mixed that tradition is. Just what *is* being invoked when we make an appeal to Trent? One objection of the Inquisition to a formulary agreed by Roman Catholics and Anglicans was that justice was not done there to transubstantiation, the wondrous and unique conversion of which Trent spoke (p. 2). But just what *is* it that has not had justice done to it? If we accept the Inquisition's remark, how much are we supposed to accept of what we have so far seen in the older tradition?

I am obliged to pursue the theme of *corpus mysticum* because of my attempt to elucidate the Eucharist in ritual terms. The rite signifies the unity of those who share it: so I cannot hold that the suggestions I make about the Eucharist are indifferent to the Church within which the Eucharist is celebrated. In particular, I am obliged to consider the far-reaching ritual changes there have been over the last quarter of a century in the Church of Rome. The older and newer rites of the Mass; the older and newer accounts of the eucharistic presence; the older and newer styles in what can be seen in the Church: how are all these connected? At the start of the third chapter, I wrote of the unhappiness of Julien Green at a preacher's scepticism over a biblical narrative. We shall see that his unhappiness is an unhappiness shared by others: ritual innovations and reservations over stories in the Gospel are seen as symptoms of a dissolution of so much that was ancient, firm and precious in a uniquely enduring Church. Yet it is just as true that for others there is unhappiness of a different sort. They saw the changes in ritual as part of a spirit of renewal and life brought by the Second Vatican Council. But the promise of those days has not yielded the fulfilment for which they had hoped, and things seem to them to have slipped back to their old ways. Whatever side in present disagreements we take, we have to agree that there is unhappiness. And the unhappiness points to the need for an examination in some detail. We can hardly be content with saying something like 'the rite and the accounts and the

Church have remained substantially the same, although some of the accidents are different'. We have seen far too much of substance and accidents to be able to accept anything as brief as that. We shall need to set about seeing something, in concrete terms, of how ritual and belief are connected, and how past and present are related in them. We shall have to extend to the Church the kind of questions we have been putting about the Eucharist. We must, in both settings, be prepared to encounter topics like insulation, the shadow of the past, and what I pointed to when I distinguished between 'Aquinas' and Aquinas. I have divided themes met so far into three groups, and in doing so I pointed out that they had run through all the previous chapters. They will run through what follows as well, and we shall find that the three groups will not be kept apart.

27   I BLUSH, THEREFORE I AM

A past that is revered shewed itself to be unsatisfactory with peculiar force in the final section of the preceding chapter. Not only was the account offered by Aquinas alien to a shared and communal ritual; it proved all too willing to talk in physiological terms of an eating of Christ camouflaged by prudence and tact. The words he used – still more, the words others used – have dark associations, and embodied the shadow of the past in eucharistic belief. These darknesses are absent from the accounts recently offered in terms of presence, giving and naming. In them we are emancipated, brought out into the light, released from embarrassment.

But ought we to be emancipated? If the older account has to be kept clear of cannibalism, have not the newer accounts to be kept clear of banality? The tea-and-a-biscuit, the old bricks for the new bridge, the presence in our affections of a distant friend, the coaster serving as an ash-tray – none of the authors we have seen regards these analogies as adequate, but do not these words also leave us with unwelcome associations and resonances? Is not a mystery in danger of being eliminated in favour of what is pedestrian? I have called this section 'I blush, therefore I am' because I think embarrassment is something that cannot and should not be eliminated in these matters: embarrassment is the best starting-point for trying to understand them. At the same time, I stand by my observations on what I have called 'the shadow of the past'. It is understandable that those bizarre texts from Aquinas should have been forgotten, that

'Aquinas' should not be Aquinas here, but the forgetting does not mend the system of thought that led to their being written in the first place. The position I am trying to maintain attempts to hold to the need for embarrassment, without going along with speculations that have led to the grotesques we have encountered. As I warned, the balance is uneasy; I must try to spell out more of what I hold here. And I begin by looking beyond the topic of the eucharistic presence to a theme which can produce still greater embarrassments. It is a theme that is not confined to debates within the Church of Rome, and I go for an example of it to Dr Johnson.

On 3 June 1781, he dictated at Boswell's request some thoughts on original sin and on the atonement. Concerning the first he found no problem, in that human corruption (whatever be its cause) is all too evident. But concerning the second he spoke at some length, and I abbreviate his remarks. Vicarious punishment as such may raise difficulties, but the universal practice of sacrifice shows that mankind has always accepted the propriety of punishment. God needed to make known his utter detestation of moral evil. At the same time the purpose of punishment is to propagate virtue by warnings rather than to exact vengeance for crimes committed. The divine justice and its detestation of evil were therefore best shown in that 'it was necessary for the highest and purest nature, even for DIVINITY itself, to pacify the demands of vengeance, by a painful death; of which the natural effect will be, that when justice is appeased, there is a proper place for the exercise of mercy'. To which statement it is proper to add that Johnson on his death-bed recommended the sermons of the reputedly Arian Samuel Clarke (+ 1729), 'because he is fullest on the propitiatory sacrifice'.

Catholic and Protestant disagreed over the Eucharist at the time of the Reformation, but both sides agreed that what Christ did upon Calvary was a sacrifice or propitiation; indeed, much Protestant dissent was due to the belief that what was being said of the Mass compromised what ought to be said of the cross. The exegesis of texts in the New Testament touching the redemptive work of Christ does not concern me here, it is enough that doctrines I have in mind were long read into them. The doctrines do concern me, for they constitute the wider setting for the Eucharist and for disagreements about it. And just as the setting is wider, so its embarrassments go deeper. At the risk of appearing to reduce complexities to absurd over-simplifications, I want to state and to reflect upon some examples of what has been said over the centuries about Christ's saving work.[1] There is and could be no question of giving adequate descriptions, I seek rather to exhibit what I would call the varieties of embarrassment in some accounts of this wider theme. To reflect on the varieties will, I hope, lead us to an appreciation of how mixed a past there is here too; and so lead us also to a better understanding of the place of embarrassment in our own eucharistic topic.

I begin with the *Catechetical Address* of Gregory of Nyssa (+395), because he gives clear expression to the view, found also in other patristic writings, that Christ's work lay in a deceptive inducing of the devil to overreach himself. Man is changeable by nature, had been deceived by the devil and was now his legitimate slave – he could not justly be set free by violence, but needed to be bought back. This was achieved by Christ, whose human nature was the bait concealing his divinity. The devil overreached himself in his turn when he seized Christ, thinking it is a good bargain to exchange the human race for him. Life thus dwelt in death and we are released. (The course of the argument is in chapters 21 to 24 of the *Address*: 45 MG 57–65.)

I set beside what Gregory wrote the line of thought in the work on the Blessed Trinity by Augustine of Hippo (+430), whose writings on grace and redemption were to affect Latin theology so deeply. Here too we have a rescue from diabolic power, but also a stress upon balance and equity. In Book IV, Augustine had written of the way in which a knowledge of our weakness can help us, can make us seek – even amid things that change – eternity and happiness (*De Trinitate* IV 1; 42 ML 887). In Book XIII, the pattern of our redemption by divine love is shewn. There was 'a certain justice' in our being made over to the Devil by original sin, a sin inherited by all descendants of Adam who are sexually procreated. The devil, like all the wicked, lusts for power; it was therefore not by power but rather by justice that he should be overcome. And so it came to pass: the devil kills the virginally conceived Christ, sinless though he was, and so not in his debt; and so those who were indeed the Devil's debtors were released (XIII 10–18; 42 ML 1024–32). Notice that Augustine still writes as Gregory did about human changeability and the quest for happiness.

---

[1] When investigating the topic of eucharistic sacrifice in the middle ages, I studied the theme of atonement, and only a fragment of the result appeared in FitzPatrick 1991a. To what I accumulated then I have returned for this part of the chapter, but I gladly acknowledge again here the guidance I found in Rashdall 1920 and Rivière 1909, for the investigation of older sources.

Notice too that he still displays the theme of deception towards the devil that Gregory used. Indeed, in a sermon on the Ascension he refers to the cross as a mouse-trap and to the Lord's death as the bait (38 ML 1210).

Considerations of equity were to be developed in the dialogue *Cur Deus Homo?* ('Why did God become man?') of Anselm of Canterbury (+1109). Anselm denies any rights to the devil over fallen man, and so abandons the language of overreaching and deception. He elaborates instead a dialectic of offence and justice. God made us for happiness; the debt of honour we owe him we failed to pay; so a recompense over and above the debt is due to him. God's justice demands that it be paid; man in his fallen state cannot pay it; God alone can satisfy, man must; so satisfaction is given by God made man. Christ surrenders his life as something not already owed to God; and the recompense now owed by the Father to the Son is given to those for whose salvation he became a man. (The *Cur Deus Homo* is found at 158 ML 359f., and its economy and verve won it great popularity. The line of argument I have summarised can be found in I 10–23 and II 7–19.) The apparent tightness of the deduction makes all the more welcome a question put by Anselm's interlocutor in the dialogue: why does not God live up to what he commands about forgiveness in the Lord's Prayer (I 12)? The salutary jolt encourages reflexion on the accounts so far given.

If we press the older exposition, we seem to be committed to a celestial war-game embarrassing in its details. On the other hand, its very picturesqueness may discourage us from taking details over-seriously, and its general pattern can suggest how Christ was exposed to the full onslaught of evil, and met the onslaught with something different in kind. Anselm's account does not embarrass us by picturesqueness, while its talk of justice and equity links it with things we recognise in other settings. But now even greater embarrassments await us. Anselm's calculus of affronted honour and exacted debt seems to exchange the older dualism of God and devil for a dualism of obligation – as Jove was subject to the Fates, so is God bound by the demands of justice. And if we seek to avoid the dualism by placing the demands within God himself, our embarrassment is even worse: the Father now seems to be assuming the rôle once played by the devil. It is not surprising that, in the generation after Anselm, an account was offered which sought to remove these embarrassments altogether.

Abelard (+1142), in his commentary on the Epistle to the
Romans, shared Anselm's rejection of the older notion that the devil
has rights over us – we could not hand over such rights in the first
place, he is no more than our gaoler. But Abelard goes on to reject as
cruel the idea that Christ's death was pleasing to God: the purpose
rather of the incarnation and of the cross is to give us an example that
binds us in love (the second book of his commentary contains much
on this theme; I found material at 178 ML 834f.). I interpose at once
an admission. I have never been able to understand why Abelard's
account (whatever be thought of it) should be taken as putting an
end to earlier embarrassments. Surely talking in terms of example
only pushes the question further back – why was such an example
deemed necessary? Example given is indeed part of the story, and
later on Aquinas incorporated such 'Abelardian' considerations into
his own account, but the embarrassment is not eliminated, it is only
postponed. But there is a response to Abelard that I want to notice,
because it will lead us to the next stage in our reflexions.

The response is not that of Abelard's best-known adversary,
Bernard of Clairvaux (+1153) in his *De erroribus Abaelardi*.
For Bernard, Abelard would have Christ only teach justice, not give
it by the redemptive shedding of his blood. To the charge of cruelty,
Bernard replies that what pleased the Father was the will of him
who freely died, not the death itself. The Father did not demand that
blood, but accepted it when offered; in the blood there was more
than an exhibiting of love, there was salvation itself. (*De erroribus
Abaelardi* v, 182 ML 1063, gives a good sample of Bernard's objections,
and of the objectionable language of that objectionable man.) What
is much more interesting, and much more temperately expressed, is
an estimate of Abelard by a former pupil, Gaufridus of Clairvaux,
a successor to Bernard as abbot there. In an Easter sermon, Gaufridus
explained the differences between the two by going to what is written
in Exodus xii about eating the Passover Lamb. *Caput cum pedibus et
intestinis vorabitis* runs the Latin: 'ye shall eat its head, with its feet and
entrails'. Abelard, he comments, commanded us to eat the feet and
the entrails (Christ's example in doing good is in dying for us); it was
Bernard who added the commandment to eat the head, thus
acknowledging that human redemption was accomplished in Christ,
and was more than a matter of example (180 ML 331–2).

I must ask the reader to be patient while I give my reasons for
finding the remark of Gaufridus an excellent introduction to what

follows. Notice first that there is *no arguing* about it: he simply offers two pictures, and invites us to agree that Abelard is not so much positively wrong as inadequate. Notice next that the two pictures are of *eating*, itself a pre-argumentative activity concerned with the sustenance of a mortal body: we are being invited to see human life in its fullness, a physical life shared with other living creatures on Earth. Notice now that *another living creature has been slain* to provide the food, food which has also been subjected to the human process of *cooking*: if we share the Earth with other living creatures, we have powers and skills that they have not, and our life can be sustained through a death that we inflict among them and through subsequent practices that they lack. Notice that the sustenance with which the two pictures are concerned is a *sacred meal*, the Passover, for which commands have been given by God; and that Bernard, unlike Abelard, is presented as obeying them to the full: there are *stages* in the process. And now see that both the weakness and the strength of the pictures will teach us something about the various accounts of Christ's redemptive work we have briefly surveyed. I go first to the weakness.

The weakness of what Gaufridus offers lies in the ease with which his pictures can topple over into the undesirable. His adjurations about eating head, feet and entrails arouse associations that are both ludicrous and indigestible – one thinks of the 'cow-pies' relished by Desperate Dan. But this propensity to topple over is just what is noticeable in all the accounts of the atonement we have seen. Gregory of Nyssa gets all too close to a dualistic war-game between God and the devil, and his image of bait and hook is far too persistent for comfort. Augustine, while retaining the imagery of deception (and what *can* his congregation have made of the mouse-trap?), adds considerations of equity and debt. But what measure is being used for them? What support is offered for the account of original sin as coterminous with sexual descent from Adam? The pictures are of book-keeping and of a cosmic drama, but neither one nor the other has any rules to keep it in check, and both are vivid enough to assume an unwelcome life of their own. Vividness is even more of a trouble in what Anselm writes, and in the way I suggested earlier – his calculus of offence and recompense seems to call in its apparent water-tightness for a change of rôles between the devil and the Father. The crudity of tricking the devil has been avoided – but only as the cost of a repellent scenario of tit-for-tat.

Let us retain this lesson from the weakness of what Gaufridus writes: any of the accounts of the redemption can lead to what we do not want, just as Gaufridus' pictures of eating the Passover can; all have the tendency to be *prolonged*, to take on an independent life, to develop. How the tendency is to be restrained we have yet to see, although we might notice at once that picturesquenesses like baits and mouse-traps, and the details of Anselm's calculus, seem to have dropped out of the minds of Christians today. I turn to what is more important here and now: the strength in what we have been examining in Gaufridus and in the others. And this calls for a longer journey, because it touches the whole human condition and the needs of us all as human beings. There are texts and to spare on the point in the Bible, but I prefer to go elsewhere; the witness, by its very difference in origin, should be all the stronger. I have described myself as a Greek come up to worship at the Feast; I go to Greece for my witnesses.

'It is a strange picture that you offer, and the prisoners are strange!' So exclaims a listener when Socrates utters the parable of the cave: the underground prison; the prisoners chained and shackled; their gazing at the shadows on the wall in front of them, cast by puppets held up between them and the light of a distant fire; the guesses made by them at what will appear next on the wall; their utter unawareness that what they see is no more than shadows and illusion. The picture and the prisoners are indeed strange – *atopos* is the word Plato uses (*Republic* VII), 'out of place' or 'uncanny'. But, Socrates answers, 'they are like us'. We are all *atopoi*, unaware of the deceptiveness in our state of life. If we are reasoning beings – and the whole force of what Plato writes is to insist that we are – we are also strange and deluded prisoners. Release is difficult: the parable goes on to speak of a prisoner who is unchained, of the agony and bewilderment he undergoes when turned round and forced to gaze at the fire, and of the still greater agony when he is dragged up to the surface into daylight. No release is permanent – the description of the cave begins by saying that it is 'open all the way along at the top': it is always possible to fall back. And when the released prisoner returns, he meets with incredulity and a desire to kill him.

'All human beings by nature reach out for knowledge.' So declares Plato's pupil Aristotle at the start of his *Metaphysics*, and he goes on to shew how knowledge can be relished for its own sake, and how it is distinguished by generality and depth. But he than asks whether anything so exalted is not beyond what is human, and whether in consequence it can be sought by us: would not the gods be jealous, and have we not a *doulé physis*, a nature enslaved, and in many ways? The first question he dismisses as a poetic fiction, but over the second he remains silent. As we shall see, he is well aware of its force.

'Mighty things there are many; but none more mighty than man.' So sings the Chorus in Sophocles' *Antigone*. *Deinos*, which I render as 'mighty', has connotations of wonder and dread, and the Chorus goes on to give examples: the conquering of distance and the seasons by travel; the cultivation of crops and the domination of other animals; speech and reason; the foundation of cities. All-devising, man is at a loss for nothing that may befall; from death alone will he devise no refuge. But the Chorus ends by stating that his gifts can be used for good and evil alike, and the play itself spells out what the gifts mean for the city of Thebes. Death is ineluctable; marriage has been contaminated; a father has cursed his sons; brother has killed brother; a sister's faithfulness runs against what the city's ruler has decreed, and she has gone to her death; the end is a sorrow that cannot be mended.

The examples are ancient but what they point to we find throughout human history. There are outrages done in the service of greed, of power, of beliefs. There are hopes that come to nothing and there are lives that are broken. We all know, in settings less dramatic and more familiar, things that tell the same story. Our very strengths can breed weaknesses; habits constrict as well as support; we are selective in our endeavours; time builds up only to take away; death puts an end to all our devisings, even to our acceptance of it. And death exhibits what is both *deinon* and *atopon* – mighty and out of place – in what we are. Our hopes and desires are ever new; 'nature' for us is an exercise, not a fixed formula for a limited range of action as it is for the other animals. It is because we are unlike them that we lack the inbuilt safety devices which could limit the damage we can do. What is *deinon* in us exposes us to temptations that are simply different in kind from the fenced-in desires and aggressions of the other things that share the Earth. We know we shall die, and we have striven and hoped and seen so much when we come to die, that our death can be an affront in a way that theirs cannot be. But it is also an affront in that the life which is to end includes all too much of the *atopon*, the out of place, that is in each one of us.

The Greeks are often charged with thinking too much in terms of securing knowledge, and too little in terms of wrong knowingly done. The texts I have offered may serve as a corrective. At all events, Aristotle shows an awareness of just how much is demanded of us if we are to live as we ought. Much of his *Nicomachean Ethics* depicts right conduct in terms of a mean between excess and defect: we judge rightly in practical matters when we hold the balance between, say, stinginess and prodigality. But later in the work, the picture of holding a balance is replaced by something more demanding. The happiness that is perfect, he writes, will be an activity according to what is best in us, which is either divine itself or the most divine thing about us. To live according to this activity is to live in a way that is beyond what is properly human. Having said that, Aristotle moves to a language of unaccustomed urgency:

There are those who tell us that we are human, and so should think things that are human too; that we are mortal, and so should have thoughts that are of what is mortal as well. But to such advice we should not listen. Rather we should, as far as is open to us, strive to be immortal, and do everything in our power to live according to what in us is highest... It would seem that this highest thing is what each of us really *is*. (Book x, chap. 7)

The image of the prisoners is strange, but they are like us. Our nature, seeking for knowledge, is in many ways enslaved. Among all creatures on Earth, man is most mighty, but the strength in him can easily be turned to ill. He is doomed to undergo the extinguishing of death, but he must strive as he may to be immortal, going beyond any holding of a balance between excess and defect. Such witnesses from Athens can easily be supplemented with others from Jerusalem: think of the text that declares the heart to be deceitful above all things and desperately wicked (Jer. xvii 9). The prophet goes on to ask who can know it – and receives the answer that the heart is searched by the Lord. The whole project of construing virtue in terms of knowledge is seen as inadequate, for there is far more to be known than we like to think, including how much our very sight is darkened. 'I blush, therefore I am': embarrassment should not surprise us if we are concerned with what matters most and goes deepest, embarrassment is a sign that we are facing up to the full reality of our condition. If we take that reality as our starting-point, we can come to some better understanding of what the accounts of Christ's redemptive work have, for all their oddities, been rightly anxious to preserve; and so come to some better understanding of the eucharistic ritual, which is a sign of that work.

28 THE PLACE OF SACRIFICE

> Our Lord and Saviour Jesus Christ, saving his people from their
> sins as the Angel promised, shewed us in himself the way of truth,
> by which we might attain to the happiness of undying life in the
> resurrection.

With these words Aquinas begins the third part of his *Summa
Theologiae*, and he goes on to state the plan of that part: first, the
Saviour himself, beginning with the mystery of the incarnation and
proceeding to the events of Christ's life, death and resurrection;
second, his sacraments, the means of our salvation; third and last, the
destiny of immortal life which, in the resurrection, we reach through
him. The passage I have just given expresses the larger context of the
eucharistic texts I have been citing. I wrote at the end of the
preceding section that facing the reality of our condition is the first
step towards a better understanding of what has been said of the
redemption and of the Eucharist. It is in the very setting of that
condition – our *doulé physis*, our nature in so many ways enslaved –
that Christ's work for us needs to be seen. 'He shall save his people
from their sins': Aquinas goes back to the mystery of the Word made
flesh, to Gabriel's words addressed to Mary at Nazareth. Christ
shewed us the way of truth: we are to face reality, face what is most
true and follow it. But there is more to the facing than learning about
a model for imitation, because we are concerned with a way that lies
beyond what human endeavour alone can reach. From death we can
devise no refuge, but now the way of truth lies in Christ himself, a way
by which we are to attain in the resurrection the happiness of a life
that is undying. Our whole selves are to be restored and transfigured;
we are to be released from illusion and shadows; our *doulé physis* is to
be set free. 'Because I live, ye shall live also'; whatever we say about
the redemption and the Eucharist, we must say it in the setting of the
life that Christ shares with us, where he is the vine and we are the
branches.

But we know that following him means taking up the cross;
whosoever shall lose his life for Christ's sake shall find it. This call too
we are to place within the setting of what he himself did. He faced the
reality of things, and the facing cost him all that he had. The nature
of death is such as to elude at the last whatever provisions we might
devise, for it ends all our devisings. We are left with nothing to grasp,
no object of wit or of foresight. So it was for Christ: the sight of his

mother and his few friends; the words of the thief; even the torment of his own pain – a time came when they were to be his no longer. In giving his life, he had to give everything to which our language can put a name. Death he taketh all away, and with a desolation aimed at the very heart and soul of those who have to go into the dark. 'My God, my God, why hast thou forsaken me?' Those words were no pretence, they were as real as the death that was closing in at that moment.

The light shineth in the darkness, and the darkness did not grasp it – where 'grasp' (John has *katélaben*) could also be 'understand' or 'overcome'. Light and darkness are set one against the other, not just by way of contrast, but by way of content. The life is the light of men, and life is what came to be through the Word, the *Logos* – light goes with creation, with life, with eternal thought and utterance. The darkness, on the contrary, is incapable of anything beyond incomprehension and failure. If Christ is the light of the world, then in him will be displayed the absoluteness of the contrast between good and evil, between the life-giving light and the darkness that cannot seize it. The contrast must go beyond any terms drawn from knowledge or the lack thereof: evil will indeed have ignorance and deception as characteristics, but it goes deeper into us than they do, the bondage of our *doulé physis* reaches our very hearts. The happiness of the risen life achieved for us by Christ calls for a resurrection, a restoration and transfiguration of what we are. Just so, it calls for a confrontation that is supremely real, between the love of God and mankind's need for release from the power of evil and of death. And the reality of the confrontation is shewn in the concrete reality of Christ's passion, death and resurrection.

I submitted in the preceding section that embarrassment in matters to do with Christ's redemptive work is not surprising, and I also gave examples of how various accounts of the work can lead to consequences that are not desired. The Eucharist is a sign of that work, so embarrassment can be expected here too; it is my submission that a right acknowledgment of the embarrassment is the starting-point for what we should say of the eucharistic presence. In the previous section, after shewing weaknesses in the various accounts of the redemption, I turned to shewing their strengths. I promised that this would be a much longer job, and so it has proved – we are not through with it yet. I began it by adducing witnesses to what is dark in the human condition. I have gone on to exhibit the saving work of

Christ as a confrontation with that darkness, and as a calling of us to a life of happiness lying beyond what our own condition can achieve. My next step must be to consider more of the embarrassment that is associated with the accounts of what Christ has done, and in particular with the description of what he has done in the terms of satisfaction and of sacrifice. Once more, it is embarrassment that points the way we should go.

I gave in the preceding section Dr Johnson's account of Christ's propitiatory sacrifice. I now give an objection against such accounts, made in 1859 by the nineteenth-century churchman Benjamin Jowett, then Master of Balliol, in an essay forming part of a commentary on the Epistle to the Romans:

The doctrine of the Atonement has often been explained in a way at which our moral feelings revolt. God is represented as angry with us for what we never did; He is ready to inflict a disproportionate punishment upon us for what we are; He is satisfied by the suffering of His Son in our stead... The death of Christ is also explained by the analogy of the ancient rite of sacrifice. He is a victim laid on the altar to appease the wrath of God.[2]

As I have put it less elegantly, accounts of Christ's work in terms of a calculus of satisfaction present us with a repellent scenario of tit-for-tat. I now notice that some recent writers on the redemption have themselves turned away from what Jowett denounced. A few examples will suffice. Sykes notices the movement of some testimonies to Christian belief towards 'a morally monstrous saga in which God engineers human salvation by the ritual slaughter of his own Son' (Sykes 1980: 74; he denies, of course, that Christian belief is committed to such a view). More than one writer dwells on the text 'God was in Christ, reconciling the world with himself' (2 Cor. v 19), which lacks the opposition between Father and Son suggested by texts like 'The redemption that is in Christ Jesus, whom God hath set forth to be a propitiation through faith by his blood, to declare his righteousness' (Rom. iii 25) – an opposition suggested too in the accounts offered by Augustine and Anselm. Rather, it is the unity of

---

[2] I have taken this text from p. 209 of the anthology of his theological writings made by his biographer Lewis Campbell (Jowett 1906). Campbell reprints the text of the second edition (1859) of Jowett's commentary on some Epistles of St Paul. The first edition contains material omitted in the second, including this sentence: 'No slave's mind was ever reduced so low as to justify the most disproportionate severity inflicted on himself: neither has God so made his creatures that they will lie down and die, even beneath the hand of Him who gave them life' (printed in Abbott and Campbell (1897: 1, 234).

the divine purpose that is stressed. For Aulén, the atonement is a divine warfare against evil, and the triumph of Christ (Aulén 1970: 146); for Young, God 'took upon himself the consequences of evil and sin' (Young 1975: 125). It is enough for me here to state that I find these suggestions speaking to my condition, but that I do not find in them an adequate facing of an obvious problem: how have the older accounts, with their oddities and repulsivenesses, come to be accepted for so long among those who reflected upon the work of Christ? My contribution to the discussion takes the form of attempting an answer to the problem. The answer may seem disappointingly inconsistent, because it makes the notion of sacrifice be the clue both to the grotesquenesses in the accounts and to the insights they severally display. I turn to spell out this contention, and I begin with texts from Augustine and Aquinas.

I have pointed out that in Book IV of his treatise on the Trinity, Augustine writes that we are not so cut off from unchanging joy as not to seek – even in changeable things – eternity, truth and happiness; insights are given to us by God that what we seek is not where we are (*De Trinitate* IV 1; 42 ML 887). In Book XIII, before beginning his account of Christ's redeeming work, he writes that the nature of human life makes our desire for happiness involve faith in the eternal possession of a life that is blessed (XIII 11; 42 ML 1025). Augustine here is yet another witness to the paradox of the human condition, with its *deinon* and *atopon*: its powers, its being out of place, its hopes and its closure by death. But witness is also borne in the matter by Aquinas. His treatment in the *Summa* of the virtue of religion contains reflexions upon sacrifice, and to that question I now turn.

He contends that sacrifices are natural, and found everywhere. The defects man feels within himself are the grounds on which he concludes that he should be subject to something above him, by which he can be helped and guided. It is this that is everywhere called God; just as signs of honour are used to earthly superiors, so they are to God, in ways that custom dictates (*ST* 2/2.85.1 and ad 1). God is our origin and the goal of our being made happy, and sacrifices do but express the offering of ourselves to him (*ST* 2/2.85.2). Any good act has something sacrificial about it, in that it shews our desire to share his fellowship (*ST* 2/2.85.3 ad 1); but actions specifically sacrificial are those specifically directed to revering him (*ST* 2/2.85.3). Of these, the chief is the offering of what is good in ourselves (*bonum animae*, literally 'the good of the soul'), such as devotion and prayer; next come martyrdom, mortification etc; and last, the offering of material things – either directly to him or giving them to others in his honour (*ST* 2/2.85.3 ad 2). A distinction can be drawn, he writes, between sacrifice in the strict sense (*sacrificium*) and offering (*oblatio*). The former connotes the doing of something concerning things offered to God: animals were killed, bread is broken and blessed and eaten – by sacrifice, *sacrificium*, man 'makes something holy' (*facit aliquid sacrum*). Offering in its primary sense connotes the giving of something to God, even though nothing be done to it: money or loaves are offered on an altar (*ST* 2/2.85.3 ad 3).

These texts from Augustine and Aquinas all follow the pattern already mentioned, in that they take the defects and aspirations of our condition as the starting-point for movement towards God. What Aquinas goes on to write of sacrifices also falls in with this pattern – they are an acknowledgment of our condition, they are an expression of our hope and of the struggle it involves. Anthropology would welcome the acknowledgment by Aquinas of the variety in sacrificial ritual, and of its shaping by custom. Indeed, it is plain that investigations into sacrifice do not suffer from a scarcity of material but from a confusing superabundance of it. And so, although I venture some remarks upon sacrifice, I offer them tentatively, reserving for a footnote some references to more solid material.[3]

I begin by noticing that when Aquinas gives examples of sacrifice, he leaves the offering of material things until last. 'Any good act' is in a way sacrificial. Among sacrifices properly so called, 'the offering of what is good in ourselves' comes first, with devotion and prayer as examples. Things like the sacrifices of animals come at the end, and are referred to in the past tense: Aquinas has in mind here the ceremonial usages of the Old Testament, and the rites he would have known from pagan authors like Virgil and Livy. The 'sublimation' of the notion of sacrifice, if I may use the word, he would have encountered in biblical texts such as 'I desired mercy, and not sacrifice; and the knowledge of God more than burnt offerings' (Hosea vi 6). In my opinion, this sublimation is just as important in

---

[3] Burkert 1983 I have found rich in information and in profitable suggestion; my use of it in this chapter touches only a few of its themes. For the theme of sacrifice in the Old Testament, de Vaux 1961 gives ample accounts, on sacrifice as well as on all other 'institutions' of Ancient Israel. I add that I have used translations for both these works – the graceful versions by Peter Bing and John McHugh respectively.

its own way as the rites of sacrifice themselves: some Greek reflexions on the rites reached similar conclusions, and I understand that the Persian sage Zoroaster also denounced the taking of life for these purposes. But – again, I write with hesitation on all this topic – the sublimation comes as the result of a process, and that process has for its origin the sacrificial ritual in all its crudity.

I have throughout this chapter been concerned with the place of embarrassment in what is said of our redemption. But embarrassment has been encountered as well in language used of the Eucharist, which is the sign of our redemption. In both settings, I have objected to things we have met – in eucharistic language, to the associations of cannibalism in the scholastic account; in language to do with the redemption, to the scenario of tit-for-tat. These are objections that I stand by. All I want to point out here is that what we have encountered has not been accidentally encountered. Body, blood, food, drink, death – our journey has led us into places where the encounter was inevitable. We have been concerned with more than what we can do and say and resolve of ourselves, we are concerned with the heart of our being and with its enlargement. And this concern is one that, in its immemorial antiquity, finds expression in sacrificial ritual and language.

Gaufridus of Clairvaux, we saw, used the picture of eating the Passover Lamb. When describing his picture, I said that it was concerned with the pre-argumentative activity of eating; that eating itself shewed our bodily dependence on the Earth; that here the sustenance of human life was obtained by taking the life of another creature; and that the taking of the life, the cooking of the meal, and its subsequent consumption, could be made to constitute a ritual action. Following what I understand to be claimed for sacrifice, I place its force in the *ambivalence* it displays, an ambivalence found in Gaufridus' picture. Blood is shed and life is lost – and yet thereby our own lives and possibilities are sustained. Aggression has been necessary – and yet aggression must be contained if we are to survive. We acknowledge our dependence on the Earth and the life it yields – and yet our encounter with it has led to the destruction of life. This pattern of destruction and sustenance repeats itself when sacrifices are made involving agricultural produce – the cycle of burial and rebirth becomes even more palpable, while the preparation of what the Earth has yielded demands its destruction by grinding, pressing, cooking and the rest. The need to consume is endless, yet nourishment cannot ward off death forever; so the sacrificial ritual can express – whether by sharing the meal with the gods, or by some ceremony of initiation – an acknowledgment of dependence and a hope for sharing in what goes beyond the human condition, of which death must be the ending.

I have already warned against imposing a uniform description upon the ancient multiplicities that attend on the notion of sacrifice. Thus, the sacrificial rituals of the time of Christ cannot be reduced without more ado to the primitive descriptions I have given; the temple-ritual was the produce of a lengthy and complicated evolution, and its place in the life of Israel was just as complicated. My purpose in offering the descriptions is to submit that sacrificial language and ritual can go very deep into those who use them, deeper than the users can articulate; and that the nature of sacrificial language and ritual makes them confront us with the fundamental realities of human life – its constrictions, its darkness and its hopes. Christ's redemptive work is presented by Aquinas in the context of the whole process of freeing from sin and of bestowing everlasting life in the resurrection. That is, Aquinas sets down both the acknowledgment of our darkness and our hope of transcending it, so that the language of sacrifice used of Christ's work displays both, in the way I have tried to describe. To go back to the phrase used earlier, the language of sacrifice here is an acknowledgment of our *doulé physis*, our nature held in bondage; but the bondage is acknowledged to be more than illusion and misapprehension, it is a darkness that touches the very heart of our being. And so it is that the ambivalent associations we have seen in sacrifice – body, blood, food, life, death – are united with the light shining in the darkness, with the absolute contrast between good and evil, with the work of the one who promises that, because he lives, we shall live also.

But if the language and ritual of sacrifice bear witness to the bondage in which our nature is held, and to the darkness that is within us, such language and ritual will themselves be touched with that darkness. I wrote earlier of the 'sublimation' of sacrifice found in Aquinas, and referred to the denunciation of temple-sacrifices by the prophets. I called the sublimation a process, I saw it as protracted in time. Here, I submit that the use of sacrificial language about Christ is inevitable, but just as inevitably doomed to topple over into what we do not want. The language brings out, with depth and richness, the holiness of God, the contrast between good and evil and the light and life offered us in our darkness. Anselm's dialectic of offence and reparation bears witness to all this, as does the language of Augustine. But if what the two write is taken at its face-value, we are indeed impelled towards the 'morally monstrous saga' rightly denounced by Sykes and others. Gregory of Nyssa's bait to the devil – even Augustine's mouse-trap, if the reader can take it – bear witness to the divine condescension and love expressed in the Incarnation, to the reality of Christ's surrender of his life and to the ultimate negativity and overreaching in evil. But it is not necessary by now to dwell further upon the results of taking those images as descriptions of some sort of celestial manoeuvres. After all that, Abelard's contention that Christ's work lay in setting us an example may seem refreshingly simple. But his theory still leaves unanswered the question why such an example was necessary, and it fails to acknowledge the depth of the plight of those for whom the example was intended, and the fulness of the hope that is now theirs: example needs placing in the wider content of the salvation Christ came to bring.

'A past both revered and unsatisfactory.' We have come back to the phrase yet again, this time in the context of language used about Christ's saving work. We first met it when examining the attitude of newer authors to older accounts of the eucharistic presence. The phrase points to the tension between present and past, and we shall be meeting the phrase and the tension ever more over the rest of the book. We have an inheritance – scriptural, scholastic, patristic, ecclesial and the rest; the heritage enshrines what we believe to be precious; but if we press any part of it hard (be that part an argument in Aquinas or Anselm, a passage in Augustine, a text of Scripture or a council's decree) we shall end up where we do not want to be. We may talk of holding a balance, but that is little more than optimism; we are concerned with matters that go beyond balances and means – as indeed a text of Aristotle has in its own way already suggested (p. 186). It is nearer the mark to wonder how many conflicting attitudes we can support simultaneously, for our very attempts to utter these things are touched by the darkness in which we live and hope.

Of such attempts, more remains to be said. Here and now, it is the next stage in the chapter to which we must press on. The chapter's argument began with the suggestion that embarrassment is not something to be eliminated in these matters. Rather, I went on to propose, we should start from the embarrassment that goes with our condition as human beings and our hope of salvation. Having dwelt

on the embarrassment in various forms, I passed in the present
section to the way in which Aquinas places the redemptive work of
Christ within the whole setting of the incarnation; and I took, as a
specific example of embarrassment, the use of sacrificial language to
describe his redemptive work. I hope that the investigation has
taught us something about the 'placing' of religious language here,
and why it is that the apparently materialistic imagery of cookery,
eating, death, life, body and blood should play the rôle it does. But
imagery of this sort, and the indispensable awkwardness of sacrificial
language, point to what is involved in an elucidation of the eucharistic
presence in ritual terms.

29   THE WAY OF RITUAL

'Do this in memory of me': Luke's Gospel agrees with Paul's account
in First Corinthians in having Jesus give that command to those who
were eating with him at the Last Supper. The early testimony of
Justin Martyr (*c.* 180 AD), which also records it, shews that the story
was taken then by Christians as including a command to carry out a
ritual eating and drinking. What Aquinas has to say about Christ's
choice of the occasion is worth setting down at the start of this section:

The last things to be said, especially by friends who are about to leave us,
are those that are best remembered. At such a time, our love for our friends
is greatest; and what we love most is what sinks deepest into our hearts.
(*ST* 3.73.5)

We have seen that Aquinas considers the Eucharist and the other
sacraments in the setting of the saving work of Christ, and of the
happiness to be shared by him with us in the resurrection to eternal
life. The darkness and illusion that wait upon our impeded human
nature, our *doulé physis*, are to be mended; we have a promise of
deliverance through the encounter between light and darkness, life
and death.

   That is also the setting for what we have just seen Aquinas write
about the human pathos of Christ's farewell to his friends. 'Only for
a little while am I with you now' (John xiii 33) – the sense of urgency
is there, as the power of darkness is about to be exercised upon him;
the general terms of the opposition between good and evil are about
to be particularised in what he is to undergo. The hope offered of life
and deliverance is now to be achieved, but at a cost. And the ritual

Christ now bequeaths to the disciples he is about to leave comes itself
in the setting of a ritual familiar to them already – the Passover meal,
the commemoration of the ancient preservation and liberation of
God's people. It is in this ritual complexity, inherited from a distant
past, developed by Christ, and enjoined upon those who follow him,
that I see the best way towards an understanding of his eucharistic
presence. The way is of a piece with my earlier claims about the rôle
of what embarrasses, and about the place of sacrifice and of sacrificial
language. I go first to texts of Aquinas about the saving work of
Christ, and about the relation borne to that work by the Eucharist.
I then turn to a series of rituals in whose cumulation, I shall submit,
the eucharistic presence is encountered by us and is in some measure
indicated.

For Aquinas, Christ is our mediator with God, and through his
offering we are reconciled with God and made partakers of the divine
nature; he is in the supreme sense our priest (*ST* 3.22.1). His
priesthood is eternal, for although his offering was made but once, its
power endures for ever, and the glory promised to those who
persevere comes through him (*ST* 3.22.5). The offerings made in the
Old Testament prefigured the offering made by him. In particular,
the offering of bread and wine ascribed to the priest Melchizedek in
Genesis xiv is a type or prefiguring of Christ's priesthood, as is
claimed in Hebrews vii. It is so because it is a type of our sharing in
the sacrifice of Christ; Melchizedek's bread and wine signify (Aquinas
is here following Augustine) the unity of the Church, and that is made
by our sharing in Christ's sacrifice (*ST* 3.22.6). For Aquinas there
is no salvation outside this 'unity of the mystical body', of which the
Eucharist is the sacrament or sign (*ST* 3.73.3). Without faith in the
passion of Christ there can be no salvation, and so there had to be at
all times a representation of that passion. The Passover Lamb was its
chief representation in the Old Testament; in the New, the
representation is the Eucharist, which commemorates the passion,
just as the Passover Lamb prefigured it (*ST* 3.73.5.)

Let us prescind here from asking just what kind of belief Aquinas
thinks is involved in this faith in the saving work of Christ. That
question raises matters to do with what Christians of his day thought
about the possibility of salvation for those not of their faith, and some
light on these things will be given by other texts I shall cite. All that
concerns us here is that the saving work of Christ is seen by Aquinas
as something touching our very being, going far deeper than example

or imitation, lying beyond human endeavour, and offering a destiny past human imagining. Of this saving work the Eucharist is a representation and a commemoration: it is not another sacrifice (*ST* 3.22.3 ad 2); just as what represents someone can be called by his name ('That is Cicero', we say, pointing to a bust), so we can call the Eucharist a sacrifice (*immolatio*) because it represents the passion of Christ, which was a sacrifice. Moreover, we can so call the Eucharist because through it we share in the fruits of the Lord's passion (*ST* 3.83.1). The life of the spirit is of the same pattern as the life of the body, because bodily things have a likeness to spiritual. Bodily life needs both generation and nourishment; to these respectively correspond the sacraments of Baptism and of the Eucharist (*ST* 3.73.1).

Those texts display the Eucharist as representing the saving work of Christ, as a sign of our union with him, as a means of our sharing in what he has done for us, a means that is analogous to bodily nourishment. But there are other texts of Aquinas in which this likeness is spelled out in a way that deserves separate notice: these display the Eucharist as subordinate to something more fundamental, as subordinate to that union with Christ of which it is a sign. I go to a text from the *Commentary on the Sentences* (there are related texts in the *Summa*, such as *ST* 3.80.1, but I do not find them as clear). The text I now translate, lettering its paragraphs for future reference:

(a) Christ is the spiritual food of the elect, not by being turned into others, but by turning to himself those whom he feeds. So to eat Christ spiritually is to be incorporated into him, and this happens through faith and love.

(b) Since Christ in himself is spiritual food, he is signified and contained in sacramental food.

(c) Christ's being spiritual food by nature is prior to his being spiritual food contained in the Sacrament. The reason is that for something to have a property because of its own nature is prior to its having a likeness of that property associated with it by a sign. So not everyone who eats Christ spiritually also eats this Sacrament spiritually. (In 4 *Sent.* dist. 9, art. 2, qu.la 4; 371/68)

Aquinas is concerned here with drawing various distinctions that allow physical reception of the Eucharist to be kept apart from sharing in it with profit. He applies the distinctions to an objection about the Patriarchs of the Old Testament. They had faith and love, and faith and love are the means by which we eat spiritually, being incorporated into Christ: see (a). Yet the Eucharist was not yet instituted in their day. Consequently, they surely cannot be said to have partaken of the Eucharist spiritually – that is, they could not share in it with profit, for it was not there to be shared in (see In 4 *Sent.* dist. 9, art. 2, qu.la 4, obj. 2: 368/43). In his reply to the objection, Aquinas makes the observations under (c) in the text I have cited. 'Eating spiritually', in the sense of having faith and love, is more fundamental than the sacramental eating which signifies it: the patriarchs cannot indeed be said to have eaten the Sacrament spiritually; but they can be said to have eaten Christ spiritually, in the sense of an eating that is simply the union with him by faith and love necessary for salvation (in 4 *Sent.* dist. 9, art. 2, qu.la 4 and ad 2; 372/68–71).

As I promised, this text throws some light upon what Aquinas took for granted about the need for faith in Christ's saving work. We can see that he attributes to the patriarchs an anticipatory belief in the New Testament that we find at odds with our sense of history. But the general drift and force of what he writes is not touched by this. 'Spiritual eating', as described in paragraph (a) of the text, is sharing in the saving work of Christ. That work is the context of all that Aquinas goes on to say about the redemption and the sacraments. 'Eating' here reverses the usual relationship: it is a transformation of ourselves, the eaters, that is brought about. And this transformation has for its object the release and eternal life which will consummate the deliverance Christ came to bring. It is in this consummation in glory that spiritual eating reaches its perfection; at present we have it only imperfectly, as signified in the Eucharist (*ST* 3.79.2). We hope to be united with Christ in glory, through perfect love and clear vision; here, we are united by faith (*ST* 3.80.2). And paragraphs (b) and (c) of the text place the Eucharist with respect to this 'spiritual eating', and bring us back to a text of the *Summa* quoted earlier: the Eucharist is the sign of our unity in Christ, outside which there is no salvation (*ST* 3.73.3). The Eucharist is the goal of all other sacraments, for it is the supreme act of worship (Aquinas refers back here to *ST* 3.63.6). But it is not necessary for salvation that we receive this Sacrament. Spiritual food transforms us to itself, and this transformation can be effected by a longing of the mind for Christ (*ST* 3.73.3 ad 2).

It is this 'spiritual eating' that I take as a guide in approaching the eucharistic presence by way of ritual – the spiritual eating which is the union with Christ by faith and love that is indispensable for salvation, a union that has the Eucharist for its sacramental sign in his present life, and the life everlasting for its consummation. To say that I take this union as my guide means that I place what I write of the eucharistic presence in the setting of what Christ's saving work does for us. But it does not mean that I claim to isolate some concept of eating so general that it can be either 'physical' or 'spiritual'. Such a claim is absurd, because our union with God by faith and love goes beyond what our human language and life can adequately express. We must rather begin by looking at the human activity of eating and at its ritual employment. That is the starting-point of what I call 'the Way of Ritual': the Way is an approach towards the eucharistic presence through ritual's successive stages. The presence cannot be seized by direct description, for both the sacramental sign and that which it signifies exceed the range of what can be properly expressed. Indeed, to write 'looking at the human activity of eating' can mislead, by suggesting that we are able in some way to stand outside the ritual activities I choose as the path, in order to consider their merits and demerits. And this, I have insisted, is what we cannot do. Moreover, the phrase suggests that *looking* is where the clue and direction to the presence are to be found; whereas in my submission it is in the ritual itself of the Eucharist that they lie. Comment and reflexion may be necessary, and obviously are necessary in pieces of writing like this. But they are and must be seen to be subordinate to the ritual with which they are concerned.

The path has been indicated in the preceding section, where sacrificial language about the saving work of Christ was linked with a long tradition. In sacrifice, both the limitations and the capacities of human life were acknowledged and embodied, along with the intertwining of life and death, of violence and its containment, of our dependence upon the Earth and our special place among the other lives the Earth supports. In some forms of sacrifice there was expressed a hope for what goes beyond the cycle of birth and death which sets boundaries to all living and striving. Human life has expressed in a variety of ritual forms the desire for God, the quest for what is not touched by the destructive forces of time and change. Generalisations here are both imprudent and misleading, but I venture to point out a recurrent strangeness in the quest: that which is sought reveals itself as seeking our friendship, as open and almost vulnerable to our love. Here, any form of words will fail to satisfy –

more than that, the words will take on an undesired life of their own, in the way we have already met. But I offer a distinction, based on one borrowed from Plato's *Sophist* (254a), between two sorts of difficulty that language faces in topics like ours. One difficulty is due to darkness and negation, to deceptions that hide themselves in gaps and emptiness. And difficulties of that sort lie deep in the human condition, in ways we have seen: the gulf between promise and fulfilment, the *doulé physis*, the nature held in bondage that is ours. It is in this darkness that we encounter the problem of evil, and our language can do little after a while except halt. But there is another sort of difficulty. Here once more we are at a loss to know what to say, but this time because of abundance of light; we are confronted by excess. Here, I suggest, the problem we face is what I would call 'the problem of interest' – why does the Almighty seek our love? Our perplexity here is not engendered by the darkness of deception, suffering and wrong-doing; rather, it is the dimension of the love and of its calling that embarrasses.[4]

---

[4] Anything anyone writes here misleads, and will recall for others what they find odd in writers like Meister Eckhart and Angelus Silesius. And I find such things odd myself; only I cannot help thinking that the oddities are pointing – although in a curious way – to something of the first importance. I have used the phrase 'the problem of interest'. I fill it out with a poem by Rilke, from his *Vom mönchischen Leben* (Rilke 1955: 31), which some readers will know already. Of such a poem, a translation gives less than a shadow; but I think that even the dream of a shadow puts things better than I can; and so I give that as well. First then Rilke:

> Was wirst du tun, Gott, wenn ich sterbe?
> Ich bin dein Krug (wenn ich zerscherbe?)
> Ich bin dein Trank (wenn ich verderbe?)
> Bin dein Gewand und dein Gewerbe,
> mit mir verlierst du deinen Sinn.
>
> Nach mir hast du kein Haus, darin
> dich Worte, nah und warm, begrüßen.
> Es fällt von deinen müden Füßen
> die Samtsandale, die ich bin.
>
> Dein großer Mantel läßt dich los.
> Dein Blick, den ich mit meiner Wange
> warm, wie mit einem Pfühl, empfange,
> wird kommen, wird mich suchen, lange –
> und legt beim Sonnenuntergange
> sich fremden Steinen in den Schooß.
>
> Was wirst du tun, Gott? Ich bin bange.

And now for the other:

> If I die, God, what will you do?
> If I, your jug, in pieces flew?
> If I, your drink, turned bitter brew?

'I blush, therefore I am': we can now see more clearly why this embarrassment and its acknowledgment have expressed themselves in the rite of a meal. A ritual meal embodies these paradoxes and tensions. The consumption of food displays the incomplete nature of our lives, which need regular replenishment, and yet which will eventually perish, despite all their replenishings. It displays the dependence of our lives upon the Earth and upon what the Earth provides, while at the same time bearing witness to the skills and force which we bring to bear upon the Earth and upon what it supports, in order to prepare the food we need. Among the works of man described by Sophocles in the *Antigone* is agriculture: 'The highest of the Gods, Earth the imperishable and untiring, he vexes with the turning plough, year in year out, with horses.' The obtaining and preparation of food call for an assignment of rôles in the community that is to eat it; and so the meal is a communal acknowledgment of our needs, our abilities, our dependence upon each other, our mutual trust. Given all that, it is natural that a ritual meal should have been linked with the quest for God and with the awareness of God. In a meal we share something pleasant, which expresses both our needs and our achievements; we now make a meal into an occasion where our sharing is with what lacks our weaknesses, surpasses the reach of any skills we can possess, and yet for all that is open to and desirous of our friendship. Just as the sharing of a meal is at the heart of a shared human life, so we make this special sharing into a means of uniting those who eat, uniting them with what is greater than any life with which they are acquainted.

Generalisations, I have suggested, are foolish in matters like these: that much at least I have gathered from sources written by those

I am your robe, your practice too;
My loss will all your sense deny.

With me not here, you've no house by,
Where close and gentle words may greet.
There fall from off your weary feet
The velvet sandals that am I.

Your ample cloak away is torn.
Your glance, that on my cheek now laid
I keep so warm and soft arrayed,
Will come, will seek me, and, delayed,
Will when the sun goes down be made
On alien stones to rest forlorn.

What will you do, God? I'm afraid.

more competent here than I am. As I pass to the next stage, the specific instance of a sacrifice and ritual meal that is the Passover, I feel on firmer ground – if only because reflexion on its specific setting and details will serve to keep apart the rite itself from any attempts at reducing it to something else. We cannot call the Passover a repetition of the rescue from Egypt: the point of the ritual would be lost if the rescue turned out to need achieving all over again. Nor can we make the Passover into a simple recollection of the rescue, for that would not distinguish it from activities like reading appropriate passages in the book of Exodus. We must rather learn to *look* at the rite for what it is, and not attempt to reduce it to an ornamental flourish on a text which already says all that matters. The rite is inherited, handed down and commanded to be carried out each year. The command came from the Lord, the same Lord who gives bread to eat and life to all creatures on earth, and who set our forefathers free. By their freedom, we are alive to eat the meal ourselves. Just as it was the Lamb's blood on their door-posts that marked them off as a people protected by the Lord, so their privileges are ours, their meal is ours also; we are one people with them, the people the Lord has chosen as his own. The present tense in this brings out what I have claimed already for this 'Way of Ritual': it is the rite itself that is and must be what is primary; comment and reflexion must lead towards it, not develop a life and direction of their own. And this claim I repeat for what I now want to say about the next stage on the Way, the Last Supper.

What I have called 'the problem of interest' is heightened in the mystery of the incarnation. We saw that Aquinas gave first place to the love and promise of eternal life in the Word made flesh, so that all that follows in the third part of the *Summa* – redemption, sacraments and the rest – must be seen in the setting of that love. Just so, the involvement in our world of the Word made flesh displays the tension between the transcendence of God's love over anything we could achieve of ourselves, and the historical and material particularity of his sharing his life and love with us through Christ. 'Born of a woman, born under the Law', Christ takes the rite which he and his friends have inherited, and goes beyond it in a way that only he can. The old Passover ritual, by which the saving and liberating power of God was remembered and embodied and shared, is now transformed; the new age of the deeper rescue is inaugurated by a sharing in something greater. He and his disciples had come to know each other in many ways during their time together. One of these ways was the sharing of meals in the ordinary course of life, with all life's hopes, joys and disappointments. For them, such sharings were the setting and the preparation for sharing in Passover rituals, the ritual in which they shewed themselves to be part of the people whose very existence as a nation was due to God's liberating call. But, just as the Passover ritual both embodies and transcends their ordinary meals, so did this Last Passover they shared with Christ both embody and transcend the Passover meals which they, like their ancestors, had shared over the years.

The ritual associated with the meal, and with the liberation that followed – the lamb, the unleavened bread, the cups of wine, the blood put on the door-posts or sprinkled over the people in the Sinaitic covenant – all that was the means Christ both used and surpassed in what he instituted at the Last Supper. The ritual language of the Passover, already taking up and transcending the day-to-day significance of eating, is put to a new use by the Word made flesh, and now proclaims his death for our salvation. He gives the Passover bread to his disciples – they are to eat, it is himself, the Lamb of the new Passover, given up for them. He gives the cup to them, as the Passover ritual prescribed – they are to share it, for it is his blood shed for them, and sealing the new Covenant, greater than that of Sinai long ago, between God and his people. They are to do these things in memory of him – so he commands, in the last hours before his arrest and condemnation. For those who first passed on this rite, he was the Risen Lord, the first to break the power of death and to enter into the freedom promised to them through what he had done. And, in passing on the rite, they were to shew forth his death until he returns in glory.

This is the Way of Ritual along which we must proceed, because it is only by doing justice to the successive ritual settings of what Christ said that we shall do justice to his eucharistic presence. The Way leads us towards what lies beyond anything human activity could achieve of itself, or human words express; but the Way uses and respects the place of ritual in human life, it does not commit the Fallacy of Replacement and deny the nature of ritual by talking in terms of appearances, or by denying the meaning of the words that we use. We must start from the basic significance that eating has in human life; go on to the associations of a ritual meal; go further still, to the meaning of the ritual of the Passover; and only thus approach the transcending of this ritual by Christ at the Last Supper. By proceeding along this Way of Ritual, we proceed in the direction of the mystery of the eucharistic presence. The Way of Ritual does not eliminate the mystery: on the contrary, it acknowledges the mystery by its very inadequacy. We cannot make the Way of Ritual *explain* the eucharistic presence, as if what Christ instituted could be reduced to a special Passover, or to some other ceremony that enabled us to remember him. Reductive accounts of the Eucharist are always attractive, because they are couched in terms of what we ourselves can provide; they can never satisfy, because we are faced here with what only God's love can provide. Newer accounts of the Eucharist are sometimes blamed for reductivism; it is worth recalling that the older account is in its way reductivist too. It conceives of the eucharistic conversion as the admittedly miraculous shuffling of elements which it claims to have distinguished. Mystery is thus reduced to the 'technique' by which substance and accidents are manipulated; better, mystery is reduced to conundrums of our own making. The Way of Ritual I am suggesting is reductivist in neither of these senses. It neither translates the Eucharist into human terms, nor makes it into a divinely induced rearranging of human distinctions that have become dissections. It takes seriously the successive stages of which I have written, and so obliges us to admit that we are concerned here with the saving work of the Word made flesh, and that his presence exceeds anything explicable in terms of memory, fellowship, or devotion. But, because we take the ritual stages seriously, we do not reduce the ritual used by Christ to appearances. What words we do use will have resonances that go far beyond our powers of verbal expression, but we must not therefore deny them their minimal meaning. Once more, what is exalted does not replace what is humble.

In the fourth chapter I found fault with both older and newer theologies of the eucharistic presence, on the ground that they confused signs with disguises. What I have called 'the Way of Ritual' is an attempt to shew how we can use the category of sign here, without falling back either into the language of camouflage that menaces the older account, or into the denial of meanings to words that menaces the newer expositions. A sign is not a disguise; we must respect a sign for what it is; we must respect the reality both of what signifies and of what is signified by it. We must approach the eucharistic presence, not as a concealed presence of Christ linked only extrinsically with ritual, but as a ritually achieved sign of his presence among those with whom he already shares his risen life and the hope of glory. The Way of Ritual, by its succession of stages, exhibits the Eucharist as built on but going beyond what is expressed in human rites and actions, exhibits it as a sign of the saving work of Christ, the light in our darkness.

To reflect on the Way of Ritual will recall for us themes we have already met, and point forward to some we have still to meet.

The language we use of rituals is out of joint by its nature – ritual is not primarily a matter of words, and (here as elsewhere) verbalisation can lead to a self-consciousness that is alien to celebration. But language, like ritual itself, can invite the listener here to join in, can point towards what eludes adequate expression in words. Yet such pointing does not involve denying ordinary words their ordinary meaning. Poetry provides a useful analogy: it allows words to work to the full, in order to suggest what goes beyond them. Thus, Shakespeare's eighteenth sonnet begins with the question 'Shall I compare thee to a summer's day?', and then hunts out the deficiencies of the comparison. It invites us to see in the uncertainty and turn of the seasons an image of the tragic lot of love and youth and beauty, and it presents the challenge that poetry can make to that tragedy. The comparison and its rejection have become both the vehicle for what we want to say about a bondage of our nature, and the means of suggesting what goes beyond our saying. But neither way do we deny the force of the words that we are using. How could we? The poem's power lies in accepting their force and directing it.

The Way of Ritual invites us to set out on a journey towards the rite instituted by Christ. But a journey of the sort cannot consist in denying meaning to the words describing its course, any more than the poem can exercise its force by denying the words that compose it. We must let the stages on the journey keep their significance, we must take seriously the complex associations of the eucharistic rite. We must accept that it is a rite of eating and drinking, that it is bread that is eaten and wine that is drunk; and that this rite has, in the way I have tried to present, been made by Christ into an eating and drinking of his body and blood. The Eucharist is Christ's body given up for us, his blood poured out for many; it is a ritual signification of Christ's saving work and of the unity achieved thereby. A mystery does not suddenly appear when the elements of the Eucharist are considered; the mystery is there as soon as we start thinking about the presence of Christ in the members of his body, by which they are made sharers of the divine nature. An account of the eucharistic presence must begin with this signifying function; it cannot start with the elements used, and go on to seek in them a presence of Christ that is not essentially a matter of sign or ritual at all. It is because ritual and sign are essential that we need to do justice to the reality of what we see and touch, the reality which is ritually used as a means towards the far deeper reality to which we can only gesture. Aquinas, following Augustine, uses the rich and multiple associations of human eating to point towards a transforming union with Christ which is far closer. It is the reality and associations of the starting-point in eating that give content to what follows, and provide the means for suggesting what lies beyond our conceiving. Once more, the humbler creation is not all the story; but there would be no story at all without it.

The Eucharist is a ritual sign, and we have seen something of the human and historical fittingness of the ritual Christ chose. It is to his concrete ritual we must return, not to abstract considerations borrowed from natural philosophy or from personal and linguistic relations. The ritual is not just a sign of Christ's saving work in the sense that an 'x' can be a sign of a rejected solution, for that would reduce it to convention. It is not just a sign in the sense that a smile is a sign of welcome, for that would reduce it to an indication – embodiment, if you will – of human feeling. And it is not just a sign in the sense that food and drink offered are a sign of hospitality, for that would reduce it to shared human activity. The Eucharist is a ritual sign of Christ's saving presence in us, a sign where he acts in and through us, where – by sharing with us the ritual meal he has built upon inherited rites – he unites himself to us in a way that cannot be reduced to friendship, to memory or to any activity or convention of ours.

I have insisted on the defects of language here, and so upon the ultimate lameness of the Way of Ritual. It ends in a confession of defeat – but the defeat is profitable, in that it sends us back to the ritual itself. Older and newer accounts, I have submitted, have in common a divorce between appearance and reality that is incoherent, and the divorce does give them an attraction that my account lacks, specious though the attraction be. But no account of the Eucharist in terms of disguise and concealment can do justice to ritual. Ritual is not and cannot be a matter of disguise. A disguise conceals what is in itself straightforward, all that puzzles is the mode of concealment. Ritual signifies and leads on to what is not straightforward because it goes too deep – here, the mystery of God's love for us shewn in Christ. (The 'problem of interest' comes, as I said, from excess of light.) We must recognise the eucharistic ritual for what it is – not as a matter of prudent concealment, not as calling for a denial of what words mean, but as an activity that makes sense as it stands, and so can be given a greater and manifesting sense by the Word made flesh, a sign of his saving actions, and a sharing in his body and blood, given up for all that they may have eternal life. The Way of Ritual obliges us to start in the right place; it takes the link between eating, ritual meals, the Passover and the Eucharist, and makes it into a progressive illumination, not a disguise. To move along the Way of Ritual is to respect both human nature and the history of human salvation. We have seen how a shared meal has been ritually used in human history as an embodiment of a hope for union with what transcends human existence. Of that hope Christ is the fulfilment, and we share in the life he has gained for us when we share in the one bread and cup.

I have warned more than once that to reject what I called 'insulation' in eucharistic theology is to condemn oneself to a posture that is uncomfortable. The discomfort I described as going with the holding of an uneasy balance, and it is this tension and lack of ease that attend on the Way of Ritual I have proposed. The Way acknowledges the reality of the stages through which it invites us to pass. In other words it takes seriously Schillebeeckx's Principle of the Givenness of Reality, while refusing to follow him into a denial of objectivity to what we perceive. The Way of Ritual obliges us to take ritual on its own terms; to accept that ritual is distinct from ordinary activity, and yet cannot be divorced from that activity; to accept that ritual is touched by what we make of the world, while going beyond the world, and yet touching the way the world is to be dealt with by us. This is not insulation, it is openness; and the openness has further consequences we have yet to meet.

But the tensions and discomfort go deeper. The Way of Ritual tries to exhibit the Eucharist as the sign of God's love shewn to us through Christ in our great need and darkness, our *doulé physis*. But our flawed nature shews itself even in the phrases and imagery we use to describe our redemption: they lead us whither we would not go. We must expect the same in the rites which make up the journey along the

Way of Ritual. Ritual means can exhibit disgusting brutality, as an acquaintance with classical paganism will shew. It is the same Dionysus, the 'god poured out for mortals', whose power leads in Euripides' *Bacchae* to madness and murder. The Passover itself goes with a story of the slain first-born (for his mercy endureth for ever) and the Egyptians drowned in the sea (whither they had gone because the Lord had hardened Pharaoh's heart). And the Passover lamb eaten at the Last Supper would presumably have been immolated amid the scenes of mechanised temple butchery against which the prophets raised their voices. 'A past which is both revered and unsatisfactory' – we have come back to the phrase yet again, and can now see more of the unfinished business it obliges us to acknowledge.

A final unease goes deeper still, and recalls the theme I called *corpus mysticum* at the start of this chapter. The Eucharist, which is one sense of that name, signifies the Church, which is the other sense. I have claimed for the Way of Ritual that it is touched with uneasiness. What uneasiness will there be then in the Church and in its relationship to the world in which we live as human beings? I have just claimed that the ritual tradition leading to the institution of the Eucharist is marred with the very darkness from which we hope for deliverance, a deliverance of which the Eucharist itself is a sign. What corresponding darkness do we find in the Church? I also made a disclaimer: the Way of Ritual cannot claim exemption from the limitations and undesirabilities I detected in all language used in this field. Are we to make similar disclaimers for language used in the Church? If our past is both revered and unsatisfactory in eucharistic belief, what of past and present in the Church itself?

Those questions call for answers, and the answers will take us beyond this chapter into the next. But we must begin the answers from the right point. I have claimed that reflexions on the Eucharist must bring us back to the ritual itself, and I have also claimed that we shall need to see something, in concrete terms, of the ritual changes in the Roman Church. And so I go in the next section to the rite that was for so many years the sign of union in that Church: I go to the Old Roman Mass.

30 CULTIC PICTURES

Stately, plump Buck Mulligan came from the stairhead, bearing
a bowl of lather on which a mirror and razor lay crossed. A
yellow dressing-gown, ungirdled, was sustained gently behind
him by the mild morning air. He held the bowl aloft and
intoned: *Introibo ad altare Dei.*

And so begins the century's greatest novel. And so began the Old
Roman Mass. And annotations to *Ulysses* have now to insert an
explanation at this point, because the Old Roman Mass has passed
into the realm of footnotes.

I am concerned with more than writing footnotes in this section.
Ritual has been presented in this chapter as part of our response to
the call made by God's love to us in our great need. I have insisted
that ritual needs to be acknowledged for what it is, and not be
subordinated to categories drawn from natural science or from
human relations. My insistence takes concrete form in this section,
where I examine an ancient rite.

Any tradition of belief shews itself in a multitude of ways –
customs, reticences, priorities, idioms, styles of artefact, the kinds of
appeals made and the kinds of excuses allowed. The Old Roman
Mass was not a ritual expression of theological speculation, nor was
theological speculation the result of reflexion upon that form of
worship. An inheritance in religious belief is not like that: it is
essentially plural, heterogeneous and extended over time in its
different manifestations. 'Religious language' in this wider sense
is only partly verbal, and can never be wholly of a piece – there is
always liable to be a 'looseness of fit' between one part and another.

Among the variety of manifestations in eucharistic belief, I consider
here the Old Roman Mass – not only because of the central place I
give to ritual, but because of what ritual manifestation of belief is like.
Ritual, being innately conservative, can embody quite disparate
elements from different ages.[5] And being more than verbal, it can
express inherited beliefs more vividly than any abstract formula

---

[5] I anticipate here what is still to be dealt with and give an example familiar to all who know
the Roman Rite today. Resistance is being exhibited to the introduction of 'altar-girls' to
serve Mass, and the resistance can at least claim a great deal in the Roman Church's past
as a precedent. But that same Church now permits women to act as special ministers for the
distribution of the Eucharist. In other words, females are barred from presenting the wine
and water to the priest, but not from administering the Lord's body and blood. Ritual is like
that – so, of course, is the Church of Rome.

could. To what is expressed in ritual I give the name *cultic picture*, and I want to display what I think is a cultic picture exhibited by the older rite of the Mass. There may be other pictures; I am trying to obey the command 'Don't say what it *must* be; look!', and trying to express what I see.

So let us go back in time – to the late fifties, say. Let us eschew the past tense and see what we can find in a church where Mass is being said.[6] The church is an essentially simple structure – an oblong, with benches in the nave for the congregation, and the sanctuary at one end, set at a distance and fenced off by the communion-rails. The sanctuary's structure is also simple. There is an altar up against the wall, with a tabernacle in the middle for reserving the Blessed Sacrament. A crucifix will be above it, usually in some kind of superstructure allowing the consecrated host to be displayed in exposition or benediction. There will also be a pulpit, sometimes away from the sanctuary altogether. To these simplicities of structure corresponds a simplicity of posture by the congregation. They come into church for Mass; they make no responses of any sort during the Mass; they remain kneeling all the while, except during the gospel, when they stand (*RG* XVII 2; in some places they would sit during the offertory-rite).

The priest's rôle is both all-absorbing and in effect just as simple. Not simple in the sense that his rôle involves no ceremonial, it involves a good deal. But the complexities of what he has to do are in great measure concealed from the congregation by his posture of what I have to call *undifferentiated dorsality*. He turns every now and then to address them briefly (and the rubrics direct that he keep his eyes down the while – his voice too, in some cases). For the rest, he

---

[6] In trying to look at the eucharistic ritual, I am obviously indebted to its classic history in Jungmann 1952. I cite it by part and section, which the English version also follows. Those who celebrated the Old Mass will not need me to tell them about the labyrinth of rubrics and commentary thereon wherewith it was surrounded. It is enough here to recall, for those unfamiliar with the stuff, that there were four primary sources of information. There was material given in the course of the recited texts themselves (the material was printed in red, whence 'rubrics'). There were general instructions about the rite and the choice of Mass (*Rubricae generales*, 'General Rubrics'), printed at the beginning of the Missal. These were followed by two other items there. *Ritus Celebrandi Missam*, 'The Rite of Celebrating Mass', gave a detailed description of what had to be done. *De Defectibus*..., 'On Defects...', was devoted to what measures had to be taken if anything went wrong. The four sources disagreed just enough among themselves to keep experts gainfully employed; I give references to them by their acronyms, adding numbers of section and paragraph. Readers should be warned that – for reasons to me obscure – a revised version of the Roman Missal was produced as late as the 1960s, which took away much of the fun. All my references are to the old original.

remains with his back to them, and the actions he has to perform are thus largely hidden. I call the Priest's rôle 'all-absorbing' because his solitary recitation makes no distinction between different parts of the Mass. Some are personal prayers of preparation (the initial 'prayers at the foot of the altar', *Introibo ad altare Dei* and the rest). Others are recitation of Scripture, now done by a reader ('the Epistle'). Others again are responses now shared between reader and people ('the Gradual'). Still others are now recited or sung by the people as an entrance chant ('the Introit'), or as antiphons and chants during the Mass ('the *Gloria in excelsis*', 'the offertory verse', 'the Communion verse'). One and all in the Old Rite are said by the priest, and said by him alone. The server does indeed make responses here and there, but any difficulty in these is past when the prayers at the foot of the altar are over. And the specifically 'priestly' parts – the offering of the bread and wine, the central part of the Mass ('the canon') – are all said secretly: that is, so that the priest can hear them but others cannot (*RG* XVI 3).

Let us now look at the canon, but first let us recall some texts from Aquinas about the eucharistic presence. In the first chapter, we saw that the categories he used in his account – themselves closer to what we should call science than to philosophy – were alien to considerations of ritual. In the final section of the fourth chapter, this lack of connexion with ritual became more obvious, and more disconcerting. The Eucharist was said by him to be achieved 'in the consecration of the matter' (*in consecratione materiae*); its use by the faithful is not of the essence, but something 'following on the sacrament'. In Christ's words themselves, the command 'Take, eat' is not essential – it connotes 'the use of consecrated matter', which is no more than 'a certain completion of the sacrament'. The consecrating minister has 'no action to perform beyond the pronouncing of the words, just as in any other sanctification of matter'. Can we find anything in our cultic picture that recalls this primacy of transformation over distribution?

We find it first in the typography and rubrics of the book ('the Missal') from which the priest reads the canon, just as he reads everything else. The narrative of the Last Supper is there, and words uttered by Christ are usually set in large print. But the chief break occurs before *Hoc est enim corpus meum* ('For this is my body'), the words we saw Aquinas hold to be alone essential. Both text and rubric and the Instructions (*RCM* VIII 5) exhibit a break. The words themselves are set in much larger print; and the Instructions tell the priest to take up the host, to bow low, to rest his elbows on the altar, and to utter the words 'distinctly, reverently and in silence'. He is then to stand upright and after a genuflexion to elevate the host for the people to adore (*RCM* VIII 5–6). A similar break, and similar instructions, occur in the words to be uttered over the chalice.

We find the same primacy in what follows. After elevating the host, the priest must keep together the forefinger and thumb of each hand because they have touched it, and he must so keep them until he washes his fingers after giving communion. They are also to be rubbed over the chalice after any further touching of the host, in case any particle of it adheres to them (*RCM* VII 7, IX 3). Before consuming the chalice, the priest is to wipe the 'corporal' (the square of linen on which the host has rested) with the paten (a golden disk), to retrieve any stray particles of the host (*RCM* X 4). Should the host fall to the ground, or any of the chalice be spilt, elaborate procedures are given for scrapings, washings and burnings, and for the pouring away onto the earth of what results (*DD* X 5–15; I pass over a fair proportion of what can be found there by the curious).

But we find this primacy of transformation over distribution most of all in what the Missal has to say about the reception of the Eucharist by those who are present at Mass. The rubrics in the text itself give no details for reception whatever. After the drinking of the chalice by the priest, there simply follows 'if there be any to be given communion, let him give them communion before he purifies himself' – that is, before the server pours wine into the chalice for him to consume. If we want more details, we have to go to the end of the instructions for the priest's own reception of the Eucharist, and for what follows it (*RCM* X 4–5). The instructions about distribution are in effect a tail-piece, and their opening words shew as much: 'If any are to be given communion at the Mass…' Indeed, these instructions refer in their primary sense to a distribution quite separate from the Mass altogether.

To see this, we need go no further than the *Rituale Romanum*, the 'Roman Ritual', the service-book devoted to the administration of the sacraments. Here, the section devoted to the Eucharist takes it for granted that the distribution will take place separately. The priest is to see that enough particles are reserved in the tabernacle 'for the sick, and for the communion of the other faithful'. For distribution, he vests in stole and surplice, not in Mass-vestments; a confession of sin is made by the server on the people's behalf, and absolution given by the Priest; all receive kneeling, when a particle is put into the mouth of each. The distribution concludes with a response and prayer by the priest, who replaces in the tabernacle the vessel containing the particles and gives the people a blessing.[7] What is to be found in the Instructions in the Roman Missal is simply an adaptation of this – distribution begins with the confession and absolution, and when it is over the priest is instructed 'not to say anything' when returning to the altar (that is, to omit the response and prayer), and not to give a blessing (the concluding blessing mentioned above) – 'for he is to give a blessing at the end of the Mass' (*RCM* x 6).[8]

'A primacy of transformation over distribution': I think this phrase is a fair description of what the cultic picture of the Old Roman Mass exhibits, just as it was a fair description of what we found in scholastic texts. Indeed, the cultic picture shews itself in the fact that the reception of the Eucharist was attenuated to a point where little remained ritually of the actions recorded in the New Testament. The talk there of the Lord's taking bread and *breaking* it

---

[7] When Gerald Manley Hopkins gives, in 1879, the Bugler his First Communion, in his poem of that name, the setting appears to be outside Mass, involving only the pair of them. The boy

> ... begged of me, overflowing
> Boon in my bestowing,
> Came, I say, this day to it – to a First Communion.

Hopkins will have been at the altar, and the boy kneeling at the rails

> in regimental red.
> Forth Christ from cupboard fetched, how fain I of feet
> To his youngster take his treat.

The poem is notorious for containing the rhyme 'Boon he on – Communion'. Theologically too it confirms Hopkins as a true poet, in that his lapses are *cosmically* dreadful.

[8] The eminent rubrician O'Connell, understandably anxious to encourage the distribution of communion within Mass, cited the Roman Ritual in support of such distribution (1941–2: II, 154). That is not what the text he cites says. We have already seen how the Roman Ritual takes for granted that the distribution will take place outside Mass. All it does at the point O'Connell cites is add a paragraph to the effect that, when communion *is* distributed at Mass, it should be given after the priest's communion, not after Mass. What the ritual has in mind is the custom of distributing communion before Mass, during Mass (beginning quite early on) and after Mass. Some prayer-books adapted their devotions to these several contingencies. I feel obliged to add that O'Connell's own treatise on the celebration of Mass nicely illustrates the cultic picture I have been discerning. His account of the distribution of communion is relegated to the second appendix in what he writes about saying Mass (the first appendix is devoted to Faults in Celebration): O'Connell II: 138. In fact, the cultic picture here has continued to survive, in the practice of many priests who 'give communion' at Mass with hosts already stored in a tabernacle. Use of consecrated matter...

was no longer appropriate. Not only were the particles only bread by courtesy, there was no breaking to be done. The large host was indeed broken, but the priest was instructed to consume it all himself, and only in an emergency (e.g., danger of death) to share it with another. Indeed, it was rare for people even to receive particles that had been consecrated along with the large host; priests kept a supply in the tabernacle, and what was already there would naturally be distributed before anything else. There was naturally no question of any share in the *chalice* for the people, even though Christ had given it to the disciples; nor could they be said to '*take*' the particle – it was placed on the tongue by the priest. As for Christ's command to *eat*, it has to be added that many regarded biting the particle as irreverent, and it was sometimes allowed to dissolve in the mouth (which for some moral theologians scarcely counted as eating, and so such communions were doubtful. Strait indeed was the gate).

I suspect that some readers may feel I have made things easier for myself by returning in spirit to a 'Low Mass', a mass said, not sung, and with no solemnities added. I can see what the objectors have in mind, and hope to do it justice in due course. But here I can only say that the poverty of the older cultic picture is even greater for me in more solemn celebrations – whether the *missa cantata* (Mass sung by one priest), or the *missa solemnis* (where the priest was accompanied by deacon and subdeacon). I deal in turn with two things that are made to stand out even more sharply here than in a Low Mass: the poverty of the place given to Scripture, and (once more) the primacy of transformation in the Eucharist over distribution.

Lent and Easter Week provided new readings from scripture for each day. For the rest of the year, saints' days had readings chosen from a small and everlastingly repeated selection; other days simply used again the Sunday's readings – which were themselves a very mixed bag, the end-product of just as mixed historical circumstances (details in Jungmann III.2.2). This narrowness of range was made all the more evident at a solemn mass, by the ceremonial with which the meagre passages of Scripture were draped. The epistle was sung by the subdeacon with his back to the congregation, the gospel was sung by the deacon facing the north wall of the sanctuary. Once more, the origins of these fooleries were mixed. The ancient positions had allowed all to see and follow. They had been overlaid by the removal of the altar to the east wall, by sheer misunderstanding, and by arcane symbolism – among other reasons, the north had demonic connotations (details are in Jungmann III.2.3.). But the office of deacon and subdeacon here, maimed already as it was, received a further diminution. What I called earlier the 'all-absorbing' role of the priest absorbed here too – he had to read the epistle and gospel himself first, in an inaudible voice at the altar. High Mass here was but Low Mass made worse.[9]

It was still worse in its separation of sharing in the Eucharist from the celebration of Mass: by and large, at a 'Solemn High Mass' there was no communicant at all. The practice was due in part to the need to fast from midnight, but that was not the only reason. 'Communion' was something received at an early mass; it was not done to 'go at the eleven o'clock' – I recall being rebuked by a parish priest in the 1950s for having suggested to people that they should communicate at such a mass. Indeed, time was when communicating at a mass for the dead was explicitly forbidden ('May communion be given at Requiem Masses?' 'Certainly not': Reply of the Congregation of Rites, 22 January 1701). The reasoning behind the prohibition nicely sums up the cultic picture I have been discerning. Communion at Mass means communion given when the Mass is over; which means following the ceremony described in the Roman Ritual; which means ending with a blessing; which is incongruous, because the priest at a Mass for the dead is wearing black vestments. *Quod erat demonstrandum.*[10]

After all that, I hope that readers – even those who disagree with me – will not be surprised when I say that I find it hard to follow all the contentions of those who claim that the changes in worship in the Roman Church have robbed the Mass of its mystery, have shifted the

---

[9] Some of my readers who are in holy orders will recall a rite even more preposterous: the celebration of a *Missa coram*, a Solemn Mass in the presence of some 'Greater Prelate', who was provided with a throne on the Sanctuary and appropriate attendants. Of the many farcical complexities engendered by a *Missa coram*, one sticks in my memory. The subdeacon is singing the epistle (with his back to the congregation of course, but let that pass). While he is doing so, the celebrant is quietly reading the epistle for himself, and the greater prelate is doing likewise at his throne. Both, of course, appropriately attended.

[10] Incredulous readers can pursue the theme, not only in the reply already given (see Rites, Congregation of, 1815), but in Merati's revision of the classic work on rubrics by Gavantus (Gavantus and Merati 1736–8, vol. I, Part II, Tit. x *de ministranda Eucharistiam* [do not blame me for the Latin] *intra missam defunctorum* No. 28). That title translates as 'on distributing the Eucharist within a Requiem Mass'. Gavantus held to the prohibition and gave the grounds I have cited; Merati claimed it had fallen into abeyance. A later reply of the congregation (27 June 1868; see e.g. Rites, Congregation of, 1879) was meant to cancel the prohibition, but the memory of it lingered on. Other readers may recall that attempts in the 1950s at a College in Rome to introduce communion at Solemn Requiem masses (instead of before them) foundered on, among other things, the supposed prohibition.

emphasis from the divine to the human, and have in effect carried out ritually what modern theologians of the Eucharist are supposed to have carried out theoretically – surrendered the objectivity and absoluteness of Christ's eucharistic presence for a transignification that makes the presence into a function of what the Christian community believes. I say that I find it hard to follow *all* these contentions, because there are some that I do not find in the least difficult to follow, and I will try in due course to say what I think about them. Of those I do find hard to follow, some are complaints made by the anthropologist Mary Douglas. I consider these, partly because of the humanity and shrewdness that distinguish her book (Douglas 1970, especially the first and third chapters) and partly because what I have to say in reply forms a natural part of the course of my argument.

Douglas makes observations about the power of ritual that are similar to those I have already made in this book. She goes on to claim that in the Eucharist the condensation of symbols is so great – union, atonement, nourishment, renewal and so on – that those accustomed to elaborated forms of speech (as priests are) will not take kindly to it, and will move towards an internalising of religious experience; thanksgiving, togetherness and the rest will be given pride of place over the transformation of the bread into the divine body. But it is the pastors who are straying, not the flocks; these are more at ease with what ritual involves, because of their less 'verbal' upbringing.

With Douglas' general observations about the importance of ritual and symbolism, I am in complete agreement. With her contention that many of the clergy have been antipathetic to such things I am also in agreement – although I shall be suggesting other causes for the phenomenon. It is not so much disagreement I voice as bewilderment – where on earth can she have gone to Mass? Certainly, the symbolism in the old rite could be elicited by those who knew how to see beneath the surface uniformity, beneath its atrophy of gesture and movement, beneath its preservation of historical accidents as apparent inevitabilities, beneath its lack of justice to Scripture, beneath its downright ugliness at times. Those who knew where to look could indeed see how, beneath all this, the fossil's origin could be discerned. But that is not symbolism, that is matter for detection – we are back to Holmes seeing clues where Watson does not, we are back yet again to the confusion between signs and disguises. Liturgy is meant to communicate ritually, not to provide liturgists (or anthropologists, come to that) with obscured patterns of significance to decipher. The Eucharist does indeed condense a multitude of symbols, as Douglas claims, and I have tried to bring out something of their range and variety earlier in this chapter. But, to repeat my expression of bewilderment, where can she have encountered all this, ritually communicated, at a celebration of the Old Mass?

I press the point by taking up the description she gives of 'a closed social group', where a 'positional' code appeals to the status each individual has in the group, and makes the group at ease with ritual. The justice of the description I am not competent to appraise, but I do submit that 'positional' is the last word to associate with the Old Mass. 'Positional', like 'closed social group', suggests a structure and a differentiation of rôles and places. How much of the sort can be seriously associated with the structure of the Old Mass? Only this much – a series of *polarisations* (I italicise the word, for we shall be seeing more of it). The unstructured body of the church is set against the sanctuary. The altar is set against the rest of the sanctuary – it serves alike for the readings from Scripture and for the prayer over the gifts. The priest is set against everything else – his rôle is all-absorbing, his undifferentiated dorsality blurs everything except the opposition between his place and the (again undifferentiated) place and posture of the congregation. The canon is set against all else in the rite – the bell and the silence and the rest against the all too familiar brevities of epistle and gospel. In the canon, the words of consecration are set against all else – set against them typographically and rubrically, as we have seen. And, as we have also seen, the transformation of the bread and wine is set against their reception by all others at Mass except the priest. I have described my own position as one that interprets ritual in terms of ritual. I think I am now entitled to submit that the ritual of the Old Mass is not the best place to begin the work of interpretation.

Introibo ad altare Dei. The Old Roman Mass has passed into the realm of footnotes. How much has passed with it? What significance have the 'polarisations' that the Old Mass ritually expresses? Is it the same Church? Our examination of the older cultic picture will prove of help as we try to answer these questions.

31 THE GALILEAN PRESENCE

At the end of the preceding section, I mentioned the simplicities and polarisations that go with the Church and sanctuary associated with the older cultic picture. But to the simplicity there is one exception. I described the altar as being up against the wall, with the tabernacle for the reserved Sacrament in the middle, and some kind of superstructure behind it. Here and here alone in the sanctuary was something designed with its own specific purpose in view – the display of the consecrated host in services like 'exposition' or 'benediction'. To this purpose, the altar itself had exchanged characteristics of a table for those of a sideboard or shelf. The priority of transformation over distribution, already expressed ceremonially and typographically, received architectural embodiment, so that space and physical structure made a contribution they had not done previously. However high the Mass, however rubrically perfect its execution, it was conducted in an area which lacked a differentiated structure and at an altar designed with other things in mind. Is it any wonder that it was only when Benediction began and the lights and candles went up that such altars and sanctuaries came into their own? Then it was that the older cultic picture expressed most forcibly its eucharistic attraction; so it is the nature of the attraction we must now consider. And I start by recalling things we have already seen.

I have accused older and new accounts of confusing signs with disguises, and have associated the confusion with the Fallacy of Replacement, by which exalted predicates are deemed to compete with and to replace predicates that are humbler. The trouble with the Fallacy, I claimed, is that the exalted predicates are supposed to be competing with what I called 'the humbler creation', the kind of presence that is for us the clearest and most basic of all, so that what is exalted has to take on the spatialisation and 'dimensionality' of this basic presence. Dimensionality was the unwanted destination to which reasonings over 'presence by way of substance' were led, and the appeal made by newer accounts to the status of a risen body fared no better. What apparent vividness the older and newer accounts possessed was a vividness bound up with confusion. But, as I have observed more than once, the confusion engenders a specious attraction, for it seems to offer us a definite if invisible presence to be affirmed or denied. And, just as the older cultic picture exhibits analogies to the older accounts of the eucharistic presence, so it too shares in the attraction possessed by them, as by any account in terms of concealment and disguise.

But that is not all the story. The attraction of the older cultic picture has more to it than imaginative vividness derived from speculation gone astray. The attraction does indeed have to do with the confusion, but it is also an attraction both understandable and not unworthy of its setting. The attraction lies in associating the eucharistic presence with a presence of Christ, imperceptible indeed, but resembling the way in which he was present to those with whom he walked and talked in Galilee. It is this 'Galilean Presence' which is cultically pictured in the Old Mass, and brought into even greater prominence by the physical structures directed towards exposition of the consecrated host. And that such a presence should be attractive needs no proof. We have seen something of how the human quest for God manifests itself. Belief in the incarnation combines this quest with the vividness and tangibility of an encounter with another human being. 'That which was from the beginning, which we have heard, which we have seen with our eyes, which we have looked upon, and our hands have handled...' – the opening words of the First Epistle of John enshrine the grace of that encounter in Galilee, the unique grace that lives on in the memory of the writer. The presence I call Galilean is quite simply the most vivid and basic presence we have yet encountered; it was in such a presence that the disciples came to know and to love their Master; what more understandable than to think in terms of such a presence, when we think of our eucharistic sharing in the Lord's body and blood?

Indeed, I would go further. I claimed as a merit for my Way of Ritual that it had an uneasiness and incompleteness about it; I now make the claim again. I cannot offer anything as attractive as the Galilean presence, no account can that takes the notion of sign seriously. The Eucharist is a sacramental signifying of the 'spiritual eating' which is the union of Christ with believers, a union that is the purpose of his saving work and that it touches our very being. The mystery of the eucharistic presence, I have insisted, does not start when we consider in isolation from ritual the perceptible elements; the mystery begins with the whole pattern of God's love for us in the Incarnation, of which the achievement is the happiness of eternal life in the resurrection. But the hope and promise here do not have and cannot have the vividness that goes with what I call the Galilean presence. They point to something far greater than such a presence, but the pointing calls for faith, it offers no sight. Unease and incompleteness are and must be part of any account in which the Eucharist is allowed to be a sign: what we are to be hath not yet been revealed. (Mercifully, I should want to add: the unease I associate with the Way I propose is very real.)

All that supposed advantage I willingly concede to the Galilean presence. But I repeat my claim that to confuse the signifying power of the Eucharist with a process of disguise will lead, whether we want it to or not, to a spatialised account of the presence, and to the fantasies we have met of appearances as camouflage prompted by prudence or tact. The result was embarrassing, but the embarrassment here is not in the face of divine generosity but in the face of misunderstanding run riot. I gave samples of how far the misunderstanding can go, and called them 'the shadow of the past'. I now submit that the 'Galilean Presence' associated with the older cultic picture, despite its understandable attraction, is touched with the same shadow. Our legacy of belief concerning the eucharistic presence resembles the legacies of belief concerning redemption, and sacrifice, and ritual meals. All those legacies touch our hope for release from our darkness, but they are themselves all touched in turn by that darkness, and in this way bear witness to the very *doulé physis* whose emancipation is their aim and concern.

To spell out this submission will bring us back to the theme of 'Present and Past', and of the tensions between them. At the start of this chapter, I set the theme beside the theme I called *corpus mysticum*, where 'mystical body' suggests the link between Eucharist and Church; and I wrote later that I should have to extend to the Church the considerations I have been making in a eucharistic setting. This extension I reserve for the next chapter; here and now, I mean to examine specific examples of the tension between past and present in eucharistic belief. We have already seen a good deal of how mixed a past we have in the matter. We shall now see the mixture cultically expressed, and can notice the tensions set up by it – all that will take us to the end of this section. In the next section, I pass to a range of techniques by which these tensions can – apparently – be eliminated, and a recalcitrant past accommodated to present concerns. The techniques I then set beside a specific case of tension between present and past, by describing a cultic picture which in my opinion is displayed by the newer rite of the Mass. And this eucharistic example of tension will, I hope, convince the reader that accommodation of the past cannot be enough. The tensions between present and past need acknowledging, not disguising: and some forms the acknowledgment might take I offer in the last section of this chapter. Once again, unease and embarrassment will point the way forward – the way, indeed, into the final chapter of this book. Because it is in the final chapter that topics like accommodation of the past will be applied to the Church, and one sense of *corpus mysticum* be seen as exhibiting analogies to the other.

And so for some examples of our mixed inheritance. I go first to an appeal made to the past by Pope Paul VI in his encyclical letter *Mysterium Fidei*, which reprobated attempts to reduce the eucharistic change to 'transignification' or 'transfinalisation', attempts that did not mention the wonderful conversion of which Trent speaks (and here the pope cited the phraseology of Trent's canon on transubstantiation, see p. 2). Later in the encyclical, the pope referred to a medieval testimony to correct eucharistic belief:

it is helpful to recall the firm faith with which the Church unanimously opposed Berengarius, who gave way to difficulties raised by human reason and first dared to deny the eucharistic conversion. (Paul VI 1965a: 768; §52)

Berengarius or Bérengar (+1088), a teacher at Tours, was accused more than once of contravening eucharistic belief, was more than once obliged to retract, and seems after every such occasion to have resumed his former opinions. Two of his retractions are to be found in Denzinger and Schönmetzer's collection, and I give a brief extract from both. First, from what he was forced to declare at a council in Rome in 1059:

I Berengarius... profess... that the bread and wine which are placed upon the altar are after the consecration not only a sacrament [*sacramentum*], but also the true body and blood of our Lord Jesus Christ, and are in a sensory fashion [*sensualiter*], not only in a sacrament [*sacramento*], but in truth [*veritate*] touched and broken by the hands of priest and crushed [*atteri*] by the teeth of the faithful. (DS 690)

In 1079, at another council in Rome, he had to make this declaration:

I Berengarius... profess... that the bread and wine which are placed on the altar... are substantially converted [*substantialiter converti*] into the true and proper and lifegiving flesh and blood of Jesus Christ our Lord, and after the consecration are the true body of Christ, which was born of the Virgin... and the true blood of Christ which was shed from his side, not just by the sign and power of a sacrament [*sacramenti*], but in their own nature [*in proprietate naturae*] and in the truth of substance [*in veritate substantiae*]. (DS 700)

If the encyclical claims that the Church unanimously opposed Berengarius, then both professions of faith will be part of the opposition, and – as the encyclical puts it – it will be helpful to recall them both. Readers will have noticed that I have added the original Latin in places. I have done so to bring out the difficulty raised by the words in which the opposition was couched. Our inheritance is indeed a mixed one. If it is 'helpful to recall' it, the helpfulness can hardly be the straightforward appeal that the encyclical seems to have had in mind.

Appeals to our inheritance can be found in other utterances of Paul VI. In 1971, on the eve of Corpus Christi, he spoke of the institution of that feast 'after the miracle of Bolsena' (Paul VI 1971 : 139). Some readers will have seen Raphael's fresco of the miracle, in one of the Stanze in the Vatican (reproductions in Jones and Penny 1983, plates 127–9): a priest celebrating Mass is cured of his doubts about the eucharistic presence by seeing the consecrated host drip blood.[11] Paul VI had visited in 1964 the Cathedral at Orvieto, where the blood-stained linen is preserved. He spoke there of listening to the medieval account of the miracle as to '*una storia*' (the Italian is conveniently ambiguous), but gave no details (Paul VI 1964: 753). A brochure available in Bolsena itself in 1972 is less reticent, and I quote its English text, correcting the spelling:

The moment of consecration came and [the priest] raised the particle to heaven. And then – behold – there came the divine answer to his desperate prayer: the particle was not any more a piece of unleavened bread: it was living flesh, dripping blood. The priest, bewildered, wrapped the particle in the corporal and left the Altar, taking refuge in the Sacristy. A few drops of blood marked his progress on the floor. (Bolsena 1963)

I hope that no reader will object that the recitation of unclean nonsense like this is an unfair disinterment of obsolete eccentricities. Such objections will really not do, and by this stage in the book we ought to have outgrown the belief that they might. We saw that medieval speculations about the eucharistic presence exhibit a propensity to conceive of it in terms of camouflage, and that Aquinas, for all his insistence that Christ is not in any way injured in the

---

[11] Browe devoted two monographs to topics to be mentioned here: Browe 1938 deals with eucharistic miracles, Browe 1933 is concerned with the veneration of the Eucharist in the middle ages. He has accumulated in both an astonishing amount of *curiosa*.

Eucharist, does have texts himself which exhibit the propensity. Miracle stories like that of Bolsena are but spelling out the implications of camouflage in a picturesquely disgusting way. Nor should the stories be dismissed as mere eccentricities, the tradition of them goes back far further than Aquinas. How far, I do not know; the earliest I have come across is found in the *Vitae Patrum*, a series of anecdotes about the fathers of the Church, going back to the sixth century – here a doubter sees a small boy on the altar when the loaves are placed there, sees him cut up by an angel when the bread is broken by the priest, receives a piece of bloody flesh, ceases to doubt, and the flesh appears as bread once more (v.18.3; 73 ML 979). The middle ages were fertile with such visions: St Dominic saw Christ's blood pouring into the chalice at Mass, nuns saw an infant appear. Indeed, the general direction of the apparitions received embodiment in the art-form known as 'the mystic wine-press' (there is a famous example in Paris, in Saint-Étienne du Mont): Christ's blood is being tapped into barrels.[12]

Here indeed is the shadow of the past – but the shadow is not only camouflaged cannibalism, it is the *reductio ad absurdum* of that separation of transformation from distribution that has dogged the older account. The general drift of it all is towards treating the host as a *commodity* – not in the sense of irreverently, but in the sense that the host was linked only by way of supplementation with being distributed, and was seen as possessing in itself a power that could be used for a whole range of other purposes. Already in the twelfth century, the particles for distribution had been made in the form of a

---

[12] We can notice a difference of emphasis in the early story, which distinguishes it from its medieval successors. First, neither the appearance of the miraculous child, nor its cutting up, is centred on the words of consecration. Secondly, the story ends with the receiving of the Eucharist – the medieval anecdotes do not.

Aquinas considers the question of such eucharistic apparitions at *ST* 3.76.8, and it is a tribute to his good sense that he seems (or so I think) somewhat ill at ease with them. Where the miracle is of short duration, God miraculously affects the spectators' eyes. Where it persists, it is an appearance in the accidents that he creates. In neither case is the flesh or blood of Christ visibly perceived. He adds – Newmanesquely, I fear – that there is no deception here, because the miracle is done in favour of the truth that Christ is really present. I add that this text of Aquinas, because it speaks of a miraculously effected modification of our perceptual apparatus, was invoked much later by theologians who followed Descartes in philosophy. With him they denied the objective reality of properties like taste and colour; the text of Aquinas allowed them to reconcile this with orthodox eucharistic belief by thinking of transubstantiation in terms of something like the disguised presence of Christ on the way to Emmaus. We saw that analogy used in the early middle ages (p. 32). Its revival in the seventeenth and eighteenth centuries I mention again, briefly, in footnote 19 to the next chapter.

coin (details in Jungmann IV.1.4.); the elevation of the host, unknown at the end of the twelfth century, had become almost universal by the middle of the thirteenth – a black veil was sometimes extended behind the altar, to throw the sight into greater relief; the host was sometimes shewn to the dead; it was customary to communicate before fighting a duel.[13] And this seeing of the host as a commodity bred its own tale of miracle stories. A heretic at the stake had by the power of the devil resisted all attempts to burn him alive – the Host was brought along 'and he went up like straw'. Hosts long neglected in tabernacles remained miraculously fresh – I saw one such 'relic' as late as 1948, in (I think) Sienna Cathedral. And the shadow was darker yet, for eucharistic miracles became embodiments of anti-semitism. Pope Innocent III (+1216) tells of a Jew who, wishing to abuse a consecrated particle, put it in his strong-box, only to find later that all his coins had been turned into particles. The *Catholic Encyclopaedia* s.v. 'Host', mentions miraculous hosts in the church of Sainte-Gudule in Brussels which had survived 'the perpetration of many outrages by the Jews in 1370'. Just what such tales led to can be best seen in *The Jewish Encyclopaedia* s.v. 'Host, Desecration of'.

The last example I offer is the language of some prayers in the Missal. It will be enough, I think, to set down some in English, leaving to a footnote their sources and the original Latin of them. 'We are fed and given drink by the heavenly mystery': 'we have been nourished by the holy gift'; 'what we have touched with our mouth'; 'we have been fed, Lord, with the delights of your precious body and blood'; 'we who are about to be fattened with the body and blood of our Lord Jesus Christ'. The last of the prayers I cannot bring myself to put into English in the main text, so give it here in Latin:

caelestem nobis praebeant haec mysteria, Domine, medicinam: et vitia cordis expurgent.

Readers without Latin will, I suspect, have still been able to guess what imagery is being used – at all events, a version is in the footnote.[14]

---

[13] The particles were given *heraldic* significance at times. The Goncourt diaries (4 May 1868) tell of a pious nobleman (a contemporary of theirs?) who always communicated with particles stamped with his own coat-of-arms. On one occasion, the chaplain found to his alarm that there were none of the right sort left, and was obliged to administer '*une hostie commune, plébéienne*' to his master. He covered up his confusion with '*A la fortune du pot, monsieur le Comte!*'

[14] I give the original Latin of the phrases I have quoted in English, adding a reference to where each can be found in the Old Roman Missal. *Caelesti mysterio pascimur et potamur* (Postcommunion for Christmas Eve); *sacro munere vegetati* (Postcommunion for eighteenth

Readers, Latinless or not, will surely agree by this time that there is a variety in our eucharistic inheritance, whatever else there be. What do we do about it and what should we do?

32   ACCOMMODATING THE PAST

There is a curious difference between the Prayer Book Psalter and the Latin Vulgate in their renderings of a verse in the twenty-fifth Psalm. Coverdale – and here the Authorised Version is very close to him – has the Psalmist ask the Lord not to remember 'the sins and offences of my youth'. For the Vulgate (which of course counts the Psalm as the twenty-fourth), it seems to be the sins and ignorances of that period which the Lord is requested to forget: *delicta juventutis meae et ignorantias meas*. Psychologically at all events, the Vulgate has the advantage. Oecumenism with one's past is never easy, and what we take to be our accumulation of knowledge over the intervening years contributes greatly to the difficulty. Was my ignorance really so gross? Can I ever have believed this? Not known that? Failed to link that with this? Affirmative answers here can be hard sayings, and the peculiarities of autobiography bear witness to the hardness.[15] We should then not be surprised that accommodating the past should be a regular activity in eucharistic belief or in the Church, for it is regular everywhere. Here and now I start with four varieties of accommodation, to which I have given names: adjustment of the record, supervenient isolation, redirection of the force of the record, and interpretation of the record by analogies. The four varieties will prove to have things in common, which will introduce what for me is the most powerful of all accommodations – to which I give the name of *selective amnesia*.

Sunday after Pentecost); *quod ore contingimus* (Postcommunion for *Sapientiam*, a Common of many Martyrs); *pretiosi corporis et sanguinis tui, Domine, pasti deliciis* (Postcommunion for the feast of St John Cantius); *Jesus Christi Domini nostri corpore et sanguine saginandi* (Secret Prayer for Holy Cross Day). The prayer I confined to its original Latin in the text is the Secret Prayer for the twentieth Sunday after Pentecost. Its English is: 'Lord, may these mysteries provide us with a heavenly medicine; and may they purge out the vices of the heart.'

15 A citation from the first editor of the *Dictionary of National Biography* seems appropriate here. 'We do not wonder when a man gives a false character to a neighbour, but it is always curious to see how a man continues to present a false testimony to himself. It is pleasant to be admitted behind the scenes, and to trace the growth of that singular phantom which, like the spectre of the Brocken, is the man's shadow cast upon the colossal and distorted mists of memory.' Leslie Stephen wrote this in his *Studies in Biography*; I found it in Augustine Birrell's admirable essay 'A few warning words for would-be autobiographers' (Birrell 1930).

1. *Adjustment of the record*. We saw that the first recantation imposed upon Berengarius contained the phrases that after the consecration the bread and wine are 'not only a sacrament, but' the true body and blood of Christ, and that these are handled and crushed 'in a sensory fashion [*sensualiter*], not only in a sacrament but' in truth. In the *Summa Theologiae*, Aquinas comments upon the recantation, at a point where it provides the objection that Christ is therefore cannibalistically eaten in the Eucharist. His reply we should be able to anticipate by now: breaking and the rest touch only the sacramental form under which Christ is present, they do not touch Christ himself (*ST* 3.77.7.obj.3 and ad 3). I am not concerned with the justice of this reading of the recantation, but with the text of the formula that Aquinas had to face. It had already been adjusted, because the phrases I have just given in quotation marks had been omitted. It is not hard to see why, and we can draw from the omission our first moral. Accommodations of the past bear witness in their own way to what was believed later, by shewing what later on was proving awkward.

The eucharistic feast of Corpus Christi itself provides another example of textual adjustment (the reader is welcome to use a harsher word). A passage from St Augustine was recited during the third Nocturn of Matins for the Feast. Augustine's eucharistic theology proved (not for the first time) to be a *mauvais coucheur*, and I translate a sentence of the text as found in the Breviary, putting square brackets round the spurious clauses:

So whoever does not abide in Christ nor have Christ abide in him certainly does not [spiritually] eat his flesh or drink his blood [although carnally and visibly he does press with his teeth the sacrament of Christ's body and blood].

Whoever perpetrated the forgery might at least have tried to imitate Augustine's Latin.

But moves of this sort call for effort, and a much commoner adjustment lies in what calls for no effort at all: a simple silence. Berengarius' first profession was not printed in any edition of 'Denzinger', the widely used collection of texts, until Schönmetzer's revision of it in 1963; only the second and less rebarbative profession used to be given. An almost as widely used edition of the *Summa Theologiae* was published in 1948 by Marietti. It gives in footnotes an abundance of material, from Councils and so on, for all topics in the

Summa. But it has nothing to say about the adjustments made to the first profession by Berengarius, for the excellent reason that it says almost nothing to suggest that the first profession so much as exists. Its collection of eucharistic decrees at *ST* 3.75.1 gives only the second profession. At *ST* 3.77.7, as we saw, Aquinas deals with an adjusted text of the first profession in answering the third objection. But all the footnote there prints is 'Can.*Ego Berengarius, de Consecr.*, dist. 2.' Readers familiar with the canonical collection made by Gratian (+ *c.* 1151) would have been able to follow up this enigmatic note, but then such readers would hardly have needed the reference. I think the move may be fairly described as the preservation of simple silence.

Nor is this the only silence on the point. In the previous section I cited a passage from *Mysterium Fidei*, the Encyclical Letter of Paul VI in which newer accounts of the eucharistic presence were reprobated. It will be remembered how the Letter claimed that it would be 'helpful to recall' the unanimous condemnation of Berengarius. But the reference given here in the encyclical is to his second profession only; the pope follows the example of Denzinger and Marietti and passes over the first profession in silence. Silence too has begun to be observed over the 'miracle of Bolsena', of which we saw the same pope make mention. Already the older *Catholic Encyclopaedia* (1907ff.) had written with extreme caution and admitted that the source-material is late and dubious (XI 332f; s.v. 'Orvieto'. I owe this reference to Browe, who, however, seems unaware of just who made that admission – the author was Umberto Benigni, the arch-conservative henchman of the reactionary Pius X. If he could doubt, who could still believe?) As for the *New Catholic Encyclopaedia* (1967) it simply preserves, as far as I can see, a profound silence on the whole business. I have dwelt on this point because the accommodating power of silence is so great. Those who try to decipher Latin and Greek inscriptions will know the force of *damnatio memoriae*, the order to erase every occurrence of someone's name throughout the whole Empire. Rejections and doubts in religious belief at least have to mention what is no longer acceptable. The best adjustment of all is the *damnatio memoriae* of the past by silence; it taketh all away.[16] Bolsena here is a paradigm case, both in the lack of detail in

---

[16] As I write this, a serio-comic thought strikes me. Could the curial official who wrote *Mysterium Fidei* for Paul VI have used Marietti's *Summa* and an old edition of Denzinger? Odder things have happened. Simple silence would then be replaced by sheer ignorance;

the papal reference to it, and in the sinking of the tale without trace in a work of reference. There were many such occurrences in the middle ages (the old saying 'as sure as God's in Gloucestershire' is supposed to refer to some eucharistic relic there). Where have they all gone? After all, eucharistic miracles of the sort were mentioned in instructions to children down to our own day – certainly I was taught about them at school. In their original context, instructions of the sort would have named names and mentioned places. But the context had petered out; silence, for all its power, is necessarily uninformative. And the deeper silence now preserved tells us even less.

2. *Supervenient isolation.* I have just given examples of beliefs where the original context has petered out. This is but one instance of a whole family of adjustments and accommodations where what is believed now has been detached from a mass of other things once believed along with it; it has been *superveniently isolated.* I explain with a homely example. Suppose I am approached by a vendor of almanacs, who urges me to buy one on the grounds that, in 1963, he forecast the death of President Kennedy. In face of my doubts he produces a dog-eared copy from that year: sure enough, there is the prediction 'This year, the President of the United States will be assassinated.' I am entitled to be impressed; but I am a good deal less entitled if I subsequently discover that he makes the same forecast every year. The significance of what I read in the 1963 edition was acquired by *supervenient isolation* – I was impressed by it only because it had been removed from the whole series of forecasts made by the astrologer.

It is not difficult to think of examples of supervenient isolation in our inheritance of religious beliefs. Years ago, when I was examining claims for a continuity of belief in the Church about birth control, I noticed it time and again. The appeal made to tradition for the subordination of intercourse to procreation was fraudulent. It made the impression it did only because it was superveniently isolated from a whole array of opinions about sex and marriage quite alien to what is now believed, and in flat disaccord with the present official sanction of methods that are designed to separate intercourse from the procreation of children (FitzPatrick 1966: 172–7). In our own topic here of eucharistic belief, we have already encountered supervenient isolation, in what I called 'Historical Insouciance' in

the *damnatio memoriae* would still be there, but the responsibility for it would be pushed further back.

the third chapter: the scholastic terminology of 'substance', 'accidents' and the rest was treated by some recent authors as if it were detachable from the tradition in which it had grown up, and then without more ado guaranteed to mean something when put into a quite alien context. I reprobated the move there, but I recall it as an example of the strength which supervenient isolation apparently possesses. A vocabulary – especially a vocabulary which seems to stand half-way between common sense and philosophical speculation – gives the appearance when so isolated of being emancipated from dependence on a context that has become old-fashioned; the isolation apparently does it nothing but good. I have given reasons and to spare for thinking that the eucharistic terminology of substance and accidents is nowhere near common sense and just as remote from coherent speculations. But I admit that the move to isolate the terminology superveniently is a tempting one, because it seems to preserve our adhesion to what we deem mandatory in a eucharistic belief inherited from tradition, while at the same time allowing us to distance ourselves from what we dislike in our inheritance.

3. *Redirection of the force of the record.* If supervenient isolation removes items of our inheritance from the context of what else we have inherited, the manoeuvre we now consider lies in accepting what we have inherited, but in adjusting its force and its purpose. For example, we can devise a presentation of what we find awkward in the inheritance, and then set the presentation at a distance from what we hold really to matter there. Near the start of the second chapter, I cited a spirited ridiculing by de Baciocchi of 'an imaginative solution' with which transubstantiation 'is often confused', but which (he says) is quite different. The imaginative solution is, of course, in terms of 'the inflated skin of accidents', and I have given my reasons for thinking that the picture has all too much to do with transubstantiation. For all that, the move of redirection can be effective, given the strength of the wish to eliminate the embar-rassment of a clash with the past. Just as effective can be moves where awkward items are given descriptions that apparently lessen their importance. The first and apparently cannibalistic profession of Berengar can be called 'harsh', and his second profession can be seen as 'correcting' it. Stories like that from Bolsena are 'popular expressions' of true faith; medieval practices concerning the host are 'manifestations' of belief and reverence; and so on. What is inherited is preserved, but its force is redirected. Moves of that kind are not in

themselves dishonest, but they must be seen for what they are –
accommodations of what embarrasses in our past, not dispassionate
examinations of former beliefs.

4. *Interpretation of the record by analogies.* Things that disturb can look
less grave when shewn to have precedents; the changes that have
beset the Roman Church over the last quarter of a century have been
duly provided with them. I have seen the passing away of the Old
Roman Mass likened to the superseding by that Mass of medieval
usages like the Sarum Rite. And Schillebeeckx himself presents, in the
very first pages of his book, the great medieval scholastics as offering
a quite new elucidation of the eucharistic presence, an elucidation
which had something shocking in it, but of which popular piety was
unaware. Had that age been as free in communication as is ours, he
goes on, the theology would have provoked an explosive disturbance,
with its impression of novelty, modernism and of hollowing out the
faith (7[11–12]). The analogy has an obvious use there, given the
seeming novelty of the eucharistic account which Schillebeeckx
himself goes on to elaborate. A more general move of this kind is to
retroject the acceptance of this or that disputed innovation: what is
being said now amounts to what has already been said; the innovators
are pushing at an open door; we have long held what they are
proposing. The move is popular in other contexts, and we should not
be surprised to find it used here – perhaps some readers have already
employed it, to accommodate what I have been writing in these
pages.

Are moves and analogies of this sort fair? At present the fact of these
adjustments and isolations and redirectings and interpretings matters
more than their morality. To see *why* all these things are done will
lead us to the most pervasive accommodation of all – and to an idea
of why neither it nor any of the others can be all the story.

I wrote that oecumenism with one's own past can be a difficult
business. Even more difficult is the relationship that needs to be
cultivated between present and past within a shared body of belief
and practice. 'Let each one worship the Gods according to the
custom of his city': so declared the Pythian Oracle (Xenophon,
Memorabilia I 3). The heritage of belief and practice is one into which
we have entered, to which we must make our own contribution, and
into which we must initiate those who will possess the heritage when
we are gone. No wonder that the very words and perceptible forms of

the heritage assume an importance of their own: to use them is to align ourselves with a tradition of which we cannot grasp the whole. But if we cannot grasp the whole, neither can we approve of the whole – as long, that is, as we regard what we have inherited as sharing in some measure our language and imagery, and as making some claims upon how we should live. The life we live is given structure by this heritage; but life itself provides questions and challenges for the heritage we take for granted. The accommodations I have described are responses to the tension that is set up in this way between past and present. But the tension is a sign of life; museums may engender melancholy, but they do not accept the challenge of what is new – that is not their job. If a religious heritage is to be other than a museum, there must be tensions in our possession of it.

We have seen much by this time of where the tension can arise. The expression of Christ's saving work can lead to images of bait for the devil or of punishment inflicted on the innocent by God the Father; the tradition of sacrifice harbours violence and brutality; the pattern of the ritual meal includes madness and murder; the Passover is touched with what it jolts us to remember; the ritual of eating used by Christ has been taken by a theological tradition in ways that topple over into cannibalism. These traditions and images have to do with God's plan for our release from the darkness of our enslaved nature, our *doulé physis*; but they are all touched by the limitations of that nature. We cannot press the words and images too hard. We must check their propensity to take on a life of their own. *We must learn to forget.*

Put like that, the command sounds paradoxical. But all we have here is something mentioned much earlier: the need to subordinate words and speculation to ritual and practice. The subordination proves natural enough. Prayers in the Missal that used language with unseemly physiological suggestions had long been recited; but their general drift was part of a sharing in the Eucharist, so that details could be overcome by inherited form and ritual stateliness. The attractions of the 'Galilean Presence' can lead to an apparent camouflaging of Christ in the Eucharist; but the terminology of substance and accident seemed to offer a way of fencing off Christ from the indignities bound up with the fate of food. It is a quenching of development in words and images that is sought when we accommodate the past, a damping-down of consequences, a return to ritual. That is why a sense of fittingness among those who worship can effect this accommodation, even without any abstract reflexion. By a certain instinctive tact, we learn to forget. Human kind, the poet tells us, cannot bear very much reality. Which, presumably, is why human kind has been given an almost limitless faculty for disregarding what is unacceptable in the real. To repeat the phrase I gave earlier, human kind has been given the gift of *selective amnesia*. The gift has been used in all the contexts I have mentioned – and it will prove to be used in many more.

I have called the next section 'Beyond accommodation', and the title is meant to suggest that more is necessary than what has been mentioned so far – or, to put things more accurately, what has been mentioned so far has more to it than what has so far appeared. I have described several ways in which the tension between past and present is eased, and agreement between them claimed. Now a conspicuous example of tension in the Roman Church today is provided by the changes there in ritual. I set down in an earlier section the 'cultic picture' I discerned in the Old Mass. I want to set that picture beside what can be discerned in the new rite. If we keep in mind a specific example of the difference between present and past, we shall be able to judge all the better in the next section the techniques of accommodation we have been examining in this.

One important difference between old and new cultic pictures is that the newer pattern of ritual is not fixed and uniform in the way the older was. My remarks are therefore bound to be incomplete; they can at least represent possibilities that are present in what we now have.

What is most conspicuous about the newer rite is the *differentiation of rôles* that goes with it. The differentiation shews itself in what is said and done, in the physical setting of these activities, and in those appointed to execute them. The disposition of the building itself allows a proximity of the congregation to the sanctuary: the two are distinct but are not remote. The sanctuary itself has a structure to exhibit the differentiation. The altar, which had once served alike as book-stand and as a place for the gifts, is now reserved for this latter rôle only; the readings from Scripture have their own place, namely the lectern.[17] Their reading is distributed between more than one

---

[17] In the old rite, the epistle and gospel were also, on Sundays and Holy-days, read in translation. But they were not read until the priest had left the altar and gone to the pulpit. There, they were preceded by 'The Notices' – feast-days, masses that had been paid for, jumble-sales and the rest – and were then read one after the other. They were followed by

person, with the gospel alone reserved for priest or deacon; the range of Scripture read bears no comparison with the repeated portions once prescribed; the lectern is given a conspicuous place, and what was once negatively called 'The Mass of the Catechumens' (that is, the part of the service open to all) is now 'The Liturgy of the Word'.[18]

The priest himself no longer absorbs all other rôles. The 'undifferentiated dorsality' of his posture in the Old Mass has given way to movement and change of position prompted by the different parts of the rite. The chair at which he sits or stands is his place, as the one who presides – but presides at a celebration in which a plurality of agents is perceptibly involved. It is from that place that he conducts the penitential rite with which the Mass begins; from there too that he leads the others in the *Gloria in excelsis* and recites the collect; but it is also at the chair that he sits and listens with the others to what is read at the lectern, and responds with them to any Psalm led by the reader. The book of the gospels is carried from the altar, on which it has rested, for the principal reading at the lectern; there is now in reality what had been only a fossilised remnant of a procession in the Old Mass, where the server moved the Missal from one side of the altar to the other.

The newer rite is familiar enough to make unnecessary a detailed enumeration of all the contrasts. I mention some – the reader can think of others. There is the procession of members of the congregation with the gifts, which will in due course be distributed (from the start, the link with distribution is present). There is the position of the priest during the central part of the Mass – facing the people, uttering aloud the Canon, his gestures visible and intended to maintain and to strengthen the bond between himself and the congregation. The isolation of the words of consecration that was part of the 'cultic picture' of the Old Mass has departed. It is the

the sermon, for which some priests removed the maniple, a strip of cloth then worn on the left arm – a cultic picture of the lack of connexion between the Mass and preaching. Some made the picture even more colourful by removing the chasuble too (a film about 'Father Brown' shews Alec Guinness preaching thus attired). I leave until last what in its way is the most vivid cultic picture of how little was made of the reading of scripture in the Old Mass. Priests were accustomed to read out the translation of epistle and gospel from a book that gave the extracts for each Sunday and Holy-day. Occasionally, a feast would occur on a Sunday that called for other extracts instead; they carried on regardless. (Has the clerical vocation even the *remotest* of rivals for things to get away with in?)

18 In the days of the Old Mass, I once used a stop-watch to see how long various parts of it took. One Sunday morning the Introit (nominally the entrance-antiphon) took 24 seconds; the gospel (the principal reading from Scripture) 1 minute 12 seconds; the prayers at the foot of the altar (in origin a private preparation by the celebrant) 2 minutes and 38 seconds.

whole narrative – the words of institution, with their command to take and eat – that is now thrown into relief. And the command shews itself when the distribution of the consecrated elements is made: all alike receive under both kinds, taking both host and chalice; and the office of distribution can be shared by special ministers of either sex.

Perhaps the reader noticed an awkwardness in the vocabulary I used when discerning the cultic picture displayed by the old rite. 'Low Mass', 'High Mass', 'Sung Mass', 'Communion at a Solemn Mass', and others were indeed awkward for me, because the distinctions and practices implied by them have no analogues in what we now do. Obviously, celebrations can and should differ in their degree of solemnity and elaboration; but those words and distinctions were part of a whole picture that we now find alien.

How alien? Let me complement what I have written about the newer rite with two citations to do with the older. The first is from someone who deplored the changes. At Easter 1964, Evelyn Waugh (+1966) set down this reflexion in his diary:

When I first came into the Church I was drawn, not by splendid ceremonies but by the spectacle of the priest as a craftsman. He had an important job to do which none but he was qualified for. He and his apprentice stumped up to the altar with their tools and set to work without a glance to those behind them, still less with any intention to make a personal impression on them.

Now for what the older rite meant in practice to the Jesuit C. C. Martindale (+1965). He was staying with his father, who was not a Roman Catholic, and had gone out early one Sunday to say Mass. His father asked him at breakfast if he had had a good congregation.

He answered that he had not looked, but presumed no one was there, that he had gone there early to be alone. Naturally this was more than his father could understand. Cyril then explained himself, but in terms he knew would puzzle his father even more. Mass was a sacrifice, something between him and God...(Caraman 1967: 212–23)

The two passages do not by any means say all that needs saying about the older rite, but I think they nicely fill out the comparison I have made between old and new in celebration. And I submit that they reinforce what – I hope – is the moral of the comparison: that 'same' and 'different' may label problems here but cannot solve them; and that, whatever be the virtues and vices in our means of accommodating the past, we must also move to what lies beyond accommodation.

33 BEYOND ACCOMMODATION

This section might seem superfluous, for surely the accommodation of the past we have been examining cannot even pretend to be enough? Tampering with texts; simple silence over awkward pieces of evidence; shiftings of the supposed force in such pieces of evidence; removing terminology from the setting of which it formed part; devising picturesque descriptions of belief – 'Aunt Sallies', we might call them – from which we can then without more ado regard our own beliefs as comfortably distanced; simple forgetfulness: those and other accommodations do possess advantages, there is no doubt of that. But are not the advantages of the same kind as (to use Bertrand Russell's phrase) 'the advantages of theft over honest toil'? I hope that this section will shew that there is much more at stake than honesty or dishonesty. Our investigation will bring together much we have already met, and will prepare us for what we have still to meet in the final chapter.

The preceding section began with four methods of accommodating the past: adjustment of the record, supervenient isolation of it, redirection of its force, interpretation of it by analogies. I went on to claim that a tension between past and present is inevitable when the present is living; that the themes with which we are concerned encourage a prolongation of language that is unseemly; and that we must build on the existing sense of fittingness we possess in using words and ritual, and – as I put it – 'learn to forget'. I then wrote of selective amnesia as the most powerful of all methods of accommodating the past. Selective amnesia in fact underlies other methods mentioned earlier. Thus, supervenient isolation occurs when other testimonies have been forgotten, and the force of the record can be redirected (or domesticated by a convenient analogy) only if the concomitant inconveniences in the record are not remembered. But there is one method which does call for separate treatment here, and that is what I called 'adjustment of the record'. I shall consider it first; it will lead naturally to what is involved in the 'learning to forget' that is part of selective amnesia.

In one sense, little needs saying about adjustment of the record. Tampering with awkward texts is a piece of dishonesty that is liable to have its own punishment built into it – we can rarely be sure of the plausibility or the consequences of our fabrication.[19] But in religious matters we have to do with something that goes much deeper than tinkerings with evidence. We have to do with something well described in 1905 by von Hügel, at the time of the 'Modernist crisis', namely

the slow, very late, very difficult, never simply spontaneous growth and persistence, in the human race and in any one soul, of the sense and practice of mental accuracy, with regard to the apprehension and attestation of *factual* things and events. (von Hügel 1926: 43)

To which description I add a consequence drawn in a work of which (rare distinction!) the joint authors are a theologian and a logician. Modern knowledge, they write, answers questions that earlier ages could not even have put. But the price paid has been heavy. Since the growth of modern knowledge from the seventeenth century onwards, it has become obvious that we do not possess a unitary knowledge of mankind and the world. Earlier ages thought they did, but were wrong; we know enough now to renounce that claim, in the name of 'a tragic sense of truth' (*Wahrheitspathos*; I have gone for the contentions to Kamlah and Lorenzen 1967: 144–6).

With these remarks I associate myself, and I notice a further characteristic of modern thought. The enormous expansion of historical, literary and scientific knowledge is due to and in its turn strengthens habits of mind like willingness to question and to doubt, perseverance in absorbing and often expensive enquiries, openness in free and irreverent debate, and refusal to grant privileged exceptions to what has custom on its side. These habits can be ignored – falsification and self-deception become ever more elaborate as means of investigation increase – but the habits themselves are bound up with any progress in knowledge. Yet – and this is the further characteristic I want to notice – these habits sit very uneasily to religious belief. Athens and Jerusalem here are remote from each other's concerns. When it is a matter of the relation between past and present, we cannot expect things to run smoothly between those who

---

[19] The Roman Breviary was reformed under Pius X in this century. Part of the reformation concerned itself with some (only some) of the legends therein to do with the saints. In the unreformed version, St Sylvester (+335; Feast 31 December; Bishop of Rome in the time of the Emperor Constantine – *il primo ricco patre*) baptises Constantine and cures him thereby of leprosy. The reformed version, after removing other fables, makes the baptism cure Constantine 'of the leprosy of heathenism'. In fact, Sylvester never baptised Constantine at all.

profess allegiance to both Athens and Jerusalem and those whose concerns are essentially ecclesiastical. The latter are likely to be prone to habits of accommodation, so that past and present may be rendered straightforwardly harmonious in the service of religion. The trouble is that life is not straightforward, and resists all attempts to make it so; adjustments and other accommodations are symptoms of a persistent tension, and the tension will be especially strong in the Church of Rome, given its immense antiquity and its variegated past. I shall be considering in the next chapter what is impeding that Church from accepting the *Wahrheitspathos*, the tragic sense of truth. Here and now, I turn to what I described as the most powerful of all accommodations of the past: 'selective amnesia'.

The peculiar power of this method comes from its being so congenial to our instincts. I cited in an earlier footnote the sombre remarks of Leslie Stephen about autobiography, but they apply in due measure to all the tales we tell ourselves about our own past; our capacity to forget and to reshape can be frighteningly strong.[20] An immediate disadvantage of the process lies in its very selectivity – we can easily be unaware of just how much we have forgotten. Schillebeeckx himself provides us with an example, when he contrasts the account given of the eucharistic presence by great scholastics like Aquinas on the one hand, with popular medieval beliefs on the other. He cites texts of Aquinas we have already seen – texts in which the rebarbative profession of faith imposed upon Berengarius is robbed of its grossness (see above, p. 226). He claims that Aquinas, by the exposition he provided of the eucharistic conversion, gave something which

quietened the 'perceptual temptations' of priests who fell into torturing doubts when they drank the consecrated wine, because they tasted *wine* and not *blood*. (Schillebeeckx 1967: 10 [1968: 15])

Whatever one thinks of the account Aquinas offered, it seems odd to write of its quietening temptations, when these turn out to be

[20] I commend here a book on this theme that appeared anonymously in the 1930s (Anonymous 1932). It narrates, intelligently and arrestingly, the plight of a man whose capacity for amnesia extended to everything that had happened between about 1910 (his last memories went down that far) and 1931 (when he came to and discovered his loss of memory). Although retaining sharpness of mind, he was even unaware of the First World War, and wondered where he had acquired the wound of which his body still bore traces. His eventually successful struggle to regain his own past, which is excellently told, turns on two things: one is that his capacity to repress awkward memories has to be acknowledged; the other, that the capacity is not limitless and can be overcome. And both things are of concern to our theme.

uneasiness that what has just been drunk tastes as if it were wine rather than blood. It makes sense to say that someone is tortured by doubts that he may have drunk blood rather than wine – what sense is there in doubts that run in the opposite direction? But, of course, the priests supposedly consoled by Aquinas would have been just as nauseated as ourselves at the thought of having really drunk blood. Their doubts make sense only through selective amnesia – through a process that diminished the content of what they were saying. And the way Schillebeeckx reports their feelings suggests that he is himself in some measure a victim of the same process of diminution.[21]

But there is much more to be said of amnesia than that, its setting needs to be noticed. Forgetting is a part of the whole procedure by which we live within the inheritance that is ours and which we in our turn develop. That procedure has far more to it than forgetting. It includes changes in what we see as important in the past. It includes what I have called in these pages 'the Theaetetus Effect', where what is done later exercises a new placing upon what went before. The procedure also includes what experience has taught us, or what seeing the lack of experience in others has taught us: both can affect what we make of our past. And it includes likewise the practical resolves we make to direct our energies to what needs doing now, rather than to contemplations of what might have been done once upon a time. All this vast and continuous process, just as it touches individuals, touches also groups and societies. It does so especially when matters like religious belief and ritual are at stake, for religion runs deep and ritual is innately conservative. I cited the oracle's command that we are to worship the gods 'according to the custom of our city'. But if our city is something other than a museum, then inherited religious custom and present urgencies may need some kind of reconciling. And the reconciling – because of the character of religion and of ritual – will be a vivid example of the tensions and resolutions that are always there, whenever human beings are engaged in activities which they regard as important, and which are protracted over a period of time.

---

[21] A cruder example occurs in an essay of Ronald Knox. The prayer of the Missal that I left untranslated in the last section contains a medicinal image, and the same image is found in the second part of the *Pilgrim's Progress*, when Christiana and her party reach the Palace Beautiful. Knox twits Bunyan for using such imagery – but, when reprinting the essay as a Roman Catholic, he failed to notice that Bunyan is here no worse than a prayer Knox would have recited himself (Knox 1928: 215). The Missal encouraged amnesia, and Bunyan did not.

I wrote near the end of the previous section that we had to move to beyond accommodation, that we had to attempt more than the methods I had mentioned so far. But I then corrected what I had written: 'to put things more accurately, what has been mentioned so far has more to it than what has so far appeared'. In other words, the methods of accommodation I have described are more complicated than they look. They have wider implications, and the reflexions made upon them in this section should have taught us more of just what is bound up with the methods, given our own historical setting and preoccupations. I have given particular attention in this section to two such matters – 'adjustment of the record' and 'selective amnesia'. I set down here what I think the reflexions on each have to tell us.

Tampering with texts or silence over them brings home the distance that separates us from the roots of a religious heritage that goes back so far in time. We have lost our innocence; we have the burden of the *Wahrheitspathos* to bear, the tragic sense of truth. We are aware of the difficulties bound up with accuracy. We are bereft of the comfortingly unitary view of the world that once prevailed, because we know of too many kinds of question that can be put: Athens makes demands that once it did not. It is not that we are always honest today, for time and again we are not; it is that we have awarenesses about evidence and about its transmission that have not always been present in our religious heritage. For us, such methods of accommodation can no longer work. They have rather become topics for our study, in order that we may understand past practices and mental habits we do not ourselves share.

'Selective amnesia' proved to be part of a much wider process of tensions and resolutions, between what is and what has been. But, once more, our increased knowledge makes a difference. Our knowledge enlarges the range of our questions, and questions touching the relationship between past and present can touch the very process of selective amnesia itself. Our forgetting, if I may so put it, has to be *self-conscious*. That is the point of what I wrote in the preceding section: 'we must learn to forget'. The claim sounded and sounds odd; I go on to explain it. I would in any case admit that a danger lies in reflecting on ritual overmuch: self-consciousness can impede the celebration of inherited rites, just as it can impede other things. But I now go on to submit that a measure of self-consciousness is part of the price we pay for the extension there has been of human knowledge. The self-consciousness I have in mind touches many activities nowadays. We take delight in a work of art – but our *musée imaginaire* of photographs presents a bewildering and numbing variety of art-forms from every place and age. We pursue a historical topic – but cannot help being aware of fierce debates as to what historical knowledge really amounts to. Scholars give themselves to this or that academic pursuit – and are for ever being asked to describe the worthwhileness of what they are doing. We take part in a tradition of worship – and may well know of the multiplicity of such traditions and of the forces (often not distinctively religious) which have shaped the words and ritual that we ourselves use. We are obliged, so to speak, to step into and out of activities: to be prepared to reflect when necessary on what is being done, on why it is so done, and on how it might be done better; but also to be prepared to step back into the activity and simply take our share in it. Such is life, and that this can be difficult to do is no proof that it ought not to be done. Indeed, it is easy to see that the burden imposed by self-consciousness follows a pattern we have been meeting time and again: the pattern of unease and embarrassment.

In putting forward what I have called 'the Way of Ritual' as an approach to the eucharistic presence, I have repeatedly denied it the vividness of the 'Galilean Presence' associated with any account in terms of disguise. In making use of notions like sacrifice and ritual meals, the Way of Ritual does not deny the very mixed origins and connotations of them, and so is obliged to hold a precarious balance – uneasiness is inseparable from it, and is part of the embarrassment I took as my starting-point (I blush, therefore I am). There is embarrassment at the bondage in which our nature, our *doulé physis*, is held; embarrassment at the love of God extended to us; embarrassment at the means of deliverance taken by His love; embarrassment at the sacramental signs of the means. But I submitted that those very means of deliverance are expressed by us in ways which are themselves touched by the *doulé physis* that is ours. Images and language can acquire a life of their own, topple over into the grotesque, become a 'Shadow of the Past', and demand to be selectively forgotten. Once more, unease and awkwardness have been part of the pattern of it all.

'A past that is both revered and unsatisfactory' – that phrase and others like it have recurred ever more frequently, and we should by now be clear as to why they have: the phrase points to something that is inseparable from our inheritance. Just as the theme of 'Past and Present' has run through the book, so the varied and chequered nature of the past we inherit has emerged. What seemed at first sight a homogeneous account of the eucharistic presence in Aquinas turned out to straddle the boundaries of disciplines as we know them, and to contain themes that have been quietly dropped from common memory. The medieval eucharistic tradition itself proved to be a colourful miscellany of reflexion, devotion and miracle stories, and the miscellany also prompted forgettings. The Old Mass was venerable in age and association, but the cultic picture associated with it exhibited imbalances that resembled imbalances we had found in texts of Aquinas. The sacrificial tradition within which the Eucharist was established is older than recorded history; but that same tradition not only embodies the human hope of deliverance, it contains things that prove the need for deliverance. Our past is indeed chequered, with light and darkness intermixed everywhere. And that is why our past – revered and yet unsatisfactory – goes with the ever-recurring pattern of unease and of a balance precariously maintained. The self-consciousness of which I wrote is simply the need to share in the tradition, while being prepared to survey it and to estimate its strengths and weaknesses. And so we should not be surprised at the demands this self-consciousness makes; it too is part of the unease with which we have to live.

I have set much store by unease. A quest for ease – an ease that is attractive, even though false – is at the back of the methods of accommodation I have been considering, and there for me lies the inadequacy in them: their common effect is to remove all friction between present and past, and such a removal cannot be effected without in some way maltreating evidence. I gave the old Roman name of *damnatio memoriae* to the method of accommodation that simply obliterates or ignores what could prove embarrassing in what we have inherited. The peculiar strength of *damnatio memoriae* can point to the moral we should draw: we must let the past speak to us in all its variety. The past is no more infallible than the present, and any choice of evidence we make might have been made otherwise; for all that, an openness to the sheer variety and quantity of the past is indispensable for any worthwhile attempt at surveying it and at estimating its light and darkness. Such openness touches the present as well as the past, for it strengthens us against thinking in terms of a frictionless 'everlasting now', a timeless and seemingly inevitable present. For obvious reasons, a present like that is congenial to any large and powerful body, and the Roman Church is no exception; *damnatio memoriae* and other accommodations there will be just as congenial. Congeniality is not enough: we need awareness of the past if we are to keep our head in the present. In the next chapter we shall be meeting examples of the need, but we can notice one example here and now. I have mentioned the distress there has been among some Roman Catholics over the last quarter of a century. The distress has many causes, but one has surely been the persistent ignoring of the complexities of history that prevailed for so long in their Church. It is not accidental that this ignoring led to pain in ritual matters. The central form of worship, undoubtedly venerable, just as undoubtedly marked with gross deficiencies, and in any case a product of the chances and changes of time, was identified with religious loyalty to a faith deemed exempt from what time brings. And then the authority which had encouraged alike the identification and the exemption denied them both.

I would call the moral I have just drawn 'the liberating power of history'. I go on to draw another, this time about religious language – we might call it 'the acknowledgment of limitations'. The dangers of prolongation here we have seen, and seen too the ways in which religious practice can cope with the dangers. But our practice needs complementing by more general admissions. We need to acknowledge that language in these matters is concerned with what passes adequate expression. We need to acknowledge that 'language' here is more than verbal – words are only part of the whole cultic picture that communicates, and there can, as I have put it, always be a looseness of fit between one element in the picture and another. To all this we must resign ourselves, and resign ourselves as well to accepting that, if we do point out the defects in language used, the pointing-out is itself a part of religious language – and so is itself in need of having its limitations acknowledged: there is, once more, no stepping out of the arena.

To acknowledge the limitations of religious language in this way is to accept that the *style* of speculation here should not suggest inevitabilities inappropriate to this area of discourse. I offer two texts from Aquinas which in my view nicely illustrate what a difference style can make. Both concern the redemption, but their content matters less than their respective 'tones'. One is from the early

Commentary on the Sentences, the other is from the *Summa Theologiae*, the mature work of Aquinas.

In the former, 3 *Sent.* dist. 20, art. 1, qu.la 2; 614/23f., conclusions are presented as if they were consecutive theorems. It was fitting that Christ should restore us by satisfaction – God's justice is shewn in the abolition of a fault by punishment. Christ alone could make this satisfaction – no creature could, because of God's infinite majesty. Christ had to make it by dying – all other punishments are directed to death, and anything less would not have been sufficient with respect to the kind of punishment, for the debt of death had to be paid for the human race. And the death was suitably a shameful one – the satisfaction was not only for original sin but for all subsequent crimes.

The *Summa Theologiae*, which treats of the same theme in 3.46, exhibits on the other hand what I have to call a relaxed good humour. Why bring in justice as well as mercy, when mercy alone would have sufficed? Well, nature gives us two eyes, not one. Why should Christ's death have been violent and not natural? Because he who healed the sick should not suffer such things himself. Why upon a cross? The four elements are thus sanctified, the tree in Paradise is matched, and many 'types' of the Old Testament are fulfilled. We have here no attempt at the 'dialectic' found in the *Commentary*, no *prolongation* of what is said. We have what I have called 'the acknowledgment of limitations' – of the limitations of religious language and of the limitations of argument in matters like this. And we have something else in the *Summa Theologiae*; the mature thought of Aquinas here has exchanged the abstract dialectic of the *Commentary* for a placing of reflexion within the setting of the saving work of Christ – both the concrete circumstances of that work's achievement, and the hope it offers to us.

I have contrasted two sources in Aquinas to illustrate the acknowledgment of limitations that I think necessary in religious language. But there is another contrast in his writings, and it may by this time have already obtruded itself on the reader. The contrast is, quite simply, between what we have read from Aquinas in the present chapter and the texts of his we met earlier on. In this chapter, his texts have shewn an awareness of ritual and of what goes with it: how the origin of sacrifice lies in the sense of deficiency among mankind; how the Eucharist is a commemoration of Christ's saving work, just as the rites of the Old Testament prefigured it; how it echoes our need for food, just as Baptism echoes our birth; how there was a personal urgency in the institution of the Eucharist, for Christ was bidding farewell to those he loved; and how the Eucharist is a sign of 'spiritual eating', our union with Christ that is the way to salvation and is consummated in glory. But in the texts seen in earlier chapters to do with the eucharistic presence, there is very little about ritual at all. Aquinas, as we know, takes terminology to do with change from the Aristotelian tradition, and adapts it to express the conversion of the substance of the bread and wine into the substance of Christ's body and blood. With the coherence of the adaptation I am not now concerned, it is the absence of ritual seen time and again that I recall: the 'quasi-scientific' speculations in the first chapter, the problem of 'presence by way of substance' in the third, the bizarre speculations in the fourth that I had to call 'the shadow of the past'. There is a real contrast – what can we learn from it?

I see in the texts from earlier chapters the damage which can be done by *prolongation* in religious language. The reason for prolongation there is not hard to see. Aquinas had at his disposal the body of distinctions and definitions in the Aristotelian tradition. They needed to be maltreated if they were to be put to eucharistic employment, but the maltreatment did not rob them of their vigour. On the contrary, it turned them into so many 'dissections' of the bread and wine to be consecrated, and thus gave them a new degree of independence. We should not marvel at the elaboration of the reasonings over the eucharistic presence put forward by Aquinas, we should rather marvel that he stopped when he did. But with the texts we have seen in the present chapter, things have been different – above all, there has not been the same drive to *deduce*. I discerned a 'relaxed good humour' in what Aquinas wrote in the *Summa* about the saving work of Christ; it can also be seen in those passages of the *Summa* from which I cited texts to do with the rite of the Eucharist and its institution. For example, we saw that he is quite prepared to say that we can call the Eucharist a sacrifice because it represents the sacrifice of the Cross, just as we can point to a bust and say 'that is Cicero' (p. 197). Taken by itself, the analogy sounds like a reduction of the Eucharist to no more than a memory or picture of Calvary. But Aquinas is able to use the comparison without letting this consequence impose itself, because his whole presentation of the Eucharist here is of the *rite* as a means of sharing in the saving work of Christ: instituted by him, it is a sign of the 'spiritual eating' wherein we share his divine life. The ritual setting here is too strong for the comparison with 'that is Cicero' to take on a life of its own. At the same time, the age in which Aquinas lived was not propitious to ritual under-standing, in that the manner of celebrating the Eucharist known to Aquinas exhibited its own ritual sense only imperfectly. And so, I suggest, it comes about that his remarks on the sacrificial character of the Eucharist are, for all their perceptiveness, scattered and brief. Whereas the quasi-Aristotelian heritage of terminology to do with the eucharistic presence was not only massive, it had no essential link with ritual at all, and so was not touched by defects in ritual practice. The two simply stood apart (for more details, see FitzPatrick 1991a: 138–41).

The moral I draw is that those who reflect on the Eucharist cannot afford to cut themselves off from the concrete reality of the ritual on which they are reflecting. The reality of this ritual is a reality that is historical, with its roots in the past and with the chequered background to its evolution that attends upon all our searchings for God. I discerned in the cultic picture of the Old Mass a primacy given to transformation over distribution, and an atrophy of the differentiated and historically evolved structure of the rite. I then submitted that there is an analogy to be drawn between this cultic picture and the speculations we had encountered in Aquinas about the eucharistic presence. I now submit that it is not unreasonable to see, in this ritual poverty and lack of historical awareness, an obstacle that impeded Aquinas in his reflexions on this topic. There was, we might say, not enough in the way of ritual and of history to counterbalance the vigour and attraction of the Aristotelian vo-cabulary to do with change. Prolongation was only to be expected.

I have been reflecting in this section on ways of going beyond accommodation. In one sense, the quest is vain; we live in our present, there is a past we have inherited, we must in some fashion make sense of them both. But it should have become clearer that what can go wrong with accommodation is that we should fail to estimate its complexity and power, and fail to learn from it what we should. That is why I claimed that we need self-consciousness in our accommodation of past and present: we need a knowledge of the past, access to evidence, a grasp of how what we now hold has evolved from what went before it. Our knowledge here should extend to the methods of accommodation themselves – which is why I used the expression 'self-consciousness' in the first place. But if it does, our knowledge will bring obligations with it – the kind of obligations I linked earlier with our tragic sense of truth, our *Wahrheitspathos*. The methods of accommodation – ranging from crude tampering with texts to redistribution of the weight in tradition and so to selective forgetfulness – are so many activities by which a recalcitrant past is domesticated for the present. The task of our self-conscious reflexion will be to acknowledge that all these methods involve a confrontation with the past and a revaluation of it; then, having made that acknowledgment, we must let the revaluation become explicit. The revaluation is of a past that, although unsatisfactory, is revered; and so the revaluation cannot be painless. The methods of accommodation aimed at easing the pain, but they paid the price of confusion as to just what the revaluation involved. Confusion is a price that has to be paid when facts are not faced; what I have called self-consciousness demands that we face them. As we face them, we must face up to what else our examination in this section has revealed: the liberating power of history, the limitations of religious language, the need to keep the historic reality of ritual at the centre of our concern. Most of all, perhaps, the remoteness of thoughts like these from the concerns of those to whom our religious heritage goes back. Let those conclusions go with us into the final chapter of the book.

CHAPTER 6

'*Corpus mysticum*'

34 TWENTY YEARS AFTER

It is, more or less, as I begin this final chapter in 1991. Hans Küng's attack on the common notion of infallibility in the Church was published in 1970, its English translation in 1971. In 1972 Karl Rahner edited a volume of essays by various theologians who were in various degrees critical of Küng's position; it included a reprint of Rahner 1971, his own original dissent from Küng. In 1973 was published Küng's massive riposte: a collection of contributions from different authors, preceded and followed by essays from Küng himself, and terminated by a prodigious bibliography of the whole controversy. The tumult and the shouting dies, and readers may be assured here and now that I have no intention of appraising the debate and its ramifications. What concerns me in it is what will concern me in other debates and disagreements we are going to meet in this final chapter – the nature and the implications of what is being debated.

I wrote at the start of the preceding chapter that three themes had emerged from what had gone before, would become ever more conspicuous in what lay ahead, and could not be kept apart: the relation between the ritual and belief, the relation between present and past and the relation between the two senses of *corpus mysticum*. So it has proved. My dissatisfaction with older and newer accounts of the eucharistic presence went with my proposal to approach the ritual of the Eucharist in ritual terms, not in terms drawn from categories resembling natural science, or from personal relations. But this 'Way of Ritual', as I called it, involved an examination of how past and present stand to each other. The older heritage of eucharistic belief turned out to be more of a mixture than it promised, and the mixture harboured shadows that disconcert. The newer accounts shewed at

247

times an historical insouciance in its own way just as disconcerting. Yet old and new were and are more than pieces of abstract speculation, they touch things central to inherited belief. The cultic picture going with the Old Mass embodies what that inheritance has been, it is not just an ornament; ritual shapes and is shaped by those who celebrate it.

I conceded that the Way of Ritual does not offer the apparent clarities of the older and newer expositions I have disagreed with. To set out on the Way, to try to take ritual for what it is, to keep signs apart from disguises, is to resign oneself to an uncomfortable posture. But I submitted that comfort is not everything, that embarrassment and not insulation points whither we should go, and that we must move beyond techniques for accommodating past awkwardness. At the same time, I said we should not forget why those techniques were used. They were meant to insulate and so to defend something valued, namely the inheritance of a shared religious tradition. And so it is that the first and second themes necessarily involve the third. Those who celebrate the ritual of the Eucharist are celebrating the *corpus mysticum* that is a sign of the mystical body, their union in Christ; the relations between ritual and belief, and of past to present, cannot fail to touch the Church, which has celebrated the Eucharist over the centuries.

In the course of this chapter, I shall be considering several disagreements in the Church – over the Bible, over infallibility, over the Church's past, over the cultic pictures in older and newer forms of eucharistic ritual, over the social implications of Christianity, over the content of Christianity itself. My consideration will be directed to the *nature* of the disagreements, because it is their nature that, in my opinion, points to things amiss in the Church and to what might mend them. I have chosen to start from the disagreement between Küng and Rahner because it will lead naturally to the wider topics that concern us. The present tensions and unhappiness in the Roman Church will be elucidated by eucharistic analogies. The relation of our religious inheritance to our present belief will receive specific application, in an enquiry as to what this book has made of our eucharistic inheritance. Eucharistic belief in its turn will appear as involving matters going beyond what we usually regard as distinctively religious – in particular, the language involved in ritual. In other words, each sense of *corpus mysticum* will illuminate the other, and ritual will prove once again to be central to the account I have to offer.

And so I turn to reflect upon the nature of the debate between Küng and Rahner. What concerns me is that the two disputes exhibit a common pattern: the pattern is one of adopting a stance that turns out to be not so very adopted after all. I shall endeavour to trace the pattern in Küng first and then in Rahner.[1]

Küng challenges his opponents to support their case with scriptural evidence. For him, it is the biblical message that is the norm of belief, a message that is not identical with particular sentences in Scripture, but which did receive its initial precipitate in the New Testament. The message cannot be reduced to the level of conciliar or papal utterances; it and it alone is the ultimate criterion (*norma normans*) of belief. We might call this appeal of his to the primaeval expression of the Christian faith the *argumentum ab initio*, the 'appeal to the origin'. If we so call it, we can call the position adopted by Rahner the *argumentum a praesenti*, the 'appeal to the present'. For Rahner, the present faith of the Church is a starting-point that must be respected by any Catholic theologian, and that faith includes belief in the kind of infallibility which Küng has denied: the belief is but a more specific form of our confidence that Christ is with the Church always.

Argumentum ab initio, argumentum a praesenti: the difference between them seems sharp enough. But when we come to practice, when we try to *look* rather than to say what it *must* be, we find things a good deal less sharp. Küng, for all his talk of placing the ultimate criterion for belief in the biblical message, does not pretend to be a fundamentalist, does not defend the inerrancy of Scripture, and accepts findings of biblical criticism. He must in consequence be prepared to dissent from claims as central to the New Testament as the imminent return of Christ in glory and the prophetic force of passages in the Old Testament removed from their context. He must in general be prepared to take in a cautious and critical way what

---

[1] I examined the controversy, and expressed my dissatisfaction with what both sides took for granted, in FitzPatrick 1974. The contrast here between Küng and Rahner is real, but naturally both disputants put forward a more elaborated and qualified thesis. Useful and conveniently brief texts are in Küng (1973: 54–6; 379–80) and in Rahner (1972: 53, 58–62). For Küng's attack on infallibility I have used the translation by the late Edward Quinn. I take the occasion to express my esteem for the work done here and elsewhere by that scholarly priest, and commend Quinn 1983 for an interesting reminiscence of his experiences in translating Rahner.

have been read for centuries as straightforward narratives, and these very exercises of caution and criticism will set him apart from the general spirit and style of those who composed the Scriptures. Küng is, of course, not alone in being thus set apart. But Küng has made the biblical message the norm of belief, in his *argumentum ab initio*. For him it is the ultimate criterion, the *norma normans* – and yet the material embodiment of this message proves vulnerable and incomplete when faced with demands made on critical and historical grounds. The stance adopted is not so very adopted after all.

But neither is the stance adopted by Rahner in his *argumentum a praesenti*: this too proves more pliant than it looked. The matter here is more complex, and will take longer to explain, but examining it will lead us to themes that are central to this chapter. The illustration I offer concerns changes in Rahner's views about the origin of mankind. I have divided what I write into two parts, the second of which I shall take up in a later section, 'Facing the past'. Here and now, I consider changes in Rahner's views about *polygenism* – the claim that mankind goes back, not to one primaeval pair (*monogenism*) but to a whole group or 'population'.

In 1950, Pius XII's encyclical *Humani Generis* had cautiously given house-room to discussions over the evolution of the human body, but had declared that polygenism was certainly not open to such discussion; in no way was it clear that polygenism could be reconciled with the doctrine of original sin (as defined at Trent, for instance) – which 'comes from a sin really committed by one Adam, passed on to all by descent, and present in each one as his own' (*inest unicuique proprium*) (Pius XII 1950: 576; DS 3896–7). In a writing of 1954, Rahner conceded that monogenism was *presupposed* by the Council of Trent, but denied that Trent had *defined* it. However, he writes that the pattern of salvation as shewn in Scripture is in terms of one single stock; polygenism sits very uneasily to the doctrine of original sin, whereas monogenism is intimately bound up with it (Rahner 1962: 294, 299; ET 269, 273). Original sin in the proper sense is not thinkable without an historical origin in the action of one real individual in the beginning (Rahner 1962: 307; ET 281). More will be said of this distinction between presupposing and defining, but Rahner remains here close to *Humani Generis* – and to much else, as we shall see.

But by 1958 he has introduced the concept of *historical aetiology*. Aetiology states a cause (Greek '*aitia*') of something, perhaps in mythological terms (I suppose Kipling's *Just-So* stories provide examples). Catholic theologians may not abandon the objective references in Scripture. But they may take statements there as historical aetiology – as accounts which hark back to genuine historical events, but present them in a garb that does not derive from the outward visible features of the events themselves (Rahner 1965: 36–44). The distinction between an event and its outward features obviously allows a great latitude of interpretation, and the latitude is needed in the next writing I take from Rahner, composed in 1967. Here, it is admitted that polygenism is widely accepted, and the question is put the other way round: how can evolution be accepted *without* polygenism, given that a 'population' is needed for the evolutionary process to operate? The unity of mankind can be at the level of a specific and limited population (1967: 32–3). And even this last qualification goes later, when Rahner writes that it is becoming ever harder to think of 'the "cradle" of mankind as confined to a small circle': the unity of mankind is guaranteed rather by their mutual dependence, and their ordering to the one Christ (1969b: 106). Whatever Pius XII declared in *Humani Generis*, Rahner has moved on from it.

I need to complement this illustration of the pliability of the '*argumentum a praesenti*', as I have called it. I need to do so in order to meet the objection that *Humani Generis* is after all not an infallible decree. The objection points towards much that lies ahead in the chapter, but I can make three observations at once. First, *Humani Generis* itself condemns the objection – even non-infallible papal pronouncements demand assent, and remove their object from free discussion among theologians (568; DS 3885). Secondly, notice the *nature* of the pressure which has made Rahner and others change their views here – it comes from secular physical sciences. What Rahner makes of inherited belief is touched by his present knowledge and concerns – the 'Theaetetus Effect' is with us once more. Thirdly – and most important – we must ourselves take care not to think about the choice between monogenism and polygenism as some professional dispute among theologians, brought on by scientific discoveries, remote from scriptural considerations, and of no importance to the inherited substance of belief. To think that is to fall into something like the 'Historical Insouciance' for which I blamed newer authors in the third chapter. They wrote as if technical terms and distinctions about the Eucharist could without more ado be transferred to wholly alien contexts; here, the suggestion seems to be that the Christian belief in original sin is *modular* – that its elements can be detached or replaced while all else remains unaltered. At the very least, the suggestion needs proving, not taking for granted. Just what the suggestion involves here we shall see when we return to Rahner in the later section. But we can notice in what we have seen so far of his views that he seems on firm ground in the earliest of these items, when he stresses the intimate link monogenism has with the biblical conception of salvation-history, and expresses his intention of shewing that it is more than 'a marginal notion to Scripture' (Rahner 1962: 298–9; ET 273–4).

So both Küng and Rahner have proved less constant in their adopted stances than we might expect, and have modified their views for reasons of an external character – the exercise of critical techniques upon the Bible, the findings of natural science. But if Küng and Rahner exhibit this pattern of withdrawal and adaptation, what substance can there be to the appeals they respectively make? Are not they both being inconsistent with positions originally adopted?

I think they are being inconsistent, but I also think that the inconsistency points to a better way. What this better way is we can begin to see by noticing another inconsistency, present this time in many others as well. Roman Catholics who are prepared to accept the methods of biblical criticism are very much less willing to apply similar methods to the utterances of their Church. Rahner does, as we have just seen, move on from *Humani Generis*, and we have yet more to see of where the move takes him. But in his debate with Küng, where his *argumentum a praesenti* was opposed to Küng's *argumentum ab initio*, both were in agreement from the start in rejecting biblical fundamentalism. Which makes the very bulk (and at times the asperity) of their controversy a sign of how differently the two sorts of criticism are regarded. Indeed, a more recent example of the difference will bring out the contrast, and in a disconcerting fashion.

The year 1984 saw in England various events of real or imagined theological significance: an episcopal appointment in the Church of England that was taken to compromise orthodox beliefs; the fulmination of the cathedral where the bishop was to be consecrated; and a widely discussed programme on the television which expressed scepticism over (among other things) the biblical accounts of the Resurrection. For one Catholic writer in the *Universe*, Anglican disarray had the lesson for Roman Catholics of 'a sense of humble gratitude for the guidance we have in the Church for our Faith as well as a deepening fidelity – which is also a trait of true ecumenism' (Burridge 1984). But the guidance actually available to Roman Catholics might be thought to deserve less gratitude, humble or otherwise, when we look at the 'Official Catholic Response' to the television programme, composed by a group of scholars at Cardinal Hume's request. Among its admissions I mention these. Some or all of the titles like 'Son of God', 'Son of Man' and 'Messiah' were not used in Jesus' lifetime, and in a sense he never intended to found a Church. In what they contain about the resurrection, Matthew and Luke 'embellish' Mark's account, and have 'meditated on it more deeply' – so that Luke replaces Mark's young man in a white robe with two men in brilliant clothes, and Matthew replaces him with an angel. And although the empty tomb and the appearance are the only adequate grounds for the Resurrection faith developing in the minds of the first Christians, they are not absolutely essential to the Christian faith (Cathnews 1984, parts 2 and 3). Once more, I am not concerned to pronounce upon the elements of this debate, be it the bishop, the programme or the Response (or the fulmination, come to that). I am simply concerned to point out just how much the Response was prepared to abandon of traditional belief about the gospels, in its concessions to biblical criticism, and just how little it contained of analogous concessions to do with the Church, in which the traditional belief had been taught for so long. Tradition concerning the resurrection seems more expendable than tradition concerning infallibility. What we found with Küng and Rahner, we have found again here. The oddity is disconcerting; to follow it up will be profitable, and must be our next step.

At the start of the third chapter, we left Julien Green deploring one Sunday in 1966 the changes in the Church as he had known it, and expressing bewilderment at the scepticism voiced in a sermon he had heard on the raising of the widow's son at Nain. We can now set beside this the entry for 9 March 1968 in his *Journal*. Jacques Maritain came to luncheon, and Green said that another Catholic had recommended to him a book by Bultmann. Maritain laid down his fork (*posa sa fourchette*) with a look of horror, and murmured '*Bultmann, l'écrivain le plus néfaste...*' For once, Maritain had succinctly expressed a thought that mattered: given his beliefs, he was quite right to describe Bultmann as the most abominable of writers. The rightness, I add, lies for me not in the particular opinions favoured by Bultmann about mythological elements in the Gospels. For me, the rightness lies in something that goes deeper – so deep that it gets taken for granted all too easily nowadays. It lies in the very concept of a critical reading of the Scriptures. The pressures in favour of biblical criticism come from considerations that are not specifically religious at all – literary, philological and historical investigations of various kinds. Once admit these pressures, and you are allowing the religious heritage to be appraised by external standards; and once allow *that*, and there is no reason for confining the appraisal to biblical text, while leaving ecclesial declarations untouched. Maritain's instinct, given his own beliefs, was sound – you may start with the Bible but you cannot offer rational grounds for stopping there. The breach has been made, and its consequences have to be faced. The Roman Church has in my view scarcely begun to face the consequences, so I mean to spell some of them out – they touch the heart of my contentions, about Eucharist and Church alike.

I begin by drawing another analogy between beliefs about the Church and beliefs about the Eucharist. Since the second chapter, we have seen a good deal of what I call the Fallacy of Replacement – the belief that a presence which is exalted and profound *competes with* and *replaces* a presence that is simple and workaday. The Fallacy we met in a eucharistic context, but in the third chapter I claimed to detect it in a wider setting, when noticing what is sometimes written about biblical narratives of the marvellous. The allegation is made that, in such contexts, simple workaday questions to do with events, times and places cannot be put. My objection there to the move was partly logical (recall my comments about *Gulliver's Travels* at p. 109), but I made another observation, to which I must now return: I pointed out that generations of believers had taken the narratives as allowing the simple questions to be put, and as allowing them to be answered in a favourable sense. And it is the very simplicity of the questions that now causes – or ought to cause – embarrassment. Because the trouble with a critical reading of the Bible is that, time and again, it reveals the authors of biblical narratives as unable or unwilling to preserve accuracy concerning simple propositions of this sort, even though propositions of the sort are intimately bound up with the more exalted claims that the authors are eager for us to accept. I turn to a specific example of the kind of trouble I have in mind, taking up themes I raised in FitzPatrick 1985.

I wrote earlier that some theologically significant events for England in 1984 touched what is to be found about Jesus in the Scriptures, and in particular what is to be found there about his resurrection. Once more, I abstain from passing judgment upon the debate; once more, my purpose is to notice the *nature* of the disagreement. And I do so by going back to what the New Testament presents as the first public preaching of the resurrection, the discourse of Peter on the first Whit Sunday (Acts ii 14f.). Jesus was crucified, he says, but God raised him up, for death could not hold him; as David wrote in the Psalms, 'neither wilt thou suffer thine holy one to see corruption'. Now David is dead, and his tomb is well known; but, being a prophet, he wrote what he did about the resurrection of Christ; and of that resurrection Peter and his companions are all witnesses. The chapter goes on to describe the effectiveness of this preaching, but the narrative prompts in me rather a more homely question – what possible notion of proof or of evidence or of investigation can the author have had, or the audience have had to whom his account was addressed? That the resurrection means more, indescribably more, than what is open to human investigation, is obvious. But just as obvious is the author's failure here to grasp that the claims being made did have connotations that are open to human investigation; and that the investigation should have more to it than fanciful exegesis of scripture, and more than an appeal made to the existence of David's tomb without a word spoken about the existence and characteristics of the tomb of Jesus himself.

I understand that the narrative in Acts ii is now attributed to preachings in the eighties and nineties of the first century. So be it; its origins have nothing to do with my contention. Neither has the 'literary form' of the passage – the nature and purpose of the piece of writing, its intertwining of texts from the Old Testament with the proclamation of the Risen Lord. Yet again, I prescind from judgment upon all such matters. My concern is to recall what I pointed out in the preceding chapter: our age has the burden to bear of the *Wahrheitspathos*, 'the tragic sense of truth' (p. 236). It is not that we are morally superior (or inferior) to those who went before us. It is that we have to live with a greater awareness of the complexity of the past and of the remoteness of some of its patterns of thought. We have to live with habits of mind to do with accuracy and with free historical and literary inquiry, habits that are simply alien to so much in our religious past, a past that includes Bible and Church alike. Yet again, that past turns out to be 'revered but unsatisfactory'. If we find the sermon in Acts ii embarrassing, we ought to be just as embarrassed by the tradition that accepted it without demur for so long. If we find the Official Catholic Response a comfort, and feel a humble sense of gratitude for the guidance we have in the Church, we ought to ask ourselves what gratitude would have been felt for the guidance by the generations in the Church for whom the Gospels were a straightforward narrative of things that happened. And if we do ask questions like that, we shall be embarrassed – we have applied secular canons of criticism to a biblical text, and the application has revealed limitations in the text. But it has thereby also revealed limitations in the tradition within which texts of the sort have been read and believed: the Church, which is supposed to provide the guidance, turns out to be just as limited as what it is meant to be guiding us about. And so yet another analogy between Eucharist and Church emerges. Appeal was made to the account of eucharistic belief in Aquinas – but that account contains things that are part of what I called 'the shadow of the past'. Just so, appeal is made here to the tradition of belief in the Church concerning biblical narratives – but narratives and belief alike display limitations. We are, I repeat, embarrassed.

Unless of course we take measures not to be. We have already seen something of the measures in a eucharistic context, but must now think of them in the wider setting of the Church's life as a whole. The debate between Küng and Rahner has shewn the tensions in the positions they respectively adopt. It has also shewn that the Church seems to come off better than the Bible when concessions are made for external reasons. We have yet more to see in the next section of how the difference comes to be made. I shall submit that, for Church just as for Eucharist, embarrassment is profitable and insulation is not.

35   A PICTURE RECALLED

Vatican II: *Gaudium et spes*, On the Church in the modern world. 7 December 1965 (Vatican, Second Council of the, 1966e).

§36 In any discipline, investigations pursued in a scientific way and according to the norms of morality can never really

Pius IX: *Letter of 21 December 1863 to the Archbishop of Munich* (DS 2875–2880). Some Catholics among those engaged in higher studies... have not been deterred, in their claim for a deceptive and false freedom of knowledge, from being drawn away beyond the limits which should not be crossed, given the be opposed to faith, because the objects of secular knowledge and of faith come from the same God...We may here lament certain habits of mind – found among Christians themselves at times – which are due to a failure to recognise the legitimate autonomy of science. The habits gave rise to confrontations and controversies, and have led many to be of the opinion that faith and knowledge are opposed to each other.

§59 [The Council acknowledges two distinct orders of knowledge: faith and reason]...It...affirms the legitimate autonomy of human culture and especially of the sciences...In consequence, with due regard paid to the moral order and to the public good, anyone may freely seek truth, express and make known his views, and pursue any of the arts; it also follows that he has a right to be informed of public events.

§92 The Church has the mission...of uniting all men...into one spirit. She is thereby a sign of that brotherhood which permits and encourages a sincere dialogue. What this calls for in the first place is that we foster in the Church itself mutual respect...acknowledging all legitimate differences, so that a more fruitful conversation may be established among...the one people of God.

Vatican II: *One of its closing messages of 8 December 1965 : That to men of thought and of science* (Vatican, Second Council of the: 1966f).

A special greeting to you, seekers after truth, men of thought and of science... your road is ours also...We are friends of your calling as searchers...Continue your search...But do not forget that, if thought is something great, it is in the first place a duty. Woe betide those who deliberately close their eyes to the truth! And thought is a responsibility too; woe betide those who darken the spirit, darken it with those tricks and devices that lower it, puff it up, deceive and

obedience due to the Church's *Magisterium*, which was divinely established to preserve the integrity of the whole revealed truth...
We should like to believe that they did not wish to limit the obligation [to submit to Church decisions] – binding all Catholic teachers and writers – to only those things which are proposed by the infallible judgment of the Church as dogmas of faith to be believed by all. [The same submission must be given] to what is taught as divinely revealed by the ordinary *magisterium* of the whole Church...
It is not enough to receive and to venerate such dogmas of the Church. They must submit to the decrees of the Pontifical congregations [of the Roman curia] to do with doctrine...

Congregation for the Doctrine of the Faith [i.e., the Inquisition]. *Instruction of 24 May 1990 on the theologian's calling within the Church* (Inquisition, the Roman; 1990). [The Extracts that follow are taken from §§15–17 (the different interventions of the Magisterium) and §23 (what response is demanded by each).]

§15 Christ promised the...gift of infallibility...The gift is exercised in various ways.
[a] In a special way, when the Bishops [of the Church, in union with the Pope] proclaim a doctrine by a collegial act, as in a General Council. Or when the Roman Pontiff...proclaims a doctrine *ex cathedra*.

   §23 [Assent demanded:] *theological faith*.
[b] The Magisterium can definitively make pronouncements which, although not among the truths of faith, are intimately connected with them...It can pronounce on the natural law. (§16)

   §23 [Assent demanded:] *such a truth is to be firmly embraced and believed*.
[c] Divine assistance is given to bishops

deform it. What else is the first principle for men of science, except to struggle to think aright? For that – without seeking to impede your steps or to dazzle your vision, we come to offer you the light of our mysterious lamp of faith... Thanks be to God, there perhaps has never appeared as clearly as today the possibility of a deep harmony between true knowledge and true faith – servants, one and the other, of the truth that is unique... Do not impede this precious coming together. Have confidence in faith, this great friend of the intellect.

and especially to the Roman Pontiff... when – even without making an infallible or definitive pronouncement – they teach what leads to a clearer perception of revelation. (§17)

> §23 [Assent demanded:] *A religious submission of will and intellect*; not simply external or disciplinary, but moved by the obedience of faith.

§17 Account must be taken of the particular nature of any intervention of the Magisterium... but... all these interventions come from the same ultimate source – from Christ... Decisions of the Magisterium, even when not endowed with the gift of infallibility, are not... lacking in divine assistance, and call for the assent of the faithful.

We seem to have come full circle. Pius IX reigns as Pope in 1863, and theologians are admonished concerning their duties. John-Paul II reigns as Pope in 1990, and theologians are admonished concerning their duties. The two sets of admonitory words could be comfortably interchanged; and neither one nor the other bears much relationship to the extracts printed in the left-hand column from the Second Vatican Council. The extracts from the council cannot seize all the qualifications in the full text; but they seem couched in a different language altogether from the admonition of the 1860s and from the admonition of the 1990s. We seem to have come full circle.

I chose the texts – I could have chosen others – because they can sum up the disappointment felt by many nowadays in the Roman Church. Much there has changed – above all, the forms of worship, but the styles of other things as well: clerical education, life at parochial and diocesan level, relations with other Churches, involvement in public life, a concern for justice over the Earth. But the style of many pronouncements from Rome seems by contrast to have moved backwards if it has moved at all. There is a real gap, and it shews no signs of narrowing. The disappointment is just as real, and it shews no signs of mending. Of course, it goes back a long way. Küng's book on infallibility opens with 'A candid preface', where the first sentence complains that the renewal of the Catholic Church sought by the Second Vatican Council has come to a standstill. But, as the previous section pointed out, a score of years has gone by since the debate over Küng's book. The gap is not only real, it has proved to be durable. For better or worse, utterances at the Second Vatican Council are not of a piece with utterances of today, just as they are not of a piece with utterances of nearly a hundred and thirty years ago. What is to be said?

Various things have already been said. Küng himself ends the main body of his book with a section entitled 'The pope as he might be': such a pope would see the Church in a way 'genuinely evangelical' rather than 'juridical-formalistic and static-bureaucratic'; he would foster legitimate diversity, and liberate the centre from unnecessary unwieldiness; he would not be against the law but against legalism; his would be a primacy of service (Küng 1971: 244–7). An American contributor to Küng's 'riposte' proposed analogies for the papal office drawn from presidential government, and from the leadership given in his own country towards ending segregation in schools (Greeley 1973). Some years before the debate, a writer in England put forward as a model the conducting of a seminar (Wicker 1966: 274–5). The trouble with all such suggestions – one of the troubles rather – is that we already have the papacy as a going concern, and that the things in it to which exception is taken are part and parcel of the way in which it has come to be what it is. I am not just thinking of the centripetal tendencies in any large organisation, although these play their part. What I have in mind is rather an historical pattern that has shaped the papacy, a pattern to which a phrase I have already used may be extended: 'supervenient isolation'. Time and the course of time have removed counterbalancing powers, initiated centralising and isolating tendencies with a life of their own, concentrated in the papal office what was once distributed and variously shared.[2] It is not that I lack sympathy for

[2] In a footnote I can be more specific. I have long held six figures to be the founders of the Roman Church as we know it: the Emperor Claudius, Gregory the Great, the Prophet Mohammed, Martin Luther, Napoleon Bonaparte and Sir Charles Wheatstone. Claudius (+AD 54) established the Roman civil service, which is the ancestor of the curia, the administrative organisation of the Roman Church; moreover, by recruiting it from the dregs of society, Claudius ensured that its loyalty would be directed without intermediary to the imperial figure. Gregory the Great – 'Consul of God', as his epitaph rightly described him – was able, amid a distracting life, to look Westwards towards new work rather than towards the Christian East (aided, it must be added, by his intellectual limitations – he had little understanding of classical literature, and had lived in Constantinople for years without learning any Greek). As Gregory (+604) looked West, so the rise and diffusion of Islam from the 640s onwards weakened the ancient Eastern Churches – by the end of the middle ages there was no practical rival to Rome. The divisions of the Reformation in the 1500s could not but make of the papacy a tangible expression of adherence to the old religion, while the sweeping away of so much by the French Revolution, and the reshapings

the suggestions I have been recording. I have a good deal of sympathy, but I do not think that their proponents grasp as they might just how much is involved in suggestions of the sort. There is a time-honoured pattern of argument called *modus tollens*: 'if such-and-such be the case, so-and-so must also be the case; but so-and-so is *not* the case; therefore neither can such-and-such be.' I am concerned to point out that impugning the papacy as we now have it involves something analogous to a very large *modus tollens* indeed.

Let me state here and now that the *modus tollens* goes far beyond personalities. It should be fairly evident by this time that I do not find congenial either curial utterances or the personal style of the present (John-Paul II) pope, and the lack of congeniality will become more evident as this chapter goes on. All the more reason then for me to insist that I am not bothered about my personal preferences, and that the *modus tollens* I have in mind goes far beyond assigning the tiara to some liberal shepherd, who will style himself Gallio I (see Acts xviii) and canonise Erasmus. I should be amused by such a turn of the wheel of fortune, but in no way satisfied. Much more is amiss. The *modus tollens* I have in mind goes deeper, and I shall be explaining it by eucharistic analogies.

In the preceding chapter, I introduced the notion of what I called a 'cultic picture' – the pattern of beliefs and preferences embodied in a tradition of ritual and ceremonial. I submitted that the Old Roman Mass offered a cultic picture, and I stated what I thought were the main characteristics of it. Later in the chapter I turned to the cultic picture presented by the New Rite, and pointed to the contrasts between it and the picture presented by the Old Rite. My contention now is that the unease felt in the Church over the patterns of behaviour and pronouncements by pope and curia is only to be expected, because forms of worship have their own inner logic. Cultic pictures express a significance that can touch more deeply those who worship than any purely verbal exposition could. And the significance of the newer cultic picture is simply at odds with the pattern

in Europe by what followed it, left the figure of the Pope isolated and dramatised in a new way altogether. Pius VI may have died in exile in 1799, and Pius VII (+1823) been a prisoner of the Napoleonic eagle; but the papacy survived into something more than denominational (and, incidentally St Malachy thus scored two more bull's-eyes: *Peregrinus Apostolicus* and *Aquila Rapax* – 'Apostolic Wanderer' and 'Rapacious Eagle'). Sir Charles Wheatstone (American readers might prefer Samuel Morse) produced the first practically usable form of the electric telegraph. Given that, Rome could be as near a bishop as could the neighbouring diocese; communication, here as elsewhere, began to fashion what was communicated.

and drift of so much that is associated with Rome; it is at odds with it because papal and curial interventions are still of a piece with the older cultic picture. Yet again, ritual turns out to be central to the thesis I am propounding: the inner logic of the newer rites, if those rites be deemed legitimate, must be allowed to operate upon the organisation of the Church at all levels; ritual needs catching up with.

To make explicit what this contention amounts to will take time, but it is not difficult to set down at once some ways in which the Roman style of things resembles what we saw of the older cultic picture. Recall some characteristics we noticed in the last chapter. The physical setting of the Old Mass was starkly simple: all structural differentiations were reduced to a 'polarisation' between altar for the priest and nave for the people, where they remained in silence and for the most part on their knees. The priest's rôle was all-absorbing, in that he had taken over functions which were originally distributed and shared among others. His posture was one of 'undifferentiated dorsality' – his back to the people, without regard to what actions he was performing, his downcast eyes on the occasions when he briefly faced the congregation. His words and actions during the central part of the Mass, though in themselves complex and elaborate, were concealed from the people by his posture and by the silence of his recitation. The amount of Scripture read was small; the transformation of the gifts was stressed rather than their distribution; and the lengthy and complicated history of the rite was subordinated to the conception of it as an inherited and untouchable whole. It is surely not unfair to see analogies in all this to what can be found in the central organisation of the Church. There is the polarisation between the papacy and all else. There is the concentration at Rome – by that supervenient isolation I have referred to – of what was once distributed. There is a 'dorsality' in Roman interventions, a conceiving of them as essentially a monologue which calls for no response other than acceptance. And there is a concealment of the machinery of administration and dissent that leaves in isolation what is finally given the seal of approval. Small wonder surely that the Roman style today should seem at odds with so much else in the Church: the Roman style today is still of a piece with the Old Roman Mass.

The analogy I have drawn may still seem fanciful, so I support it with two illustrations of how the older style of ritual finds correspondence in the present style of the Roman Church. The first example is the once popular practice of *allegorising* the ceremonies of the Mass, the other is the *concept of substance* we have seen in the older expositions of the eucharistic presence. I deal with the examples in turn.

Allegorisation, which goes back to the ninth century, is now mercifully dead, but I think quite a few readers will remember it from schooldays or sermons. The ceremonies of the Old Mass were taken as symbolising the actions of Christ before and after his passion and death. I refer readers who want details to *ST* 3.83.5, where (to give but one example) Aquinas makes the triple sign of the cross over the elements before their consecration signify the selling of Christ to the priests, the scribes and the pharisees; and makes the double signing that then follows represent Judas the seller, and Christ the one sold. And so on; indeed, why ever stop? (Note that Albert the Great, the teacher of Aquinas, had strongly disapproved.) The effect of allegorising was the imposition of an appearance of uniformity – even of inevitability – upon a ritual that had in fact been developed over many years, from many sources and in many different ways. Historical complexity was blurred and obscured by allegorising, and it is in this blurring and obscuring of history that I find an analogy to what is happening in the Roman Church today, and happening there in a novel fashion. The novelty will throw light on why biblical criticism seems so much more acceptable than a similar critical approach to the Church.

The Reformation offered a challenge that concerned a text, namely the Bible. Small wonder that Rome's reaction was to keep a strict control of the Scriptures, and that their use in worship and devotion was severely limited. The advent of biblical criticism also offered a challenge concerning a text – criteria of a secular character were applied to sacred writings, and the limitations of the writings were made painfully evident. Small wonder that Rome's reaction was an attempt to stifle such criticism. In each case, a powerful organisation was being confronted by something alien, something that revealed in a new way a gap between past and present, something that called for a revaluation of what had been taken for granted. What more natural than that the organisation should try to strangle the challenge at birth? But the second of the challenges has apparently turned out to be a defence against the first, and Chesterton's claim seems to have come true – it is sometimes better to have two enemies than one. Biblical criticism, so long resisted by the Church of Rome, can now be welcomed as reinforcing the claims that Church makes: by bringing out the limitations of the Scriptures, it seems to leave the Church without a rival in determining what is to be believed. The tension between what is now taught and what is to be found in the gritty particularity of a biblical text seems to have been overcome, and overcome by the very critical activity that was frowned on for so long. But if there be anything to what I have been claiming so far, this acceptance of biblical criticism is no more intellectually coherent than its former condemnation. If it makes no sense to deny the complexity of the relations between present and past, it makes just as little sense to allow the complexity, but to fence off privileged areas as exempt from it. Once more, Maritain's instinct was sound – you cannot start with biblical criticism and hope to stop there. I do not agree with those who would reject a critical reading of the Scriptures, but I respect their position for its coherence. It is a coherence I do not find in the greater willingness of theologians to speak in critical terms of the Bible than of the Church, or in the general persuasion found here and to be found again: that the Bible may be approached in ways quite alien to ways in which it once was approached, and all else remain unaltered.[3]

I wrote in the previous section that the Church of Rome had scarcely begun to draw the consequences of its having accepted biblical criticism. Why it has not drawn more will now be clearer, but I turn to another and very modern reason for Rome's failure to draw them. It is in this reason that I see the analogy to the allegorising of the ceremonies of the Old Roman Mass, which blurred and obscured the historical development of the rite. And the modern reason is quite simply that Rome, to a degree both difficult and uncomfortable to appreciate, is adapting itself to modern media of communication and above all to television. Television has many capacities, one of which is the provision of pictorial immediacies; it has many defects, one of which is an inability to articulate a rational analysis of what looks so

---

[3] Incoherent the persuasion may be, but I can bring out its attraction by going back to Molière's *Le Malade Imaginaire* for an analogy: biblical criticism resembles the art of medicine, criticism of the Church resembles surgery. Biblical criticism has an array of terms like 'literary form', which can keep what we are dealing with at a comfortable distance – just as M. Diafoirus is believed by Argan when he utters gibberish to cover up a wrong diagnosis. But criticism of the Church seems to come closer – just as when Argan's servant Toinette, disguised as a doctor, recommends that her master have an arm off, he is at once perturbed.

close upon our screens. Roman Catholicism can be displayed there in terms of a powerful and powerfully visual figurehead; such display seems to circumvent the problem of time, for pictures have no past to jar with the present. Television for the Church is what allegory was for the Old Mass – a temporally extended reality is obscured and overlaid by a speciously attractive attempt to defy the complexity of present and past. Neither the obscuration nor the defiance can do justice to things as they really are. You can televise a travelling pope; you cannot televise the Communion of Saints.

I turn to the other analogy I draw between the Church today and the older cultic picture: the *concept of substance* that has proved so direly convenient for scholastic speculations about the Eucharist. Concerning the concept it is enough here to recall what I wrote earlier, that the theological usefulness of the concept of substance for accounts of transubstantiation varies inversely with its philosophical coherence. The debate between Selvaggi and Colombo considered in the first chapter shewed the deceptive attraction of what I later called the 'splendid isolation' of Colombo's notion of substance, a notion which removes all considerations touching substance to the 'metaphysical order', and relegates to the order of accidents whatever can be discovered by physical investigation into the nature of things. It is in this insulation that I see another eucharistic analogy to what can be found in the Roman Church. The analogy concerns techniques for accommodating the past. When I gave examples of them in the preceding chapter, I put them forward as activities in which we all engage in a variety of contexts – selective amnesia and the rest are by no means exclusively religious. But when the activities are exercised in a religious setting, when they are exercised upon the past I have been describing as revered but unsatisfactory, we face the difficulty that religious utterances do not take kindly to qualifications and hesitancies, but take all too kindly to emphatic and noisy assertion. It is then only natural that (if I may return for a moment to a culinary metaphor) we should subject to a process of marination what is awkward in our religious past, in order to render it more digestible. The process amounts to what we might call *retroactive demotion*, and is familiar enough in the activities of Catholic theologians – what we saw Rahner doing about monogenism is but one example among many. Our inheritance may look obdurate, but somehow it turns out to be not so obdurate after all. This utterance was not as solemn as it seemed; that one was directed at a particular problem which has now passed; the terms in a third do not really mean what they might be expected to mean. The analogy with a notion of substance like Colombo's is striking. Just as no physical discovery can reach the order of substance, so no accommodation of the past can reach the substance of belief. Just as physical investigations (being in the accidental order) are subordinate to metaphysics (which alone deals with substance), so all speculations concerning the faith are subordinate to what is proclaimed by Rome. At the same time, just as all subsequent developments in knowledge of things leave untouched the order of substance as Colombo proposes it, so all subsequent manoeuvres in the face of Roman proclamations leave uncompromised the infallibility (or indefectibility, or what you will) of the proclaimer. If the proclamations end by being ignored, they cannot have been infallible to begin with.

I argued that Colombo's 'insulated' notion of substance in eucharistic theology summed up a whole bundle of fallacies, philosophical and theological. I shall be submitting that similar fallacies, philosophical and theological, are summed up in this analogous attempt to insulate the teaching of the Church from what apparently impugns it. And my submission will also be that the process of insulation goes with just that blurring and obscuring of history we have also been considering. The submissions will concern me ever more as this chapter goes on. I start by briefly noticing the matter of insulation as it happens in the disagreement between Küng and Rahner.

It is notorious that Küng directed an attack upon the concept of infallibility, and we have already noted some of his and Rahner's opposed contentions. I wrote at the start of this chapter that I am less concerned with the merits of disputes like this than with their *nature*; and it is the nature of the disagreement between Küng and Rahner that concerns me here. The general verdict on the dispute, as far as I can see, is that Küng (in a manner praiseworthy or blameworthy, according to your views) is *diluting* the claims traditionally made for the Church. The traditionally strict demands for infallibility in the 'propositional' sense, to use a term of Küng's – demands still made in a subtle and nuanced way by Rahner – are replaced with a looser claim: the claim that the Church, despite individual errors, remains fundamentally in the truth (Küng 1971: 181f.). Those who blame Küng and those who praise him seem to agree in thus describing the disagreement.

I dissent from both sides. It is not Rahner who is defending the stricter demand, it is Küng. Küng it is whose claim is the crueller, Küng it is whose claim is the more obviously and more embarrassingly not satisfied by the course of the Church's history. Rahner's claim – of course, it is not just Rahner's! – is something essentially *clerical*: it looks back over the centuries of ecclesiastical history, and denies that, in the fullest exercise of its powers by pope or by council or by general teaching, the Church has been in error. What we have been seeing earlier of accommodating the past, and what we have seen just now of retroactive demotion, ought to have convinced us that a claim of that sort is not really very exigent. Presented with any candidate for falsifying the claim, we know what we shall do. We shall do what theologians and councils and popes have done in the past; we shall deny that the alleged commitment was as definitive as it looked. Things are very different with Küng's claim (or should be – I am not claiming he would go along with me here, although I think he should and hope he would). Küng talks of a fundamental remaining in the truth, which is not annulled by individual errors. But 'fundamental' connotes a going down to the roots of things, and 'truth' connotes something with a universal concern – as the scholastic tag runs, *Verum vagatur per omnes categorias*, truth is at home in all categories of reality. Küng, if I may so put it, takes the Church into the market-place by what he claims for it; and others in the market-place will not be tied down to the ecclesiastical processes of adjustment and accommodation by now familiar. They will have their own processes, but they are likely to cast a cold eye on those I have been describing. So we shall be obliged, if we want to talk in the market-place about the *corpus mysticum* that is the Church, 'not to say what it *must* be, but to *look*'. And what we find when we do look will be something very mixed indeed.

How mixed I can best shew by a simple example that will bring this section to a close. We have all heard that Pope Alexander VI (+1503) was a wicked man, and we have all learned to distinguish between admitting his wickedness and denying that he ever compromised the faith in a supposedly infallible pronouncement. Some readers may have learned something else about him – that the King of Spain presented him with the first consignment of gold from the New World, and that Alexander used it to gild the ceiling of St Mary Major's at Rome. One does not need to know much history to understand just what went to that consignment and to the consignments that followed – plunder, torture, genocide, we need not continue the list. Rahner will not be embarrassed, as far as his demand goes, for it does not cover such matters. Alexander can err all the way to St Mary Major's just as he can break all Ten Commandments simultaneously when relaxing back at the Vatican, and no harm is done in either case to the claim being made for infallibility in the sense in which Rahner defends it. But Küng has to be embarrassed, if 'fundamentally' and 'truth' are to have any meaning. And he will be more embarrassed at the gilded ceiling than at the gilded follies. And, because Küng is embarrassed, his claim has some content to it; it is concerned – to speak in Roman terms – with what witness Christ's Vicar and Christ's Church then bore to the good news Christ had come to bring. I use a word we shall be meeting again: Küng's claim connotes a *vulnerability* in the Church, it does not talk in terms of some insulated guarantee, some Colombo-like substance of faith that lies beyond any attempt to devise counter-examples. Once again, the two senses of *corpus mysticum* go together. Once again, awkwardness and embarrassment point the way forward.

A choice has presented itself to us in this section, and I have suggested how we should choose. But if we choose in this way – if we decline to ignore the mixed character of our religious past, if we refuse to insulate our claims from the abrasiveness of history – we must face the consequences. We must accept the embarrassment that history can bring, and admit the vulnerability of the *corpus mysticum*. I move in the next section to seeing where acceptances and admissions of the sort can lead us – and to seeing where we are led if we do not make them. And I do this in a tale of two visits.

36 A TALE OF TWO VISITS

Vatican II: *Dignitatis Humanae – Declaration on religious freedom of 7 December 1965* (Vatican, Second Council of the, 1966d). Extracts, cited by marginal numbers.

§1 In our time, demands are ever growing that human beings should...enjoy judgment and responsible freedom... and that legal limits be set to public authority, to avoid undue restriction of

Congregation for the Doctrine of the Faith [i.e., the Inquisition]. *Instruction of 24 May 1990 on the theologian's calling within the Church* (Inquisition, the Roman, 1990). Further extracts, cited by marginal numbers.

§35 The interventions of the Magisterium are to ensure that the unity of the Church persists...for they serve to keep it in the truth against the arbitrary freedom...The demand for freedom... touches first of all the practice of religion.

§2 The Council declares that the human person has a right to religious freedom...free from coercion...from any human power; so that no one be forced to act against his conscience or impeded from acting according to it, within due limit, privately or publicly, alone or with others. The Council declares too that the right to religious freedom is based upon the dignity of the human person...Because men...are endowed with reason and free-will...they are naturally led to seek the truth and morally obliged to do so, especially religious truth...But the obligation cannot be satisfied in a human way unless men possess freedom of mind and immunity from external coercion. Religious freedom rests, not upon the individual's subjective dispositions, but on his nature. And so the right to immunity persists even for those who fail to satisfy their obligation to seek the truth...

§3 Truth is to be sought in a way that corresponds to the human person and to the social nature of that person. That is, it is to be sought by free investigation, with the help of teaching, instruction, communication and dialogue, whereby truths found or believed to have been found are passed on, in order that there may be mutual help in the search for truth. When truth has been found, it must be firmly held to with an assent that is personal.

§12 The Church...is therefore following the way of Christ and the Apostles when it acknowledges that the nature of religious freedom is in harmony with the dignity of man and with divine revelation...Although in the life of the People of God in its journey through the varieties of human history there has at times obtained a pattern of behaviour that matched inadequately the spirit of

character of changing opinions...When such interventions seem to limit the theologian's freedom, they generate (by fidelity to the faith we have received) a higher freedom, a freedom which comes only from unity in the truth.

§36 The freedom of the act of faith cannot serve as a basis for the right to dissent. What is meant by that is not a freedom from truth but a free giving of oneself, which everyone must fulfil according to his own moral duty of embracing the truth...If the right to religious freedom is respected, the foundation is laid for respecting the other rights of man. Appeal cannot therefore be made to these rights of man in order to resist the interventions of the Magisterium. Such a course of action misunderstands the nature of the Church's mission; the Church received from the Lord the task of proclaiming the truth of salvation to all mankind; and it fulfils this task by following in the footsteps of Christ...

§31 [What if a theologian cannot give an intellectual assent to a proposition imposed by the Church?] He must abide with a mind willing to undertake a deeper investigation of the question. To one who is sincere and loves the Church, that situation may seem hard. But it can turn out to be an invitation to endure in silence and in prayer – with the sure and certain hope that truth (if it be the truth that is at stake) is bound to triumph in the end.

Extract from Canons of the Third Lateran Council (March 1179). [The canon, No. 27, deals with the declaration of a 'Holy War' against the Albigensians in Provence. It is printed in Denzinger and Umberg at 401; Denzinger and Schönmetzer, although printing another canon of the council (against simoniacal admissions to monasteries), omits it.] Although ecclesiastical discipline is conthe Gospel, and indeed was opposed to it, the teaching of the Church has always been that no one is to be compelled to believe. The... Gospel... has done much to bring about... the conviction that in religious matters [the human person] should be free from human compulsion.

John-Paul II. *Address of 9 May 1983 to participants at a conference on Galilean Studies*. (John-Paul II 1983b: 689–92)
We recall a time when great misunderstandings had grown up between science and faith... the world of science and the Catholic Church have overcome these moments of conflict... this is because a more accurate understanding has been reached of the methods proper to the different orders of knowledge... [The case of Galileo] has allowed the Church to reach a more accurate understanding of its own authority... The Church was founded by Christ... but is made up of limited people who are of a piece with their cultural epoch... We acknowledge that Galileo had to suffer at the hands of organisms of the Church... These facts confirm our persuasion that a free and open dialogue is needed between theologians, scientists, and Church authorities... Catholics have received a kind of intellectual purification...

Secretariat for Unbelievers. *On Dialogue with Unbelievers*, 28 August 1968. (Unbelievers 1968: extracts from 698–701)
That all participants believe themselves to be in possession of the truth does not invalidate the dialogue... It is enough that all those sharing in the conversation should regard the truth they hold as open to increase by means of dialogue with others. Such an attitude in believers [who share in the dialogue] should be adopted and fostered with the greatest honesty. Truths of faith in as much as they are revealed by God are complete and perfect in themselves. But they are always grasped imperfectly by be-

tent with priestly judgment, and does not inflict bloody punishments, it is helped by the ordinances of Catholic princes, in order that men, fearing the infliction of a bodily punishment, may often seek a remedy leading to salvation. [It goes on to anathematise those who give any succour to the heretics.]

Another Extract from the Inquisition's *Instruction*.
§ 12 Freedom of investigation – which is rightly prized as most precious by all learned men – means this: a mind ready to accept truth as it is, after an investigation conducted in which nothing is involved that is alien to the demands of the method appropriate to the matter under consideration. In theological science, this liberty lies within rational knowledge, whose object is offered by revelation, transmitted and explained in the Church under the authority of the Magisterium and received by faith. These elements are to be held as principles, and to neglect them would be to cease from practising theology.

A Few Items from the Roman Index of Prohibited Books.
Acta Eruditorum 1682–1757. Addison, J. *Remarks on Several Parts of Italy*. Alstedius, H. *Encyclopaedia*. Bacon, F. *De Dignitate et Augumentis Scientiarum*. Balzac, H. All Novels (*fabulae amatoriae*). Bayle, P. All works (*opera omnia*). Beccaria, C. *Dei Delitti e delle Pene*. Bentham, J. *Traité de Législation*. Bergson, H. *Essai sur les données immédiates de la conscience*. Berkeley, G. *Alciphron or the Minute Philosopher*. Charron, P. *De la sagesse*. Condorcet, J. A. N. *Progrès de l'esprit humain*. Cudworth, R. *The True Intellectual System of the Universe*. Descartes, R. All philosophical works. Diderot and D'Alembert, J. (eds). The *Encyclopédie*. Gibbon, E. *The History of the Decline and Fall of the Roman Empire*. Goldsmith, O. *An Abridged History of England*. Gregorovius, F. *Geschichte*

lievers...Not everything which Christians believe comes from revelation; dialogue with unbelievers can help them to distinguish what comes from revelation from other items...For the dialogue to achieve its proper purposes, it must obey the law of truth and freedom...A conversation about belief calls for a readiness, both to expound one's own opinion, and to acknowledge truth everywhere, even when the truth so overcomes a participant in the conversation that he is obliged to rethink at least in part his speculative and practical position...Truth in dialogue should not prevail save by the force of truth. So freedom in the conversation should be safe-guarded by law and respected in reality. [Dialogues where doctrinal agreement cannot be reached call for special conditions.] To decide whether [the conditions obtain], attention must be paid both to what the participants propose to do now and in the future, and to what past experience has shewn.

der Stadt Rom im Mittelalter. Grotius, H. All theological works. Hume, D. All works. Kant, I. *Kritik der Reinen Vernunft*. Malebranche, N. *Recherche de la Vérité*. Mandeville, J. *The Fable of the Bees*. Mill, J. S. *Principles of Political Economy*. Milton, J. [*All writings in support of Cromwell*.] Montesquieu, C. *L'Esprit des Lois*. Pascal, B. *Les Provinciales*. Pufendorf, S. *De iure naturae et gentium*. Renan, E. All works. Richardson, S. *Pamela*. Rousseau, J. J. *Emile. Du Contrat Social. Julie ou la nouvelle Héloïse*. Sand, G. All novels. Sarpi, P. *Historia del Concilio Tridentino*. Simon, R. *Histoire Critique du Vieux Testament*. Sterne, L. *A Sentimental Journey*. Strauss, D. *Das Leben Jesu*. Voltaire. All works. Whately, R. *Elements of Logic*. Zola, E. All Works.[4]

'What [they] propose to do now and in the future, and to what past experience has shewn': the concluding words in the left-hand column give us pause. There are many other values to be defended than intellectual freedom, and the ability of human beings to defend a plurality of values is notoriously limited; but the words still give us pause. It is less a matter of a choice between the two columns than a matter of what we are to make of their evident inconsistency. The two columns with which the preceding section began offered just as stark a contrast, but now we have something more to worry about. What

[4] Canonical penalties in connexion with the Index were abolished in 1966 – see Inquisition, Roman (1966). The abolition followed on the renaming yet again of the Inquisition, as mentioned in the Preface: see Paul VI (1965b). I understand that some books have since been prohibited. I made my selection from an edition published in 1930. Earlier editions would have yielded other items. Index (1828), for instance, includes a French translation of Locke's *Essay*, an Italian translation of *Paradise Lost*, and Scaliger's *De emendatione temporum*, as well as, of course, Copernicus and Galileo. Translations of the Ordinary of the Mass were also forbidden until well into the nineteenth century (details are in Jungmann 1952: 1.14; IV.4.7). Sheer malice made me include Whately's *Logic*, a once deservedly popular work published in 1826, and presumably put on the Index because of some of its reflexions and examples, which are often theological. Whately very handsomely acknowledges in his Preface that a considerable portion of the work as it now stands was composed by 'the Revd J. Newman, Fellow of Oriel College' (Whately 1870: viii).

the left-hand column now contains is confident and didactic in tone: for it, the past has been overcome, the present and future are open, a message of encouragement is offered. But tone is not enough. A teacher's credibility has to be earned, and what lies in the right-hand column shews that a great deal still needs to be earned by the Church of Rome, and that the earning is far from over. Unless, of course, we are expected to agree that Rome's past darknesses can be left unregarded and that its present policy can be a law into itself. But that gives us even greater pause. Our own age has taught us all too much about the willingness of autocracies to demolish their past and to reshape their present as they please. If we are invited to accept without demur what is in the left-hand column, we are entitled to ask what claim either column has, not just upon our belief, but upon two minutes of our attention.

Whatever claim the columns may have on us, they come from a source that is producing words at an unprecedented rate. Material from the various bodies in the Roman curia, and above all utterances and decrees from popes, are being provided ever more abundantly. The places and occasions of papal pronouncements are just varied: the two visits with which this section will be concerned are only two among so very many journeyings, each of which implies yet another set of discourses. How much of it all finds its way into print I have no idea, but the sheer physical increment of the *Acta Apostolicae Sedis*, the official 'Gazette' of the Roman Church, tells its own story. Go back to the 1930s, and the regular bulk was 600 or so pages a year. By the end of the 1940s it was pushing onto 700; it has now reached nearly 1,500, and librarians are having to split each of the years into two for purposes of binding. And that is just the *Acta*; the Vatican newspaper *Osservatore Romano* has much to offer that the *Acta* does not print. So many topics, so many words, so many places to utter them in.

I have chosen two papal visits and discourses to reflect on in this section. Both were made by John-Paul II. The first was to the Synagogue in Rome in 1986. The other was to Turin in 1988. From each occasion I want to draw lessons. The lessons are not of a personal nature, they have to do with the themes with which we have been engaged – the relations between present and past, the religious inheritance that is ours, the present tensions in the Roman Church, the choice between embarrassment and insulation. All these lessons will prove to concern Church and Eucharist alike.

I take first the visit to the Roman Synagogue, and I start by reminding readers – if they need reminding – of something that needs to be set beside the ever-increasing volume of words produced by Rome; something that, set beside this stupefying logorrhoea, can recall us to reality. I remind them of something that never saw print at all, because there was nothing to print. I remind them of the public silence of the Vatican in the face of the destruction of the Jews.

Here more than anywhere else in this chapter I must insist that I am not concerned to take sides over the various controversies I am mentioning, I am concerned rather to examine their nature. Thus, I have no intention of adding to the debate as to whether Pius XII could or should have spoken out more than he did in his wartime pronouncements. What concerns me is the *nature* of his silence. By this, I do not mean the extent to which a condemnation could be read into the Delphic obscurities of his utterances, or the very real extent of the help provided by the Vatican to enable Jews to escape their persecutors. I have in mind something more fundamental – how did Pius himself regard his silence? For an answer, I go to the address he made to the cardinals on 2 June 1945, just after the cessation of hostilities in Europe, in which he surveyed the war that had ended, and the régime that had ended with it (Pius XII 1945). Here if anywhere he could his speak his mind: his appalling dilemma no longer faced him, and a new age was beginning; what did he have to say? And the answer is that he said nothing. He spoke much of the Church's tribulations in Nazi Germany; he spoke much of the sufferings in concentration camps endured by priests and layfolk because of their loyalty to Christ; he quoted Pius XI's condemnation of the Nazi 'apostasy from Jesus and idolatry of race and blood'; concerning what had befallen the Jews, and concerning his own conduct in the face of it, he uttered not a syllable. It is as if silence were to be regarded as natural, and the fate of the Jews as peripheral to what really concerned the Church.

Forty years on from this *magnum silentium*, in April 1986, the visit to the Synagogue was made. The years between had seen in the Roman Church the summoning by John XXIII of the Second Vatican Council, and the declaration *Nostra Aetate* by the council concerning non-Christian religions. In that declaration were passages which recalled the spiritual bond between the Church and the family of Abraham; denied that the guilt for Jesus' death can be blamed upon all his Jewish contemporaries, or upon Jews of today; said that the Jews should not be presented as repudiated or cursed by God, as if such views followed from the Holy Scriptures; and deplored the hatred, persecutions and displays of antisemitism directed against the Jews at any time and from any source (Vatican, Second Council of, 1966a). What did the visit in 1986 produce from the pope and from his hosts?

I submit that from him it produced tragically little. After recalling recent acts of courtesy made by the religious authorities of the Synagogue, he said that in a way

this gathering brings to a close, after the pontificate of John XXIII and the Second Vatican Council, a long period which we must not tire of reflecting upon... We... should not forget that the... circumstances of the past were very different from those that have laboriously matured over the centuries. The general acceptance of a legitimate plurality... has been arrived at with great difficulty. Nevertheless [this acknowledgment] cannot prevent us from recognising that the acts of unjustified limitation of religious freedom [and civil oppression] regarding Jews were from an objective point of view gravely deplorable manifestations. Yes, once again, through myself, the Church in the well-known words of '*Nostra Aetate*', deplores [etc., etc., see the preceding paragraph]. (John-Paul II 1986b: 6)

He then expressed horror at the genocide during the war; recalled the price in blood paid by Roman Jews, and the significance of the shelter offered them by religious houses; made his own the other statements about the Jews in *Nostra Aetate*; and spoke of faith as a free assent that cannot be the object of external pressure.

There are just and obvious complaints to be made against all this. Against the complacency exhibited by announcing the 'long period' to be closed by his own visit and by the declaration at the council, a declaration which was very properly described by one rabbi as 'a unilateral pronouncement by one party which presumes to redress on its own terms a wrong which it does not admit' (quoted in Abbott and Gallagher 1967: 669–70). Against the complacency exhibited by the talk of a 'legitimate plurality' being reached with difficulty, when Rome itself notoriously and persistently stood out against such plurality, so that those who pressed for religious toleration are conspicuous among those we saw on the Roman Index of prohibited books. And against what is worse than complacency, when the wrongs done to the Jews are described as 'limitation of religious freedom' – the wrongs went much further than that. All that can be objected, and I go along with the objections. But the real tragedy of the visit – a visit of historic significance by any standard – is the total failure to make explicit and to follow through the successive lessons that it had to teach. So this I will now do: because the lessons are many, and they bear directly on our own theme of how we are to see the Church.

In the first place, it could have been said and should have been said that the Jewish community at Rome has a longer continuous existence than any other settlement of the diaspora in Western Europe. Whatever else Rome did, it allowed a community to survive that reaches back to the capture of Jerusalem by Pompey in 63 BC. In centuries when mistrust led to murder and violence against the Jews in so many places, they survived at Rome; some even practised medicine, and the papal physician was often a Jew. Moreover, it was from interventions by popes that protection came against what menaced their communities. Gregory the Great forbade in 602 the prohibition of Jewish ceremonies at Naples (DS 480), while Innocent III condemned in 1199 attempts at forcible conversions, defilement of Jewish cemeteries and insults offered during religious festivities – and appealed in doing so to the example set by his recent predecessors (DS 772–3). The accusation that Jews practised ritual murder was denounced by several popes – most notably by Benedict XIV (+ 1758), after an investigation made by Cardinal Ganganelli (later Clement XIV, + 1774) into accusations made in Poland (details in *Jewish Encyclopaedia*, s.v. 'Blood Accusation'). To this day in France, the most venerable relics of Judaism are to be found in the region round Avignon, once papal territory. In Rome itself, the confinement of Jews to the ghetto went with laws that protected their dwellings from expropriation by Christians. All this could have been said and should have been said; and it would have been said to a community that had been allowed to survive when others had perished in murder and destruction. The shelter offered to Jews in Rome during the war by individuals and religious houses was not wholly foreign to the traditions of the city.

But more could have been said and should have been said: darker things. Whereas the dissolute Alexander VI had allowed Jews expelled from Spain to settle, it is to the reforming Paul IV (+ 1559) that we owe the confinement of Jews to the Roman ghetto. For 200 years, the Roman carnival saw them degraded and humiliated in Rome's main thoroughfare, as part of the public entertainment. It was Gregory XIII (+ 1585) who established the practice of compelling groups of them in turn to listen to Christian sermons insulting

their religion.[5] The custom was abolished only by Pius IX ($+$ 1878)
– and Pius himself continued the restriction of the ghetto, which
ended only when papal government of the city came to an end in
1870. All this could have been said and should have been said; and
it would have been said by a pope to a community that had
persevered, over centuries of injustice and outrage inflicted by the
papacy, in the faith of its fathers.

It is to the honour of the president of the Synagogue that truths like
these were uttered – the worsening of conditions for Jews when
Christianity replaced paganism as Rome's official religion, the
defence of the Jews by some popes against persecution, the cruelty
exercised against them by popes like Paul IV, the perdurance of
restrictions upon them until the papal government itself came to an
end. Honour to him for his frankness – but what a tragedy that
history was faced on this occasion by one side only!

Yet even his facing of it was not enough: still more and still darker
things could have been said and should have been said. Antisemitism
cannot be reduced to individual eccentricity, it is too old and too
deeply rooted for that – as a Polish pope would have been peculiarly
qualified to point out, given the virulence of antisemitism in his
native country, a virulence that has healthily survived the presence of
the death camps on Polish soil and the virtual annihilation of Polish
Jewry. The causes and history of antisemitism lie beyond my concern,
but what does not lie beyond my concern is the need to point to one
source of it – the New Testament. True enough, phrases in the
Gospels and Epistles reflect domestic tensions and squabbles in the
early Church which are of a different order to the hideous use that
was to be made of them later on. True again, the structure and
composition of New Testament writings are complicated: the
writings have literary conventions for their background that need to
be borne in mind if we are to understand the point of what was
written. But what were to become sacred writings shewed an animus,
in their vocabulary and in their narratives, against groups identifiable
with those who claimed descent from Abraham and followed the Law
of Moses. For instance, Matthew xxii alters the account in Mark xii
of the scribe who, admiring Jesus, asks him a question about the Law.
He is now one who 'tempts' him; Jesus in his reply no longer recites

[5] By one of those delightful twists of fate that season human existence, one church used for the
forced sermons turned out recently to have been employed for years by a sodality of priests
dedicated to the surely supererogatory task of forging Italian currency.

the *Shema*, the central profession of Judaism; he and the scribe no longer exchange words of friendly praise. Later in Matthew, the crowd who call for Jesus' death call likewise for his blood to be upon them and upon their children. For John, 'the Jews' has become a synonym for the opponents of the (presumably Christian?) Jesus and his disciples. In Acts, they are brought on with monotonous regularity to obstruct Paul's ministry. Forget about bickerings in the early Church, forget about literary forms. Think rather of what we saw earlier – the credulity and inaccuracy which a critical reading of the Scriptures reveals in them. When we saw it, I noted the embarrassment; it has come back here, but now with horrible consequences. Those who formed the Christian Scriptures neglected accuracy and justice in the basic matters of place, time and action – matters analogous to what I called in a eucharistic context 'the humbler creation'. And their neglect created a vocabulary of contrasts that could later be read as incitements to oppression and to murder. As the oecologists rightly remind us, you can never do one thing at a time. The neglected humbler creation has taken a terrible revenge. All this could have been said and should have been said; and it would have been said by one who was confessing that his own religion had developed from Judaism in a setting touched by those darknesses.

But even that is not all: still more could have been said and should have been said. If the New Testament contains darknesses, they are of a piece with what can be found in the Old. One example will be more than enough. What Jesus taught – at all events, what the first Christians said he had taught – had a smack of novelty about it. And novelty, as we know, is something for which the Old Testament has very little time. 'If thy brother ... or thy son, or thy daughter, or the wife of thy bosom ... entice thee secretly, saying, let us go serve other gods ... thou shalt not consent unto him ... neither shall thine eye pity him ... neither shalt thou conceal him: but thou shalt surely kill him; thine hand shall be first upon him to put him to death, and afterwards the hand of all the people ...' (Deut. xiii 6–9). Readers will be able to match this with other texts, there is no need to descend into details. The heart of man is indeed deceitful above all things and desperately wicked. The hope for deliverance from his nature held in bondage, his *doulé physis*, is indeed a hope touched with the very darkness from which it promises relief. Christians have inflicted upon

Jews outrages that bear no comparison in their enormity with what Jews have done; but the intolerance and exclusivism Christians have shewn are set deep in the tradition that they have inherited from Jews. They are chips off the old block; and that too could have have been said and should have been said.

Nothing whatever of that sort was said, the opportunity passed by untaken. But the successive lessons I have been drawing ought to have made clearer why nothing of the sort was said. We have come back to what we met in the preceding section, about criticism of the Church and criticism of the Bible. But we have come back to it with what we have learned since. If our religious past is revered but unsatisfactory, it is also a past that touches our present, for we are ourselves part of that temporally extended and morally diverse reality to which the past also belongs. Revaluing the past – biblical or ecclesial – is not concerned with something remote that we can patronise; our past displays the imperfection and fallibility of our present. Revaluation here is a rending business; we are embarrassed. I have been suggesting that we should prize embarrassment, but I have also acknowledged that we like to find ways of accommodating it. And one way is exhibited in what did get said during this visit: an appeal to the Second Vatican Council. Yet again – I apologise for having to harp on the point – I am not so much concerned with taking sides in controversies here as with considering their nature. I have already expressed dissatisfaction at what that council had to say about Judaism, but my dissatisfaction matters less for me than the *nature* of the appeals that are made so often nowadays to the council. 'Vatican Two' has become for the Roman Church a phrase by which long-standing debts can be repudiated, and a present can be safely insulated from a past that it finds awkward. As a perjured witness in the Watergate enquiry put it, everything said so far 'is no longer operative'. But the past is simply not like that. What merit Vatican Two possessed lay in its attempt to face the past and to draw lessons from it in the present; and merit like that lies in a habit of mind, not in a datable enactment. To talk in terms of enactments is to talk in terms of what can be rescinded – and to see that rescinding is a real possibility, we need look no further than the right-hand column at the beginning of this section.

We have yet to see how far the lessons I have been drawing will take us, but I cannot leave this visit without an expression of deep regret. If ever there was a special occasion, surely this was – 2,000 years of history were present, and the oldest of all relations between the two Testaments. The president of the Synagogue provided dates, times and places – including an acknowledgment of the refuge granted to Roman Jews during the war, and a refusal to pass judgment on Pius XII. All the Christian side could furnish was a citation of Vatican Two, and a reference in the pompous complacencies of officialese to what had been so shameful a past in the Church. Was not this in its way just as great a silence? The waste and the pity of it!

If we have been inclined to weep with Heraclitus, we can now end the section by laughing with Democritus, as we move to the second of the two visits. It will not keep us long, but it does have an important lesson for us – that what is amiss in the Church is not only something far more than personal, it also concerns what I have called insulation.

In September 1988 the pope paid a visit to Turin, on the occasion of the centenary of the death of St John Bosco, who had founded the religious society of 'Salesians' in that city. On Sunday 4 September, he ate luncheon with the Salesians and the neighbouring bishops. His short speech (*breve discorso*) to them, made up over lunch (*improvisato al pranzo*), was sombre. Turin needs to be told of the need to convert oneself; its level of religious practice is low and its mentality secularised; many theologians today are helping people not to feel the need for conversion; the devil is real and the father of lies; he is also the prince of this world, which is a tempting title – which political party or which ideology would not want to be prince of this world?

The text of the talk was distributed to the press that afternoon, because a priest present had taken notes. But half an hour afterwards, the adjustments (*precisazioni*) to it began. The Vatican Press Office recommended that certain phrases be corrected; the motive (as seen by one reporter) being not to offend the city, which had welcomed the pope with acclaiming crowds (*folle osannanti*). The Press Office, given the incomplete transcript made by the priest, said it would be better to wait and see just what phrases had been used; this could be done by waiting for the Vatican Radio's magnetic tapes (*bobine*) first to be played back (*sbobinare*) – everything spoken publicly or in private meetings is recorded, when the pope travels – and then to be approved by the high Vatican authorities (*vertici vaticani*). And the *Osservatore Romano* did print on Monday the address in its sombreness

– except that the references to Turin's religious indifference, originally noted by the priest, had been omitted.[6]

Ex absurdo sequitur quodlibet – 'given the absurd, anything follows': the scholastic tag seems the perfect comment on all this. The absurdity is in no way personal, it is embodied in the whole preposterous apparatus which dictated the procedures to be followed. No human being, be he pope or pauper, ought to be subjected to this grotesque framework of travel, crowds, tape-recorded improvisations, press conferences and retroactive adjustments by officialdom. That is not what human beings are for, and it is not what human speech is for. If anyone be so subjected, his position will be falsified and will collapse into the ludicrous.

Consider first what was said – and then reflect on what was not said. *Of course* we need to convert ourselves, be we Torinese or not. *Of course* theologians are obscuring the need – they always have and I suppose they always will, our chequered religious past should have convinced us of that by now. We all obscure the need – men, women, priests and popes alike. And the more exalted our position, the more dangerous can the obscuring be. Thus, to speak of 'the prince of this world' as a tempting title is to speak the truth; to ask what political party or ideology would not want to possess the title is to put a fair and disturbing question; but can it be seriously suggested that Roman Catholicism itself does not come under that condemnation? What price conversion there? Consider now what followed. We have here, in one Sunday afternoon's flurry of public relations, a miniature enactment of the insulation we have so often encountered. I drew an analogy in the last section between Colombo's notion of an insulated substance and the attempts to domesticate our religious past by retroactive demotions – that is, by claims that what adjustments are made do not touch what really matters. The analogy here is as striking as it is perturbing. The *precisazioni*, the *sbobinare* and the intervention of the *vertici vaticani*, comic though they be, point to something not comic at all. Insulation is just not the point; it is not the point in the Church and it is not the point in the Eucharist. To more of this contention I now proceed; and I turn to make it of the Eucharist in the next section.

[6] For the visit to the Synagogue, I have gone to the English edition of the *Osservatore Romano* for 21 April 1986. For the visit to Turin, I have gone to the Torinese newspaper *La Stampa* for 6 September 1988. The original Italian of the *Osservatore* for the visits was unavailable for consultation.

37 ANOTHER PICTURE

So far in this chapter, we have met three inconsistencies. The first is an inconsistency over the bases of argument: Küng appeals to the biblical message, and Rahner to the present faith of the Church; but Küng is still prepared to read the Bible critically, and Rahner manages to adjust his views on the origin of mankind, despite a papal declaration that would close the topic to free discussion among theologians. The second inconsistency is over the range of criticism: biblical criticism has come to be accepted in the Roman Church to an extent far greater than criticism of that Church's own pronouncements. The third inconsistency touches what I have called 'cultic pictures'. The picture implicit in the newer rite of the Eucharist is at odds with the picture presented by so much that has come from Rome over the last years – the latter picture resembles rather the picture presented by the older eucharistic rite. But so far in this chapter we have also met examples of how the two senses of *corpus mysticum* can throw light on each other. The present pattern of church government resembles the various 'polarisations' that went with the older rite. The process of allegorisation to which the older rite was subjected resembles the blurring and muffling in the Church of history and of what history can teach. And the process of insulating ecclesiastical pronouncements is analogous to the concept of substance found in some scholastic speculations about the Eucharist.

I do not regard the inconsistencies as accidental, or the resemblances as far-fetched. If the eucharistic ritual is a sign of the union of the faithful in Christ, then that ritual should be a guide for us in judging the visible forms which the union can take, and should help us to elucidate inconsistencies like those we have been meeting. In the remaining sections of this final chapter I want to let the ritual of the Eucharist provide this guidance and elucidation, both for its own celebration and for the Church that celebrates it. I set down here the stages in my submissions over these sections.

The present section complements those that have gone before it. The older cultic picture I have discussed, and seen in it a resemblance to phenomena and tensions in the Roman Church. But what of the newer cultic picture? Wherein lies its newness? What patterns, in ritual and in the Church alike, are suggested by it? The present section explores the general demands that the newer picture makes upon ritual. It makes the exploration by following up, this time in a ritual setting, the morals already drawn about the merits of embarrassment and the dangers of insulation. These general conclusions about ritual I then apply to the Church in the next section – 'Facing the past'. I consider there the relations between present and past in the Church of Rome, the claims made for its pronouncements, and the treatment of its pronouncements by those who come after. In that section we shall be obliged, to use the phrase yet again, not to say what it *must* be, but to *look*. When we have looked, we shall be better able to consider in two further sections the relations between past and present in a specifically eucharistic setting. In the first of them, I look at the successive complexities revealed by the course the book has taken, and I try to place what I have written in its relationship with the heritage of eucharistic beliefs and practice in the Church of Rome. I call the section 'The inherited conglomerate', hoping I shall be forgiven by the shade of E. R. Dodds for borrowing the expression from his classic *The Greeks and the Irrational*. I then turn to the ritual changes that have taken place in the Church of Rome over the last quarter of a century; I call this section '*Religio depopulata?*', and will elucidate there the choice of the title and its ambiguity. The changes have had consequences that express – sometimes in a tragic way – the tensions between past and present, and I think they have much to aid reflexion upon the specific demands made by ritual. Once more, we shall see the need to keep open what we are inclined to insulate; once more, ritual will prove to be central to the course of the book, and to have consequences that go beyond what we regard as specifically religious. And the last section of all – 'A door for opening' – will consider this need to keep open what we are tempted to close; it will see the opening as touching the *corpus mysticum* in both its senses; and it will suggest some things about those who might open the door.

And so now to the topic of this section – the newer cultic picture and the general demands it makes upon ritual and will make upon the Church. The general characteristics of the newer picture were given in the previous chapter and were contrasted with what had already been seen of the older picture. The starkly simple polarisation of altar *versus* all else has given way to a more complex disposition of places, and this spatial complexity corresponds to a variety that has been made explicit in the ritual itself. The leading of the congregation in prayer, the proclaiming of the word, the various processions, the canon itself with the words of institution: these are distinct, and the structures of the building and of the ceremony now exhibit their distinctness. The activities of the rite are likewise distinct and distributed – responses, readings and the rest. The very pattern of sharing in the consecrated elements now exhibits their reception as an intrinsic part of the rite, not as a distinct ceremony that happens to be placed within it. All this we have already seen – to it I would add that the wider range of scripture appointed to be read makes new demands upon those who are deputed to read it.

The foregoing paragraph began and ended with a mention of the *demands* made by the newer rite. Those who take part in it will agree that the demands can be real enough, real in a way they never could be for the old. We have seen how Eveyln Waugh drew an analogy between the priest with his server in the old days and the craftsman with his apprentice, stumping up to the altar and setting to work, without a glance at those behind, on an important job for which none but he was qualified (p. 234). The analogy is curiously lame, for it would be hard to think of an activity for which less 'craftsmanship' was required than the Old Roman Mass. The celebration could indeed be carried out reverently or ineptly, but (as Waugh takes care to emphasise) the question of what he calls 'making a personal impression' was foreign to what really mattered. When giving the text from Waugh, I also gave one from the biography of C. C. Martindale, the Jesuit. For Martindale, we saw, Mass was 'a sacrifice', 'something between him and God'; he had gone to the church 'early, to be alone'. There is an insulation in the cultic picture seen by the two that is simply foreign to the demands made by the newer rite. The readings, the chants, the pattern of gesture and movement, the whole interplay of those present – all of that goes towards making up the newer eucharistic ritual, and to admit the uniqueness of the part played in it by the priest does not in any way amount to claiming that his part can take over the parts to be played by others. If the newer rite can rise to greater heights than the older, it can also fall into more resounding disasters. It is open, it is vulnerable to such things, it can be embarrassed. And it is with spelling out these qualities of the newer rite that the present section is concerned.

It should be clear by now that my claim to elucidate the eucharistic ritual in terms of ritual is more than a platitude. It has meant accepting the awkwardness of the redemptive setting, where the hope of deliverance offered us finds expression in pictures and formulae which, do we give them their head, take on an unwanted and unseemly life of their own. It has meant accepting that the darkness of our condition, the enslaved nature or *doulé physis* which is ours, touches even that which promises release, so that words slip and slide, and move whither we would not have them go. We need, I have been submitting, to take a harder way. We must decline the understandable but specious attractions of what I called 'the Galilean Presence' in the Eucharist, a presence conceived in terms of the spatial proximities of Christ to those who first were his friends. Such an account confuses signs with disguises, and its attraction goes with phenomenalism: that is, with a divorce between appearance and reality that is ultimately sceptical, a eucharistic presence that is insulated. Instead, I have insisted all along, we must follow a pattern by which that which is more exalted does not compete with or deny that which is more humble, as the Fallacy of Replacement would suggest; rather, that which is more humble is respected, and is taken up into that which is greater. As I put it, the Way of Ritual builds on what we know, even thought it is inevitably obliged to pass to what eludes our comprehension; and to move along the Way is to respect both human history and the history of human salvation. And, human history being what it is, and human beings what they are, the Way demands openness and leaves itself vulnerable.

The ritual openness and vulnerability in such an account we began to meet as far back as in the second chapter. There, when I dissented from the newer accounts offered of the eucharistic presence, I acknowledged the merits of suggestions made by various authors for 'placing' the Eucharist. I recall here what can be found there in texts I printed: the human significance of giving and of sharing food; the ritual heritage of the Passover; above all, the insistence by Schillebeeckx on the Giveness of Reality, its 'quasi-sacramental' revelation of God's love for us. I notice, too, that although considerations like these are met in newer authors as they were not met in the scholastic texts of the first chapter, what we have seen since in other texts of Aquinas shews that they were not absent from his thought either. The general force of all such considerations is that we are not to keep the Eucharist apart and insulated, but are to let our approach to it start from the human world, in which the history of God's saving plan for us has been revealed. My own Way of Ritual is an attempt at such an approach, and I submit that it is of a piece with the cultic picture displayed by the newer rite of the Mass. And that newer cultic picture, I have also submitted, is of a piece with much that has changed in the Church, and points to how defects in it might be remedied. These submissions may be rejected, or just dismissed as pretentious. But I have made them, and I shall go on to elaborate them. For better or worse, I am claiming that what I have written of the eucharistic presence has of its nature an application to the *corpus mysticum* that is the Church.

My own account stood apart from older and newer expositions by its refusal to talk of the eucharistic presence in terms of disguise, and the refusal meant that I could not offer anything like the apparent definitenesses of what I opposed. But I contended that definiteness here is no more than apparent, and is the product of incoherence. I also submitted that the incoherence went – even if to different degrees – with an insensitivity to ritual. But the insensitivity is no more than the price paid for the seeming definiteness of talking in terms of disguise. Such definiteness does not go well with ritual. For accounts of the Eucharist in those terms, that which appears will be an *obstacle* rather than a clue or a guide, and will be no more than *appearance*. As an obstacle, it stands apart from what it obstructs; as appearance, it is separated from the sole reality, which lies concealed by it. Insensitivity to ritual is not accidental here, because here ritual can never be more than peripheral, never more than – literally – 'a matter of appearances'. I acknowledge yet again that the newer accounts have indeed brought out ritual connotations of the eucharistic presence. But I submit that they bring them out despite what else they say, not because of it.

I must face the consequences of admitting that accounts in terms of disguise can attract by an apparent definiteness. The consequences touch more than any exposition I offer, they touch ritual itself – the unease and embarrassment I have mentioned so often must be accepted by me as inevitable characteristics of eucharistic ritual. Ritual here is bound to be vulnerable and incomplete. It must point, it must indicate, and so cannot tell a rounded-off story. It is ever liable to be taken as what looks more straightforward, either by being reduced to human activity, or by being described in terms of switching inaccessible substances or of renamings that deny ordinary words their meaning. The eucharistic ritual, taken as ritual, makes demands on those who share in the celebration. It has all the chequered associations of the stages of the Way of Ritual. It embodies its achievement, which is more than human, in the fragilities of what is truly human. It is to shew forth the Lord's death until he come, and so is in a sense caught between memorial and anticipation. Here indeed is vulnerability; openness; embarrassment. And so it is that all these must be for me the consequences of the newer cultic picture – for Eucharist and for Church.

The consequences drawn here will receive specific application, both for eucharistic celebration and for the Church that celebrates. I end this section with a reminder of something seen already, and with an image we can take with us into what follows.

I have rejected the apparent clarity that goes with accounts of the Eucharist in terms of disguise – accounts that insulate the eucharistic presence in ways we have examined. But I have also rejected attempts to insulate meanings from words, attempts that exhibited the historical insouciance I condemned in some recent authors. The two insulations here both promise an apparent clarity and definiteness; I have rejected both, and my rejection of the 'insouciance' brings us yet again to the theme of 'Present and Past'. We cannot leave language for some wordless and timeless vantage-point, as insulated in its way as was Colombo's notion of substance. We saw in the third chapter that the suggestion we might adopt such a vantage-point proved incoherent in the setting of the Eucharist. It will prove just as incoherent in the setting of the Church. But, having recalled what we have seen, I recall something more – that what I myself write is temporally limited. When I dissent from this or that in our religious heritage, I cannot take my stand outside that heritage in order to declare my dissent. There is, as I put it in the third chapter, no stepping out of the arena. The words and actions in the eucharistic ritual are touched with the defects I have repeatedly noticed; but I cannot mend matters – and I have not tried to mend them – with talk of 'the data of faith' or of 'the real doctrine of transubstantiation'; or with anything of the sort. Whatever I suggest will itself be words and actions, with their own resonances and connotations, desirable and undesirable; and my suggestions are made within the tradition I have inherited, the tradition within which and from which I am expressing dissent. The past is not only revered and unsatisfactory, it is inescapable.

Now for the image which we can take with us: it is what is traditionally called the narthex of a church. I wrote earlier in the chapter of what Küng claimed for the Church – 'a fundamental remaining in the truth' – and I saw that claim as taking the Church 'out into the market-place', confronting its history with criteria that were not ecclesiastical (p. 266). Of this placing of the Church more remains to be said, and the image of the narthex can be a guide as I go on to say it. The narthex has taken different forms over the centuries, depending upon the structure of the services and on the local weather. At times, it has been no more than the church porch. At other times, the word has been applied to an area between the street and the entrance to the building itself. What matters for me is that the notion of a narthex can recall the vulnerability and the openness which I see as inseparable from ritual. The narthex is not a part of the building in the intimate way the nave and sanctuary are (at one time, penitents were relegated to it), and yet it is not alien to the building; it both joins the church to the street and the market-place, and yet it keeps the church distinct from them; it is a route by which we pass into the church, and yet the passage itself shows that the origin of our route is not its terminus. The narthex does not *polarise*, for it is open to both street and church; but its very openness is not to be taken as a reduction of either of them to the other; it both links them and keeps them apart.[7]

It is in these properties of the narthex that I find an image of what I claim for ritual – and, indeed, for what I claim about the Church itself. The eucharistic ritual is neither a matter of camouflage, nor a matter of simply human activity; it is an inheritance from the past that is more than a preserved antique; it is a sign and pledge of what hath not yet been revealed, and yet it uses the humbler creation of which we ourselves are part. The hope it offers goes down to the very depth of our being, and to the enlargement of that being through Christ; yet the hope needs translating into how we shall live in our shared and ambiguous world, and the hope will be touched in its ritual embodiment by the *doulé physis*, the nature held in bondage, of those who share in the rite as they share in the world. After all I have written of religious language and imagery, I can hardly claim that the image of the narthex is exempt from drawbacks. Enough for me that it can recall the qualities I have attributed to the eucharistic ritual – qualities that in a sense make the task of ritual impossible

[7] For information about the different forms of the narthex, see Bingham (1867: VIII.3) and also Jungmann (1952: II.8). The entry under the word in Ducange (1688) – a lexicon of ecclesiastical Greek – shews how 'narthex' was applied with what we might call a shifting frontier: the region designated was not always the same, but it was never part of the church as the nave was.

from the start. And what I say of the Eucharist I shall be saying of the Church too; once more, the two senses of *corpus mysticum* go together.

38 FACING THE PAST

The general conclusions I have just drawn for the eucharistic ritual I must now draw for the other sense of *corpus mysticum*, the Church. The difficulty of facing the past will be clear by now, both from examples we have examined, and from ways we have seen devised for domesticating it. But we also know by now that there is more to the past than difficulty. There are lessons to be learned from it, if only we can persevere in facing what can embarrass. This section begins with an attempt at perseverance.

When I reflected on the papal visit to the Roman Synagogue, I put forward a series of lessons that might have been drawn from it. That they were in fact not drawn was understandable, given that each lesson in the series was 'undercut' by its successor. That is, it was not denied, but it was shewn to be incomplete – and the series shewed in this way a vulnerability and openness. I have seen those qualities in the newer cultic picture of the Eucharist, but the series of lessons shewed them as properties of the Church's own inheritance from the past: even in the most exalted and sacred parts of that tradition, darkness can be found along with what is valued and revered. It is this pattern of a series of lessons that I want to follow in this section. Once more, I go for my starting-point to something specific in recent ecclesiastical history; this time, to the debate there has been over what is called 'liberation theology'.

I had better give at once the assurance that I gave before drawing some morals from the disagreement between Küng and Rahner: I have no intention of embarking upon an appraisal of all the issues involved in the debate. I am in any case not qualified to do anything of the sort; my purpose is, as it has been with other disagreements in this chapter, to make some observations on the *nature* of the disagreement, and upon some things in it that both sides seem to take for granted. There are lessons to learn here, and I think they can disconcert; but they lie somewhat apart from the main line of the debate, and what I offer neither is nor could be an adequate comment upon it.

I leave to a footnote some remarks on the sources I have used, and I go to one of them – an anthology of essays – for a very brief account

of what I take liberation theology to be.[8] For Rahner, who introduces
the anthology, it is the distinctive contribution of Latin America, and
both demands and deserves a response from the European tradition.
Its starting-point is the experience of oppression and lack of freedom
in society, and it aims at a rethinking of Christian belief, where the
praxis of Christian life will be a primary source for knowledge of that
belief (Rahner 1977: 6–7). For Goldstein, who writes of links with the
Bible, Latin American theologians see underdevelopment as a
correlate of technological progress in the richer nations; they often
articulate their starting-points in marxist terms; they see in the
proletariat the front-line troops of the process of liberation; they
reflect theologically on all this, and read the Bible in this setting
(Goldstein 1977: 62). For Boff, who is one of the best-known
exponents, liberation theology was not the result of an arbitrary
choice, but part of the process by which the peoples of Latin America
became conscious of themselves. An opting in favour of the poor and
the exploited, and against the prevailing mode of society, has opened
a new way to be a Christian and new dimensions of faith; it lets
scripture and tradition be seen in a wholly new light (Boff 1977:
46–48).

It is hardly surprising that liberation theology should have
attracted opposition. Of the tangled history, I recall only that themes
of this theology appeared in the conference of Latin American
bishops at Medellin in 1968; that the themes proved alarming for
some; that the alarm shewed itself when the bishops were to meet at
Puebla in 1979; that reservations about liberation theology have
been expressed at Rome, where Boff has been investigated by the
Inquisition; and that elements in discourses by John Paul II have
been welcomed by supporters and by opponents of liberation
theology. The reservations themselves are what might be expected:

---

[8] I have not managed to find works on liberation theology in Portuguese or Spanish, and I
suspect that the *timbre* of the original is, unavoidably, dulled in the translations. Gustavo
Gutiérrez has written much on the topic, and Gutiérrez 1983 translates a work of 1979. I
have not followed the details of the controversy through the 1980s; readers who wish to do
so will find a convenient guide in the annual Indexes to *The Times* (under 'Roman Catholic
Church', 'Latin America', etc.). The years 1985 and 1986 seemed to see much debate, and
the claim made that some agreement had been reached. For all that, the debate and
disagreement continue. *New Blackfriars* for October 1991 is devoted to the matter; the *Tablet*
has further information during the same month, which indicates manoeuvres prompted by
Roman disapproval. Moreover, an honorary doctorate for Gutiérrez from the Catholic
University of Fribourg was vetoed by the Vatican in 1990 (*Tablet* 17 November 1990). It
should be remembered that such things in such places are open to veto – as are professorial
appointments and the awarding of tenure (Catholic Education 1979). Polarisation lives.

liberation theology can compromise the uniqueness of the gospel by reducing it to political and social terms; its adoption of marxist categories can lead it in directions incompatible with Christianity; the heart of the Christian message, the promise it contains, goes beyond any reformation, however praiseworthy, of social structures.

The series of lessons that I think can be learned from this disagreement starts on a humorous level. Think what you will of reproaches that liberation theology is compromising the uniqueness of the gospel with political attitudes, the reproaches come very oddly from Rome itself. Popes and curial officials need look no further than Italy to see what their own tradition of meddling with politics has successively produced: anathemas against any political involvement in the new Italy after the ending of the Papal States; then the encouragement of involvement; then the abandonment of those who were so involved, as part of the horse-trading with Mussolini; then the deployment of propaganda and anathemas in favour of the Democristiani; and so to forty-odd effete coalitions since the end of the war. Pots and kettles.

But the lessons to be learned touch far more than Vatican impudence, and two texts from the authors we have met can begin to shew just how much more. Goldstein writes of the distorted understanding of God in popular Catholicism in Latin America, and of its one-sided image of Christ, where both are products of a preaching over centuries by the Church of obedience and resignation (71). Boff writes of the bewilderment with which liberation theology is becoming aware of the question of how such social oppression could come about in a predominantly Catholic part of the world; and he contends that religious belief was manipulated in order to legitimate the power of the oppressors (61). For the zeal of such men I have every respect, but I confess my own bewilderment too – bewilderment at the innocence they exhibit in these texts. 'Distortion', 'manipulation' and 'popular Catholicism' are simply examples of what I hope has now become all too familiar – they are accommodations of an embarrassing past. The past here embarrasses because neither distortion nor manipulation was necessary, the article imported from Europe already had the qualities that Boff and Goldstein lament. Of course it had other qualities as well; of course there were those who spoke out in defence of the oppressed, just as we saw when reflecting on the visit to the Synagogue that there were popes who spoke out in defence of the Jews. But we saw much more

there, and the general picture was very different: the persistence of
the ghetto until the fall of papal power at Rome was no accident, it
was part of a tradition, the tradition to which texts I printed at the
start of that section bear melancholy witness. So it is here. What Boff
and Goldstein lament is part and parcel of what Roman Catholicism,
popular or not, has stood for. As the Old Catechism taught us
(Q.347), 'the principal virtues we are to learn from Our Lord are
meekness, humility and obedience'. If Latin America is distinguished
at all, it is simply because Roman Catholicism was given its head
there. Rahner, we saw, writes of liberation theology as the distinctive
contribution of Latin America. I suggest that the contribution would
do better to include the acknowledgment that Latin America felt the
need of it so much. Just as Boff and Goldstein would do better to
accept their embarrassment, and to conclude that there is something
very much amiss with Roman Catholicism, and very much amiss
with the whole Christian tradition of which it forms so conspicuous a
part. I wrote in an earlier section that a teacher needs to earn respect.
So much still needs earning here that my own reaction to the debate
over liberation theology in the Roman Church is not to take sides,
but to find a paradox in the fact that there should be a debate at all.

My observation can receive an answer that must be mentioned,
because it leads to the next lesson we can learn. The answer made is
that papal documents over the last hundred years have shewn
awareness of social problems and injustices; that Leo XIII's
encyclical letter *Rerum novarum* (1891) marked a turning-point in
Catholic thought; and that pronouncements from Rome down to our
own day shew how real the turning-point was. I do not deny that
some awareness like this now exists, and (for what my opinion is
worth) I rejoice at it. But, once more, the lesson I want to draw lies
apart from the evaluation of such documents, it concerns rather the
nature of the appeal that is made to them. Leo's encyclical is seen
nowadays as a turning-point: but how were his views seen by his
successor, Pius X (+ 1914)? In one of the first pronouncements of his
pontificate, Pius was rebuking (he was a great rebuker) tendencies
among Catholics involved in social questions. He reinforced his
rebuke by giving a summary of social documents promulgated by
Leo, to inculate principles such as: inequality is part of God's
establishment of society, and it is agreeable to his ordinance that there
should be rich and poor; workers, even when defending their rights,
must refrain from acts of violence; the poor should not disdain the

charity of the rich; those who take up the cause of the poorer classes should not use language that may arouse in them hostility against the upper classes. And so on (Pius X 1903c).[9] The lesson to learn is not that talk of a turning-point in Leo's pontificate is dishonest; it is that such talk is not the only kind of talk that can be uttered about him. The lesson, in other words, is that we have in the Church something we have time and again in human understanding, something we have met time and again in these pages. What is present looks at what is past; and it both shapes and is shaped by what it finds there. Pius X's view of Leo XIII is not the view which prevails today in the Roman Church; but then the view at present prevailing there in social matters would not take Pius X himself into account to begin with, nor the passages he cites from Leo, and still less the flirting of Pius XI (+1939) with fascism in his encyclical letter *Quadragesimo Anno* (Pius XI 1931). When the present looks at the past, what it makes of it is due in part to what it overlooks in it.

But of course the lesson applies to more in the past than papal pronouncements. We saw that Goldstein and Boff hold the Scriptures to be both a source of liberation theology and to be illuminated by it. An example is provided by Goldstein, who makes specific mention of something that others too (Moltmann 1967, for example) have seen as a compelling instance of the liberating power of God – the story of the Exodus, and of how the Lord brought his people out of the house of bondage (63–7). And of course the story is all this; the trouble is that it is more than all this, and that we fall into disagreements and embarrassments over how much more. Some Jewish thinkers reproach liberation theology for having wrenched the Exodus from its original setting – a setting which included the giving of the Law to Moses and the entry into the promised land (Harries 1988). Goldstein himself attaches importance to the possession of the land (63), but neither he nor (as far as I can see) any of the Jewish critics spells out

[9] There is an English translation of this pronouncement of Pius X, found in a CTS pamphlet with the remarkable title *Christian Democracy and Sacred Music*. Appearances to the contrary, the pamphlet does not explore the relationship between bank frauds and classical polyphony; it prints two documents on two different topics (Pius X 1903c and 1903b). I add that Pius might have gone further than he did in what he writes of Leo. One of the first of Leo's documents he cites also forbids insurrection against unjust rulers, even when there seems no other hope of survival; prayer and patience are the remedy (Leo XIII 1878: 373). Renan's *L'Eglise chrétienne* (1879) has in its Preface a comment on this document that shews how it was seen by an outsider: 'Has not a pope been trying to prove recently that Jesus Christ preached and died in order to safeguard the fortunes of the rich and to guarantee capital?'

what the possession was believed to have entailed: a genocide and enslavement of the very sort against which liberation theology is protesting. The story of the Exodus is indeed stirring; the trouble with it is the trouble we have found with more than one piece of religious language – it goes on too long, and it includes all manner of things that we do not want to make our own. So we read it selectively; our reading is an evaluation of the past, not just a recitation.[10]

Nor is it simply the Old Testament that we so evaluate. The New calls for such evaluation even more from those who would enlist its support for liberation theology. That Jesus favoured the poor, repeatedly warned the rich, accumulated no wealth himself and called on his followers to leave all and follow him; and that the infant Church set great store by charitable relief – things like that are present in the New Testament if anything is. But liberation theology is after other things, and those things seem starkly absent from the preaching of Jesus. The Epistles have yet more to embarrass readers today, and Goldstein is obliged to cite a tortuous exegesis of Paul's letter to Philemon (a letter conveyed by Philemon's runaway slave Onesimus, whom Paul was sending back to his master). He agonises over what degree of manumission is or might be implied by what Paul writes – while failing to face the rather obvious point that Philemon's acceptance of baptism from Paul had not affected his acceptance of slavery in the first place (73–4).

I am not blaming Goldstein for wrestling with embarrassments in the Bible, any more than I am blaming him and others for selectively reading the Exodus story, or blaming others again for selective reading among papal pronouncements. The selectivity is of a piece with the selective amnesia we have met in eucharistic as in other

---

[10] Rabbi Jonathan Sacks, in an admirable article which appeared in *The Times* on Good Friday 1991, acknowledges 'the power of religion to fuel conflict rather than reconciliation'. He notes the custom by which the Passover Seder service includes a gesture of mourning for the Egyptians smitten by the plagues. And he goes on to say that the rabbis added 'a fine touch of theology', in their commentary on the story of the crossing of the Red Sea – when the angels wanted to join in the Israelites' song of victory at the destruction of the Egyptians, God silenced them: 'The work of my hands is drowning, and shall you sing a song?'

I hesitate to cross swords with the Chief Rabbi over interpretations of the books of Moses, but we need to be clearer than this as to just what the rabbinical commentary is doing. It is bringing something into the story that was not originally there, because it feels embarrassed by the story as it stands in Exodus. The Seder ritual he mentions is the result of the same embarrassment. Neither of the results, of course, am I blaming – but the burden of self-consciousness I mentioned in the preceding chapter, the tragic sense of truth or *Wahrheitspathos*, demands that here too we face just what it is that we have inherited. And we do not need to go far in the story (whatever we think of its truth) to find, yet again, that our inheritance is very mixed indeed.

matters. It is not that accommodating the past is wrong; it is that –
yet again – accommodation cannot be all the story. We need to be
aware of what we are doing; aware that a past we revere is not only
unsatisfactory, but that this mixture of qualities runs throughout our
inheritance, no matter where we turn in it. And this awareness,
already noticed by me, can count as the next lesson in the series for us
to learn. But the series is not finished; the lesson we have just learned
we must now 'undercut', in the sense that what we have
learned raises a further question: how does so mixed a past affect
the present in which we have to live?

I write, as I have said, as a Greek come up to worship at the Feast.
So I introduce this next stage in our series of lessons with a comment
on Christian belief by one who writes rather from outside it, and who
is concerned with moral attitudes among the Ancient Greeks. He asks
at one point whether Christian belief makes an individual morally
better or worse, and replies that the answer depends upon how that
individual

interprets ambiguous and enigmatic passages in the New Testament, what
criteria he employs as a means of distinguishing between valid and invalid
religious experience, how he applies general injunctions to particular cases,
and (above all) the relative importance he attaches to different elements in
Christianity. In taking all these decisions, whether consciously or not, he is
necessarily judging Christianity by standards that are external to it. (Dover
1974: xiii)

Those words I gladly make my own, but the lesson I want to draw
demands that I add something to them. If we say we judge
Christianity by standards that are external to it, this judgment is for
me not a matter of our having a set of standards independently
acquired, against which we then measure the Christian religion. The
standards themselves – like the religion – are a heterogeneous mass of
criteria and preferences, acquired and shaped in a multitude of ways,
coherent to a greater or lesser extent, articulated in some areas more
than in others. They are what they are because of many things, and
among those things is – the Christian religion. And if this sounds
circular, so be it: life in that sense is bound to be circular.

The importance of this lesson demands that I spell out the notion
of circularity. Spelling it out will in fact shew that I have already been
proposing it, and that it is part and parcel of our making sense of
things. Some readers will have seen similar things elsewhere. I begin
by noticing the complaint I recalled in the last section, against some

recent writers on the eucharistic presence. I blamed them for an historical insouciance which made them divorce inherited terminology from its meaning, as if meaning were some entity that could be considered independently of its linguistic and ritual embodiment. This complaint I had made near the end of the third chapter (p. 130), and I recall it here:

Time spent in finding an unadulterated translation of the word [*species*, the word used at Trent that is usually rendered as 'appearances'] would be better spent in seeing what the word's connotations are, and in seeing whether the Council's purpose made sense. And whatever our verdict may be, it will have to be expressed in words that are themselves just as much open to similar appraisal. An imperfect past is appraised by an imperfect present. There is no leaving the arena.

And that is part of my contention about circularity. I mean that there is no privileged position, no Archimedean point from which we can, timelessly and neutrally, survey the debate. I reinforce this contention by going still further back in the book – back to the conclusion of the first chapter. There, I insisted that it is not possible to comment on the temporal limitations of our inheritance as if we ourselves, and our comment, were not temporally limited, and so open to comment in the same way. I made the point after examining the views of Aquinas, the earlier medieval setting in which views like his emerged, and the later reactions against the whole Aristotelian tradition. The examination had revealed what I called 'the Theaetetus Effect', the modification of earlier opinions by what comes after them (pp. 41–2). In other words, activities and changes spread out in time are not indifferent to what preceded them or unaffected by what follows them. The succession itself is something which, if it still lives, develops. Once more, there is no leaving the arena.

But if there is no leaving the arena, we need to see more of what is to be found there. The circularity with which we are concerned in religious belief involves a plurality and variety – that is the next lesson I wish to draw. Here too I can draw the lesson by going back to what I have already been claiming. I have insisted time and again that the Eucharist is a *ritual*; it is not that speculations and expositions are illegitimate, it is that they belong to something much wider, and that there will always be what I called 'a looseness of fit' between one manifestation of belief and another; words are only part of the whole cultic picture that communicates. To convince ourselves of how real the variety is, we have only to recall the sheer number of themes we have had to examine: speculations old and new; ritual and its history; the human condition and our hope for its liberation; official pronouncements by Church authorities; legends and practices that now seem alien; and the whole process of accommodating a past that is so mixed. What we have to deal with here is essentially *plural*, it cannot be narrowed down to one expression without being distorted.

But the themes I have recalled shew something else – that I have been thinking from the start in terms like these. Nor is this surprising, for there is nothing out of the ordinary in what I have been suggesting. I have introduced the idea of 'circularity' in a religious setting – naturally enough, given what the book is about – but the idea is not specifically religious, we encounter the circularity throughout our human pattern of learning, evidence, communication and testing. We do not proceed by deducing consequences from primary propositions in the way that we derive theorems from axioms. Rather, there is a whole body of activities, beliefs and revisions interconnected in various degrees of firmness and shared in many ways among many people. Consider (I have used this example elsewhere) two historians who differ over the character of Joan of Arc, one being favourable to her and the other unfavourable. Now suppose that a third party proposes to them Schiller's account of her in his play (where she escapes from prison and dies on the field of battle). We know what the historians would agree in saying, for all their differences. They would insist that any *investigation* must take into account *reliable evidence*, and must *respect the facts* that she was tried and was burned. They would allow *reasonable suppositions* when the *evidence*, though *appreciable*, is not *conclusive*; but they would add that no *serious historian* can make assertions that *collide* with all that *we know about* the *past*. The words I have italicised form a circle, in the sense that to apply one of them in any historical debate is to commit oneself to accepting others and to excluding still others. But circularity here is not the vacuous verbal circularity of saying that (as Sydney Smith jestingly put it) an archdeacon is a person who exercises archidiaconal functions. The circularity in the historical argument reflects the whole range of activities that make up the historian's task of endeavouring to understand and to evaluate the past. It is this miscellany of activities that gives substance to the series of claims that good evidence is what satisfies certain standards; that one of the

standards is that evidence should not contradict what are acknowledged to be facts; and that what are acknowledged as facts are
so acknowledged because they are supported by good evidence.

I now submit that the successive lessons to which I have pointed,
beginning from a recent disagreement in the Roman Church, can
give us a clearer view of the process by which, within that Church,
there is an interaction between past and present. The series of lessons
completes and reinforces my earlier contentions – that there is no
place to stand outside the varied activities that make up the inherited
life of the Church, no place where we may be exempt from the
temporal spread of activities that make up the tradition. Within the
tradition, we cannot be exempt from the reshaping which successors
in the tradition exercise upon their predecessors, while being shaped
in turn by what has gone before them. The succession and variety are
inescapable. The tradition exists in time and in the interconnected
circle of its manifestations: the biblical message, its several interpretations, the patterns of worship, the preferred formulae of teaching,
the range of favoured imagery, the various sensitivities and insensi-
tivities in language and in behaviour, the lessons of history and of life,
the effects of speculation and of the terms it uses, the endurance of
some beliefs and the transience of others, the interventions of
authorities and the reactions to those interventions. All this motley is
shot through with the activities of understanding and evaluating
what has been inherited, activities that are just as miscellaneous in
their forms as are the objects upon which they are exercised. To say,
as I have said so often, that the religious past is revered but
unsatisfactory is to point to the miscellany of activities by which it is
both esteemed and found fault with – activities which will themselves
in due course become part of the past. There is, as I have put it, no
leaving the arena. Or, as Neurath's famous simile puts it, we are like
sailors who have to repair their ship without putting into harbour.

We may be like them, but we may still be inclined to long for the
stability of a dry dock (as I am sure Neurath's sailors would). The
attractions of what I called earlier an Archimedean point are very
great, and the abandonment of belief in one can seem a loss that is
very real. Indeed, without such a point, what stands in the way of
total scepticism? I can best begin my answer by making a more
general remark. The citation from Neurath can serve to tell some
readers what other readers will already know – that the approach I
have been favouring resembles other treatments of knowledge and

enquiry in our century. In more than one philosophical tradition there has been a turning away from the quest for some ultimate and (to use my own word) insulated certainty, of the sort associated with Descartes. It is not that the quest has been abandoned as beyond our powers – rather, the whole notion of such a quest has come to be regarded with disfavour. The details of this philosophical shift do not concern us, but it does represent a pattern of thought that has shewn itself repeatedly in this book. We shall be seeing yet more of the pattern, and I offer at this point some specific examples which can help us to discern it. The examples are all concerned with change in religious belief, and we can look at them in the light of what we learned from the case of liberation theology. We can then, I hope, draw morals from them, morals concerning the relation between present and past in the Roman Church; and the morals we can apply in the next section to eucharistic contexts.

The first of the three examples takes us back to Rahner, and to the shift in his views about the origin of mankind. We saw that the shift took place despite the pronouncement by Pius XII that polygenism was not open to discussion, on the grounds that there seemed no way of reconciling it with the doctrine of original sin. Pius described this doctrine in words taken from a decree of the Council of Trent, and I cite the passage: the sin of Adam is 'one in its origin, passed on by generation and not by imitation, and present in each one as his own' (Sessio v: DS 1513). But the council says more. It condemns any who do not profess that

the first man Adam, when he had disobeyed the commandment of God in paradise, lost at once the holiness and justice in which he had been established; incurred by this disobedience the anger and indignation of God; incurred indeed death, with which God had threatened him; incurred along with death captivity under the power... of the devil; and the whole Adam was changed for the worse, in body and soul, by that disobedience. (DS 1511)

Then the council goes on to deal with the effects of this on Adam's descendants. It condemns all who assert

that Adam's disobedience affected him alone and not his descendants; lost holiness and justice for him only; or that Adam... handed on death and bodily penalties only... and not sin, which is the soul's death. (DS 1512)

So much for Trent: let us now set beside it what Rahner ends by holding on the topic.

We have already seen that he will accept polygenism – so there need be no one individual Adam. He will also accept that there was no Paradise to begin with, and that the appearance of Adam (whether as individual or group) was not different from ours – so there is no change for the worse in body and no change in the fact of death; rather, immortality and the rest would have been bestowed if he (they) had not disobeyed (Rahner 1965: 102–5). He also holds that original sin is only analogously sin if we compare it with personal guilty actions and with the guilty state they lead to; original sin is not an extension to us of Adam's personal guiltiness, whether 'Adam' be taken as an individual or a group (Rahner 1970: 269, ET 257). Holiness, as primordially imparted by the holiness of God and meant to have been handed on by physical descent, is now not so handed on – *this* can rightly be called a state of sinfulness, and this is what original sin means for each of us (1970: 268, ET 256. A similar account, in English, is in Rahner 1969a).

We can surely agree that the identity between what Rahner holds and what Trent decreed is not self-evident. So let us return to the claim he made in the earliest of these writings, that Trent *presupposed* monogenism but did not *define* it (p. 250): the distinction, if legitimate, might accommodate the shifts there have been in his thought. I give the gist of his exposition, inserting letters to clarify a difficult text. Let D be a definer (a Council, etc); let A be defined by D; and let B be part of the content of D's mind in making the definition. B *is defined along with* A if its content stands to A in a relationship so immediately perceptible and indissoluble that D's assertion of A extends with all its weight to B. On the other hand, should the relationship exist, and even be demonstrable, yet not be immediate and so not explicitly seen, then B cannot be so described – it will be a *presupposition* or *consequence* of the definition, but it will not be asserted by D with the absoluteness with which D asserts A. And what Rahner intends by all this can be seen from how he goes on. On this second hypothesis, he writes,

we should put this question to D: do you assert B just as absolutely as you assert A, what you explicitly define; and on the grounds that you are defining A? And D would then have to reply: 'I must think about that; I must first reflect on the relationship between A – what I have defined – and B, which is in fact primarily just present to my mind with A.'

Which Rahner concludes amounts to saying that D did not define B, but might do so later (1962: 266–7; ET 242–3).

I have laboured over this text because it embodies with such unhappy felicity what I am opposing. The presuppositions and implications of assertion can indeed have complex relations with what is asserted, and they are a legitimate topic for logical investigation. But we have something quite different here – a defiance of history. Who are supposed to be the participants in this conversation? Ourselves and the Council of Trent, perhaps? But what meaning can be attached to such an hypothesis – if it be not the idea that we (and the council) can step out of our respective selves and converse at some timeless rendezvous? In what way is the council (how assembled?) supposed to conduct the reflexion of which Rahner writes? Or to know that it has been successfully conducted? How do we know what answer it will give? And will the council be permitted to interrogate us in return? The questions have only to be put to display the picture as incoherent. Rahner's distinction between definition and presupposition only masks what is really going on. It depicts us as engaged in scrutinising something ('the definer's mind') to see just what its contents are, and how close is the relationship between them. But that (even if it makes sense) is simply not what we are doing. We are in fact engaged in revaluing our inheritance in the light of what claims are being made by, among other things, physical sciences: we are reshaping our past and re-ordering its exigencies and priorities. It is being subjected by us to the Theaetetus Effect.

If our inheritance of belief were modular, there would be no difficulty – removals and replacements would be effected, and all else remain as it was. But modularity is alien to the whole business. We do not have pieces that we may separate, marking off some as defined and others as only present at the definition. We have a story in Genesis; we have in the Western Church a series of reflexions sparked off by it and by passages in the New Testament. And now we have (not only in Rahner, of course!) a series of changes by which the *feel* of the story is deeply affected and even more the general *drift* of the reflexions. The one Adam has gone, the unity of stock has gone; the initial state of Paradise has gone; the primal fault is indeed still there, but its aetiological representation tells us nothing of its nature; original sin is only analogous to the sins we personally commit. That original sin is not personally committed by us, I naturally do not deny. What I want to bring out from obscurity is that the whole drift of the tradition is touched by the style of Rahner's presentation. Trent was appealing to an ancient heritage when it spoke of slavery to the devil, penalties of the body, and the death of the soul. Think of one example among so many. Christmas Matins in the Old Breviary had a Sermon of Leo the Great (+461) in the Second Nocturn: Christ's birth stands apart from what is read (he cites a version of Job) of all others – no one is clean of defilement, not even an infant that lives but a day upon the Earth (the original is in 54 ML 191).[11] That is what our past is like. And that is why I have used words like 'feel' and 'drift'; I think that they represent how the heritage of belief touches us. My purpose is to insist that we need to *look* at what is being done here, done to an inherited belief. Our past is revered but unsatisfactory; Rahner finds it unsatisfactory here, for reasons drawn from physical science, history, and (I suspect) morality; so he revalues it. But he needs to state what he is doing for what it is. All the more because of the place he gave to the Church's teaching in his debate with Küng.

My second example of change in religious belief can, fortunately, be given in a much briefer compass. What I have in mind is change there has been in belief about the resurrection. We have already seen what positions were adopted by an 'Official Catholic Response' about it (p. 253), and I hope I do not need to convince readers that the response embodies changes – and with a vengeance – from beliefs long held. We can set beside the response what, in the fourth chapter, we saw Aquinas write about details of the resurrection (p. 140). These speculations of Aquinas are not identified by me with Christian belief; but, once more, I point out that he took the biblical narratives of the resurrection, and other biblical texts, in a way that so many others have done, but that many of us now do not. For better or worse, we are cautious over certain narratives; which is why we are bewildered as well as amused by the deductions he makes, and by the colourful details with which he fills six questions of the *Summa Theologiae*. But do not let us allow our amusement to deceive us – the caution we exhibit goes further than we are likely to realise. In the New Testament, the resurrection is not, if I may so put it, an isolated

---

[11] This is more than rhetoric for the older belief. Recall from p. 140 how for Aquinas Christ on Good Friday left in Hell (that is, in the 'place of waiting' of Old Testament Saints) infants too young to have had faith in him as their now heaven-bound parents had. Add that for Augustine (*Enchiridion ad Laurentium* 93; 40 ML 275) unbaptised infants are eternally punished, even though very lightly. And then appreciate a pleasant cultic picture in the New Breviary. Leo's sermon still appears in the night-office for Christmas – but the passage I cited has been replaced. Modularity lives.

wonder. Matthew tells us of other resurrections, occurring at the death of Jesus (Matt. xxvii 52), and the disciples have already been told by Jesus to raise the dead (Matt. x 8). For Luke, Jesus has already raised up a dead man, at Nain (Luke vii 11f.). For John, there has already been a species of rehearsal in the raising of Lazarus (John xi). The place we give to the resurrection obviously involves more than the details with which the different Gospels narrate it; but for many the narrative is now dissociated, in reading and in thought, from the concomitants I have just mentioned. We have what we have had before – our belief in the resurrection has been superveniently isolated from what were once its accompaniments. Of course, we need not have this supervenient isolation – Julien Green for one would reject it. For him, scepticism over the miracle at Nain raised questions about (and note the conjunction) the raising of Lazarus and Christ's resurrection itself. I repeat my expression of respect for the coherence of thought shewn by those who think as Green does, and I repeat my cautionary observations to those who take biblical criticism in their stride: they must face up to what they are doing and to the consequences thereof. When we in the present try to make sense of the past, we must not refuse the burden of evaluation, and we must not refuse to acknowledge that our belief and life are temporally extended, and everywhere limited. And so we must accept that, having read critically what Scripture says of the first Adam, we cannot draw back from a critical reading of what Scripture and Church tradition alike have made of the Second Adam and of his saving work.

I have examined two changes in religious belief, changes of which we have already seen something earlier in the book. But there is a third item of belief which now calls for examination, given all that I have been saying about the relations between present and past, about the profundity of the changes which time can bring, and about the very mixed inheritance that is ours in the Church. What of the claim that the Church possesses, and possesses most sharply and perceptibly in the papacy, the gift of pronouncing infallibly under certain conditions concerning faith and morals? It might be thought that, after all else that I have said – indeed, after the whole direction and style of my arguments and suggestions – there can be nothing left for me to say about this claim. But I think there is, although part of it must wait until the next section, where I turn to the specifically eucharistic inheritance that is ours. Meanwhile I go once more to eucharistic analogies, to express something of what I have to say here and now.

The first of the analogies illustrates an admission I make at the outset – that there is an attractiveness in the idea of an infallible guide, and in the idea of the definiteness such a guide can give to what is proposed for our belief. The analogy I draw here is between this attractiveness and an attractiveness I have already admitted – that of conceiving the eucharistic presence in terms of a switch of substances beneath the veil of the accidents. The 'Galilean Presence', as I called it in the last chapter, attracts by seeming to offer a definite choice for belief – Christ is either present or he is not. Just so, an infallible authority seems to provide us with something definite – such and such is part of our faith or it is not. The machinery of tran- substantiation is matched by the machinery of an infallible authority. I did not deny the attractions of the Galilean presence, and I do not deny now the attractions of what I see as corresponding to it in the claim made by the Roman Church. But, just as I rejected the machinery in the setting of the Eucharist, so I reject the machinery proposed here.

Readers may once more relax. I am well aware of the controversies there have been over infallibility in the Church – the debate prompted by Küng's book is only one among a long succession. I have no intention of treading ground so over-trodden already, and no intention of revisiting the rogues' gallery in which – as supposed counter-examples to the sharpest form of the claim to infallibility – certain popes are exhibited as having made mistakes in solemn pronouncements: Honorius and his unsoundness on the dual will; Liberius and his signing a heterodox formula about something or another; Zacharias (my favourite – I hope the tale is not apocryphal) and his denunciation of the existence of the Antipodes; and others of the sort.[12] If things like that were all that could be dredged up from

---

[12] It is in fact the *antipodeans* that Zacharias rejected – 'other men, or another sun and moon' at the antipodes – but other authors were unfavourable to the antipodes as well. I owe this information to a subsequent reading in the twelfth chapter of Leopardi's work on common errors among the ancients (in e.g. Leopardi 1945: vol. II, p. 361), and I give the matter a footnote for two reasons. The first is that, in recording Zacharias' condemnation (in a letter to St Boniface [89 ML 946–7]), Leopardi – poor Leopardi – qualifies it at once with 'speaking as a private teacher, not as head of Christianity': an unsought example of my 'retroactive demotion'. The second is that, when St Augustine rejects the antipodeans because descendants of the first man could not have sailed so far, he adds that Scripture 'produces belief in its narratives of the past by the fulfilment of its predictions about the

over so long a period, papal infallibility – or ecclesial infallibility, if you wish – would be doing rather well. My own objection may seem naive, but at all events it is different. Once more, to repeat the phrase, I do not want to say what it *must* be, I want to *look*. There are many places where I can look – I go to one that affected our own country.

I began the book with talk of the Royal Declaration against transubstantiation, which every English sovereign once had to make. I go now to an oath once exacted on occasions from his subjects, the oath of allegiance to the monarch, which – along with other things – denied the power of the pope to depose sovereigns. Questions to do with its possible lawfulness for Roman Catholics in England had been raised early in the reign of James I. Robert Persons, that ubiquitous Mr Fixit, wrote to his fellow Jesuit Henry Garnet in 1606 that he had taken opinion on the point from Roman theologians, and that these had denied that the oath could be sworn: 'the reasons are many, but all reduce to this that the Popes authoritie in chasteneing princes upon just cause is *de fide* [i.e., part of the essence of the faith]' (quoted in Clancy 1961: 211). Their opinion was not surprising, for had not papal practice exhibited this authority? Indeed, had not James's predecessor Elizabeth I been so deposed by Pius V? And had not Boniface VIII in 1302 solemnly pronounced 'We therefore declare, state and define that it is utterly necessary for salvation for every human creature to be subject to the Roman Pontiff' (*Unam Sanctam*, conclusion; DS 875)? Unsurprising indeed – and so to more persecution in England and to the penal laws.

I have taken the example as something to which an obvious and ready reply can be and is given; so that I may draw lessons from why I find the reply so unsatisfactory. The reply will be well known to many readers and is to be found in many places. I go for it to an article by Bishop Christopher Butler, which appeared in the wake of Küng's book. The article was concerned with the scope and limitations of infallibility, and in it the author cited with approval the profession of Baron von Hügel, the philosopher of religion and mysticism, that he accepted 'whatever the Church had finally committed herself to' (Butler 1971: 399, col. 2). From which the reply to the example I offered follows easily enough – the Church did not commit herself finally to what the Roman theologians told Persons, and the course of history shews that she did not. Human

future' (*De civitate Dei* xvi 9 [41 ML 487–88]). Which is just as unsought an example of what I claim about the shift there has been in our views of the Bible.

society has changed, and the life of the Church with it; there has been development in doctrine; the weight of pronouncements in the Church is something that becomes clear only with the passage of time (Newman is often cited at this point). In a word, the example I have given is ludicrous – Persons and Boniface VIII are all a very long time ago. None of which answers, of course, I deny; the trouble for me is that we all end up being a very long time ago. Here and now we are in the present, just as there was a time when Persons and his Roman theologians (and even Boniface VIII, presumably) were in the present. And it is with the present that I am concerned, for it is in the present that demands are made upon our belief by the Church. If we now believe that demands once solemnly made are in fact no more than antiquated excess, how can that belief leave untouched our response to the demands now being made by the very same authority? The contention that our response should now be one of submission, on the grounds that what was formerly demanded was no part of the faith, but only politics or something, does nothing but beg the question. If words and emphasis and practice mean anything, claims were being made in past time to privileged and authoritative utterances. But words and emphasis and practice have not saved from revaluation what was then claimed to be privileged; why should words and emphasis and practice in our own time fare any better?

A second eucharistic analogy can be of use in pressing the point I am making. We have seen recent authors like de Baciocchi disown what they hold to be a caricature of transubstantiation, and the disowning is understandable. But if there be anything to my contentions about the view he and others put forward instead, it is transubstantiation itself that they should be disowning – the caricature is of a piece with what they are trying to keep apart from it. Just so, those who dismiss embarrassing claims made in the past as so much antiquated excess should rather be looking at claims to infallible utterance being made in the present. To face the claims is to have a chance of becoming clearer over the relation between utterance and response in the Church. I will try to shew more of the relation in what follows in the chapter, as I try to spell out more of the relationship between the two senses of *corpus mysticum*. What I have to offer may or may not prove acceptable; but those who baulk at facing these problems raised by clashes between past and present must ask themselves whether they have anything better to offer – anything apart from what we might call the Watergate Disclaimer.

And in order to face what is actually claimed by the Roman Church for its pronouncements, I go to a third eucharistic analogy. We met the analogy earlier in this chapter: I drew it between our retroactive demotion of inconvenient utterances once made by authority, and the view of substance presupposed by Colombo. I said that, just as for him no physical discovery can touch the metaphysical order of substance, so no retroactive demotion can ever touch the substance of our belief. But I can now take the analogy further. The insulatedness of substance as seen by Colombo leaves it inactive in its splendid isolation: it is only natural that, by way of compensation, all else should be demoted, and physical science be relegated to the order of accidents. It is not hard to shew that the belief in infallibly guaranteed utterances calls for – and gets – a similar demotion of all else in the Church.

To shew it, we need go no further than the right-hand columns of the two sets of parallel texts I printed earlier in the chapter (pp. 256–8, 267–70). What is in those columns is concerned with submission as well as with truth, and with submission demanded in a variety of ways: Catholics must accept not only dogmas infallibly declared, but what the ordinary *magisterium* of the Church teaches as divinely revealed; they must submit to decrees of the Roman Congregations; the magisterium can exercise the charism of infallibility (which calls for theological faith), can make pronouncements in a definitive way (which must be firmly accepted and held), and enjoys on other occasions divine guidance (which calls for a religious submission of will and intellect, not just an external response). Moreover, freedom of the act of faith cannot justify dissent; and, to reinforce all this, the faithful were threatened over centuries with excommunication if they read any prohibited books. Submission in all this is demanded, and submission on the ground of the various forms of guidance provided by God for the teaching Church. It is in this range of demanded submissions, if I may so speak, that I see the general demotion of all else in the Church, a demotion analogous to the demotion by Colombo and others of physical science. The nature of the demotion I can best bring out by going back to the article by Butler already cited. When Butler supported there von Hügel's position that he accepted 'whatever the Church had finally committed herself to', he was expressing concern about a phenomenon in the Church which he himself described as 'creeping infallibility' – a process by which 'a higher note of truth or obligatoriness [is attached to] a piece of doctrine than the Church herself actually assigns to it' (Butler 1971 : 374, col. 2). With the drift and details of Butler's complaint I am not concerned. My concern is to claim that an infallibility which does *not* creep is not worth having. I go on to explain this claim of mine.

When the First Vatican Council declared the pope to possess on special occasions the gift of infallibility, it gave a description of those occasions.[13] The text I leave to a footnote, what concerns me is its *length* and its *solemnity*: its length opened the door to claims that the full tale of conditions had not been satisfied; its solemnity, to claims that the occasion was not sufficiently serious to count. Both were a boon to apologists who worried about Boniface VIII or the antipodes; but both, by the very exaltedness they bestowed upon the declarations, gave them a splendour that was all too isolated. Just as Colombo's substance was insulated at the cost of becoming inert, so the defences of papal infallibility insulate it by keeping its horizon ever on the move. Whatever might impugn it is demoted; should a counter-example touch anything, it no longer counts as one. But here too the insulation has to be paid for: infallibly guaranteed utterances are always vanishing round the next corner. To draw for once a mathematical rather than a eucharistic analogy, the divine guidance turns out to resemble a point of convergence that is approached but never reached. Von Hügel may well accept whatever the Church has finally committed herself to: but what counts as a final commitment remains (as von Hügel's own practice superabundantly shewed) curiously elusive. It is therefore no more than natural that the demands for submission should be extended, and that the claims for divine guidance should be multiplied, in the way we have seen happen. Call the process 'creeping' if you will – but what content in practice would the claim to infallibility have without it? The effect,

[13] 'We therefore, faithfully adhering to the tradition received from the start of the Christian faith, for the glory of God our Saviour, for the exaltation of the Catholic religion, and for the salvation of Christian peoples, do – the holy Council approving – teach and define to be a divinely revealed dogma: that the Roman Pontiff, when he speaks *ex cathedra*, that is, when exercising his office as shepherd and teacher of all Christians, he defines with his supreme Apostolic authority a doctrine concerning faith or morals to be held by the whole Church, enjoys by the divine assistance promised to him in Saint Peter, that infallibility with which the divine Redeemer wished his Church to be endowed in defining a doctrine concerning faith or morals; and that therefore definitions of that sort by a Roman Pontiff are of themselves, and not through the consent of the Church, irreformable. If anyone – which God forbid – should presume to contradict this Our definition, let him be anathema' (Vatican I (1870), cap. 4; DS 3074–5). There is of course much more to the decree: I have printed only what concerns us here.

of course, is this general demotion of all else in the Church – all else must wait obediently upon what emerges from a peremptory but inconstant centrality. Indeed, yet another pleasingly clear example of 'creeping' is provided by this Instruction from the Inquisition on the theologian's calling. We saw earlier the responses demanded there to the various pronouncements by popes and bishops. But another section goes even further:

§ 18 The Roman Pontiff carries out his universal mission with the help of the Congregations of the Roman Curia, and in a special way with the help of the Congregation for the Doctrine of the Faith [i.e., the Inquisition] when matters arise to do with faith or morals. It follows that documents issued by this Congregation, and expressly approved by the Roman Pontiff, share in the ordinary magisterium of the successor of Peter. (Inquisition 1990: 1558)

Readers familiar with the vocabulary of Roman theology can note here what they may well have noted already elsewhere: a shift in the application of the phrase 'ordinary magisterium'. It was used at one time for the day-to-day teaching of the Church in general; it has now been 'polarised' upon papal and curial pronouncements. I suggest that this shift is complemented by another: the introduction of the words like 'meditation'. The 'Official Response' used it to describe the elaboration of the Easter-stories (p. 253); 'reflecting upon' occurred in the papal speech in the Roman synagogue (p. 273); 'meditating' occurred near the start of the very first address made to the Cardinals in John-Paul II's pontificate (John-Paul II 1978). Such words have associations that are essentially individualistic and private – the associations of communal, open discussion are accordingly weakened. Just as the shift in 'ordinary magisterium' extends privilege at the centre, so words like 'meditation' lessen spontaneity anywhere else. All outside are supposed to wait upon, as I put it, a peremptory but inconstant centrality.[14]

---

[14] That the centrality is inconstant as well as peremptory raises problems for those who would try to describe what form the response to it should take. Rahner struggles with the matter, unsuccessfully in my opinion, in his earlier essay on monogenism (1962: 274; ET 250). The only sources known to me that really face the issue are Örsy 1990 and McHugh 1969. I hope they will not take amiss my suggestion that the very honesty of what they write exhibits the incoherence of what they are writing about. For just *what* is being suggested by this 'religious submission of will and intellect', which none the less is open to subsequent change? What are we supposed to *do*? Gwendolen, in *The Importance of Being Ernest*, is asked whether she can doubt what her suitor asserts, and answers 'I have the very gravest doubts about it; but I intend to overcome them. This is no time for German scepticism.' Is that it? Or must we go to the example provided by King and Matthews 1990? This narrates the *volte-face* imposed on the Communist Party in this country when the treaty between Hitler and Stalin was

When I offered my criticism of Colombo's notion of substance, I said that it was ultimately sceptical. I would say the same of this general demotion of all other things in the Church. It is no accident that, in the two parallel columns on pp. 267–70, the right-hand column should contain extracts from the Index of Prohibited Books, or that the left-hand column contains apologies for how the Church of Rome has at times regarded human investigations. Only 'at times' misleads. The right-hand column shews that the times have been and are our times too. If we do not say what it *must* be, but *look*, we see that this is what the tradition is like, and that 'creeping' in Butler's sense is the only way of continuing it. His complaint at creeping infallibility provides yet another example of the analogy with de Baciocchi's disowning what he claims to be a caricature of transubstantiation: de Baciocchi and Butler are both repudiating what in fact gives life to doctrines in which they do believe. I have claimed that de Baciocchi's manoeuvre will not bear examination. I now make a similar suggestion about Butler's manoeuvre here: those who worry about creeping infallibility should worry rather about infallibility itself.

In this section as in others, I have drawn analogies between the Eucharist and the Church. In the next section, I turn to the specifically eucharistic inheritance that is ours, in the light of all that I have been proposing in the book about Eucharist and Church alike. What general morals should we carry over to it?

We have learned, I hope, something more about the value of facing the past, and something more about the difficulties in facing it. I gave earlier my reasons for attaching importance to the acceptance of a critical reading of the Bible, and I hope we have learned here something more of the force of those reasons. It is a critical reading of Scripture that brings us up most insistently against the *otherness* of the past, and prepares us for accepting that otherness in the past of the Church. There, as in any other community, many things encourage us to homogenise past and present, as if we could live in some everlasting now, exempt from time and from what time brings. We must resist the temptation. The past is not an encumbrance, nor is it an ornamental archive. It is part of what we are, it helps to make up

signed. Some members thought that silence from them in the face of it would be enough (just as Newman described Roman pronouncements as purely external; Ward 1913: 349–50). They were disillusioned: Moscow demanded an inner change of heart. The parallels with Rome, even in vocabulary, are striking; the work would repay examination by theologians.

our humanity. The past does not impose a *quietus* upon reflexion and decision, but those activities would not make sense without it. The past can liberate: an awareness of it gives us insight into the origins and development of what we do and know; we can learn how we have come to be what we now are; we can discern patterns of change, choices among alternatives, and both the wisdom and the folly of the dead. That autocracies should attempt to tame and even to obliterate the past is no accident – without a past, we are but slaves of the present moment. But it is not autocracies alone who are to blame, for the quest to understand and to evaluate the past is not easy. The past can exert its proper power only if it can stimulate and embarrass, only if we allow it to speak to us on its own terms. And there is more to the quest than hard work – there can well be anguish. I wrote earlier of the *Wahrheitspathos*, the 'tragic sense of truth' that is a burden for our time. We should be able to see by now that the burden can be very real, and that the revaluations we make of our religious past can go very deep. The next section, with its specifically eucharistic themes, should bring home to us even more what we have seen in this section: that there can be a rending quality in religious change, and that all the manoeuvres over clashes between past and present are endeavours to ease matters. But ease, as we have seen and shall see again, cannot be enough.

39   THE INHERITED CONGLOMERATE

Readers with good memories might – just might – still remember something that happened in the first chapter. After giving the first instalment of my objection against the scholastic account of transubstantiation, I rehearsed a protest against those objections: they were pedantic and superfluous, for what matters in eucharistic belief is what has always mattered, namely that the reality of what we receive is the Risen Lord; and what matters in the belief is not constricted by the categories of obsolete modes of thought, and not compromised by the incapacity of language to seize it. My reply to the protest was not a straightforward rejection of it, but rather an insistence that things were just not so simple; that the protest was multiply ambiguous; and that the rest of the book could be seen as an attempt to disentangle the ambiguities and to follow up the many questions raised by them. Whatever be thought of the contentions I have since been making, readers can at least agree by now that the journey has been a long one, and that it has led us into a greater variety of contexts than we might have expected. The present chapter and its predecessor have been concerned with the themes on which the book's whole range of preoccupations has converged: the relations between present and past; the place of ritual in eucharistic belief; and the analogies between the Eucharist and the Church. And these themes in their turn have brought us repeatedly to the contention that insulation, as I have called it, is attractive but is achieved at too high a price. In the Eucharist, the *corpus mysticum*, insulation confuses signs with disguises, and leads to a divorce of appearance from reality that is ultimately sceptical. In the Church, also the *corpus mysticum*, insulation hinders us from seeing just what is the complex relationship between present and past in the community of believers. But, just as the analogy between the Eucharist and the Church makes insulation something that menaces both, so the analogy also suggests a better way. The newer rite of the Eucharist displays a cultic picture, as I have called it, which can serve as a pattern for what should be found in the Church. The picture has an openness and a vulnerability, and the Church needs to acknowledge those qualities in itself, even though the acknowledgment may be difficult and painful.

All this and much more I have claimed, but I seem to have created thereby for myself an obligation impossible to fulfil. I have laid stress on the need to face the past in all its complexity, and to acknowledge – in Eucharist and in Church alike – the protraction over time of what we are engaged in. But for the Roman Church, that protraction includes something which appeared at the very start of the book – the decrees of the Council of Trent on the eucharistic presence. I mentioned there too the Royal Declaration against transubstantiation, as a testimony to how Trent's term was regarded by those who were not Roman Catholics. I mentioned Ruskin's *gaucheries* with the French girl, to shew how the term continued to be associated with the Roman Church. And I mentioned the Roman Inquisition's complaint in our own time, as bearing witness to how that term is still seen as a touchstone of true belief. I also promised there to say something later on about what Trent had decreed, but after all I have written since, have I left myself with anything to say? I have charged with incoherence the classic account of transubstantiation found in Aquinas. I have rejected the whole pattern – whether in older or recent sources – of setting appearance against reality and of letting the former survive without the latter. And I have, in what I have written of the Fallacy of Replacement, insisted that a respect for ritual demands that we allow ritual itself to respect the reality of what it uses. Set all that beside the texts from Trent at pp. 2–3, and there seems little left for me to add now beyond an acknowledgment of incompatibility. I have barred the way – even if I wanted to take it – to effecting a reconciliation through a transference of Trent's expressions into some novel context where they can prove more pliable: such historical insouciance would come rather late in the day after all I have said against it. And even the very notion of seeking a reconciliation now looks odd – have I not also rejected, as an example of insulation, the Roman Church's claim to make infallible pronouncements? What is there for me to be reconciled with? I have complained often enough about implicit scepticism in those from whose views I have dissented. Have not my own views led me to a similar destination?

I want to approach these problems indirectly, in a way that will link what I have to say of Trent with what I have been saying already. I make my approach from something we have met more than once – disagreements and changes in religious belief. And about them I put the question: how do such things arise, and how do they die away? Let us see where the question leads us, by taking some examples.

Consider first two cases where argument used to be intense but is so no longer: one is the relationship between divine grace and human freedom; the other is the existence of post-scriptural miracles. Both topics, of course, can still provide material for debate, but neither of them plays the part it once did in the fabric of religious life. In the seventeenth century, some Christians seem to have thought or written of little else except election, grace, reprobation and all the rest of it. And well into the nineteenth century, belief in post-scriptural miracles was seen as dividing Catholic from Protestant, so that in 1864 Newman devoted much space to the topic in the fifth appendix to his *Apologia*, and in 1851 had disputed on the matter with the Bishop of Norwich. Why have both debates petered out? I suggest that boredom (that all-powerful and underestimated force) had a good deal to do with ending the former: boredom at the increasing speed with which argument was found to lead to dead ends, and boredom at the lack of connexion between the texture of debate's language and the practice of the Christian life. The language, for all its complexity and ingenuity, seemed to lead back into itself and

nowhere else – life could and did go on without it. As for the other
debate, it did not so much peter out as be taken up into other
investigations and disagreements. The Scriptures, as we have seen,
are no longer fenced off; the range of acknowledged actions and
achievements to do with healing has widened; the logical complexities in the term 'miracle' have become plainer; the nature of
narrative in other civilisations has been examined; in other words,
the conversation has become wider. And if neither boredom nor
absorption into wider concerns seems a distinctively theological
reason for the cessation of religious disagreements, so be it. We are
back to the openness and vulnerability we have met so often: there is
interaction here between belief and more general things. Better, we
see belief as part of a whole engagement over time of a complex
religious tradition with a variety of forces, forces which it shapes and
by which in turn it is shaped.

Those two examples were of controversies that have died out, but
the same pattern of engagement with varied forces is found too in the
origins of controversies. Here our examples can come from what we
have already met. Whatever be thought of debate over a critical
reading of the Bible, it undoubtedly owes its origin in part to forces
not specifically religious, and just as undoubtedly it raises questions
which could not have been asked earlier – questions which in their
turn can touch what else has previously been believed. And whatever
be thought of disagreement over liberation theology, it too owes its
origin in part to forces that lay outside religious belief. Christians
confronted human wretchedness in a setting where their own faith
had been given its head, and where other attempts were being made
to remedy the wretchedness – attempts of a politically revolutionary
character, and so regarded by some as hostile to religion. We have in
each of the examples both novelty and continuity. It would be absurd
to claim that people had never previously wondered about the Bible,
or never previously tried to remedy the lot of the poor. But it would
be just as absurd to claim that the questions now put, and the debates
now in progress, could have arisen without the engagement of
believers with things that were new arrivals. The questions and the
debates alike are a tribute to the openness and vulnerability of what
is believed.

My claim here, of course, is involved in all that I have been saying
of the religious past, and of the way in which the patterns of interest
alter over the years. The imagery of one age can prove an

encumbrance for the next – we can recall the language used at times of sacrifice and of the redemption, and those elements in eucharistic belief that I called 'the shadow of the past'. It is not that embarrassment is to be avoided – I have spent much time insisting that it must not. It is rather that we have to hold an uneasy balance between unacknowledged accommodations of the past on the one hand and giving free rein on the other to the independent life our language and imagery can take on. The encounter of belief with varied forces can make believers sensitive in ways that once they were not, so that lines of thought among them can die away or rise up. Thus, if we now pass over elements in the medieval expression of the eucharistic presence, we also dwell on elements in our inheritance that medieval thinkers passed over – recall the reflexions I suggested earlier on relations between Christians and Jews.

I said that what I am claiming here is involved in all that I have written about the relations between past and present in religious belief. It is in fact no more than an example of that 'circular' pattern I traced in all our beliefs: we both shape and are shaped by what we encounter. It is no more than an example of the 'Theaetetus Effect', by which the significance and general order of precedence among what we have inherited are changed by our present preoccupations. I introduced this term in the first chapter, when setting the eucharistic theories of Aquinas beside the speculations of earlier and later thinkers. But do not let us forget that, in the very process of recalling what Aquinas held in these matters, we ourselves exhibit the Theaetetus Effect: we stress some themes and pass over others. As I put it, the 'Aquinas' of our citations does not altogether match the Aquinas who wrote on those topics, for there are some things he wrote that we do not care to cite. And just as there is a shadow of the past in our eucharistic inheritance, so there is in what else we have inherited. The picturesquenesses of Persons' theologians on the deposing power, or of Boniface VIII's claims for his office, are nothing to be surprised at; we should not be surprised either at the way in which they have been accommodated. My own thesis has been in a sense no more than a call to acknowledge what we are doing for what it is. We cannot disregard the past, but neither is the past exempt from what time brings – just as we ourselves are not and shall not be so exempt.

It is with this awareness of time, so often stressed in these pages, that I approach what the Council of Trent had to say about the eucharistic presence. 'Approach', I fear, recalls the legendary editorial in an Irish provincial newspaper ('We have our eye on the Emperor of Russia'). Whatever the Council said on the topic, it deserves far more space than I give, and calls for much greater competences from its critics than I possess. I write what I do well aware of my previously expressed dissents, and still maintaining them. I write it to shew at all events how one dissenter reads the Council, and I hope that what I write will say something about what dissent in these matters amounts to. I am glad to have been able to use here the monumental work of Hubert Jedin on the Council's history. For my specifically eucharistic topics, I have gone with pleasure to a remarkable monograph by another German scholar, Josef Wohlmuth. My admiration for these two works will be evident from the reliance I have placed upon them; I shall cite them as 'H' and 'W' respectively.[15] I set down here at the outset that the council began in Trent in December 1545; migrated (when typhus broke out) to Bologna in March 1547, where in September 1549 it was suspended; met in Trent once more from May 1551 until April 1552; and finally, after a gap of ten years, met in Trent again from January 1562 until December 1563. The canons that concern us were first drawn up at Bologna in 1547. The debate was reopened when the council assembled again at Trent, and they were promulgated – in a form very similar to what had been reached at Bologna – in October 1551 (details of chronology are in DS at p. 363; for some reason, however, there is no mention of the Bolognese discussions of our topic

[15] Jedin's work is indeed monumental – the labour that it must have involved over thirty-five years is daunting even to contemplate. But the book also reads well, and manages to keep the thread of the story going through the long complexity of the materials the author has used. I notice here that the Acts of the Council of Trent have been in process of publication since the last century, by the Görresgesellschaft, but that (as Jedin points out) the source-materials are incomplete, and some remain in manuscript. I give references to Jedin by 'H', with book and section: these apply to the English translation too. (I cannot cite Jedin as 'J' because that is already taken for Jorissen's book.) I have followed up references in the Görresgesellschaft edition for myself (volume v is of special relevance to our themes), but I thought it less pretentious to confine myself to references to H and W. (I could have done with a general guide to the edition – is there one?)

    Wohlmuth is concerned with Trent's canons on the eucharistic presence, but he begins with an admirably full survey of recent opinions. He has gone to much manuscript material as well as to the Görresgesellschaft series, and uses it to luminous effect. My one complaint of substance touches his book's lay-out – he ought to have linked more perspicuously its erudite and helpful footnotes with the page numbers of his main text. Another observation on the lay-out is not a complaint. The book appeared before the advent of the word processor and is composed in photographed typescript. It thus provides a startling example of the Theaetetus Effect – to eyes in the 1990s, this scholarly work of 1975 looks as if it had emerged from the *scriptorium* in Wearmouth or Bobbio.

until p. 384). And so I turn to set down what I have found in examining the debates and decisions of the council.

What I find first is *a sense of urgency*. Proposals for reform in the Church had been voiced for a century and a half, and councils at Pisa, Basle and Constance had clashed with Rome over how the reform should be effected, and how far it should go. Jedin has to begin, ominously, with a long treatment of 'The struggle for the council' – a struggle with the Roman curia and with successive popes, for whom a council would have to be securely domesticated at Rome, if it were not to menace Rome in the way the councils at Basle and Constance had; considerations of power here played a pre-dictably large rôle (H 1.3). Whatever else can be said of the council, a reading of the debates leaves no doubt as to the determination of its participants to set their house in order. For details of all the struggle, see H I and II. Jedin also gives a pleasing confirmation of what I have said about cultic pictures. When the council eventually did meet, the regular celebration of the liturgy followed – as it had not done at Basle or Constance – the order observed at the papal court itself (H III.12).

What I find next is one form that the determination took – *an attempt to reach back to older sources* beyond the debates of the previous centuries of the medieval Church: to Scripture itself, and to early witnesses to Christian tradition. The attempt was the council's engagement with the new challenge faced by the Church of Rome – the challenge of a dissent which consciously separated itself from the scholastic theology that had dominated speculation for so long. Luther's own attack on transubstantiation, as reported by the council, had written of 'the Thomistic, that is the Aristotelian Church' (W, e.g., Tafel IX (2), column 1); something new was needed by way of reply. A return to Scripture was advocated by speakers; and one witness to the return can be seen in the very tortuousness of the council's debates over how to square the New Testament with Rome's denial of the chalice to the laity. Whatever be thought of the arguments, they at least shewed that Scripture was seen as able to make specific demands upon belief (for details, see H IV.2; opposition to the dominance of scholasticism was voiced by some, see H III.3 – where it is significant that an eloquent opponent of it was a monk, see my remarks on Baldwin of Ford at p. 31).

But I find too *an inevitable limitation to this reaching back*. The council's engagement was, we might say, with a novel and disturbing present;

the novelty called for an appraisal and revaluation of the past; but the formation of those at the council set severe bounds to the appraisal and to the revaluation it could bring about. The sheer material requisites for historical work, such as critical editions and chronologies, were still to come; what history there was in religious matters was seen as polemic; the whole idea of struggling to understand the development of belief was in great measure alien to the minds of those who debated over the decrees which the council was to enact. Indeed, the very form of those decrees bore witness to all these limitations. The canons were meant to be condemnations of views expressed by reformers like Luther and others, but the setting and purpose of what these had said was not adequately considered. Moreover, the whole plan – a very venerable plan – of letting the deliberations of the council end in condemning positions judged to be heretical was itself a limiting factor. It set bounds to what could be done in the way of a positive exposition of true belief that would take into account what points had been made by the reformers. Of course, there is no question of surprise or blame here. Awareness of the demands of history and of interpretation of documents was not to come until later. When it did develop, one of the factors leading to the development was surely the struggle that Trent had come to embody – the painful encounter between Rome on the one hand and on the other the appeal of the reformers from Rome to what was older. We cannot expect Trent to answer questions it was unable to put.

I find next in the council the *scholastic presuppositions of the participants*.[16] It is not that Trent identified true eucharistic belief with what the scholastics had speculated about it – the attempt to reach

---

[16] In the third chapter I took exception, and at some length, to what Schillebeeckx had to say in a discussion about the terminology of 'substance' and 'species' used in Trent's decree on the Eucharist (pp. 125ff.). I noted then that the discussion, reported in Trooster 1963, took place some years before the publication of Schillebeeckx's own book, and I expressed my belief that his opinions changed in the interval. To shew the change, I offer two passages from his book that have to do with Trent's terminology. First, a general statement about formulations of belief:

We never find God's word *neat* [Schillebeeckx uses '*a l'état pur*']. Expressions like 'the outward vesture of dogma' may be appropriate when we look back on the past, but are fundamentally misleading. They give the impression that we can put on and take off the vesture of a dogma as easily as children dress and undress a doll. (1967: 17 [1968: 25])

Then in particular of the council itself he writes:

We cannot demand of any single individual that, while situated at a particular point in the general development of human thought, he should distance himself from his own thought (his own flesh and blood!) and run ahead in history – about five centuries ahead in this case!

back to older sources shews that the identification was not made. But the whole range of illustration, analogy, form of argument and terminology recalls time and again what we have seen already in Aquinas or in other medieval sources. The resemblance between the text of what the council decreed and what Aquinas wrote we noticed at the start of the first chapter. Here, we can notice scholastic presuppositions in the course of discussions at the council – I offer a few samples from Wohlmuth's book. Visdomini recapitulates the distinctions between transubstantiation, generation, annihilation (W 230, with its footnote 29). Aquinas writes of this at *ST* 3.75.4 and 3.75.8; see p. 14; notice how Visdomini elaborates the distinctions drawn by Aquinas, in a way not uncommon among later scholastics. Seripando gives a series of alternatives concerning the interpretations of 'this is my body' (W 243–5) – the series is meant to lead to the conclusion that the whole substance of the bread is converted, and is clearly based on what Aquinas wrote in *ST* 3.75.2 and 3.75.3; see related texts at pp. 11–13. Catherinus, in a debate over the use of 'contained' about Christ's eucharistic presence, faced unease among some members (I noticed an echo of the unease in chapter 3, footnote 5). He explained that the term was employed 'not circumscriptively' (W 131). We can recall what we saw Aquinas make, or rather not make, of a similar qualification in texts like *ST* 3.76.1 and 3, in what he writes of 'presence by way of substance' (see pp. 114–15). If Trent faced a challenge that was new, it also had been shaped by what was older.

And along with all this there is naturally something else I find in Trent – *distinctively scholastic limitations*. Of these limitations we have seen a good deal already – they might be summed up as a propensity to treat the eucharistic ritual in terms of what we should call a primitive natural science, and to neglect to treat it in terms of ritual. So it proved at Trent. Consilii feels able to draw an analogy between the introduction of the term 'transubstantiation' and the invention of words to describe some newly created animal or plant (W 235). Leoninus deals with the objection that Paul in First Corinthians uses 'bread' of the Eucharist; he answers that the rod changed by Moses

The Aristotelian doctrine of substance and accidents was, although with variations, the contemporary way of thought for all these Fathers of the Council. (1967: 42 [1968: 56])

These are but two among many. I do not agree with all that Schillebeeckx writes on this topic, but I gladly concede that he is no longer 'painting himself into a corner' as he was in the earlier item.

into a serpent is still called a rod (W 228). More picturesquely still, Lombardellus argues that the substance of the bread cannot survive – if it did, consuming the host would break the celebrant's fast, so that he could not then receive the chalice (W 232–3). Wohlmuth calls this argument 'home-made' – *hausgebacken*. But see *ST* 3.75.2; and we met similar views in the first chapter, to do with *panitas*, Indians living off the smell of apples, and the rest (pp. 33, 36). That ritual is alien to the whole texture and thrust of scholastic arguments like these hardly needs proof, but there is a deeper witness to just how alien it was, and this was the council's decision (taken just before its migration to Bologna) to separate the treatment of the presence of Christ in the Eucharist from its treatment of the sacrificial character of that rite, postponing the latter until all the Sacraments had been discussed (W 116–17; H III.11, but without comment; McHugh 1991: 159–60). I have written against the scholastic account of the eucharistic presence; I have drawn a contrast in the preceding chapter between what Aquinas writes of it and what he writes of eucharistic sacrifice; I have placed there what I called 'the Way of Ritual' in the setting of a sacrificial tradition. After all that, there is no need for me to dwell now on the way in which Trent's decision to separate the two themes shaped and limited from the start how those themes were to be treated. Medieval eucharistic theology had said much of the eucharistic presence and little of eucharistic sacrifice, so the separation was not surprising in its context. But the separation shews how very much bound by that context the council was.[17]

---

[17] What I wrote earlier of medieval miracle stories and devotional practices (pp. 222–4) also bears witness to where most interest lay then. The attack by Luther in the 1520s on the notion of sacrifice in the Eucharist was all the more of a shock, and the first stages of the Reformation saw a concentration on this theme by Catholic theologians like Schatzgeyer (I offer some more details on all this, and on the place of eucharistic sacrifice in the middle ages, in FitzPatrick 1991a). But Luther's attack was followed by the more radical dissents of Zwingli and Calvin, where the accepted understanding of the presence was impugned; it was natural that the theme should receive emphatic treatment, after all that the scholastics had written on it. I welcome, as a confirmation of my own conclusion, the judgment of Wohlmuth upon the council's decision to separate the two themes – that there was no ritual praxis at hand which drew its life from holding the themes together (W 117; compare my remarks on Aquinas at pp. 243–5).

McHugh 1991 gives a lucid account of the stages in which the topic of sacrifice was eventually considered by the council, displays the human toil and historical chances involved in it all, and shews that important material for Trent's history is still being discovered. For me, two other things stand out in what he writes: the lack of agreement over what was meant by the claim that the Eucharist is a sacrifice; and the change in balance and in tone that came over the council during the eighteen years of its existence. He rightly deplores the separation of the two themes of presence and sacrifice, but I think his descriptions of the decision might mislead. For him, it 'seems to us today an extraordinary

How bound, I would indicate by what I next find, and find not only in Trent itself but in what was to come soon after: and this is the *treatment of ritual*. There was undoubted progress made, in the zeal to abolish superstitions and abuses in the celebration of the Eucharist, and a decree on the subject was promulgated in 1562, along with the canons to do with the sacrificial character of what was celebrated. (The decree is not in DS; it can be seen in a footnote at ST 3.73 in the Marietti edition I have used. Newman appealed to it in Tract XC, when trying to shew that Article XXXI was not against the Mass as such.) But the abuses were only part of a wider impoverishment of ritual, with a liturgy of the Mass largely silent, removed from the understanding of the people by the posture and language of the celebrant, and biblically meagre. Given the means available for historical research, there could not have been any coherent attempt to investigate the development of the rite, and to see how its shape and pattern might be made more evident. Demands had been voiced for changes, especially concerning the vulgar tongue and the giving of the cup to the laity, nor did the council reject the demands outright. But it took them in terms of discipline rather than of ritual, and by the time the council closed, discipline had become all-important. A very mixed liturgical inheritance had received a purification from some gross abuses. What survived had now become a matter for defence, and the proposal of changes was seen as disloyalty to what needed defending. It is no surprise that, seven years after the council's closure in December 1563, Pius V (+ 1572) should promulgate a form of the Mass in the *Missale Romanum*, which (with the *Rituale Romanum*, see above, pp. 212–13) was to be for almost four centuries the standard and standardised ritual expression of the Roman Church. Of the 'cultic picture' it offered I have already written, and of its fate I am to write in the next section. Here and now, I turn from the Council itself to the next stages in the conglomerate we have inherited.[18]

judgment for Catholics to make. Indeed, it is to us unthinkable...' (159). For all that, the still standard work of reference *Dictionnaire de théologie catholique* divided the themes ('Eucharistie' and 'Messe'): perhaps Trent's separation obliged it to? It is pleasant to record that, with just but infuriating symbolism, each of these articles is itself physically divided in half by the usual bindings of the *Dictionnaire*.

[18] I express my appreciation of Wohlmuth's book by noticing some items in it. He gives, in a preliminary chapter, an admirably full account of recent eucharistic debates. I came to it after making my own investigations, and am very impressed by his command of the sources (I cannot refrain from noting that he has unearthed yet another article by Schoonenberg with *tegenwoordigheid* in its title). But I am less sympathetic than he is to manoeuvres made

'Stages', not 'stage' for we must not think of what came after Trent as homogeneous. We saw in the first chapter that Colombo takes the declarations of Trent in such a way as to make the scholastic tradition seem inevitable, and he is of course only one among many. Schelfout, in fact, an adversary of Vanneste, whom we met in the second chapter, holds that justice cannot be done to Trent's teaching by any account of transubstantiation that fundamentally deviates from the thomistic (cited in W, footnote 122 to page 30). However readers judge my dissent from things like that, they ought not to forget that views of such severity are rather recent arrivals. In the centuries following Trent, accounts of the eucharistic presence were not as tied to Aquinas as they were to become tied by the scholastic revival in the nineteenth century, especially after an official status was allotted to Aquinas by Leo XIII (+ 1903). Earlier writers would sometimes follow Descartes in any speculations they offered about the eucharistic presence: that is, the survival of the appearances of bread and wine was attributed, not to accidents existing without a substance, but to a divine interposition upon our sensory organs. In this, they were even able to appeal to the texts of Aquinas we met in chapter 5, footnote 12 – those to do with miraculous appearances in the Eucharist. Others adopted other accounts, also differing from

by authors he examines. He rightly describes Colombo's concept of 'the metaphysical order' as abundantly obscure (*reichlich unklar*, W 16). I should want to say the same of other distinctions he records, such as that drawn by Ratzinger between a metaphysical and a physical concept of substance (W 49). I notice in what else he cites from Ratzinger an excellent example of the Fallacy of Replacement: the consecrated elements lose their fundamental 'substantiality' because they are now *signs* in their reality whereas before they were *things* (W 50). And I notice, as something I have found fault with in old and new accounts alike, that amid many speculations he cites from Sala about the human fashioning of the world of signs, there is not a word said of ritual (W 41–7). For better or worse, my own more radical dissent pre-empts a place outside the suggestions and disagreements among modern authors.

I notice last some minutiae in this admirable book. It is concerned with the canons themselves, but I should have welcomed some incidental remarks on the status of the 'chapters' with which Trent's decrees begin; can the significance of the canons themselves be kept wholly apart from them? (For information on the point, see H v.3; I gather from Jedin that the chapters were designed for pastoral purposes, and so – as we shall see – use more picturesque language.) I am puzzled that, while citing at considerable length the original Dutch of some authors, Wohlmuth should cite Schillebeeckx in a German translation. At vol. II p. 98 he queries the reading *innicalcho* in a MS source; he is right to doubt, for the true reading will be *auricalcho* – 'oricalch', a kind of brass. And (would you believe it?) our old friend from chapter 4, *dessous de bouteille*, turns up in the same volume at p. 100, and is translated this time as 'bottle' (*Flasche*). One pictures de Baciocchi's rationalistic friend knocking the neck and shoulders off a bottle, and then using the jagged base as an ash-tray. Smoking can injure your bottles.

Aquinas.[19] I have given some details in a footnote, and make in the text the general observation that we have here what we have had so often: the present engages with the past; time brings changes that the engagement tries to accommodate; the conversation takes a new turn. Indeed, it has taken such a turn in the thirty-odd years since Colombo and Schelfout wrote as they did. Neither scholasticism nor Aquinas enjoys the favour then bestowed on both. And because neither does, the Theaetetus Effect has made itself felt, and protests in favour of transubstantiation cannot be what they used to be. The Inquisition may indeed appeal to Trent's use of the term, but the term no longer has what it had then – the setting of a generally accepted pattern of speculation and distinctions. That pattern has gone; the word may survive, but it is a marooned survivor. It has been superveniently isolated, and its use has become a matter of discipline rather than of theological reflexion. One thinks of Trent's attitude towards ritual. One thinks – yet again – of the contents of our right-hand columns (pp. 256–8, 267–70).

My own objections, stated in previous chapters at such length, I stand by, and readers will have seen how much further they go than a confrontation with this or that in Trent's terminology. I have objected to the pattern of a divorce between appearance and reality,

---

[19] For something on the complexities in the revival of scholasticism, see FitzPatrick 1982. I add a word of warning. The study of the complexity is made more difficult by the fact that theological text-books were 'adjusted', as the nineteenth century went on, to align them with scholasticism in general and with Aquinas in particular. Dens, for instance, once a popular text-book, gives a Cartesian account of the Eucharist in the edition of 1812; by 1853 his tooth is drawn and the book mentioning him on its title-page has become Thomistic. I do not know whether this manoeuvre has ever been investigated; for changes in French catechisms and text-books designed to increase the power of Rome, see Michaud (1872).

Details of Cartesian accounts of the Eucharist are beyond our concern here. Armogathe (1977) gives a very interesting analysis. Notice that what reprobations there were did not prevent the speculations from being taught. Ushaw College Durham possesses MS copies of such lectures, delivered in the eighteenth century at its ancestor, Douai College (here as elsewhere I am indebted to the librarian, the Revd Michael Sharratt). Notice too that the Cartesian account of the eucharistic appearances was linked at times with a view ascribed to Orthodox Greeks – that the accidents themselves do not survive. Leibniz mentions the view in a letter of 20 September 1712 to Des Bosses (Gerhardt edition II: 458); I have tried to disentangle the references in FitzPatrick 1989. As I have already noted, the analogy with Emmaus was invoked. The tradition of non-scholastic accounts of the eucharistic presence lasted a long time. As late as 1862, Salvatore Tongiorgi, in the 'Cosmologia' of his text-book of philosophy, gave an account of the eucharistic appearances which he explicitly set apart from the whole scholastic tradition, citing the Roman theologian Perrone in support of the lawfulness of what he did (Vol. II; 311–16). And Tongiorgi lectured in philosophy at the Gregorian University (Collegio Romano) at Rome. Yesterday's claims about the place of scholasticism in eucharistic theology certainly reflect part of the past, but they do not reflect all of it.

a switch of realities beneath the veil of appearances, a persuasion that what is exalted competes with and replaces what is humbler, and a persistent neglect to take ritual in ritual's own terms. To the extent that any account of the eucharistic presence – old or new – follows this pattern, I find it unacceptable, no matter what its source may be. For instance, some defenders of transubstantiation seek to emancipate it from unwanted philosophical associations, by pointing to the occurrence of the word in writings earlier than Aquinas. And of course there are such earlier occurrences – we met some in the first chapter. Other supposedly equivalent expressions are attributed to even earlier authors. The occurrences may be of historical interest, but they do not touch my objections: early or late is not the point. Antiquity is no more of a safeguard against foolishness than is modernity – we have seen enough of shadows in the past to convince us of that.

But if Trent fares no better than the Bible as a final sticking-place for belief, am I not even more condemned to the scepticism I have claimed to detect in the views of others? No more than I am condemned to be a sceptic if I reject Descartes' quest for some isolated, absolutely transparent point of certitude. Scepticism is an essentially solitary business: the gap between evidence and con- clusion, or between appearance and reality, is contemplated in isolation from all else, while the very idea of thinking in terms of gaps is left unexamined. Life is not solitary, it is a multiple and shared business, where the debates and doubts make the sense they do because of the pattern of common activities and presuppositions within which they occur. I have often cited the command from the *Philosophical Investigations* – not to say how it *must* be, but to *look*. I venture to complement it with another injunction, conceived I hope in the same spirit: 'Don't say what it *might* be; *live*!' We have looked a great deal at the manoeuvres involved in religious belief in its spread over time, and we have seen belief to have as great a multiplicity of expression as life has – ritual, practice, formularies, imagery, speculation, forms of art and architecture, and all the rest. The heritage of our belief is unsatisfactory, but that does not stop it from being revered, and what I have written of the heritage – whether the eucharistic ritual, the Scriptures, or Trent's decrees – ought to have shewn as much. Again, the multiplicity of belief's expressions makes for a looseness of fit between them; but that does not destroy what has been inherited, any more than it destroys tensions and disagreements among those who are the inheritors. As I wrote earlier, tension is unavoidable if those who believe – the *corpus mysticum* – are to be both something more in the world than the custodians of a museum, and also something more than simple reflexions of what the world is like round about them.

I have found fault with techniques that secure an apparent relaxing of this tension by what I call 'insulation'. In them, a seeming homogeneity between present and past belief is obtained by our neglecting elements in the past that now embarrass. We forget selectively, and elements we favour we superveniently isolate from the setting that once helped to make them what they were. My complaint has not been at the forgetting and the isolating as such, but at the refusal to acknowledge them and their rôle in belief. I have contended that we need to be aware of just what is being done; that this self-consciousness is a burden peculiar to our time; and that the awareness can be hard to acquire and painful when reached. I offer here a description that I think can make the acquisition easier, because it displays in a less misleading way what we actually do: *we adjust the unit of significance.*

We have here nothing novel. Those who learn French have to remember not to translate the negative in '*je crains qu'il ne soit malade*', but simply to write 'I fear that he is ill'. The unit of significance in French includes both '*crains*' and '*ne*', it does not give them separable rôles; the unit in English here does not here match it. And differences like this go much further than grammar: gestures, works of art, social practice and ritual can all shew them. Eucharistic belief, as we have seen so often, touches matters that go very deep, and uses expressions that can take on an independent and undesirable life of their own. Neither the depth nor the undesirability should be muffled; we need to admit that we have adjusted the unit of significance, so that this or that in our heritage does not play now the part it once did, but simply goes to make up a larger whole, a whole where further details lack significance.

If we do not admit that adjustment, then amnesia and isolation will encourage from the start a misleading picture of change in religious belief. They will make us see belief as we have found others see it – as modular, as composed of parts that may be removed as 'inessential' or replaced with others, leaving all other parts as they were, much as pieces of a jigsaw can be removed or replaced. The picture I propose

instead goes with the Theaetetus Effect, with its reordering of what
we have inherited, as we try to make sense of what we now confront.
To talk in terms of confrontation, and of adjusting the unit of
significance is not always comfortable. I have used the word 'rending'
of change in these matters, and the process of adjustment can be just
that: we are dealing with what is more than a mosaic of detachables.
To talk in terms of confrontation and adjustment means to abstain
from the kind of claims we have been meeting: that such-and-such in
the past *always really meant* the so-and-so that we believe in the
present; or that so-and-so is the *heart* of such-and-such, or its *essence* or
something; or that anything in such-and-such over and above so-
and-so is no more than *antiquated excess*, or *popular devotion*, or
something else just as easily discarded. Adjustment of the unit of
significance is not a process conducted from a point outside the
temporal spread of belief; it occurs within that spread, and both
appraises and continues it. It encourages us to face facts such that
what was once believed is believed no longer, or that what is now
believed was at one time not believed. In doing, it calls upon us to
look; it does not promise that the looking will be easy.

   I have said that the idea of adjusting the unit of significance is not
novel. In fact, all that I am writing here is lacking novelty; I am
concerned to invite the reader to *look*. Thus, in what I am myself now
writing, I am providing an example of the circularity I traced in
human reasoning – I am returning to themes in earlier chapters,
while bringing to them now what has been learned on our long
journey. As part of the return, let me recall the charge I made against
the newer opinions in the second chapter – that they end by divorcing
appearance from reality in much the way that older accounts
divorced them. I also made there an admission, which I make again
here: the divorce can seem very natural to those who believe that we
are called to what exceeds our unaided grasp, and that what is most
real and most precious passes our understanding. The divorce, I have
conceded, is a distortion of something good – the acceptance of what
I called 'the Givenness of Reality' in Schillebeeckx's writings, as well
as in sources that are not theological at all. Those who think in this
way will have an instinct for the mystery of the Eucharist, the mystery
which is a sign of the still greater mystery of the divine life, shared
with us through Christ in the 'spiritual eating' we met in Aquinas
(pp. 197–9). The sign is the sign of that which hath not yet been
revealed, a sign where we walk by faith and not by sight. And this

sign, and this mystery, and this instinct of reverence for what passes knowledge, are what make a divorce between appearance and reality seem natural to believers. The language of disguise seems to express their most deeply felt sense of the mystery. Which is why such language, whatever our journey has taught us about its defects, can point in its way to what matters.

In repeating this admission, I am in no way withdrawing the objections I have made to the language of disguise. Rather, I want to bring out more clearly something else we first met in the second chapter – that talk of the eucharistic presence in terms of disguise and concealment is given strength by two parallel but quite different forces. One of them we have just recalled – the acknowledgment of mystery; and this acknowledgment my own Way of Ritual makes, although (in my judgment) in a way less liable to mislead. But the other force is that perpetual temptation, not in itself religious at all, to create conundrums which set appearance against reality. We have seen, seen all too much, of the multitude of senses that the contrast can have – fools' gold, vaporised gold, white paper under a red light, deception by false friends, scientific versus popular classification, learning by bitter experience, private opinions and public utterances, sweet things that taste sour to those who are sick, sticks that look bent in water to the healthy as well. All we need retain of this gallimaufry is the impossibility of fitting the examples into one class. 'Appearance versus Reality' deceives from the start by suggesting a simple opposition where we have a multitude of complexities. But simplification perennially tempts, and this simplification is especially tempting. In the catch-all of the opposition it proposes, and in the disguise it suggests, it seems to do justice to that sense of mystery in the face of reality, that acknowledgment of reality's 'givenness', to which religion and so much else bear witness. We should not be surprised that eucharistic theology has found the simplification perennially attractive. Nor should we be surprised at the attraction long exercised by the distinctions drawn in the matter by the scholastics. The distinctions were only an abuse of philosophy, but they did seem to offer a machinery for bringing about the disguise which the simplification had suggested. And the disguise in its turn – as we saw when reflecting on the 'Galilean Presence' – seemed to give a definiteness to what was concealed by it.

That the two forces are wholly different does not need to be argued again here, but I readily admit that they can be very difficult to keep apart. I have given an unfavourable evaluation of what older and more recent authors have written about the eucharistic presence, and that evaluation I stand by. But to let my evaluation amount to no more than a flat condemnation of what they wrote – or of what Trent decreed – would be inapposite as well as pompously absurd. I am suggesting rather that we should adjust the unit of significance, whether in what we have inherited from older sources or from Trent, or in what we can find in recent authors. The 'Way of Ritual' I have suggested lies in starting from what we know and feel about the human condition, and then moving through the ritual stages to the manifestation of God's love through Christ, and to Christ's giving himself to us in breaking of bread, a manifestation and a giving that elude both our own powers and the powers of our language. All this we have seen already in the preceding chapter. My point here is that the Way of Ritual can accommodate the other views by refusing to let their details have any independent significance, refusing to let their divorces of appearance from reality be more than misleading ways of acknowledging the mystery in the Eucharist.

The refusal is still a refusal. I am not claiming that the Way of Ritual is really no more than the essence of what Aquinas wrote, or of what Trent decreed, or of what the recent authors have suggested. Nor am I claiming to remove from these other sources the divorce between appearance and reality, so as to leave only the acknowledgment of the mystery. I reject such modularity, I am indeed dissenting from those other sources. But I am also claiming that, if their details be deprived of independent significance (some readers might prefer the metaphor of blurring the focus), the sources can be accepted by those who accept the proposals I have made. The refusal, of course, is hardly likely to commend itself to those at whom it is directed. The refusal simply goes with what I have already written about the 'non-absoluteness', if I may so speak, of Scripture, the Church and everything else. Yet again, the two senses of *corpus mysticum* go together.

But in the face of all this, two general difficulties present themselves. One touches identity. What of the identity of belief over time, and what of the boundaries of identity for belief here and now? The other touches decision. What of the determining of true belief in the face of dissent? Who is to make decisions? If nobody is, what cohesion is left? The two difficulties are obviously related, and I shall consider them in turn. I shall then suggest that they point towards something else, which does indeed matter – something that will occupy us in the next section.

For the difficulty concerning identity, I go yet again to the command to *look* rather than to say what it *must* be. Let us look at what we have met, and put questions of identity there. Are all or any of Rahner's successive accounts of the origin and fall of man identical with what Trent decreed? What of identity between the accounts in the four Gospels about the resurrection, and the 'Official Catholic Response' on the subject? Or between the two columns I printed earlier – both sides containing authoritative utterances in the Roman Church? We have only to put these questions about specific cases to see that they cannot expect the kind of answer that the difficulty suggests they ought to get. They can, of course, be given answers in terms of essential sameness or legitimate development or antiquated excess or something of the sort – I have already given my reasons for finding such answers unsatisfactory. Time has intervened, new forces have arisen, the conversation has gone on further. To describe the relation between present and past in terms of adjusting the unit of significance is to accept that the adjustment is a claim, a suggestion, a way of continuing a conversation into which we have entered; and that it is not a scrutiny of the essence of what was previously believed, or a discernment therein of what those in the past would have said to us, if only we had travelled through time to ask them what their belief amounted to. Acknowledgments like this can hurt, just as the acceptance of a loss can hurt, or the admission that in the past we have been blind. But the pain has its own value as a witness to what matters. The pain is a sign that we value our membership of the tradition we regard as imperfect; that we prize the link with those who went before us, even when we disagree with them; that the past, though mixed, is something we acknowledge as part of a temporally extended story to which we ourselves belong. (Some readers may agree with me in finding here something analogous to what has been claimed by philosophers for the 'inheritance' of proper names.) Identity is not just a matter of measuring present utterances against past – it involves the claim to membership of the tradition in which past and present utterances have been and are being made. The tradition itself is built up by, among other things, the claims made to belong to it.

But, the second difficulty urges, how far can the claims and the dissent go? How are decisions over identity and difference and membership to be made? Once more, we need to *look*; but this time we also need to recall the other piece of advice – not to say what it *might* be but to *live*. Scepticism draws its apparent force by isolating itself from any shared life in which doubts and disagreements can be proposed or resolved. Just so, an equal isolation goes with attacks on scepticism that appeal to some self-evident truth, reached in the privacy of one's mind. We need to turn away from both, and to look at what actually takes place in what we are examining. We need to recall ourselves to the essential multiplicity and temporal protraction of the activities in which religious belief is embodied. True enough, among those activities are the pronouncements of councils and of popes. True enough, my denial of absoluteness to what they pronounce does not (how could it?) deny that conciliar and papal utterances exist and have force. But what force they are deemed to have, and what force they succeed in having, are among the questions that go to make up the continuing conversation and life of those who belong to the tradition that councils and popes also belong to. And the answers the questions get will not always be the same, because the questions and answers – like the councils and the popes – are parts of the conversation, not comments upon it from some Olympian vantage-point. Moreover, the part played in the conversation by the pronouncements of councils and of popes is of its nature an isolated part – their very eminence removes them from the essentially plural and shared nature of the manifestations of belief. Which means that the isolation, while increasing the dignity of the pronouncements, limits their force. Councils and popes will make more noise, but a greater noise is of no guarantee of a more enduring effect. Endurance involves time, and time involves the whole varied array of the tradition, a tradition inherited, shared and continued among the whole motley of believers.

But there yet is another disadvantage peculiar to isolated pronouncements of that sort. I have already reflected – in what I wrote of the Synagogue visit – upon the tradition of religious intolerance. Another and even more disturbing topic for reflexion is the tradition of religious overstatement. As I see it, part of the burden of the *Wahrheitspathos*, the tragic sense of truth, is the need of our time to acknowledge that religion tends to make up for an underdetermination of matter by an overdetermination of manner; that the tendency is deep-rooted; and that it can shew itself in many ways. The complaints we recalled from Küng and others at the start of this chapter were against the present style of papal and curial government in the Roman Church. I have sympathy for the complaints, but they should not be presented in terms of pained surprise. On the contrary, the complaints are being made at just the sort of thing religion is always liable to throw up, in one form or another.[20] But if religion is liable to produce such results, it also exhibits their limitations. Centralised pronouncements are liable of their very nature to this overdetermination, because their isolation and privileged status accord an apparent sharpness of definition to what is being pronounced on. But religious belief invokes a multitude of shared and varied manifestations, it cannot escape distortion when this plurality is forced into the pattern of a single, separated pronouncement. We must get back to the life and activities of those who share in the tradition they both inherit and continue. Once more, the *Philosophical Investigations* can provide a useful warning. We find at §107 in it a caution against what looks like a clarity got sharply into focus, but turns out to be idle: 'Back to the rough ground!'

But this recall to what is shared points to something else, and to reflect upon it will be a natural link with the section that follows. Another theme in the *Investigations* is that the force of shared life and activities goes with a reasonable amount of agreement in the results reached by what is shared in. As one example puts it, the point and place that weighing objects now has would cease to exist if an object put onto the scale gave widely different results on different occasions. The practices and concepts we have make the sense they do because there is a good measure of agreement in their employment – there would be no placing of them in our lives without this (§242). But what then is to be said if the agreement fails? Or is present much less than it was? What if extraordinary things started happening, things that challenged what we have taken for granted in our dealings with the world, so that the challenge called into question the whole framework of expectancies that give our lives the sense they have (pp. 223–6. And see *On Certainty*, §§513f.)?

[20] I have by oral tradition a story concerning Cardinal Bourne (+1935) which bears narration here. He called upon some parish priest with whom he had a difference of opinion. Words grew sharp and voices were raised, until the parish priest rang for his housekeeper. 'Bridget, His Eminence is unwell. Kindly conduct him to a room where he can lie down.' And the flabbergasted Bourne was led away. Which things are surely an allegory. The many dissensions and debates I chronicle in this chapter – and in this book – need their temperatures lowering. The disputants should not be grappling with the 'data of faith', which are usually in no better condition; they should be ringing for Bridget.

As some readers will know, Wittgenstein was preoccupied by problems like these even in his latest writings, and I shall return to them in the setting of our preoccupations in this book. Here and now, there is an obvious analogy to be drawn between his hypothesis of a general challenge to what we take for granted, and the challenge there has been over the last quarter of a century to what, for so long, was taken for granted in the Church of Rome. A vivid example lies at hand. I introduced what I had to say of the Council of Trent with an expression of obligation to the work of Hubert Jedin on its history. The prefaces to the four volumes in which Jedin's work appeared span twenty-six years; and they embody, movingly embody, what has happened. In 1949 it is the labour involved, the difficulties in war-time Rome, and the free access granted to the Vatican archives that are recorded. In 1957 there is mentioned the impatience of many there has been for the second volume, the delays caused by administrative work and by ill-health, and the renewed belief that an impartial statement of Trent 'as it was' can be and should be attempted. But in 1970 we seem in a different world. This time, delay has been due to Jedin's own part in the Second Vatican Council. He has learned much from his labours there about the working of a council and about the forces that operate; but he was often asked whether he still meant to persevere with his history. He expresses his determination to do so; states his belief that a general council issues by its highest authority pronouncements that are binding; and sets down his conviction that it is divine holiness alone that can resolve the present crisis in the Roman Church, just as it resolved it in the century of Trent. The final preface, in 1975, after matters to do with the author's ill-health and with the still incomplete array of sources available, gives a more general reflexion. When he began the work, a history of Trent written in a cool hour seemed possible. Now that the work is over, Trent has become a theme for confrontation inside the Roman Church itself.

Is it that we only seem to live, but really are dead, picturing our dream as life? Or is it rather that we are living and that life is dead?...Our hopes are buried hopes, like those of dead men; all things have been turned upside down.

Those words were written in the 390s by Palladas, a pagan who lamented the boorish intolerance and brutality of the Christians, and longed for the old days (*Greek Anthology* x 82 and 90). Sixteen hundred

years later, they seem to express what can be discerned in the pattern
of the prefaces that Jedin wrote, in what we have read in Julien
Green's diaries, and in what has been felt by many others. So much
that was taken for granted is now gone; so much agreement has given
way to dissent; is there any rough ground left to go back to?

40   *RELIGIO DEPOPULATA?*

I wrote that we cannot expect the Council of Trent to answer
questions it never put, and the point is of general validity – what
questions are asked is a measure of the questioner. Which is why I
recorded the fact that Jedin was often asked during the Second
Vatican Council whether he meant to go on with his history of the
Council of Trent. That question was indeed a measure of those who
put it – not just in its crude lack of sensitivity, but in the estimate of
the past it revealed. I can hardly be charged by this time with excess
of respect for Trent, but that council is part of what the Roman
Church has been and is; its study surely cannot be regarded as a
luxury of antiquarianism – unless we are prepared to regard the past
as an ornament which the present may doff before it gets down to
business. Such a view of the past has its attractions, and we have
already met it more than once, in the all too convenient appeals made
to 'Vatican Two'. But why does the council lend itself to appeals like
that? Why was Jedin quizzed there in the way he was? And why did
his book fare as it did? The first two volumes obtained an English
translation. Then came the council, and Jedin's prefaces to the third
and fourth volumes – but those volumes remain untranslated.
Questions like these are worth asking, and I begin my own answer to
them by putting yet another: to whom should we attribute the
Second Vatican Council as we know it?

In one way, a question like that is as off the mark as any other
attempt to reduce the multiplicity of human causes to a single factor.
But it can be taken in a better way, taken as an invitation to choose
someone or something as a symbol of what the Council was and is.
One obvious choice for such a symbol would be Pope John himself,
both for his having summoned the council and for having been the
kind of person he was. Another answer might go further back in time,
and recall the biblical scholars and theologians who – in the face of
injustice and disfavour – persevered in thought and in a hope for
better things. A third would point to the changes brought about in

the world during the twentieth century, and the sense of a new beginning at the end of the Second World War. It is not a matter of disagreeing with these answers, for the question invites a variety of responses. Let me then offer mine. For me, the council indeed is what it is because of a pope, but that pope is not John XXIII; it is Pius X.

At first sight, the suggestion seems not so much a paradox as a bad joke. Pius (+1914), with his régime of toadyism and delation; Pius, with his imposition of disingenuousness and torpor upon the life of the mind in the Roman Church; Pius, with his defiance of justice in the treatment of those who dissented there – what has or could have the man to do with anything we associate with the council? I understand these objections, but I persist in my claim. To explain it will give us food for thought about the council itself.

Throughout this book I have contended that the eucharistic presence must be understood in terms of ritual, and that in ritual lies a better model for what the Church might be. I have argued that the pattern of the ritual now used – the 'newer cultic picture' as I call it – is at odds with the pattern still found in the central administration of the Church, a pattern which resembles rather the cultic picture in the older rite. But, like it or not, it is to Pius X that the origins of the newer cultic picture go back. I have already mentioned the reform – limited but real – effected by him in the Divine Office: one result was to enlarge the variety of Scripture read there. Another reform touched the Kalendar: the celebration of Sunday was allowed to emerge from the welter of saints' days and 'octaves' which had obscured it. More important still were the changes touching the eucharistic rite itself. Just as the speculations of Aquinas gave a primacy to consecrating the elements over (to repeat his ominous phrase) 'the use of the consecrated matter', so a ritual analogue to this primacy has been seen by us in the older cultic picture. But it was Pius who began to change the picture. He reduced the recommended age for children to receive the Eucharist. He called for those present at the eucharistic celebration to share in it by reception. Most of all, he insisted that the people should not be mute spectators of the rite, and that active participation in the Church's public worship was the primary and indispensable source of the true Christian spirit – and in pursuit of this aim he encouraged instruction in the traditional plainsong of the Latin Church.[21] Whatever the success of those

---

[21] The original Italian of Pius X 1903a has the insistence at p. 331. Oddly enough – or not oddly at all – the official Latin translation weakened the demand: 'primary and

endeavours, they were undoubtedly made, and so the first steps were taken towards the newer picture. And we have seen enough now of cultic pictures to know that they are more than spectacles – they have a force and direction of their own, which go further and deeper than verbal formulae. What Pius did here was moving towards what we know in worship. Which is why he has his unique place in what we have come to associate with Vatican Two.

But of course there is more to the place he has than that. I have mentioned the disasters in the Church that were due to Pius. They might be summed up as a defiance of the effects of time, and a persuasion that agreement may be secured by centralised legislation. The defiance was notorious in the policy pursued in biblical and historical matters, but it touched philosophy as well. We saw how scholasticism came to dominate eucharistic speculation in the nineteenth century, and how Leo XIII bestowed official favour on Aquinas. Pius gave all this an administrative embodiment, and the division of the curia responsible for education promulgated twenty-four Thomistical theses in 1914, as 'safe directive norms' for Catholic institutions (see Studies, Congregation of; DS 3601f.). These and other lunacies are in sharp disaccord with the implications of what Pius was doing for public worship in the Church.[22] I do not intend to take the kind of step I condemned in Rahner at pp. 298–9, and ask what Pius would answer if we asked him about the disaccord (I admit that the speculation is tempting). But, after what we have seen of the force of cultic pictures, I think I am entitled to claim that the disaccord was real and unresolved in Pius, and that it involved the

indispensable' became 'prior', and 'active' was dropped (388). For some information, see Lamberts 1990. Pius not only encouraged plainsong, he had a new edition prepared of the chants in the service-books, establishing a Commission for this purpose on 25 April 1904. I mention this in order to notice a small anachronism in *Ulysses*. During the conversation in the Public Library, a monologue by Stephen is interrupted by the intonation of the *Gloria in excelsis* ('Scylla and Charybdis'; Joyce 1954: 186). But the intonation follows Pius' edition, which would not have been available on Bloomsday, only two months later. Presumably Joyce used whatever service-book was at hand in Trieste; and Trieste, being no Vienna, could not provide an appropriate version.

[22] I state here without argument what I argued in FitzPatrick 1973. The oddity in what Pius imposed in philosophical matters was all the greater because of the problems then facing those in the Church who wanted to think. The biblical crisis called above all for an analysis of problems to do with history and with understanding the past. In the nature of things, a philosophical tradition appealing to the scholastics could hardly have much to contribute; historical problems of the sort did not preoccupy the middle ages. Even those in the tradition more willing to innovate had nothing to say. The future Cardinal Mercier of Louvain wrote much on epistemological questions – none of them, as far as I can tell, touched the problems raised by history. Indeed, he seemed unaware of just what the problems were; as George Tyrrell forcefully pointed out, in his 'Medievalism' (Tyrrell 1908, an open letter to Mercier).

'insulation' we have met so often. In one area – public worship – change was encouraged, and change of a kind that had implications for other things. But the implications were denied, and the fencing-off of worship from other areas was enforced by a system of centrally promulgated edicts. And this disaccord, I suggest, has endured into the Second Vatican Council and into what has followed it. Once more, Pius X has a special place in what we associate with that council.

The claim may still sound odd, but there is in fact nothing very novel in it, after all else that I have been claiming. I am certainly not denying that the Second Vatican Council opened doors that seemed definitively closed, asked questions that had been forbidden, and offered a picture of the Church that was unfamiliar. These things are indeed opposed to what Pius X enforced, and it is of course with these things that the newer cultic picture is associated. But – I go back to the saying yet again – it is not possible to do one thing at a time; willingly or unwillingly, the council did other things. So great shifts in emphasis could not fail to throw into sharper relief than ever the rôle of the central administration in the Roman Church. Not only was the council itself an example of centrality, it had been summoned in a Church which had for decades been thinking in terms of centrality, and which had been forced by policies like those of Pius X to ignore the reality of time and of the demands made by time. The results of the council have shewn as much. The appeal now made to Vatican Two as a means of disowning an inconvenient past is indeed disreputable. But that it should be made is not in the least surprising. You cannot legislate into existence a due acknowledgment of the past. Acknowledgments like that go deeper, and they call for wider things than what laws can achieve. You can indeed propose a new picture, call into question what was held to be unalterable, and attempt to respond to the needs of a changing world; all that – and much more – the Second Vatican Council attempted to do, with varying degrees of success, and I rejoice that it made the attempt. But all that calls for a response just as novel as the attempt itself. It calls for a response which cannot be reduced, either to punctual acceptance of authoritative enactments, or to a general disowning of things as they were. There is need rather for an acknowledgment of the relations between past and present, and for a facing up to the heritage – revered but unsatisfactory – that is ours. Unless the response includes such things, how can the council avoid giving yet more force to the centralisation that so many of its members were so anxious to diminish? The council has notoriously led to disagreements, but the disagreements rest on a deeper agreement – both sides look to what is central in the Church's structure. For those who hold to the older ways, the divisions since the council encourage an adherence to the centre, as to a focus of certainty and loyalty. For those who seek what is new, an appeal to Vatican Two seems to allow a complex past to be ignored in favour of what is present. But that present is one in which the central power is being vigorously exercised; and so the wish to innovate leads in the same direction as the wish to conserve. The Second Vatican Council is often contrasted with the First, whose general drift is nicely summed up in a remark attributed to the pope of the day, Pius IX: '*La tradizione sono io*' ('Tradition? *I* am tradition.'). But an appeal to Vatican Two as to a new beginning amounts to a denial that there is any tradition to be reckoned with. I cannot see that we have gained much by the alteration.

We have, of course, gained a great deal in what the council has accomplished – I am concerned rather with a danger which of its very nature runs through all that has been achieved. The danger shews itself in things we have already met so often: forgetfulness of what is inconvenient, isolation of claims from their original contexts, and a belief that the life of the Church is *modular*, so that we may detach this or that part without affecting anything else. The question put to Jedin was in its way as symbolic of the Council as anything else suggested might be, for think of Vatican Two as issuing fiats that release us from confronting the past, and what is there left for him to do? And that is why I claim to find in the Council, for all its merits, the unresolved disaccord I found in Pius X. On the one hand, it has moved in the direction I associate with the newer cultic picture. On the other hand, it has encouraged the belief that the complexities of past and present in the Church can be overcome by edicts centrally promulgated, obeyed at large, and regarded as new beginnings.[23] And, I shall submit, nowhere has this disaccord been more palpable than in what the council has done for public worship.

[23] An allocution to Roman institutes of higher studies spoke of the dissents there had been, and of the adjustments (*precisazioni*) that had followed. 'Things have taken up their proper placings, and we are now beginning to pass from the "negative phase" to a "positive" actuation of the Second Vatican Council' (John-Paul II 1979a: 603). This is a legitimate declaration of personal preferences and policies; it should not present itself as a description – descriptions are judged by other standards.

Pius X may have taken the first step towards the newer cultic picture, but far greater steps have been taken in the years since the council assembled. More than anything else associated with the council, the changes in worship have aroused strong feelings of favour or disfavour. I suppose I can take this as confirming my general thesis about the central place of ritual, but the disagreements surely present me with a question I need to answer. I have welcomed the newer cultic picture, and have seen in it a model for the Church itself. I have even suggested – rightly or wrongly is beside the point here – that the positions defended in this book can be seen as an elucidation and explication of the direction of the changes in ritual. But I have just now been complaining at defects in the council with which these changes are associated, and I have claimed to find an unresolved tension in it and in what has followed it. What consequences do my claims and complaints have for the evaluation I have made of the new rite, and of the cultic picture that goes with it?

Abroad has always been a dubious place for the English – George V once supported his dislike of it by saying that he had 'been there'. One eighteenth-century view of Abroad is Hogarth's *The Roast Beef of Old England, or the Gate of Calais*. In front of the gate of the town, an English sirloin of beef is being carried by a bearer who strains under its weight. Ragged, soup-drinking onlookers gape at the splendour of the joint, and a gross friar rubs his fingers on it and prepares to lick them. But in the background, through the arch of the guarded gate, can be seen another sign of Abroad – a eucharistic procession is taking place. In its way, a ceremony like that seemed to set apart Roman Catholicism from all else, much as the Royal Declaration did; the procession ritually expressed the transubstantiation which the monarch was obliged to abjure. And the Church of Rome thought as much. Trent's sixth canon on the Eucharist denounced those who rejected such processions as idolatrous, or who claimed that Christ was not to be adored in the sacrament (Sess. xiii, can. 6; DS 1656). Eucharistic devotions in fact – processions, exposition, benediction and the rest – seem to provide a clear criterion for true belief: if Christ is present, he is to be adored; if he is not, adoration would be idolatrous. With things like processions, we seem to know where we are – Abroad or At Home.

The trouble is that we have seen too much of clear criteria already. In the preceding chapter, I expressed my sympathy for what I called 'the Galilean Presence', but I still insisted that such a presence, supposedly accomplished by a switch of substances beneath the accidents of the bread, is no more coherent than the transubstantiation of which it is the product (pp. 218–20). Eucharistic devotions do not remedy the incoherence of the Galilean presence, they simply give ritual expression to it. And in so expressing it, they cannot but reveal the very mixed heritage that lies behind eucharistic belief. It is enough by now to recall briefly from earlier pages just how mixed it is: the incoherence of transubstantiation; its expression in terms of primitive natural science; the forcing of the terminology used into dimensional categories, with the unwanted consequences thereof; the presence of speculations in Aquinas and others that need violence doing to them if they are not to be read as camouflaged cannibalism; the grossness in miracle stories, legends, professions of faith and phrases in the *Missale Romanum*; most of all, because most pertinent to matters like eucharistic processions, the separation of the consecrated elements from the eucharistic rite, and their treatment as a commodity only accidentally linked with their being shared in the rite. I have conceded ('contended' might be the word for some readers) that professions of belief like that found at Trent can be accepted if we adjust the unit of significance. That is, we can take them simply as witnesses to belief that Christ's eucharistic presence is a reality not reducible to a loving memory, or to a human giving, or to anything whatever achievable by or depending upon our means alone. But the whole point of adjusting the unit of significance is to deny an independent meaning to details – and it is just such details that are crystallised in ceremonies like those I have mentioned.

It is not difficult to give examples of this removal of the eucharistic elements from their ritual setting, in their becoming the object of further actions: moved over the sick, used to trace the sign of the cross over the congregation, exposed for lengthy periods to be looked at, carried through public places in processions. I used 'commodity' in describing the drift of such activities, because the word links them with the medieval heritage we examined earlier. There is an obscuring of the sign-giving function of the Eucharist; an obscuring of how the *corpus mysticum* in its sacramental sense ritually displays that unity in Christ which is the other sense of the phrase. That is, there is an obscuring of the way in which the sacramental eating is a sign of the 'spiritual eating', by which we share the life of the Risen Lord and are transformed into his likeness (see p. 197). I wrote, when comparing older and newer cultic pictures, that the physical disposition of the older style of altar was designed more for exposing the consecrated host than for the Mass itself. The elaboration of periods of exposition ('the Forty Hours', to use the traditional name) gave further stress to this preference, and so obscured still more the primary meaning of the Eucharist. Indeed, the very name 'Forty Hours' obscured it – the number was based upon a computation of the time spent in the tomb by Christ. As for the general direction of this rite, it can best be seen in the name originally given to the display of lights and flowers that was customary – *teatro sacro*; and also in the injunction that any masses during the period should be celebrated in a low voice, so as not to impede devotion (for these and many other details, Ortolan 1923 and McKenna 1936 are richly informative). Bishop Creighton records Walter Pater's notorious description of Roman Catholic churches, with their eucharistic reservation, as having 'all the sentiment of a house where lay a dead friend' (Creighton 1905: 1112). Pater's words have been dismissed as so much dreamy misunderstanding; dismissals like that are hardly in order. As for eucharistic processions themselves, Trent's canon in their favour should be complemented by what that council stated in the fifth of the 'chapters' that preceded the canons (for something on their purpose, see footnote 18 to this chapter). After stating the fittingness of such things, it adds:

It was right that victorious truth should in this way celebrate a triumph over falsehood and heresy, so that its adversaries – put in the presence of such splendour and in so great a rejoicing of the universal Church – might wither away, weakened and broken, or come at last to their senses through shame and confusion. (Sess. XIII, cap. 5; DS 1644.)

And so the processions continued to be seen. Some readers will have heard of the fate in France in 1766 of the Chevalier de la Barre; in our own century, a 'eucharistic congress' held in London in 1908 planned a procession as a show of Catholic strength, but the government very properly forbade it. In Nazi Germany, parodies of them were held as shows of counterforce; a photograph, reproduced from the *Osservatore Romano*, is in Micklem (1939: 196). Force and counterforce alike distorted the significance of the Eucharist. The whole point of ritual processions should be to express the incompleteness of what is done in ritual, and of the Church which celebrates the ritual. It is a journey we are on, not a demonstration; just as it is a sign we have, not a commodity.[24]

'Supervenient isolation' is a concept we have met already. We can meet it again if we go to an 'Instruction' concerning these matters that Rome issued in 1967. Things have indeed changed. The faithful are to be taught that the primary purpose of reserving the Eucharist is to ensure its administration to the sick and the dying; the ceremony of exposition must express this primacy in a perceptible fashion; all such rites must be subordinate to the Mass; the local bishop must carefully decide whether public processions are advisable (Rites, Congregation of, 1967: 566–73, §§49–67). Which is all now very understandable, given the introduction of the newer rite with its newer cultic picture; but it can hardly be contended that the ceremonies endorsed by Trent and by subsequent practice have survived intact. What ritual the Instruction does recommend is now isolated from the setting which once gave force and sense to it and to other eucharistic practices. To think that the isolation leaves all else untouched, or to think that the ceremonies are only ornaments to a belief that remains unaltered, is to think in terms of a 'modularity' in religious belief. I have submitted that modularity will not do here. The cultic picture is different: Abroad is not what it used to be.

And yet. And yet. If the older style of sanctuary and altar gave priority to exposition over the Mass itself, it at least enabled the ceremonies at exposition to be displayed to the best advantage. And in those days ceremonies were present in a way that they were not present at Mass. The virtually uninterrupted and often silent monologue there of the priest gave way here to a rite actively shared in by all the congregation. There were hymns, while time and again at Mass there was nothing of the sort. There was incense, abundant candles, flowers – all things associated with Roman Catholicism, and

---

[24] One procession of the sort I have never forgotten; it took place, as far as I recall, in the 'Holy Year' 1950. All imaginable pomp was displayed, as a platform was carried round St Peter's *piazza*, bearing Pius XII apparently kneeling before the exposed Host (apparently – he was in fact seated, but the gigantic dimensions of his cope were meant to conceal the fact). The procession eventually reached the steps, where a temporary altar had been erected, at which the pope knelt, surrounded by cardinals, bishops, canons, monsignori and the rest – every hue of vestment under the sun. And then, in stark contrast to this herbaceous border of successful old men, a drab figure in black and white appeared and departed. This was one of the infinitely minor clergy of St Peter's, and to this servant of the Servant of the servants of God was committed the chore (after the pomp was over) of removing the host and replacing it in some tabernacle. Well, one must hope that any heretics present either withered away or came to their senses.

yet so often wholly absent from the celebration of the Old Roman
Mass. There was a mixture of tongues, with both Latin and English;
there was a basic structure of service, which could be elaborated as
desired; and there was the opportunity for recollection and for silent
prayer. One does not need to prefer the older cultic picture, or indeed
to have any enthusiasm for exposition and the rest, to see what it was
in services like this that touched the hearts of so many. Or to see what
has grieved those hearts in changes they have experienced in the
years since Vatican Two. I have cited Julien Green's *Journal* more
than once in these pages, and I shall go back to it in what follows.
Here as elsewhere, it is the *nature* of the disagreements that I want to
explore. My own preferences I do not wish to conceal now any more
than earlier in the book, but my first aim is to display as I can just
where I think lie the dissensions and the distresses that have been a
feature of the Roman Church over the last quarter of a century.

'Sisters, you will have noticed that I did not genuflect before the
Blessed Sacrament. That is now over and done with.' Such, according
to one article Green had been reading, were the opening words of a
retreat-father in a convent (2 December 1969. They were also the last
– the Mother Superior gave a rap with her gavel and the retreat came
to an end.) A correspondent narrates a brief dialogue: 'Father, I
missed Mass'; 'That doesn't matter at all.' She adds that she felt her
faith turned upside down (19 October 1965). 'One no longer knows
what to believe' writes another (6 October 1966). And Green himself
records what he saw in a Parisian suburb:

The antique-shops are full of objects from churches that our modern *curés*
have no time for: old silken copes, carved tabernacles from the eighteenth
century, statues of saints... The sadness of the things, discarded along with
the beliefs they signified. (14 April 1968)

I have written much of the newer cultic picture. I have also cited
more than once the prophecies of St Malachy concerning the popes,
and the title of the present section is the motto he assigned to Benedict
XV (+1922, of the Spanish influenza; an underestimated man).
Religio depopulata is usually translated as 'Religion laid waste', and
taken as a description of the results of the First World War. But does
it not also describe, all too accurately, what has distressed Green and
so many others? And if the newer cultic picture can lead to religion
laid waste, ought we not to go back to the older?

I have much sympathy for the distress, but my reply has to be what it has already been in these pages more than once: things are not so simple; they are more complicated – worse, if you will – than the question would have us believe. And I start my reply by noticing an ambiguity in the motto. It can indeed mean 'Religion laid waste'; but the Latin can also be taken as 'Religion having laid waste'. The reader may not agree with me in finding the motto in this other sense apt enough for Benedict, given what had been inflicted on the Church by his predecessor, Pius X, and indeed on Benedict himself, who had been at the receiving end of some of it. But I suggest that the idea of religion itself having laid waste can at all events point to the unresolved disaccord I have claimed to find in Pius X and in the council. And this theme I wish to explore further – we shall come by it to the heart of the eucharistic ritual.

I have opposed, in the Eucharist and in the Church, what I have called 'insulation', insisting instead upon openness and vulnerability. I have submitted that neither Eucharist nor Church can be seen as in some way exempt and cut off from the divinely given but flawed world in which we live and die. The Way of Ritual is indeed a way, a journey; it leads us towards that which lies beyond our being and our understanding; but it does not deny the humbler creation from which the journey begins. Just so, the Church inherits a past that is venerated but also unsatisfactory; and we are not to practise adjustment on what is unsatisfactory there, in a way that tries to insulate our heritage from the effects of time. I used – fancifully, if you will – the image of the narthex of a church to point to what I am trying to convey: that, if we are to see things aright, we can just as little reduce the *corpus mysticum*, in either of its senses, to what is no more than human, as we can insulate it from what is bound up with being human. The narthex both links the church with the market-place and keeps them distinct.

But this analogy does not solve problems, it rather shews how inescapable they are. We have here the point of logic I noticed earlier – we can agree over general principles easily enough, the trouble begins where we make specific estimations of how the principles are to be applied. *How* are we to proclaim and to acknowledge in worship the transcendence of the love of God shewn in the *corpus mysticum*? *How* are we at the same time to let our proclamation and acknowledgment be rooted in what we are, and in an awareness of our neighbours and of the world we all inhabit? Images like the narthex can at least warn us of the tension and difficulty we shall face in our endeavours to do justice, if I may so put it, to both extremities of the Way of Ritual. It is a *way* – we move along it towards what surpasses our being and our conceiving, without thereby denying the things we are able to understand. It is a way of *ritual* – so it is in ritual itself that the tensions will be accepted, and the unceasing attempt made to proclaim the mystery of faith. Generalities here, as I have said, are more easily achieved than particular applications. Let me at least give my contentions a specific turn by briefly reflecting on the initiation of children into the Eucharist.[25]

One mark of the older cultic picture was *polarisation*, and the starkness of it was displayed in the physical dispositions of the church-building, in the 'unrelieved dorsality' of the priest's position, and in the unvaried place and posture of the people. The newer cultic picture, as we saw, goes with differentiation and plurality – a distribution of rôles, a pattern of varied movement and position, a sharing in perceptible ways in what is being done. There has to be a similar plurality and movement in the entrance of children into sharing in the Eucharist. Part of the entrance is their own growth and experience, part is their coming to see that what they here share in surpasses whatever could be given by experience. Their entrance cannot help taking time, and it cannot help being touched by the patterns in the rest of the children's lives – the meals they eat elsewhere prepare them, positively or negatively, for the rite they share in here. The time needed is something essential, not just an enforced delay; it cannot be dispensed with in favour of something brisker. The entrance cannot be dissipated into accounts that go no further than what the children perceive, but neither can it be condensed into a denial of what they do perceive.[26] In other words,

---

[25] I have never believed that the grace of ordination conveys didactic competence, and my reasons for choosing this specific theme reflect my lack of belief. It gives those who know something about the topic a chance to correct my ignorance. It gives me a chance to point briefly to certain needs which touch all of us, children and adults alike. And it pays a debt. Years ago, I was asked to give religious instruction to a child preparing for her First Communion. It was then that I began the reflexions which have led to this book.

[26] I bring out the point I am making by setting together two texts. One gives, among many good things, this anecdote. A missionary held up an unconsecrated particle and asked what it was: 'The body of Christ', his congregation answered. He explained it was not consecrated and – to drive home the lesson – threw it on the floor and trod it in with his heel. 'The congregation were astonished: how dare a man destroy food and trample on something so fundamentally sacred?' (van der Hart 1973: 276). The other text can speak for itself:

At a college meal you are presented with what appears to be minced beef; it tastes like minced beef, it looks like minced beef – but it isn't. What you have been given is a meat-the entrance involves that 'circularity' I have noticed so often: the children's growth in experience shapes their encounter with the Eucharist, while itself being shaped and deepened by that encounter. Such is the life God gave us. If Aeschylus can speak of the learning that comes by endurance, Augustine is able to pray to learn about himself that he may learn about God. Learning in these matters is life-long. The Way of Ritual, we know, involves an acknowledgment of the darkness in the human condition, our *doulé physis*, our nature held in bondage. It also involves an acknowledgment that the very means of deliverance promised are touched by that darkness. It would be absurd to suggest that abstract formulations like these should be put before children. But it would be just as absurd to deny that life itself puts many things before them as it goes by, and the celebration of the eucharistic ritual should not be alien to those things. Entrance into the mystery of faith, and persistence in what has been entered, shape and are shaped by life itself; the entrance of children is only a more vivid form of the entrance which their seniors made and are still making.

In the previous chapter I tried to present the language of redemption in terms that respond to the needs and darkness in our condition, and the tragedies of our own century have probably made it easier for us to see these things. But we still have the problem of how to bring children to an understanding of the mysteries of the cross and resurrection. The recovery of a sense of the central place of the resurrection I have already welcomed, and this centrality should be displayed in what children are told. The place of the cross is indispensable, but the indispensability does not make its presentation to children easier. What needs growing into cannot without damage be simply imposed in its vividness. We face here the fact that the cross can be depicted in a way that the resurrection cannot – we have Lessing's problem about space and time in painting and poetry. I note with interest that Julien Green complained at a lack of balance here. 'We do not leave Good Friday; we ought to move on to Easter Day' (14 June 1963). Once again, I contend that it must be in the

substitute made from soya beans. It appears to be meat, even when there is no meat in it. So it is with the Eucharist. It appears to be bread, but it is bread no longer. Through the power of Transubstantiation it has become the body of Christ.

The source of this thing is called *God-Sheet*, produced in 1982 by students themselves at a Catholic Chaplaincy to a university. A fair comment on it is a third text, which is the account of the eucharistic presence given by a friend's child, when preparing for his First Communion: 'Looks like bread, tastes like bread – but is wine'.

ritual as encountered and shared that these matters are lived through. If that ritual goes back to the Last Supper, it goes back as well to the meals shared with the disciples by their Risen Lord; both should play their part, in celebration and instruction.

I return to the image I have already used, and point out that the narthex links church and market-place while keeping them distinct. The church is a holy place in a way that the market-place is not, although what I call the market-place is not cut off from God's provident love, nor without its effect upon what is celebrated in the church. Others will be better qualified than I am to offer specific recipes for this entrance of children into what is most holy, I can but hazard the unremarkable guess that there are things in the market-place that will help their entrance and things that will hinder it. One hindrance, if I may air a prejudice, is the reluctance of so much educational theory to admit the exotic and mysterious; which is a pity, because a quest for the immediately intelligible leads only to boredom. Whatever else the Eucharist is, it is a rite of immense antiquity, with roots that go back beyond Christianity to the earliest things in human history. We should not try to conceal these depths in the manner of the celebration; they are a strength, not a weakness, in touching mind and heart, as the instincts of children for play and for the mysterious can encourage us to remember. And above all we must face the fact that it is in the ritual itself that all these balances and tensions are to be lived, in the ritual itself that is to be displayed the most holy mystery, in the ritual itself that the call should be heard to live out in practice the bestowed life of which the *corpus mysticum* is the sign. And, given what the newer cultic picture imposes on those who come together for the eucharistic ritual, this 'we' must signify all of us, whatever our part in the ceremony may be. The entrance of the children into the rite is their entering into a heritage that they themselves are to play their part in embodying.

I have talked in terms of an entering into what is most holy, talked in terms of a narthex that both keeps the church distinct and yet links it with the market-place. The images, of course, are of a piece with what I have called 'the Way of Ritual', and they are meant to convey the need in eucharistic ritual for a *journey*, a journey from what is everyday to what is not, a journey on which the travellers neither disown their starting-point nor pretend that they can make the journey without leaving it. The image of a journey will not – any more than the other images I have used – decide for us just what forms will be taken by ceremony and behaviour; but it will help us to accept that in those things lies our response to Christ's giving of himself in the Eucharist. And so it will encourage us to accept the weight of our responsibility when we make this response. What we give to the rite is – for better or worse – an instruction to those who come after us. Yet again, it is not possible to do one thing at a time. And one of the plurality of things we do calls now for further attention.

From the first pages of this book, I have been concerned with *language* about the Eucharist. But any language in eucharistic matters necessarily refers to and is subordinate to the language used in celebration itself. Christ commanded at the Last Supper an action to be done in memory of him; but the action needs his words, that we may know whose the memory is. Just as I have insisted that the ritual of the Eucharist needs explaining in ritual terms, so those terms must include a consideration how the ritual uses language. And to this consideration I now turn.

The Way of Ritual refused to deny its starting-point; the Givenness of Reality was not an occasion for reducing perception to illusion. Just so, we might speak of the 'Givenness of Language': it is the precious thing we have inherited, the sharing we have in the world with those we know, with those we once knew, and with those who will be in the world when we are there no longer. This inheritance is bigger than we can consciously grasp. Just as it makes no sense to think of cutting off our language from reflexion, in order to reach some 'neat' expression of religious belief, so it makes no sense to think of cutting off our language from the resonances and associations that are part of what it is and has been, and part of what its speakers are and have been. Each language has a history, because it is human. This plurality and variety shew themselves in the range of what language is and does – it can be prosaic, imaginative, deceptive, abusive, intimate, public, jocular, ceremonial. Those who journey along the Way of Ritual must not think of denying the range and richness of human speech; without speech, there would be no journey to make and no one to make it. Religious language of its nature has to point and to suggest rather than give clear descriptions; for its pointing and suggesting it will need all that our language can provide. Religious language – and above all its heart, the language of ritual – cannot be divorced from the speech that makes us human.[27]

But because language is human, reflexions on it must touch something which is affecting humanity itself in all its expressions: the growing power of communication inside a technologically based civilisation. I wrote at the start of this section that questions are a measure of the questioner; I must now recall that the range of questions likely to be asked is affected by what means are available for asking them. I have also written in this section that the quest for instant intelligibility ends in boredom; I must now add that rapid means of communication put a premium upon making what has been communicated as accessible as possible to as many as possible and as painlessly as possible. Whatever is uttered is, if I may so put it, liable to be overheard by those for whom it was not originally meant. But the range and richness of language are not in the order of generalities; they are products of specific pieces of human history, they have grown up among groups for whom associations and resonances are to some extent a common possession, groups for whom the different 'orders' of language, from the informal to the formal, are things that can in some measure be taken for granted. It is not difficult to see that this side to language sits very uneasily with what is happening all over the Earth. What is happening, as we all know, favours what is general and what can be organised on a large scale. The favour is bound up with the very means of communication used, and it has the quest for power and profit on its side.

One of the manifestations of this force has been the spread of English as a means of international communication. The reasons are

[27] Metaphor, and metaphor in religious language, are vast topics; I recommend Cooper (1986) and Soskice (1989) for much humanity and good sense. I recall my own earlier remarks about the 'unwanted life' that some pieces of language can take on. The remarks call here for the acknowledgment that language would not be what it is if it did *not* harbour the unexpected. To bring out this, I return for a moment to what I wrote at p. 205 about Shakespeare's sonnet 'Shall I compare thee to a summer's day?' The comparisons and associations in the poem are not the result of applying some already existing technique, they are as deep and varied as the human heart. Set beside them a simple suggestion we might make in science: that the relationship expressed in a graph looked as if the curve were a sine-function. Here, we invite the investigator to concentrate his field of search by calling on him to use knowledge he has of trigonometrical functions – knowledge that will, we hope, enable him to decide how close is the fit. But we cannot press Shakespeare's talk of the darling buds of May by asking how strong the rough winds must be to shake them, and then apply our answer to the person addressed in the sonnet. The unit of significance is determinate in the scientific example to an extent to which it is not determinate in the sonnet, or in religious language; and the resonances in these are deeper and less predictable than what the scientific example provides.

not hard to find: no genders, virtually no problems over endings, a
capacity to remain intelligible under maltreatment, the best of all
languages to get by in. The drawback, of course, is that language is
more than something to get by in. Any human language is more, and
any human language in its own way shews as much. English may lack
the endings that some other tongues have. But it has an enormous,
graded vocabulary, a subtle syntax, a complex pattern of intonation,
and an exceptionally wide range of associations and resonances, a
range that comes from the exceptional richness and variety of its
growth over the centuries. Which makes its position today all the
more perilous. English more than any other tongue is exposed to the
pressure for universal and immediate intelligibility. English, more
than any other tongue, is exposed to the shaping force of means of
communication that are themselves essentially shaped by commercial
and utilitarian considerations. Those considerations are not in
themselves base – why should they be? But they are not the only
considerations that should shape language, for language has other
things to it. Religious language is no exception; indeed, its linguistic
needs are bound to be complex. The pressure here on English is
peculiarly strong.

And it is all the stronger in the Roman Church because of
something already noticed about that Church – its adapting itself
ever more to modern means of communication, and above all to
television. I saw in the adaptation a resemblance to the older cultic
picture. That is, the complexities of history are being neglected in
favour of something instantly available – in this case, what is visible
on the screen. As I put it, you can televise a travelling pope, you
cannot televise the communion of saints. But if the adaptation
obscures the nature of the Church, it is just as alien to the right use of
language in the Church's worship. Any language has a complex
history and a complex range of expression. English, which has spread
itself so widely, exists in different regions with different associations.
The problems raised by its use in ritual are difficult, and they call for
a sensitive awareness of language and of time. But the pattern now
preferred of instant pictorial availability is remote from such
awareness. And so the force of the older cultic picture, with its
blindness to history and its acceptance of an imposed uniformity, is
by no means spent, even in the newer cultic picture itself. The
disaccord found in the enactments of Pius X is by no means resolved.

I wrote that the range and richness of language do not lie in the order of generalities, and so, in spelling out the claims I have been making, I shall concern myself with the particular case of the language of worship found in England. But, the place of English being what it is, what I write here has further implications. English, I shall submit, provides a parable – a test-case, if you prefer – for the stress and disagreement that are evident today in the Church of Rome.

I turn to the particular – indeed, to the peculiar – circumstances of the ritual use in England by Roman Catholics of their native language. Cardinal Hume wrote some years ago that for the recent change in emphasis in public worship, 'England was probably less well-prepared than some other parts of the Church' (Crichton, Winstone and Ainsley 1979: vii). The charity of this daunting understatement may do him credit, but we need more here than pious accommodations of an awkward past. The story is bleak, but it needs to be faced and to be learned from.

Roman Catholic worship among the English was alienated from the course of their language as the seventeenth century went by and the religious divisions become permanent. The liturgy was in Latin, and (as we saw) translations of the central part of the eucharistic rite were forbidden. The Mass established under Pius V was taken as a timeless standard for true observance. In it, the portions of scripture read were small, and many of them were everlastingly repeated. The Rheims-Douay version of the Bible, though scoring the occasional bull's-eye, was freakishly eccentric, and could never be (what indeed it was not intended to be) a rendering of the Scriptures as a significant part of public worship. For 200 years and more the clergy were educated abroad, usually through the medium of Latin, and this exoticism shewed itself in the English prayers they composed for their Latinless flocks. Then, in the nineteenth century, immigration from Ireland became a flood – men and women pauperised, unlettered and with scant sympathy for a land they identified with their oppressors (by whom indeed – if they remembered as much – they had been robbed of their own native tongue). Their clergy were devoted but, through no fault of their own, grossly ignorant. The urban parishes where they congregated embodied the unhappy felicity of industrial culture for fastening onto whatever is hideous. The liturgy remained in Latin. Its history was as closed a book to the clergy as it was to the laity. The unintelligibility of its language was taken as a mark of the sacral, and as a sign of separation from the

Established Church that they hated. Popular prayers were soon coloured by mawkish devotions and hymns brought over from Italy, in translations that have to be heard to be disbelieved.[28] As time went on, curial policy made itself felt, and bishops were chosen largely from the clergy who had studied in Rome. That is, they were chosen from men who had been for years out of England, whose training had not been through the medium of English, whose experience of theology in the Eternal City seemed to consecrate a style of thought that went with an ignoring of time, and whose experience of worship there had been touched by the conspicuously low standards which have traditionally prevailed at Rome in the matter.

That such men should have resisted the changes in worship associated with the Council is not surprising. But neither is it very interesting: what is of interest is the nature of their resistance, the nature of its termination and the nature of the consequences. Reason had little to do with their opposition, because their reason had never been exercised upon these topics: their opposition lay rather in a pre-rational instinct that in the council the whole range of allowed topics was being changed and a world turned upside down – the passage I quoted from Palladas might fairly be applied to them in their bewilderment. But if their opposition was not founded on reason, neither was their ceasing to oppose. The old rite had been clung to, not so much because it was understood as because it was old, and so associated with the authority which their ancestors had defended. Now that same authority called for the old to be given up in favour of the new, and the authority was obeyed. Between old and new, the link was not – as it might have been – a recovery of what had been obscured, a disengagement of what mattered from later accretions. The link was essentially disciplinary, and what guaranteed continuity

[28] I go back to *Ulysses* for a moment, to let the reader share my pleasure in a minor discovery. The Old Mass in its 'Low' form was followed by what were known as 'the Leonine Prayers', so called after Leo XIII, who gave them their final shape; they alone were said in English. Their origins were polemical (Pius IX had ordered prayers that he might keep the Papal States, Leo wanted support against the *Kulturkampf*), so perhaps it was natural that the things should terminate with a somewhat military invocation to Michael the archangel, of which the last words referred to 'Satan and all wicked spirits, who wander through the world for the ruin of souls'. So it is (with a slightly different translation) in the Mass to which Mr Bloom goes ('Lotus-Eaters'; Joyce 1954: 75). Those who remember the Old Mass will recall the invocation to the Sacred Heart that followed this prayer, but Joyce was right not to insert it: the invocation was not then in use. But I do not think anyone has noticed when permission was given by Rome to add it. The date (with other particulars about the Leonine Prayers) is in Jungmann 1952, IV.4.7: it is 17 June 1904. Which is, of course, Bloomsday-Plus-One. Truly, life throws up coincidences that no writer of fiction would dare employ.

was centrally promulgated enactments.[29] The changes in worship presented what I have called the newer cultic picture, and the picture concerns the Church as well as the Eucharist. But, by the paradox already noticed, the newness itself here has given strength to elements we associate with the older picture. I have claimed that there is a tension between the implications of newer forms of worship in the Church and the style of the Church's central government. This claim I stand by; but I have now to acknowledge that we do not have here a tension between two wholly distinct things: the old picture still has the power, even in the new. Which is why I made the claim I did about Pius X. It may have sounded odd, but I can now submit that it will bear examination. The disaccord is by no means resolved.

That is how I see the resistance made in England to ritual change, and how I see the ending of the resistance. And that is how I see the consequences – a further emphasis upon the central power in the Roman Church. Similar things happened, to a greater or lesser extent, in other places. I am dwelling upon those of my choice, partly because it is they that I have lived through, partly because of the special place of English today, and partly because of what the tale can teach us about the Church and about ritual. As I said, what we have here is a parable – a test case. I go on to further reflexions upon it.

Julien Green narrates a disturbance of Mass at Notre Dame one Sunday by some who started the Latin *Credo* at a mass in the new rite, only to be drowned by the organ (5 April 1971). Twenty years later, there is pressure exercised upon bishops to permit more celebrations in the old rite, pressure by bishops to limit the use of it, and a jockeying by both sides for favourable decisions from the Vatican. There is even a 'Society of St Pius X', which has clergy and buildings of its own, and rejects the new rite completely – and, I am given to understand, much or most of Vatican Two. The title of the Society will have seemed a suitable choice to its founder, for obvious reasons. Less obvious, but I think just as real, have been my own reasons for seeing in that pope a symbol of so much in what the council has

[29] If generalities are alien to language, they are also alien to the doing of detailed justice. But any readers who think I am doing no justice at all here should read what was made of the council, and of what followed it, in the reminiscences of a prominent member of the English hierarchy (Heenan 1971). And they should complement their reading with Heenan 1951 – his vision of a priest's work, ten years before the council met. If I must take care not to do injustice, they must take care not to over-indulge in accommodations of an over-embarrassing past.

brought about in worship. I have claimed that the changes have in themselves more of the older style than might be believed, and I have claimed that history here has still not had justice done to it. In a dispute where accusations of *religio depopulata* are made, I offer something that stands apart from both sides.

I wrote earlier that the new cultic picture calls for a newer response – a response that is something more than prompt obedience to an edict or dogged dissent from it. By now, we can see that the response must reject the deceptive comforts of insulation. It must rather involve an acceptance of the reality of the past, and of its relation with the present, an acknowledgment that eucharistic ritual must have an unease about it, in its use of the things around us to convey that which transcends them. But by now we can also appreciate the difficulty of acceptances and acknowledgments like this, and the greater ease of thinking in terms of some kind of *polarisation*: the priest versus the congregation; the altar versus the rest of the church; infallibly guaranteed utterances against all else; and a eucharistic presence achieved by a switch of substances that belongs to the order of disguises rather than signs, and that has no essential link with a ritual meal. I have contended that ease is not what matters most, and that polarisation will not do. But what practical results follow from my position? I have started reflecting on the place of English in worship. Can I draw consequences from my reflexions for the liturgy?

I have rarely used the words 'liturgy' and 'liturgist' in these pages, because of the rather negative associations of them for so many. Liturgists are not universally beloved – as the now well-known distinction between them and terrorists bears witness (terrorists can be reasoned with). So let me set down at once my sympathy for those who concern themselves with the ways of celebrating the mysteries of our salvation – theirs is a hard task, and never-ending. But, as elsewhere, my first concern is with the *nature* of the disagreements I encounter, and I fasten on the word 'liturgist'. It has undergone a shift in meaning. At one time, its connotations were of historical and linguistic scholarship directed to the by-ways of ancient usages in ritual, where not everyone thought the results worth the effort ('No; neither do I collect postage-stamps' was the unkind answer of Dean Inge, on being asked whether he was 'interested in liturgy'). Time has marched on, and in our jollier age the associations of the word are jollier too – perhaps some master-of-the-revels in a holiday camp. Those associations need be no more degrading than the collection of postage-stamps, but they have one disadvantage: they involve a good deal in the way of practical devices, but very little in the way of reflexion upon what lies behind the devices. Some reflexion will prove worth while.

Those eager to accommodate the past have been known to insist that clergy trained in the old style were at all events those who brought about Vatican Two and its developments. For some of us, the claim is rather like insisting, on behalf of Lord North, that his colonial policies at all events brought about the American Declaration of Independence. But most of us will presumably agree that the training referred to here will be the years spent by future priests in the study of theology, philosophy and the rest. Indeed, I agree myself – but with a qualification that demands some personal reminiscence. I spent two years in the 'School' part of an English Seminary, in its sixth form. For the instruction I received there I was and remain deeply grateful, and I know that I am not alone in my gratitude. I then moved to specifically ecclesiastical education – and moved to Rome in the process. My views on the academic training imparted there will be clear enough by now: it was by no means all bad, and for some of it I remain very thankful. What I have to add is that the training seemed to leave virtually no place for the skills and values acquired during my education in the humanities. It was as if my years at school had little or nothing to do with what followed them – apart from having imparted to me a knowledge of Latin sufficient for the reading of scholastic text-books.

The content of ecclesiastical training has changed a good deal since those days. But there is a sense in which any ecclesiastical training – for better or worse – has already been taking place before the candidate formally embarks upon it. The humanities in the widest sense of the term lie and must lie at the heart of reflexions upon the journey to God. It is not that theological training is unnecessary; it is rather that the great divide between it and the humanities was disastrous. I insisted earlier that we cannot cut off our language, either from philosophical reflexion on it, or from the associations and resonances that go to its metaphorical use. I insist now that theological language cannot do without the acquisitions, in mind and in heart, that are gained from the humanities. I hope that nowadays there is nothing very novel in this. Perhaps there is more novelty in the suggestion that what lies at the heart of ritual celebration – what lies at the heart of the liturgists' task – is only in part theological.

Liturgists, I have admitted, are not popular among the clergy. I suggest that the unpopularity has for its root the awkward fact that neither one side nor the other is professionally concerned with what matters most in the public ordering of worship. The life and force of what is done there rest in great measure neither upon theology nor upon acquired tactics of communication; they rest upon what the humanities have to give. And we need look no further than specimens of the language and behaviour used in worship to see that at present the humanities are not giving what they might. But our problem here is nothing new – the older style of ecclesiastical training was just as alien to what they gave. Its whole drift, quite apart from the attrition of any lengthy vocational course, was towards extinguishing the awareness and sensibilities which come from a humane education (for an outstanding diagnosis, Foster 1962 is still required reading). We should not be surprised that the conflict still shews itself in the ritual changes there have been since Vatican Two – yet again, the disaccord found in Pius X refuses to go away.

Where the disaccord lies will be clearer if we reflect on where the force of the humanities lies: their force is particular, and whatever language is involved is just as particular. I wrote earlier that the associations and echoes in a sonnet of Shakespeare are not determinate in the way that the concepts and techniques of science are determinate. But they are essentially individual in a way that what science does is not. It is in this particular piece of writing, in this particular language, that this particular effect is achieved – the effect is not something that just happens to be found in one example first and then in another, much as a formula can be given more than one application. There is no finding some abstract literary excellence which we can then embody, first in Shakespeare and then in Racine. The project makes no sense, because the excellences of both – like the language and culture of both – are concrete and particular. And, as it is to the particular that we must keep returning in what concerns the humanities, so we must keep returning thither in what concerns worship and ritual.

What particularities do we find, as we reflect on the adoption of English as a ritual language, and on the unresolved disaccord I have noticed? We find in Pius X, along with many other things, the wish that the congregation should not be mute spectators of the eucharistic rite, and the wish that their active participation should include an acquaintance with the traditional plainsong of the Latin Church.

And along with this we naturally find, as taken for granted, the use of Latin in celebration, the tongue that links the worship with a past older than Christianity itself, and with centuries of the civilisation of Europe. We also find what I have just been describing – the eccentric place of English over the years among Roman Catholics in prayers and devotions. We find as well what the ritual use of English, left behind by Roman Catholics, achieved in the sixteenth and seventeenth centuries: the Authorised Version of the Bible, and the Book of Common Prayer. But now we find, looking once more in particular terms at this particular situation, that the use of Latin with its chant – once regarded as an untouchable mark of loyalty – has been discarded. We find that the discarding is seen as a manifestation of the same loyalty. And we find that, in the English chosen to replace it, the earlier achievements of that language have been ignored.

Questions asked are a measure of those who ask them. I have to come back to that simple truth, in order to place the questions that these remarks of mine are likely to prompt. I am not advocating a return to a Latin liturgy, and I do not believe that either the Authorised Version or the Prayerbook will serve as they stand in an English liturgy. That whole style of putting questions and offering choices is wrong from the start: it thinks in terms of general solutions, and it ignores the irreducible particularity of what concerns the humanities, and so the language of worship. The polarisation I associated with the older cultic picture has been and is tragically evident in the polarisation of so much to do with worship in the Roman Church: Old Mass versus New Mass, Latin versus English, this translation versus that, one style of ceremony versus another. If polarisation goes with the older cultic picture, it has secured a healthy survival in what goes with the newer. With the newer picture – this is its strength – there goes an acknowledgment of the course of history and of the changes it has brought. There also goes a willingness to let the ritual used correspond to the particular situation of those who share in it, those whom the ritual is to lead to what surpasses anything of their own devising. But those characteristics of the newer picture go with the particularity of the humanities. And the disaccord which I have been noticing lies in a tragic failure to do this particularity justice.

Perhaps an analogy here will be of use. We lament now, when it is too late, the work of yesterday's urban planners, whose confident and wide-ranging schemes ignored the specific realities of people and places – the very things their schemes were to touch.[30] We are all the more glad when we find attempts now made to do justice to what seemed once no more than inconvenient detail. Doing justice to present and to past, to particular needs and to wider demands, is not easy here. But it is not easy anywhere. We have seen time and again in these pages how real the tensions can be, and we must not expect to find the language of ritual exempt from them. Polarisation attracts because it seems to offer exhaustive choices; its attraction is of a piece with a modular view of things, where parts may be removed as we please and nothing else be affected. Neither attraction is helpful to what is alive, for life is not like that.

We must respect the particularity of what we have inherited. Respect here does not mean inviolate preservation, any more than it means an ignoring of how things have come to be what they are. But it does mean that we shall not think in terms of some general planning, for which the past is no more than a prelude to the greater present. It does mean that we shall not be afraid to admit that excellences in this world are sparsely distributed, that no age can provide them in everything and that language is no exception. It means in consequence that we shall not be afraid of patch-work, of adaptation, of a medley of styles in what is uttered in worship. The Roman Rite has long exhibited such a medley, in words and gestures alike; such is the way of things human which have endured over the centuries. To talk as I have done of the traditional chant of the Roman Church, and of the language traditionally used in its celebration of the Eucharist, is not a suggestion that we should go back to the fossilised poverty of the Old Mass; we need and must retain the shared structure recovered in the newer rite, and in a language understanded of the people. But it is a suggestion that the dissensions over worship in the Roman Church have been polarised from the start; that the polarisation was the penalty of a long refusal by that Church to acknowledge history in its worship; and that the newer cultic picture invites us to something better. Newer it is; but

---

[30] I have chosen an urban parallel because it suggests the style of liturgical change in so many places, where a mulish adherence to the past gave way to a reckless disregard of it. I am thinking of poor, silly Pius IX and the city of Rome – how he clung to his temporal power, with its darkness and abuse; how his resistance was ended by force; how United Italy arrived under Victor Emmanuel (the monarch we left in the second chapter calling for a *fiacre* and Bacciochi); and how the new government set about wantonly destroying so much that is now lamented in vain. (A final triumph for St Malachy, by the way, who gave Pius IX *Crux de cruce*, 'A cross from the cross'; Victor Emmanuel's coat-of-arms was a cross.)

the values it embodies can encourage – as those of the older picture could not – a respect for particularity and a fruitful collaboration between present and past.

I do not want to tax the reader's patience with descriptions of all that the respect and collaboration might involve. But – under penalty of incurring my own condemnation of remaining in generalities – I must say something. Ritual involves the whole person, for it is the whole person that it summons to the journey it involves. The whole person includes heart as well as head, habit and association as well as articulated speech; and the whole person is summoned by ritual within a tradition to which so many others have already belonged. There are Latin phrases and pieces of Latin which are simple, consecrated by antiquity and set to chants easily learned. Their regular use, accompanied by word-for-word translations, can become part of the distinctiveness of language in worship. That distinctiveness does not deny the language of the market-place, but is part of the whole process by which the essential *plurality of regions* in our language is acknowledged, and is used in the worship of God. Once more, to use my image, the narthex both links and distinguishes. And what I have written of the Latin heritage in the Church, I would repeat of the linguistic heritage there is in English. Acknowledging that heritage does not mean – why should it? – believing that all things in it are good, and that nothing good has come since. It means acknowledging *particularities*: such that English (like German) has an inherited translation of the Bible in a way that French has not; and that the collects of the Roman Missal, so condensed in their classic brevity, were given a classic rendering in the Book of Common Prayer. The needs of a biblical translation are as multiple as the Bible is: what is fitting for one occasion is not fitting for another; for some parts of the Scriptures, a translation nearly four centuries old is wholly unsuitable, and there can be few parts of the Scriptures where it will not need (just as the Prayerbook collects need) adjustments and accommodations. The fact remains that the play of its language can, time and again, speak to the whole person in a way that recent translations – for all their genuine illuminating of the text – cannot speak. Polarisation tempts us to choose between old and new, once for all; polarisation is as baleful here as anywhere else we have met it. If the newer cultic picture is to be allowed its force, we must respond to it in a way that is new.

That the picture has force will hardly be denied. Julien Green himself, despite the reservations he retained, wrote that his prejudices dissolved when he heard Mass celebrated in French (3 May 1970). Unfortunately, it is this very power which stands in the way of justice being done to particularities in ritual, in the ways I have been describing. A central body cannot but be wary of what seems to be independent of it.[31] The wariness will be all the greater at a time when so much tends in the direction of centralisation, whether in economics, in communication or in the everlasting quest for power. The unresolved disaccord I found in Pius X, and in the ritual innovations of Vatican Two, is most palpable in what has happened in the ritual use of English – which is one reason why I see the topic as a parable and even as a test-case. Worship is at the heart of religion: what is amiss in worship reflects the wider unhappiness in the Church of Rome. Facts about worship can point to the wider unease, for surely there is something very much amiss with both. A venerated but unsatisfactory tradition of worship received a welcome recovery of its shared structure – but the recovery has gone with an indiscriminate discarding of what deserved and deserves venerating. One mark of the recovery is that worship is to be in an intelligible tongue. Now, of all languages, English has spread most rapidly and into the greatest variety of places; what is made of it here is indeed a test-case. I have pointed to the essential *particularity* of demands made by language, and I have dwelt upon the circumstances of the particular setting of English best known to me. That other regions where English is spoken will exhibit some family resemblance to what I have described is likely enough. But that the resemblance will go with deep differences is not just likely, it is certain. Here are real and essentially particular problems, with that meeting of secular and sacred we have encountered so often. And all that the Roman Church can provide in the face of the problems is an 'International Committee for English in the Liturgy'. The solution is reminiscent of an International Committee for Taste in a Sausage, but it is the

---

[31] Pius XII, in his encyclical on the liturgy, shewed this anxiety when he blamed those who appealed to the phrase *lex orandi, lex credendi* ('the law of prayer is the law of belief'). He would have it replaced by the cacophonous *lex credendi legem statuat supplicandi* ('let the law of belief determine the law of worship', Pius XII 1947: 540–1). In enunciating the attitude it recommends, the Encyclical quotes a document of the fifth century at this point. Unfortunately, the passage quoted (from *De gratia Dei indiculus*) states the direct opposite: *ut legem credendi lex statuat supplicandi* ('that the law of worship may determine the law of belief'; DS 246). However, life is not amenable to such petulant obstinacies: Pius himself, in restoring the Easter Vigil, contributed more to an understanding of Easter than did any treatise or papal pronouncement.

essentially *old-fashioned* nature of the idiocy that I notice. How little things have changed! How once more we have come full circle! How we are back again with Pius X! Time was when Latin in the Mass was defended by the *argumentum a turismo* – that is, Japanese Catholics visiting Cape Town would find the same unintelligibility they had left behind in Nagasaki. Now, when Latin has been discarded, a committee is established to ensure that from the Shetlands to New Zealand the same English is heard in worship. We have indeed come full circle. Has the Church of Rome really nothing better to offer our time than that?[32]

A question that brings us to the last section of all.

41   A DOOR FOR OPENING

We are nearing the end of our journey. It has been a long journey, but for all that I was tempted to borrow the title of this final section from Johnson's *Rasselas*: 'The conclusion, in which nothing is concluded.' I have opposed many things in the course of these chapters: a divorcing of reality from appearance, a wrenching of terms from the context that gave them sense, a confusion between signs and disguises, a reduction of ritual to other categories, an attempt to insulate the Church and its pronouncements from the effects of time. But part of my opposition has lain in the contention that all these things offer a clarity that is no more than apparent, and

[32] Rome did indeed ask that some Latin chants be preserved, and several documents to this effect can be found in, e.g. Flannery 1975. But we have here an excellent example of the impossibility of doing one thing at a time. The ideas of combining present with past, of doing justice to language, of taking into account the strengths and weaknesses of specific situations – all that goes with a regard for the particularity of the humanities in the way I have tried to describe. It goes very uneasily indeed with the ideas embodied in the centralised bureaucracy of the Church of Rome, where we have seen the past regularly subjected to techniques of 'accommodation'; where the demands of language and time count for so much less than the maintenance of punctual control; and where the control is exercised by a disciplinary régime that sees the Church as 'polarised' in the way I have described. And so we have the absurdity by which the retention of any Latin whatever is identified with the celebration of the Old Rite of the Mass for marginal groups of the disaffected. The identification would be ludicrous if it were not tragic, and it points to the profound defects in the Roman Church's literacy – in its *humanity*, to use that word in its older sense. If this be thought too harsh a judgment, consider a reply of the Congregation of Rites given in 1970 and reprinted in Kaczynski 1976, nn. 205of. National groups of bishops had protested against the uniformity demanded in translations. The reply stated that the pope had been consulted (is there any *limit* to the follies of polarisation?), and a decision reached: uniformity is demanded for some parts, and *recommended for the rest*. The italics are mine and so is the dismay. The 'demand' can be ignored; but how does one begin to minister to the minds behind the recommendation?

that in fact they are muddles which are ultimately sceptical. The separation of substance from accidents in the 'Galilean Presence'; the emancipation of philosophical terminology from the setting and tradition in which it was devised; an expression of ritual in ways that make a camouflage of it: all those characteristics of older and newer eucharistic theology I have charged with *discohaerentia terminorum*, to use the phrase of Aquinas we met in the first chapter. That is, the words used in what I have been opposing do not hold together. It is confusions that I have been rejecting, not coherent positions to which I could then suggest an equally clear alternative. I have indeed stated what I have called the Way of Ritual; but I have insisted that the Way does not end in a claim of the sort I have opposed – a claim to point some fashion to the 'mechanism' of the eucharistic presence, whether by talking in terms of a switch of substances, or by talking in terms of a giving or naming or signifying that sets appearance against reality. Just as the Way of Ritual refuses to deny or to cancel its starting-point in the human condition, so it also refuses to claim to reach a finishing-point in what lies beyond that condition. In not making this claim, the Way does not become a choice to remain in the order of what is simply human; on the contrary, that is exactly what it denies. It is a Way, a journey: if a human starting-point is not denied, neither is it said to be more than a starting-point. The Way moves onward, suggests, indicates; it no more reaches a finishing-point than (to adopt a famous image) the eye draws a boundary between its field of vision and what lies beyond.

In other words, the clarity of older and newer accounts may be deceptive, but they do both offer the appearance of a definite answer in a way that what I have written does not. For better or worse, my contribution does not lie in suggesting one account of the eucharistic presence that can be set beside others. I claim that older and newer accounts are ultimately of a piece, are both incoherent, and are both in need of being selectively forgotten if unseemly consequences are not to present themselves. I have in effect called into question what older and newer accounts regard as common ground. But I have not proposed to replace them by something which will offer the appearance of clarity that they did. The Way of Ritual is not like that. And a similar restriction follows from the comparison I have been making between the two senses of *corpus mysticum*. I have dissented from claims made for the Eucharist and for the Church on the grounds that the claims 'insulate' what they hold to be most

important. I have submitted that we should prize rather, in the
Church as in the Eucharist, what is open and vulnerable, and accept
the consequences of facing a past that is both revered and
unsatisfactory – and of facing it from our own, limited position, not
from some privileged vantage-point. But to make submissions of that
sort is to deprive myself of the right to make claims in the style of what
I have been opposing. And so I was indeed tempted to borrow
Johnson's phrase as a title for this final section.

But I resisted the temptation, because there is one conclusion I do
draw. That the changes in the eucharistic rite have implications
which need pondering, both for the Eucharist itself and for the
Church – that much I do regard as established. If my own reflexions
fail to convince, so be it; but some reflexions are surely needed. The
changes have implications, because the newer cultic picture has a
force and a direction. I have argued that the picture is at odds with
things in both older and newer speculations about the eucharistic
presence; that it is also at odds with the present style of organisation
in the Church; and that it is at odds even with the manner in which
the newer rites have been introduced. Accept or reject my arguments
as you please, I do submit that new things are calling for new
thoughts, and that the new thoughts will not be what they should be
unless they take account of what older thoughts there have been on
these things.

As far as my own thoughts go, one thing is obvious – if they have
not won favour by this time, the pages that follow are not going to
mend matters. So I mean to draw the book to a close by offering three
considerations, which will recall what we have seen and also suggest
some lines of thought for when the book itself has ended. The first
consideration touches certain apparent advantages for the Church of
Rome in the way the world is going. The second suggests a better part
for that Church to play there. The third takes up the image of the
door there is for opening. And so to the first consideration.

I drew a contrast between older and newer cultic pictures in the
ritual of the Eucharist, and contended that the present strains in the
Church of Rome can be seen as due to the survival of the older picture
in the administration there. But I conceded that the survival is
vigorous; indeed, I submitted in the preceding section that the
Second Vatican Council itself has much in it that goes to strengthen
the persistence of what the Council was supposed to have overcome.

With this older picture I associated images like insulation, just as with the newer I associated images like vulnerability and openness; the opposition in imagery, I claimed, applies both to the Eucharist and to the Church. I now submit that there are more things yet which favour the persistence of the older picture in the Church, and so favour the polarisation and insulation I have been noticing, the gain of the centre at the expense of all else. I set down two of them here, and the first is the growth of unreason, in religion as so many other things, that is a mark of our time. Its causes and its manifestations are many, but its growth cannot but encourage the vision of the Church as an oracle, with the oracular rôle assigned to what is visually most perceptible there. Moreover, some forms of unreason have developed in areas deemed hostile by the faithful – I suppose the resurgence of fundamentalism among Moslems is the most noticeable.[33] Here, the vision of the Church as a bulwark will be encouraged, and the vision of its strength concentrated in one figure. In each case, the gain will be by the central body at the expense of the rest of it all.

The second thing I set down also touches reason, but has wider implications in its encouragment of polarisation. The encouragement it gives takes the form of lessening the likelihood of abrasion between the central body in the Church and other forces, more particularly forces to do with speculation and argument. What I have in mind is the shift there has been in the balance of population among the faithful, a shift away from Europe and the 'Western' world towards places like Africa and South America. The fact of the shift has long been acknowledged, but I think that some consequences of it for the Church are only beginning to be drawn. I can best state those I draw myself by recalling what we saw about liberation theology earlier in the chapter. The zeal exhibited by the writers was more than praiseworthy, but the arguments employed in the texts cited lacked rigour and exhibited a disconcerting innocence. There is nothing very surprising in this, because the needs which liberation theology faces call urgently for severely practical solutions – the righting of social wrongs, the achieving of a just distribution of resources, the

---

[33] Islamic fundamentalism is often dismissed by Christians as beneath the level of argument. They are wrong to treat it so, because it is today what their own religion was in days gone by. A sentence of deposition against a ruler; a sentence of death against a writer deemed to have offended against the faith – we have heard all too much of all these before. Thus, not only was the celebrated history of the Council of Trent by Paolo Sarpi (+ 1623) put on the Index, an attempt was made on the historian's life. The pun in Sarpi's comment, after he had been stabbed, is unfortunately untranslatable: 'I recognise the *stylus Curiae*.'

exploring of the international implications of the sufferings in this or that country. These problems concern management, the means of power and political pressure. Concentration upon problems like that – genuine and urgent problems – will be at the expense of attention to the theoretical and abstract problems that have traditionally exercised the minds of theologians. The shift away from Europe in population will go with a shift away from Europe in topics deemed worthy of discussion.

And that worries me. I hope it is not necessary for me to add that my worry does not imply any lack of sympathy for the wretched of the Earth whose cause has been taken up – often at risk to life and limb – by liberation theologians. And I suspect that by this time it is not necessary for me to add that my worry does not come either from any great affection for theological speculation. The reasons for my worry are secular, and have to do with history. The course of history in Europe has included a succession of interactions between Christianity and forces not specifically religious. We have met some of these interactions in the course of the book. In the first chapter, we noticed the arrival in the West of speculations from the ancient world, with Moslem and Jewish commentaries on them. Eucharistic theology was only one of the things affected by the arrival, just as eucharistic theology was only one of the things affected by another interaction we noticed in that chapter – the interaction of religious belief with the new sciences that arose in the seventeenth century. An interaction of our own time we met in the second chapter, when we examined the effect upon some eucharistic speculations exercised by the phenomenological movement in philosophy. And other interactions we have met in the present chapter and in its predecessor, when we considered the growth of historical disciplines, and in particular of biblical criticism. Here, religious belief encountered in a new way the need to acknowledge the multiplicity and limitations of its own past, and to accept the consequences of applying secular criteria to the remains of that past. We have seen that these interactions have not been peaceful; but they have taken place, and what the Church of Rome now professes to believe has been touched by them.

My worry touches the survival of this tradition of interaction. I can best shew where my worry lies by recalling yet again the description I have given of my own approach to the problems discussed in this book: I am a Greek come up to worship at the Feast. There is, as I said, nothing personal in the matter, I chose the text from St John to point to two sets of values. The sets are distinct and mutually irreducible. Both are present in the European centuries. I, like many others, wish to defend both. I have 'come up to worship at the Feast' – I seek to share in the eucharistic rite, and the Way of Ritual is one that I would walk in myself. But I am 'a Greek' – I inherit a tradition of open enquiry and free discussion. The inheritance is grossly imperfect, but it does exist and it goes back to Athens in a way it certainly does not go back to Jerusalem; and I will not forego it.[34] That other encounters will arise in the lands whither the weight of Christianity is moving, I do not doubt. I wish I were less doubtful about the prospects for what the encounters in Europe have displayed – the meeting of religious belief with a tradition of debate and enquiry. My complaint may be taken as yet another proof of the 'European' constrictions of what I write. I do not reject the charge. We all have our constrictions, and those are some of mine. I am a Greek come up to worship at the Feast, but I do not deny that others have come up too – with constrictions of their own, of course. What I insist is that encounters, both of this sort and other sorts, are necessary for the well-being of the Church. They can be uncomfortable, and the attraction of any process of 'insulation' is that it seems to offer relief from this lack of comfort. But, as we have seen time and again, insulation does not work. Processes like accommodating the past and retroactively demoting what is awkward there only muffle the way things really are in belief. Processes that polarise the life of the *corpus mysticum* cannot do justice to that life, they only impede the reflexion upon it that is needed.

I have written that the older cultic picture has a vigorous power of survival in the Church of Rome, and I have just mentioned here two more of the things which are helping it to survive. In the course of this chapter we have already seen some consequences of the survival. We

---

[34] *Quid ergo Athenis et Hierosolymis?* The defiant question, usually cited as '*Quid Athenae Hierosolymis?*' and translated as 'What hath Athens to do with Jerusalem?', was put by Tertullian (+*c.* 216), a writer horrible even by patristic standards. He put the question in his *Liber de praescriptionibus adversus haereticos, c.* 7 (2 ML 20) in the context of a reference to St Paul's attempt to convert the philosophers at Athens. I am surprised that an obvious answer has never been made: 'It has at least this much. When Paul came to Athens, we invited him to state his new teaching. Some of us laughed at it; others said they would listen to it again some other time; a few of us accepted it. But none of us stoned him, and he left the Areopagus unmolested. Jews, how did a preacher of new things once fare among you in Jerusalem? Christians, how did such preachers fare among you anywhere, as long as you had the power to harm them?'

have seen the contrasts between the texts in the left-hand and the right-hand columns (pp. 256–8, 267–70); we have seen the fencing-off of the Church from the kind of criticism accepted for the Bible, so that amnesia and demotion are applied to anything in the past that seems to compromise what we feel obliged to claim for the Church in the present; and we have noticed the paradox by which the spirit of the autocratic Pius X, with his defiance of the demands of history, can be traced in the Second Vatican Council and in what has followed it. I think there are still more consequences to mention, both for those at the centre of the Church and for those elsewhere in it. And I start at the centre.

For those at the centre, the power of insulation has produced a language in which it is virtually impossible to admit a fault. We met a failure to learn from the past, in the visit to the Roman Synagogue. But the speech made there at least mentioned the past, which is more than can be said for another, made slightly earlier and on the same topic of relations between Christians and Jews:

The Catholic Church is always prepared, with the help of God's grace, to revise and renew whatever in her attitudes and ways of expression happens to conform less with her own identity, founded upon the Word of God, the Old and New testament, as read in the Church. This she does, not out of any expediency... but out of a deep consciousness of her own 'mystery' and a renewed willingness to translate it into practice. (John-Paul II 1986a: 409)

The tragedy of language like that is due to the absence of those *encounters* I have been commending – no reality is involved by the words said, outside a closed set of terms to which the words belong.[35] But, just as great an insulation is present in some of the apparently more liberal texts I printed in the left-hand columns. They do indeed contain admissions that mistakes were made, and Galileo is mentioned. But the acknowledgment of past errors becomes a confident

---

[35] Once again, I stress that I am concerned with defects in structure, not with personalities. To support this contention, I notice an even more embarrassing failure of language concerning Jews, this time from Pope John XXIII. His own contribution to the mending of relations between Christians and Jews I readily acknowledge. It is well described in Hebblethwaite 1984, a well-informed and judicious account, which shews just what mental barriers John had to break to do what he did. His greeting to a party of Jews, 'I am Joseph your brother', has become proverbial. But the language of the greeting embarrasses on closer inspection. Take it as a gesture of goodwill, and it is admirable. Take it in any greater detail, and it becomes a piece of outrageous complacency. The patriarch Joseph had been sold into slavery by his own brothers, and in uttering those words he repaid evil with good and calmed their guilty consciences. What conceivable bearing has all this upon Christianity's treatment of Jews over the centuries? We have here, of course, an excellent specimen of adjustment to the unit of significance. Pope John's kindly words must be taken as a whole, they cannot be allowed individual lives of their own.

claim for present rectitude: the errors have been overcome and the relation between religious belief and human knowledge set to rights. The confidence rests upon a missing of the point. Galileo is comfortably remote, the encounters of religious belief that matter nowadays are not with physical science, but with the relations of present to past, and with the historical limitations of the Christian heritage. Those encounters are not in the least remote, and not at all comfortable (recall the reluctance to extend biblical criticism to an analogous criticism of the Church!), and concerning them the texts I have examined exhibit no more than a blank unawareness.[36] Indeed, the only perceptible acknowledgment lies in the practical order – the

[36] I support this claim with two texts. Both are concerned with religious belief and reasons; neither exhibits any awareness of what the problems are which touch the way religious belief is affected by time and by what time brings.

The first was an allocution delivered in Cologne on 15 November 1980, the seven hundredth anniversary of the death of Albert the Great – the eminent Dominican who was the teacher of Aquinas. The discourse praised Albert for having steered a course between those of his contemporaries who saw the arrival of non-Christian learning in the West as a danger, and those who deduced from it an unresolvable contradiction between faith and reason. Albert's own scientific work is obsolete, but the Christian intellectualism he proposed remains exemplary. Some still see a tension between religious belief and modern physical science; the Church acknowledges the errors committed in the case of Galileo, and commends the rôle of later theology in freeing belief from what is bound up with time (*von Zeitgebundenem*; John-Paul II 1981: 51). I hope it is not disrespectful to the memory of Galileo to say that in contexts of this sort he has come to play a part rather like the part played by Pope Alexander VI elsewhere in Roman Catholic apologetic – an admission of one disastrous error bestows an unargued respectability upon everything else. And I hope it is not disrespectful to Albert's memory to say that, just as his scientific work has receded into the past, so have the specific responses he exhibited in the face of religious problems that are themselves now just as remote. Too much has intervened since, the conversation has gone on too long for what he wrote to be in any detail 'exemplary' for us. We cannot expect Albert to put questions about history and time that came only later. These questions I have raised repeatedly through the book. In raising them, I was simply bringing to bear upon my topic a general awareness of problems that is part and parcel of reflexion today, as many readers will know. I cannot but lament the *ease*, if I may so put it, with which the awareness is ignored in texts like this, as if theology had but to release religious belief from what is 'bound up with time' in a matter touching physical science, for all else to be well. Things are simply not as simple.

But the ignoring here is no accident, it is just as evident in the other text – a discourse of 26 September 1979 to the Biblical Commission. The discourse speaks of 'the paradox whereby historically contingent persons become bearers of a message that is transcendent and absolute', and claims that 'the earthenware vessels may break, but the treasure they contain remains whole and incorruptible' (John-Paul II 1979c: 608). Neither phrases like 'transcendent and absolute', nor the use of scriptural phraseology, can remove a problem that faces Bible and Church alike, they only ignore the problem. But the problem refuses to go away, even as the discourse itself shews. The paradox is said to be associated with 'the revealed message and the more specifically Christian message'. The distinction drawn between Old and New Testament echoes what was declared at the Second Vatican Council, in its decree *Dei Verbum* on divine revelation (1966c). In effect, the latter is declared to be exempt from time to a degree that the Old is not (contrast there chapters 4 and 5). And when we ask why, we find ourselves facing once again the problem we tried to ignore.

insulations of theology we saw in the right-hand columns, and the administrative execution of those insulations by the authorities cited there.

The language I have been describing has a further advantage, if that be the word, for those at the centre. As it virtually excludes any awkward admissions of error, so it will suggest that what has happened is all as it should be. I cited Bishop Christopher Butler's description of what he called 'creeping infallibility': assigning to a piece of doctrine a note of truth or obligatoriness higher than what the Church itself assigns. My own comment was that an infallibility which does *not* creep is not worth having, but we can see now more clearly where the force of the creeping lies – not in any unwarranted promotion of this doctrine or that, but in a pervasive and unscrutinised persuasion that the general course of what happens in the Church is providential and is to be accepted as such.[37]

Such, I say, is the language used, and the supposed advantage it brings. But the advantage has to be paid for, both at the centre and elsewhere in the Church. Those at the centre, precisely because they are insulated from awkward encounters, will find it yet more difficult to obey the injunction we have met so often – don't say what it *must* be, *look*! A habit of self-scrutiny is acquired with difficulty and lost with ease, and a belief in the 'providentiality' of what happens will make the loss all the easier. When I described the Old Roman Mass, I said that it exhibited an 'undifferentiated dorsality' by the priest, as he engaged in his largely silent activities at the altar with his back

---

[37] In using the distinction between the two senses of *corpus mysticum*, I gladly acknowledged my debt to Henri de Lubac's great work, which examined the shift in the meaning of the phrase from 'Eucharist' to 'Church'. But even there, in the luminous and judicious conclusion to the book, the author can still write that the shift was 'good because it was normal' (*elle était normale, donc bonne*, Lubac 1949: 291). Now no one phrase can do justice to complexities in the history of belief, but the piece of ambiguous optimism I have just cited can surely do no justice to anything. (It may well be that Lubac was not responsible for it – his work at the time was being impeded by curially inspired censorship.)

From this regrettable example of 'creeping' I pass to two others; they may at least entertain the reader. The first concerns a papal election, the other concerns a papal microphone. One of the electors compared his experience to 'being eye-ball to eye-ball with the Holy Spirit'. The language embarrasses; we feel yet greater embarrassment when we think of what that elector (and others presumably) is likely to make of the way the votes go at elections: *elle était normale, donc bonne*. And so to the microphone. In the last of my years at Rome, a group of us went to send messages to England over Vatican Radio. The programme was introduced, in sumptuous Americanese, by an official of the station, who described us as a group of young Levites (or something) who were speaking 'at the Holy Father's own microphone'. I expressed mild surprise afterwards that Pius XII should employ so nondescript an instrument. I got a very brisk explanation: 'Everything in the Vatican belongs to the Holy Father.'

to those present, and with downcast eyes on the few occasions when he turned towards them. Yet again, the analogy between Eucharist and Church proves a fair one – the 'dorsality' of the central organisation is just as undifferentiated. Backs there have been turned on all else. A language in which faults can only with difficulty be admitted expresses a posture in which faults can only with difficulty be noticed. Looking is simply more difficult than it looks.[38]

Unfortunately, the analogy of 'dorsality' has to be taken further, when we turn from the centre of the Church to elsewhere in it. One of the consequences of dorsality in the Old Mass was tedium for the congregation; the dorsality in the Roman Church today is leading to an all too similar result. I have mentioned boredom more than once in these pages (quite apart from inflicting it) because I think its rôle in religion, as in other things, has been gravely under-estimated. One of the most irrefutable of arguments is a yawn, and there have come to be of late so many of them in the Roman Church. The sheer force of polarisation, let alone the pictures and the language in which it finds expression, seems to reduce the *corpus mysticum* to an assemblage in which a concern for honesty and indeed for anything else is subordinated to an apparatus reminiscent of piped music – centrally controlled, incessant in its transmissions and fathomlessly tedious. I wrote earlier that there are things in the world today which encourage this 'polarization' in the Church, and I gave special mention to the growth of unreason, in religion as elsewhere. But other things are growing as well. I referred to the movement of numbers in the Roman Church away from Europe, and I offered my opinion that the movement can produce a drift away from those 'encounters' with which religion in Europe has been associated. This drift can be strengthened by other things, including the present unease in the Church of Rome – those who might produce the encounters are simply doing their thinking elsewhere. But there is another drift, notorious and widespread, and that is the drift among so many in Europe away from the organised life of any Church at all. Make what

[38] This is neither paradox nor platitude, as can be seen from a remark made in a discourse delivered in Madrid on 2 November 1982:

> If, in moments like those of the Inquisition, tensions, errors and excesses were produced – facts which the Church of today evaluates by the objective light of history – we must recognize that the sum total of intellectual organizations in Spain (*el conjunto de medios intelectuales de España*) was able to reconcile in an admirable way the demands of a full freedom of enquiry with a profound sense of the Church. (John-Paul II 1983a: 208)

> What *is* one to say?

you will of my diagnosis of the present state of the Roman Church, you can hardly deny that, like so many other Christian Churches, it is proving unable, time and again, to reach those touched by indifference. They may well look at the polarising manifestations of Rome on television, but they are still voting with their yawns.

And a simple example can shew how much the yawning has spread, even in places where we might have expected interest. I started this chapter with a reference to the debate between Küng and Rahner. I dare say that readers will hold different opinions over it, but can any of them imagine a theological debate today arousing anything like the same concern? Twenty years after, where have all the flowers gone? The answer disconcerts. I started the book itself with a mention of the Royal Declaration against transubstantiation, and I recorded in a footnote there that the Declaration annoyed Roman Catholics. It annoyed them not just by what it excluded, but by what it went on to assume – that, in the Church of Rome, any promise made or any assertion uttered is open to cancellation by higher authority. But have we not been coming across things of just that sort – the kind of things I put into the right-hand columns? And do not the left-hand columns themselves contain things of the same sort – what we might call the Watergate appeal to Vatican Two? Once more, have we not come full circle?

Hōs ho diakonōn: 'as he that serveth'. For Luke, that is how Christ described himself at the Last Supper (Luke xxii 27). He had taken bread, and taken the cup, and bidden his friends do this in remembrance of him; he had spoken of his betrayal; now, as the others squabble among themselves as to who shall be counted the greatest, he uses those words of himself – 'I am among you as he that serveth.' He then tells Simon of his forthcoming denial and commands him to strengthen his brethren; tells them all that the things concerning himself are drawing to an end; and so they leave for the Mount of Olives, the agony in the garden and the rest. Aquinas reminded us that the last words spoken by a friend sink most deeply into the memory (p. 195), and with the words we may surely join the deeds. The new Passover; a foolish quarrel and his own gentle reproach (in John's Gospel, the washing of the feet – *hōs ho diakonōn*); a command to strengthen others, given to one who was about to fail; a view of what is now to be undergone; and the start of its undergoing, in the lonely agony. If all this is to sink deepest into our memory, how are we to shew it forth in the Eucharist, that sign of the life of him who is now our Risen Lord, a life shared with the members of his *corpus mysticum*? The question is as wide as the gospel, but some defects in our answers may be avoided if we bear in mind two points of logic we have already met.

The first point is that sharing words is easy; disagreements start when we apply or withdraw them in particular cases (p. 329). 'Service' (like 'love' and 'freedom') has been abused by religion even more than it has been abused by other things; the existence of the word in the ecclesiastical vocabulary cannot be enough. We must – yet again – be prepared to *look*, not just to say what it *must* be. Where should we look? Here the second point of logic may help, even if only as a caution: it is the distinction drawn more than once between definitions and recipes, between saying what something involves and giving instructions for how we can achieve it (see p. 40 and fn. 11). I have used imagery to suggest what I think we should aim at in the Eucharist and in the Church – vulnerability, journey, narthex, market-place – but these images are in their way descriptions, they are not specific recipes for the attainment of what I have tried to suggest by them; and so what I do suggest must be limited. Still, definition and recipes are not wholly unconnected, since spelling out what is involved in something may well suggest ways of bringing it about. The course of these chapters has already suggested some patterns of ritual and behaviour which I believe to be desirable. I go on to suggest more. The suggestions are not meant to compromise the distinction between definitions and recipes – to compromise the distinction can lead to worse than ludicrous consequences. I have used the images of narthex and market-place, just as I use the image of the door that is for opening. I think the images are useful, and will be using them again. But they are only images. I am well aware that many churches are nowhere near a market-place of any sort in the urban desolation to which they minister; and that their doors, far from being for opening, have to be kept locked to prevent robbery and destruction. I should be grieved if my use of the imagery I have chosen should be taken as a sign of indifference to a burden that many have to bear. Or of indifference to the wound inflicted on religion by the need to keep churches shut when services are not in progress.

Christ's service continues when the Supper is over and he is given into the hands of men. The agony and the rest are his own living out the rôle of the Suffering Servant in Isaiah – a rôle that leads him to surrender on Calvary all things to which we can put a name. The risen Christ still bears on his body the scars of that surrender, it is by them that the disciples can recognise him. For this is no triumphant appearance of a hero who never died after all; they recognise him as the one who was dead and is living; that is how he is known of them in breaking of bread. But if he still bears scars on his body, is there not a sense in which he still bears scars in his heart and mind? The vulnerability is real, the openness is real. Both ought to be present, in mind and heart, among those who wish to speak the good news Christ came to bring, and who wish to be, as he was, in the midst as one that serveth.[39]

The vulnerability and the openness should be present in the way the service to be given is understood by those who give it. I wrote earlier in this chapter that Küng's estimate of infallibility in the Church is, appearances to the contrary, more exigent than Rahner's because it takes the Church out into the wider world of 'the market-place'. To put the Church there is not to reduce its message to what is no more than human. But it is to concede that the market-place has much else in it besides the Church, and that the Church must learn to live side by side with many other things, things with their own purposes and priorities. If it is to be among them as one that serveth, it must not think of the service in terms of patronage; it must think of learning as much as of teaching. Indeed, its admission of vulnerability should go further. The good news is indeed good, but it is not self-contained and insulated, nor is the Church itself likely to be in better shape than was the group at the Last Supper – squabbling over precedence, betraying, denying, falling asleep when asked to stay awake and watch, and running away from danger. All this provides, we might say, an admission of vulnerability and incompleteness that ought to be the framework of whatever service there is to be done.

But the service itself, I now submit, should exhibit an acknowledgment of the same incompleteness; the vulnerability should be present

---

[39] Erasmus devoted a long letter to his friend Dean Colet (+1519), concerning the agony in the garden (Erasmus 1704). He sets beside it the death cell of Socrates, the cup of hemlock and the calmness of the philosopher in the face of death. The letter is excessively long (Erasmus could not resist the chance to exhibit his undoubted ability to write elegant Latin), but it has a real power – a power that comes, I think, partly from its defence of Christ's perturbation of mind, but partly from the very struggle that Erasmus himself exhibits in formulating his defence. He is *embarrassed* by his topic, given his admiration for Socrates. And, once again, embarrassment points the way forward. Christ here, praying that the cup may pass, is nearer to us than Socrates, for all his worth, can ever be.

in the very nature of what is done. My suggestion here leads to what may be dismissed as no more than another paradox. I introduce it by recalling what we have already seen of the Church as it is today.

I have been linking things in the present structure of the Church – the polarisation, the persistence of the older cultic picture – with manifestations of technological civilisation. The growth in conspicuousness of the papacy and curia since the nineteenth century, I pointed out, owes much to modern means of communication; the ever-increasing volume of words emitted by them goes with those means, and with modern methods of transport; the whole perceptible pattern of the Church's life is increasingly affected by the style and power of television. But I have in this section linked the present structure of the Church with something else – with the pressures exercised today upon human reason. I submitted that the general growth of unreason, and the drift of the Church away from Europe and from the traditions of enquiry found there, have this much in common: they favour the move in the balance of power towards the centre in the Roman Church.

Those are, I say, things that are touching the Roman Church as we know it. And now the paradox in my suggestion lies in this: it is in these very problems, the problems raised by technological civilisation and by the pressures exercised upon human reason, that the Church today can in my submission give distinctive service. The record of the Church in the face of these problems is imperfect in the extreme, and the imperfection is linked with what I have associated with the older cultic picture and with insulation. For all that, there is real service here for the Church to offer, and to offer in ways I associate with the newer cultic picture. That picture, we know, goes with openness and vulnerability; those qualities are present here by the very imperfection of the Church's witness in the face of the problems I have mentioned. The imperfection of it exhibits a solidarity with the weaknesses of what the Church is to serve. The imperfection can be the beginning of something better.

I spell out what I have in mind here. I first notice the link that exists between the problems touching a technological civilisation and those touching the pressures on reason. I then dwell on the imperfection of the witness borne by the Church in the face of these problems. And I then point to the reality of the service which the Church here might offer.

To link technological civilisation with pressures brought to bear on human reason has nothing paradoxical in it, the course of our century has shewn the link all too clearly. The immense and growing complexity of life; the ever-increasing impossibility of doing one thing at a time; the means which modern inventions put into the hands of those in power – those are only three of the many factors which encourage a simple abdication of reason, an abdication in favour of allegiance to what promises a solution or offers an escape. Other factors also exercise pressure on reason – they encourage, not a simple abdication of it, but a confinement of it within limits that are all the more real for being left unexamined. Thus, the spread of communication favours the immediately intelligible over the carefully qualified, crowds over individuals, pictures over words. In fact, the very power of the means available encourages reasoning in terms of them rather than in terms of ends and values. And reasoning only in terms of means and techniques encourages in turn a conversation in which the past is classed with the obsolete, and present reality identified with what can be profitably put to use.

It is just as true that mankind is becoming ever more aware of these problems, and that attempts are being made to offer solutions to them. My point here is to notice how very imperfect has been the record of the Church in these matters; and I turn first to the family of problems I have linked with technological civilisation.

The problems touch the conditions of mankind upon the Earth, and how we are to live. We have seen in earlier chapters how Christian belief does indeed concern itself with the human condition, and offers to it the hope of redemption. But we have also seen how shot through the offer is with imperfection. Traditional accounts of the redemption and of the eucharistic presence offer a hope beyond our dreaming – but they also shew how real is the shadow of the past. The good news exceeds whatever can be achieved by earthly means – but we have seen the puzzlement of the liberation theologians over injustice in places where the good news has so long been preached. That is, the gospel transcends earthly things – but a tragic use of the Fallacy of Replacement, if I may apply my phrase here, turns the gospel into yet another weapon for those in power. As for the eucharistic rite, we have seen how deep its roots lie in the needs and hopes of human beings, and of their nature held in bondage. But we have seen those roots obscured, when ritual has become disguise, the Eucharist itself a commodity, and 'the Givenness of Reality' a means towards denying the reality of what we perceive. Again, the eucharistic ritual, like the rites out of which it grew, builds on the acknowledgment of the natural world around us as God's creation. But what effect, time and again, has the ritual had upon those who celebrate it, for the care they take of nature? Yet again, the very antiquity of the rite should bring home the rôle of present, past and future in the human life we have, and in its heritage and its hope. But what facing has there been of the problems raised by time for religious belief, and what sensitivity has there been for the balance between present and past in worship and in the eucharistic rite itself? All these problems I have mentioned are religious; but they belong to a family of wider problems that concern mankind ever more today, amid the civilisation and population that are spreading all over the globe and recklessly devouring its space and its heritage. What we are, and what are our hopes; the place of the natural world in how we shall live; the place of time in our human existence – if they are problems for all of us, they do touch what witness has been borne by the Church, and that witness must in honesty be acknowledged to be grossly imperfect.

But just as imperfect is the witness offered in the matter of reason and of the pressure brought to bear upon it today. We have seen all too much of the imperfection. The foolishnesses found in our right-hand – and in our left-hand – columns are only some examples among many, the imperfection has been with us since the book began: in the incoherences of defences of transubstantiation; in the indifference of later authors to the context of the terminology they claimed to abide by; in the accommodations of the past that muffle the truth about it; in the adoption of television as a model for the presence of the Church; in the use of language that evades encounters with the uncomfortable; and in the turning of a process of self-examination in Vatican Two into a centrally executed exercise in complacency and neglect of the past. In the matter of human reason, as in the matter of technological civilisation, the witness borne is imperfect, and palpably so. Even more palpably, in fact, than the texts we have met suggest.[40]

---

[40] I have in mind things like one already mentioned – the control exercised by Rome over Catholic institutions of higher ecclesiastical education and tightened by means of other pieces of recent legislation. But I also have in mind something I have alluded to more than once: the philosophical vacuum left by the demotion of Aquinas from the place that Leo XIII and Pius X had assigned him. Here is the pattern we have seen already: ridiculous legislation is understandably discarded, but the consequences of discarding it have hardly been faced; we are back with historical insouciance and with modularity. Vatican Two, in

For both types of problem there has indeed been a change, to a greater or lesser degree, in what is thought and said in the Church of Rome: a care for the Earth we inhabit and a wish to let reason rather than violence govern our differences, are in fashion now at Rome as once they were not. We should not be surprised at the change, surprise would be in order only if we thought of the imperfections in the Church's witness as simply failure by individuals to live up to the standards their Church had taught. To think only in terms of individuals' failures is too easy an answer. We should rather see the imperfections as normal, as predictable incompleteness. In other words, no one thing can teach all the answers here, the problems we face need facing communally, and in a multitude of ways. The Church has no more of a comprehensively authoritative rôle than any other occupant of the market-place. Its rôle there is distinct and irreplacable; but it is a partial rôle, and a rôle played by what exhibits the very defects to which it seems to minister. The Church is in the market-place as one that serveth; but as a servant acquainted with infirmity.

For all that – indeed, because of all that – the service which the Church can give there is distinctive and real. The imperfection of its witness is indeed due to the incompleteness of what the Church is; but it is also due to the very nature of what it is that the Church has to offer. I have been contending all along that the newer cultic picture has tensions built into it, and the tensions lie in the process by which ritual leads us on from what is human to what is more than human. The tensions – the openness, the vulnerability, call them what you will – make the newer cultic picture less assured and insulated than the older, and make following it all more laborious and costing. But

its decree *Optatam totius* on the training of priests, writes of their needing to base themselves upon 'a perennially valid philosophical patrimony' (1966b: § 15). Details would have been out of place in the decree, but the phrase echoes ominously what we found in the first chapter, where a privileged place was allotted to a *philosophia perennis* that needs no study for its acquisition (p. 24). And the echo persists. *Sapientia Christiana*, the new constitution for Roman Catholic institutes of higher learning, cited the council's words (John-Paul II 1979b: 495); it was itself cited on the point in an address to the Gregorian University later the same year (John-Paul II 1979e: 1542), and the address complemented the phrase with unspecified reproofs of 'certain theological currents' (*certi filoni teologici*; Italian can do this so much better than English – *ottiche, visuali, linguaggi filosofici … sviluppi devianti*. All there at 1543). That year had seen the centenary of Leo XIII's encyclical favouring Aquinas (Leo XIII 1879). A papal discourse on the occasion (John-Paul II 1979d) saw the phrase cited yet again and Leo's adulation of Aquinas repeated (1475–7); but Pius XI was also cited, to the effect that honour paid to Thomas touches something even greater – the authority of the teaching Church (1480–1). Yet again, the centre has gained at the expense of all else, philosophy included. Yet again, the ghost of Pius X refuses to be laid.

the newer cultic picture does justice to the sense and power of ritual in a way that the older picture could not, and that is why the very incompleteness of what the Church is and celebrates can minister to the world in which we live. If it is true that the Church echoes the defects and problems bound up with technological civilisation and with the pressure on reason, it is just as true that those problems exist in the world, and are writ just as large there. The problems occupy the minds of many; once more, there should be no claiming by the Church of a monopoly of solutions. But it can seek to serve, to learn, to contribute. And, as I have claimed, its very defects give it a solidarity with the defective reality wherein it must work.

The forms of its work can be many, and many readers will be better acquainted with some of them than I am – acquainted by the harsh reality of the service they give. My own concern in this book has taken ritual as its heart. Ritual is no universal remedy for the difficulties that face the proclamation of the good news today, but then nothing else is either. But by this time, it will be enough for me to recall that ritual goes very deep into the human condition; that it can speak to the whole person as nothing else can; that it is involved with past and present; that it looks forward to the salvation promised; that it acknowledges the natural world, and faces the darkness in that world; that it proclaims the Lord's death and resurrection; that it falls silent in the face of the mystery of God's loving redemption. All these things, as we have seen time and again, ritual does but imperfectly; but the world for which they are done is itself grossly imperfect, and is grossly in need of the depths, the facings, the silences that the eucharistic ritual offers – and in need of them today all the more, because so much today muffles the perception that they are needed. I have over these pages written much of what I regard as distortions and lack of balance in the Roman Church. But I should not have taken the trouble to write all this if I did not believe that that Church, in its immense antiquity, in its enduring vigour, and in its capacity for self-scrutiny and for reaching out to what is new, has a contribution to make in these things that nothing else on the Earth has. The pattern of polarisation fails because of its very convenience to the central organisation of so large a body: convenience is not enough. Ritual indeed is vulnerable, but it has been so from the beginning, and its very vulnerability can point to something better. Here, in breaking of bread, this mind can be in us which was in Christ Jesus, and the Church can be in the market-place as one that serveth.

A door for opening. The image goes with other images I have used; like them, it conveys both distinctness and accessibility. Good fences are said to make good neighbours, and a door performs the office of demarcating. But the demarcation is not a barrier: this door is for opening, whether from within or without. With what thoughts can this final image leave us?

I have spent much of this book on dissent – dissenting myself, and reflecting on the dissents of others. But I have also claimed that what look like clear criteria for identity and difference can lose their clarity when examined. Definiteness in positions taken up is subject to time, and boundaries drawn in one age become blurred in another. Formulae which once divided may be shared when an adjustment in the unit of significance has been made, and the order of priorities in what belief has inherited is not constant. In making all these claims, I have had in mind the wider claim made so often by me – that religious belief is essentially multiple in its manifestations, and that no one of them can do it justice. What we can see more clearly now is that these reflexions on belief are not simply abstract considerations of something in itself purely theoretical, they touch practice and life. The manifestations we have seen of eucharistic belief constitute a whole family of activities and expressions. They include ritual itself, with its complex of expressions I have called 'a cultic picture'; they also include credal formulae, imagery in language, preferences in what has come down from the past, willingness to innovate in this or that way, and perceptions of what the belief should lead to. And all this variety is more than eucharistic, for these things, as we have seen, have their analogies in the Church itself, the body of which the Eucharist is the sign. What we have been considering is not just accidentally complex, it is essentially so. That is why questions of identities and differences there cannot be less complex, and why the complexity is not just a matter of being elaborate or difficult. Rather, it is complex because life is.

In using the image of the narthex, just as in talking of 'the Church and the market-place', I have deliberately gone to the ambiguity between 'church' in the sense of the *corpus mysticum*, and 'church' in the sense of the building that can be entered or left. I understand that the word 'church' derives ultimately from *kyriaké oikos*, 'the Lord's house'. His house has a door and a narthex in one form or another, which set his house apart, and yet set it apart as inviting entry. The house is what it is because of what gathers in it – in the deepest sense, the assembly which celebrates the Eucharist.[41] Here, I submit, is the life to which we must come back, in all its complex multiplicity. I have often recalled the advice not to say what it *must* be but look, and I have tried to carry it out. I have also ventured to complement that piece of advice with another: 'Don't say what it *might* be; live!'. The power of this was to direct our attention – to direct our activity – to the shared things which make up life. Just as simply saying how things *must* be can give us a wrong picture of life, so simply speculating as to how things *might* be can rob us of the living setting for what we say and do. Both pieces of advice can help when we reflect upon those who come together for the Eucharist, and especially when we ask questions to do with identity and difference, change and permanence.

I have cited another passage from the *Philosophical Investigations*, that which bids us leave what looks deceptively clear and return to the 'rough ground' of life and practice. I added that the dissents and distress in the Roman Church might prompt the question whether there is any rough ground left to go back to. By now, I hope that the nature of the question is somewhat clearer. We cannot lay down in advance the range of dissent that a community will find tolerable, any more than we can lay down in advance what will break a friendship – which does not mean that we shall have nothing to say about communities or friendships. Another citation from the *Philosophical Investigations* might help: in following instructions, or responding to a request, or taking up another's statement, we face the fact that there is 'a multitude of familiar paths leading off from these words in every direction' (§525). That is, all activities and commands and communications allow development this way and that. They work as they do because a community develops them in ways held in common. And to this observation I add once more a contribution of my own. The rate of going off the ways is not uniform; some directions soon lead to incomprehension, others do not; and nowhere will the lack of uniformity be as real (and as unpredictable in its consequences) as in something as ancient and as deep as religion. Ritual I have set at the heart of eucharistic belief, and the full

---

[41] And not necessarily where the Eucharist is reserved. To talk of the Lord's house in terms of the 'real presence' is as misleading as Ronald Knox's talk of the 'real absence' in churches of other denominations. This is not to deny a place to reservation, or a place to prayer in connexion with it. But it is to refuse to polarise the presence of Christ in the eucharistic community into the reserved Sacrament; and it is to recognise the great variety there has been, and is, and ought to be, in the place allotted by prayer and worship to reservation.

complexity of its content and of its effects needs to be acknowledged, not muffled in the ways we have seen amnesia and accommodation muffle it. Some who share the ritual may find that the respective paths tend to go in directions that are different – just as others, who do not share it, may find that their paths tend to converge. And one place can be the starting-point for a variety of journeys, and sometimes the variety is such as to make those who were once together agree to part. Yet those who celebrate the Eucharist together have made that journey together, at least. And that they cannot make all their journeys together does not turn this sharing into something to be forgotten.[42]

But doors that are for opening can make for draughts: openness and vulnerability are not easy to live with. They are even less easy to live with nowadays, when the chances of life (and of transport; we are back to technology) can bring into one place so heterogeneous an assembly for the breaking of bread. I expressed sympathy with the burdens for liturgists that this pattern creates; I must add that it creates heavier burdens still for those who must shape the Sunday celebration so as to reach those who share in it. Perhaps the best comfort to offer here is cold. Tensions and failures here are not surprising, they are bound up with the whole pattern of sign and ritual. Moreover we have here a journey that moves beyond what is simply human, so the capacity to verify by results is gravely diminished; patience is part of the journey. And the Eucharist, as Aquinas reminded us, is a sacramental eating subordinate to spiritual eating – subordinate to our sharing the divine life through Christ. The sharing must shew itself in how the community lives and how it

---

[42] The whole topic of identity and diversity in religion is vast. Its difficulty has not been lessened by the propensity of religionists to make claims on the theme so loose and so intemperate that they would not gain a hearing in any less exalted a setting. For a survey of the complex field, see Sykes 1984, where I was pleased to find a special place given to worship, and a caution uttered against the expenditure of fruitless ingenuity in the quest for sameness. I offer two stories that I think have a lesson here: one concerns Jews, the other concerns paintings. Evelyn Waugh was present at the immigration into Palestine of a very motley group of settlers, and was given the explanation: 'Everyone who thinks he is a Jew, is one' (Waugh 1955: 14). The story is narrated humorously, but it has much wisdom – identity and its professions are more than accidentally linked; all the more when the profession calls for a whole way of life. The story of the paintings is one of the many told of the garish art-dealer Duveen, who peddled Old Masters to American millionaires. Duveen drastically restored his wares, and it was suggested that a Dürer of his had very little of Dürer left in it. The answer was prompt if wistful – it *had* been by Dürer once (Behrman 1972: 175–6). Little more sensible is argument for identity that does not take into account the subject-matter and the multiplicity of its embodiments – argument which seeks to say how things *must* be rather than *looking*.

serves, the eucharistic celebration must overflow in this way. Its openness is more than incompleteness, because it is the openness of a channel for sharing with others what has been received. The love it shews forth is a love that can *cost*; the sharing does not leave untouched those who share.

But if charity should mark the overflowing of the eucharistic celebration, let us not forget that charity should also mark the manner of celebration itself. I wrote in the preceding section of the need to patch and to contrive, to build on what has been received, and to let old and new come together in worship. The imagery may have sounded homely, but it was seriously meant and it concerns a problem of great and increasing urgency in our time. If the Church of Rome does not give good example in the matter of balancing present and past, who on earth will? And yet one does not need to go as far as Julien Green's *Journal* to see how often the example has not been given, and how often charity has been lacking in these things. 'The general acceptance of a legitimate plurality... has been arrived at with great difficulty': the pope's words in the Roman Synagogue can be applied to worship in the Church, and will give us food for thought if they are. The thought will move out to the beliefs incarnate in worship, out to the whole life of the *corpus mysticum*. We must learn to live with each other and with our differences.[43]

But if we must accept dissent among those who are, if I may so put it, inside the door, we must never forget that the door is one for opening by those also who are outside it. The market-place has more in it than the Church, but the service which the Church can give there is both real and needed. The pattern of life today is harsh to those who fall behind in the race, and demanding to those who persevere in it. Life itself is noisy and breathless in its concentration upon

---

[43] I have deployed imagery about both the Eucharist and the Church, and I have insisted that, in both contexts, the images are not recipes. At the start of this chapter I recalled the suggestions made by Küng for 'the pope as he might be', and a similar theme is elaborated, with historical and other reflexions, in Tillard 1983. I have much sympathy for both authors, and for others who think in that way, but I find in them all a deficiency. Each seems to think of a reshaping of the papal office in terms of some ecclesiastical decision reached by ecclesiastical means. For me, such a thought is a defiance of history. When recalling what Küng had written, I gave my own list of the 'founding fathers' of the Roman Church and of the papacy as we have come to know them. One thing in common to them all is that the 'turn' each gave was given *from outside*: the establishment of a bureaucracy at Rome, the change in balance within the Church from East to West, the split in Western christendom, the end of the *ancien régime*, the advent of modern communication. In no case was the turn given by papal or conciliar enactments, nor should we expect that now. We need other things.

questions which look quickly soluble, and often blind to what goes deeper: the world indeed is too much with us. If it is, then the service will be needed all the more. I set together earlier, as problems for our time, the consequences of a technological civilisation and of the growth of unreason. One source of the unreason, and of its ugly manifestations, is an inarticulate dissatisfaction with what the civilisation gives and takes away. I also set out my belief that both the unreason and the civilisation can, in their fashion, strengthen a picture of the Church that is already only too vigorous. But the picture, I have submitted, is wrong; the Church has something better to offer, something which, for all its imperfections, goes with healing to the roots of human life, and offers, in a way nothing else can, what transcends it. That there are many other things in the market-place does not mean that the Church has not something unique and irreplaceable to offer there.

The door is for opening, but not just by those who enter to share in the celebration. It is for opening too by those who enter only when they are sure that there is no celebration taking place. Their reasons for entering will be many, but they have entered. And if there is no spoken word addressed to them by the community, they are still addressed, because the place is one where God has been sought and the ritual established by Christ has been carried out. The place, in its very silence and in its very purpose, has a word of its own to utter – better, a word not its own. Some readers will already have guessed what is in my mind: Philip Larkin's poem 'Church Going'. Those who know it will be glad to meet it here; I hope that those who do not will read it all for themselves (e.g., in Larkin 1988: 97f.). It does what poetry is about – its words enable us to think thoughts that are new, but which we recognise and welcome when they come to us. I cannot think how better to end the book.

There he stands, the lone caller who does not go to church in the other sense, gazing at the building and its furnishings, noticing this and that

> And a tense, musty, unignorable silence,
> Brewed God knows how long. Hatless, I take off
> My cycle-clips in awkward reverence.

He eventually leaves; 'the place was not worth stopping for'. But he adds: 'Yet stop I did: in fact I often do.' He muses on what the fate of such buildings will be, as religious practice recedes. Will some

cathedrals be made into museums, with the rest left to go to ruin?
Will superstitions linger on round the sites?

> But superstition, like belief, must die,
> And what remains when disbelief has gone?
> Grass, weedy pavement, brambles, buttress, sky...

Will its very last visitor be some antiquarian? Or will he rather be like
the poet, tending in his ignorance

> to this cross of ground
> Through suburb scrub...?

And so his musings come back to himself, and to the building in
which he stands (the change of tense and place should not be missed):

> For, though I've no idea
> What this accoutred frowsty barn is worth,
> It pleases me to stand in silence here;
>
> A serious house on serious earth it is,
> In whose blent air all our compulsions meet,
> Are recognized, and robed as destinies.
> And that much never can be obsolete,
> Since someone will for ever be surprising
> A hunger in himself to be more serious,
> And gravitating with it to this ground,
> Which, he once heard, was proper to grow wise in,
> If only that so many dead lie round.

References

Abbott, E. and Campbell, L. (1897) *The Life and Letters of Benjamin Jowett, M.A.* 2 vols. London: John Murray.

Abbott, W. M. and Gallagher, J. eds. (1967) *The Documents of Vatican II.* London: Geoffrey Chapman.

Ackrill, J. (1981) *Aristotle the Philosopher.* Oxford University Press.

Anonymous (1932) *I Lost My Memory: the Case as the Patient Saw it.* London: Faber & Faber.

Aquinas, Thomas (1929–47) *Scriptum super Sententiis Magistri Petri Lombardi.* Vols. I and II ed. P. Mandonnet; vols. III and IV ed. M. F. Moos. Paris: Letheilleux.

— (1935) *In Metaphysicam Aristotelis Commentaria.* Ed. M. R. Cathalà. Turin: Marietti.

— (1948) *Summa Theologiae.* Turin and Rome: Marietti.

— (1949) *Quaestio disputata de Potentia.* Ed. P. M. Pession. Turin and Rome: Marietti.

— (1965) *Summa Theologiae. Volume 58 (3a. 73–78). The Eucharistic Presence.* Latin text, English translation, introduction and notes by W. Barden. London: Eyre & Spottiswoode.

ARCIC (1982) *Anglican Roman Catholic International Commission: the Final Report. Windsor, September 1981.* London: CTS/SPCK.

Armogathe, J. R. (1977) *Theologia Cartesiana: l'Eucharistie chez Descartes et dom* [Robert] *Desgabets.* Hague: Nijhoff.

Augustinus a Virgine Maria (1664) *Philosophiae Aristotelico-Thomisticae cursus.* Vol. I. Lugduni: H. Boissat.

Aulén, G. (1970) *Christus Victor: an Historical Study of the Three Main Types of the Idea of the Atonement.* Translated by A. G. Herbert. London: SPCK.

Ayleworth, G. (1675) *Metaphysica Scholastica.* Coloniae Agrippinae: J. Friessen.

Baciocchi, J. de (1955) Le mystère eucharistique dans les perspectives de la Bible. *Nouvelle Revue Théologique* 87: 561–80.

— (1959) Présence eucharistique et transsubstantiation. *Irénikon* 32: 139–61.

Behrman, S. N. (1972) *Duveen.* London: Hamish Hamilton.

Bell, D. (1990) *Husserl.* In *The Arguments of the Philosophers.* London and New York: Routledge.

Bell, G. (1938) *Randall Davidson, Archbishop of Canterbury.* London: Oxford University Press.

Bingham, J. (1867) *Origines Ecclesiasticae: the Antiquities of the Christian Church.* 2 vols. London: Bohn.

Birrell, A. (1930) A few warning words for would-be autobiographers. Pages 3–10 in his *Et Cetera.* London: Chatto & Windus.

Blake, W. (1939) *Poetry and Prose of William Blake.* Ed. G. Keynes. London: Nonesuch Press.

Boff, L. (1977) Theologie der Befreiung – die hermeneutischen Voraussetzungen. In Rahner, K., Modehn, C., Zwiefelhofer, H., pp. 46–61.

Bolsena (1963) *Il miracolo di Bolsena 1263–1963.* [Brochure in English on the eucharistic miracle there.] [Bolsena].

Bourdillon, M. and Fortes, M. eds. (1980) *Sacrifice.* London: Academic Press.

Breviary, Roman (1629) *Breviarium Romanum...et Clementis VIII auctoritate recognitum.* Coloniae: Egmondt.

   (1925) *Breviarium Romanum...Pii Papae X auctoritate renovatum.* Ratisbonae: Pustet.

Browe, P. (1933) *Die Verehrung der Eucharistie im Mittelalter.* Munich: Max Hueber.

   (1938) *Die eucharistischen Wunder des Mittelalters.* Breslau: Müller and Seiffert.

Burkert, W. (1983) *Homo Necans: the Anthropology of Ancient Greek Sacrificial Ritual and Myth.* Translated by Peter Bing. University of California Press.

Burridge, W. (1984) What do Anglican bishops believe? *Universe* 29 June 1984: 6.

Butler, B. C. (1971) The limits of infallibility. *Tablet* 17 April 1971: 373–5; and 24 April 1971: 398–400.

Caraman, P. (1967) *C. C. Martindale: a Biography.* London: Longmans.

Catechism, Old (c. 1956?) *A Catechism of Christian Doctrine.* Leeds: Laverty and Sons.

Cathnews (1984) '*Jesus: the Evidence*' – *Catholic Response.* Westminster: Cathnews.

Catholic Education, Congregation for (1979) [Regulations for the proper implementation of the apostolic constitution *Sapientia Christiana* [See John-Paul II 1979b.]] *AAS* 71: 500–21.

Catholic Education, Congregation for *see also* Studies, Congregation of

Clancy, T. (1961) English Catholics and the papal deposing power 1570–1640. *Recusant History* 6: 114–40, 205–27.

Clark, F. (1967) The real presence: an appraisal of a recent controversy. *Adoremus* 49: 32–48.

Clark, J. T. (1951) Physics, philosophy, transubstantiation, theology. *Theological Studies* 12: 24–51.

Colombo, C. (1955) Teologia, filosofia, e fisica nella dottrina della transustanziazione. *La Scuola Cattolica* 83: 89–124.

   (1956) Ancora sulla dottrina della transustanziazione e la fisica moderna. *La Scuola Cattolica* 84: 263–88.

Cooper, D. (1986) *Metaphor.* Oxford: Basil Blackwell.

Creighton, L. (1905) *Life and Letters of Mandell Creighton, Sometime Bishop of London*. 2 vols. London: Longmans Green.

Crichton, J. D., Winstone, H. E., Ainslie, J. R. eds. (1979) *English Catholic Worship: Liturgical Renewal in England since 1900*. London: Geoffrey Chapman.

Dens, P. (1812) *Tractatus theologici de...sacramentis in genere, de...venerabili sacramento Eucharistiae*. Dublin: R. Coyne.

   (1853) *Tractatus de sacramento Eucharistiae...olim a Professoribus Seminarii Mechlinensis dictati et deinde sub nomine P. Dens typis editi, nunc vero in pluribus emendati...* Mechliniae: Sumptibus Seminarii.

Denzinger, H. and Umberg, J. B. eds. (1948) *Enchiridion Symbolorum*. Barcelona: Herder.

Denzinger, H. and Schönmetzer, A. eds. (1963) *Enchiridion Symbolorum*. Barcelona: Herder.

Doctrine of the Faith, Congregation for – *see* Holy Office.

Douglas, M. (1970) *Natural Symbols: Explorations in Cosmology*. London: Barrie & Rockliff.

Dover, K. J. (1974) *Greek Popular Morality in the Time of Plato and Aristotle*. Oxford: Blackwell.

Ducange, C. (1688) *Glossarium ad scriptores mediae et infimae graecitatis auctore Carolo du Fresne, Domino du Cange*. Lugduni: apud Anissonios, &c. [Reprint, 1943].

Duhamel, J. B. (1681) De meteoris et fossilibus; de consensu veteris et novae philosophiae. In his *Opera philosophica* [in one volume; vols. 2 and 3]. Norimbergi: sumptibus J. Ziegeri.

   (1705) *Philosophia universalis, sive Commentarius in Universalem Aristotelis Philosophiam*. Lutetiae Parisiorum: C. Thibout.

Egner, G. *See* FitzPatrick, P. J.

Erasmus, D. (1704) Disputatiuncula de taedio et tristitia Jesu... In his *Opera omnia*, Book v, cols. 1265–92. Lugduni Batavorum: Van der Aa.

Eustachius a Sancto Paulo (1649) *Summa philosophiae*. Cantabridgiae: ex officina Rogeri Danielis.

Filograssi, J. (1954) Teologia e filosofia nel Collegio Romano dal 1824 ad oggi: note e ricordi. *Gregorianum* 35: 512–40.

FitzPatrick, P. J. (1966) **Birth Regulation and Catholic Belief: a Study in Problems and Possibilities*. London: Sheed & Ward.

   (1969) **Apologia pro Charles Kingsley*. London: Sheed & Ward.

   (1972) *Some thoughts on the eucharistic presence. *New Blackfriars* 53: 354–9, 399–408.

   (1973a) *More thoughts on the eucharistic presence. *New Blackfriars* 54: 171–80.

   (1973b) Fact and fiat: one theme in the Modernist crisis. *Durham University Journal* 65: 151–80.

   (1974) Infallibility: a secular assessment. *Irish Theological Quarterly* 41: 3–21.

   (1978) A study in the *Grammar of Assent*. *Irish Theological Quarterly* 45: 155–66, 217–33.

(1982) Neoscholasticism. In Kretzmann, N., Kenny, A. J. P., Pinborg, J. eds. *The Cambridge History of Later Medieval Philosophy*, pp. 838–52. Cambridge: Cambridge University Press.

(1985) Once in Khartoum. [Concerning the credibility of the New Testament]. *New Blackfriars* 66: 113–26.

(1987a) Some seventeenth-century disagreements and transubstantiation. In Davies, B. ed. *Language, Meaning and God. Essays in Honour of Herbert McCabe OP.* pp. 120–45. London: Geoffrey Chapman.

(1987b) Present and past in a debate on transubstantiation. In Hughes, G. J. ed. *The Philosophical Assessment of Theology. Essays in Honour of Frederick C. Copleston*, pp. 129–53. Tunbridge Wells: Search Press.

(1987c) Reprint of FitzPatrick 1972 and an adapted reprint of FitzPatrick 1973a, with an Additional Note in McCabe, H. *God Matters*, pp. 130–45, 155–64. London: Geoffrey Chapman.

(1989) Leibniz and some Greeks. *British Society for the History of Philosophy Newsletter*. No. 4. January 1989: 28–34.

(1991a) On eucharistic sacrifice in the middle ages. In Sykes 1991: 129–56.

(1991b) Newman and Kingsley; Newman's Grammar and the Church today. In Nicholls, D. and Kerr, F. eds. *John Henry Newman: Reason, Rhetoric and Romanticism*, pp. 88–108, 109–34. Bristol Classical Press.

Flannery, A. ed. (1975) *Vatican Council II: the Conciliar and Post Conciliar Documents*. Tenbury Wells: Fowler Wright.

Foster, J. (1962) The culture of the feelings. *Clergy Review* 47: 641–68.

Gavantus B. and Merati, C. (1736–8) *Thesaurus sacrorum rituum a Bartholomaeo Gavanto* [edited by C. Merati] 4 vols. Rome: Typographia Vaticana.

Godefroy, L. (1924) L'Eucharistie d'après le concile de Trente. *DTC*, vol. v, cols. 1326–56.

Goldstein, H. (1977) Skizze einer biblischen Begründung der Theologie der Befreiung. In Rahner K., Modehn C., Zwiefelhofer H. (1977), pp. 62–76.

Goncourt, E. and J., (1935–) *Journal: mémoires de la vie littéraire*. Vol. i, 1851–61. Paris: Flammarion.

Goudin, A. (1692) *Philosophia juxta inconcussa Divi Thomae dogmata*. Paris: Guerin.

Greeley, A. (1973) Konsens und Unfehlbarkeit, soziologische Perspektiven. In Küng (1973), pp. 196–202.

Green, J. (1977) *Oeuvres complètes*. Ed. J. Petit. Vol. v. Paris: Gallimard.

Gregory IX (1228) *Ab Aegyptiis*. [Letter of 7 July 1228 to the theologians of Paris.] Extracts in DS 824.

Gutierrez, G. (1983) *The Power of the Poor in History: Selected Writings*. Translated by R. R. Barr. London: SCM Press.

Gutwenger, E. (1961) Substanz und Akzidenz in der Eucharistielehre. *ZkT* 83: 257–306.

(1966) Das Geheimnis der Gegenwart Christi in der Eucharistie. *ZkT* 88: 185–97.

Harries, R. (1988) Does the State of Israel need Jewish liberation theology? *Independent*, 10 September 1988: 15.

Hart, R. van der (1973) Not by words alone. *New Blackfriars* 54: 275–80.

Hebblethwaite, P. (1984) *John XXIII, Pope of the Council*. London: Geoffrey Chapman.

Heenan, J. C. (1951) *The People's Priest*. London: Sheed & Ward.

(1971) *Not the Whole Truth*. London: Hodder & Stoughton.

Holy Office. *See* Inquisition, Roman.

Hügel, F. von (1926) The place and function of the historical element in religion. In his *Essays and Addresses on the Philosophy of Religion*. Second series, pp. 27–55. London: J. M. Dent.

Huxley, A. (1937) D. H. Lawrence. In *Stories, Essays and Poems*, pp. 331–52. London: J. M. Dent.

Index (1828) *Catalogue des ouvrages mis à l'Index par le cour de Rome*. Brussels: Librairie Catholique.

(1930) *Index of Prohibited Books Revised and Published by Order of his Holiness Pope Pius XI...* Rome: Vatican Polyglot Press.

Inquisition, the Roman (1966) [Notification, 14 June 1966, of the lapsing of canonical penalties concerning the Index.] *AAS* 58: 445.

(1982) [Letter in English to the Rt Revd Alan Clark, Bishop of East Anglia, on the final report of ARCIC (*see above*), with observations on the report.] *AAS* 74: 1060–74.

(1990) [Instruction of 24 May 1990 on the calling of the theologian in the Church.] AAS 82: 1550–70.

Jedin, H. (1951–75) *Geschichte des Konzils von Trient*. 4 vols. Freiburg: Herder.

John-Paul II, Pope (1978) [Address of 22 October 1978 to Cardinals.] *AAS* 70: 919–27.

(1979a) [Address in Italian of 3 April 1979 to Roman pontifical universities and colleges.] *AAS* 71: 597–604.

(1979b) *Sapientia christiana*. [Apostolic Constitution of 15 April 1979 on ecclesiastical universities and theological faculties.] *AAS* 71: 469–99.

(1979c) [Address in French of 26 September 1979 to the Pontifical Biblical Commission.] *AAS* 71: 606–9.

(1979d) [Address in Italian of 17 November 1979, on the centenary of *Aeterni Patris*, the encyclical letter of Leo XIII favouring Aquinas.] *AAS* 71: 1472–83.

(1979e) [Address in Italian of 15 December 1979 to the Gregorian University.] *AAS* 71: 1538–49.

(1981) [Address in German of 15 November 1980 in Cologne to staff of public universities.] AAS 73: 49–58.

(1983a) [Address in Spanish of 2 November 1982 in Madrid to staff of public universities.] *AAS* 75: 279–87.

(1983b) [Address in French of 9 May 1983 to participants at the conference on Galilean Studies.] *AAS* 75: 689–94.

(1986a) [Address in English of 28 October 1985, twenty years after the publication of *Nostra Aetate* (*see* Vatican, Second Council of, 1966a), to

those concerned with fostering relations between Christians and Jews.]
AAS 78: 409–11.

(1986b) [His visit of April 1986 to the Roman Synagogue; his address there; and the address of the President of the Synagogue.] *Osservatore Romano* (English edition) 21 April 1986.

(1988) [His visit to Turin and address to clergy etc.] *La Stampa* [Turin] 6 September 1988.

Jones, R. and Penny, N. (1983) *Raphael*. New Haven: Yale University Press.

Jorissen, H. (1965) *Die Entfaltung der Transsubstantiationslehre bis zum Beginn der Hochscholastik*. (*Münsterische Beiträge zur Theologie*, part 28, 1). Münster: Aschendorfsche Verlagsbuchhandlung.

Jowett, B. (1906) *Theological Essays of the Late Benjamin Jowett*. Selected, arranged and edited by Lewis Campbell. London: Henry Frowde.

Joyce, J. (1954) *Ulysses*. London: The Bodley Head.

Jungmann, J. A. (1952) *Missarum Solemnia: eine genetische Erklärung der römischen Messe*. 2 vols. Vienna: Herder.

Kaczyinski, R. ed. (1976) *Enchiridion documentorum instaurationis liturgicae*. Vol. 1. 1963–73. Rome: Marietti.

Kamlah, W. and Lorenzen, P. (1967) *Logische Propädeutik: Vorschule des vernünftigen Redens*. Mannheim: Bibliographisches Institut.

Kempe, A. B. (1953) How to draw a straight line; a lecture on linkages. [A reprint, in a volume entitled *Squaring the Circle and Other Monographs*, of a pamphlet published in 1877.] USA: Chelsea Publishing Company.

King, F. and Matthews, G. (1990) *About Turn*. London: Lawrence & Wishart.

Knowles, D. (1962) *The Evolution of Medieval Thought*. London: Longmans.

Knox, R. A. (1928) The identity of the pseudo-Bunyan. In his *Essays in Satire*, pp. 201–19. London: Sheed & Ward.

Küng, H. (1970) *Infallible? An Inquiry*. Translated by Edward Quinn. New York: Doubleday 1971. From the original *Unfehlbar? Eine Anfrage*. Einsiedeln, Zurich, Cologne: Benziger Verlag 1970.

(1971) Im Interesse der Sache: Antwort an Karl Rahner. *Stimmen der Zeit* 187: 43–64 and 105–22. Reprinted, with a Postscript, in Küng 1973, pp. 19–68.

ed. (1973) *Fehlbar?* Zurich, Einsiedeln, Cologne: Benziger.

Lagrange, J. B. de (1675) *Les principes de la philosophie contre les nouveaux philosophes...* Paris: G. Josse.

Lamberts, J. (1990) Active participation as the gateway towards an ecclesial liturgy. In Caspers, C. and Schneiders, M. eds. *Omnes circumadstantes*, pp. 234–61. Campen: J. H. Kok.

Larkin, P. (1988) *Collected Poems*. Marvell Press and Faber & Faber.

Lawrence, D. H. (1958) *The Rainbow*. London: Penguin Books.

(1961) *Fantasia of the Unconscious* and *Psychoanalysis of the Unconscious*. London: William Heinemann.

Leenhardt, F. J. (1955) *Ceci est mon corps. Explication de ces paroles de Jésus-Christ*. (*Cahiers théologiques* 37). Neuchâtel, Paris: Delachaux et Niestlé.

Legrand, A. (1694) *An Entire Body of Philosophy According to the Principles of the Famous Renate Des Cartes*. Translated by R. Blome. London: S. Roycroft.

Leibniz, G. W. F. (1960) *Die philosophischen Schriften...* Herausgegeben von C. J. Gerhardt. Hildesheim: G. Olms.

Leo XIII, Pope (1878) *Quod apostolici muneris* [Encyclical letter of 28 December 1878 on Socialism, Communism, Nihilism, etc.] *ASS* 11: 369–76.

(1879) *Aeterni Patris*. [Encyclical letter of 4 August 1879 on the place of Aquinas in philosophy and theology.] *ASS* 12: 97–115. Extracts in DS 3135f. (C).

(1891) *Rerum novarum*. [Encyclical letter of 15 April 1891 on social problems.] *ASS* 23: 641–70. Extracts in DS 3265f. (C).

(1901) *Graves de communi* [Encyclical letter of 18 January 1901 on Christian Democracy.] *ASS* 33: 385–96.

Leopardi, G. (1945) Saggio sopra gli errori popolari degli antichi. In *Tutte le opere di Giacomo Leopardi*, ed. Francesco Flora. Vol. II, pp. 222–456. [No place given]: Mondadori.

Longley, C. (1988) Stand firm on an act of faith. *The Times*, Monday 4 April 1988: 14.

Lubac, H. de (1949) *Corpus Mysticum*. Paris: Aubier.

McCabe, H. (1972) Transubstantiation: a reply to G. Egner. *New Blackfriars* 52: 546–54.

McHugh, J. F. (1961) Num solus panis triticeus sit materia valida S. Eucharistiae? *Verbum Domini* 39: 229–39.

(1969) The doctrinal authority of the encyclical *Humanae Vitae*. *Clergy Review* 54: 586–96, 680–93, 791–802.

(1991) The sacrifice of the mass at the council of Trent. In Sykes (1991), pp. 157–81.

McKenna, J. (1936) Quarant' Ore, or the Forty Hours prayer. *Clergy Review* 6: 186–99.

Maigne d'Arnis W.-H. (n.d.). *Lexicon manuale ad scriptores mediae et infimae latinitatis*. Paris: J. P. Migne.

Mascall, E. (1972) Egner on the eucharistic presence. *New Blackfriars* 53: 539–46.

Michaud, E. (1872) *De la falsification des catéchismes français et des manuels de théologie*. Paris: Sandoz & Fischbacher.

Micklem, N. (1939) *National Socialism and the Roman Catholic Church*. London: Oxford University Press.

Migne, J. P. ed. (1844–) *Patrologiae cursus completus...series prima...Ecclesiae Latinae...* Lutetiae Parisiorum: J. P. Migne.

ed. (1857–) *Patrologiae cursus completus...series graeca*. Lutetiae Parisiorum: J. P. Migne.

Missal, Roman (1894) *Missale Romanum ex decreto SS Concilii Tridentini restitutum, S. Pii V Pontificis Maximi iussu editum, Clementis VIII, Urbani VIII et Leonis XIII auctoritate recognitum...* Ratisbon: Pustet.

Moltmann, J. (1967) *Theology of Hope*. London: SCM Press.

Montcheuil, Y. de (1939) La raison de la permanence du Christ sous les espèces eucharistiques d'après saint Bonaventure et saint Thomas. *Recherches de Sciences Religieuses* 29: 352–64. Reprinted in Montcheuil 1946.

(1946) La raison de la permanence du Christ sous les espèces eucharistiques d'après saint Bonaventure et saint Thomas. In his *Mélanges Théologiques*, pp. 71–82. Faculté theologique, Lyon-Fourvière.

Newman, J. H. (1843) The theory of development in religious doctrine. In his *Sermons, Chiefly on the Theory of Religious Belief, Preached before the University of Oxford*, pp. 311–54. London: Rivington.

(1887) *An Essay in aid of a Grammar of Assent*. London: Longman, Green.

Newman, J. H. *See also* Ward, W.

OConnell, J. B. (1941–2) *The Celebration of Mass*. 3 vols. London: Burns Oates.

Örsy, L. (1990) *The Profession of Faith and the Oath of Fidelity: a Theological and Canonical Analysis*. Wilmington, Delaware: Michael Glazier.

Ortolan, T. (1923) Adoration perpétuelle. *DTC*. Vol. 1, cols. 442–45.

Paul VI, Pope (1964) *Siamo lietissimi*. [Address in Italian of 11 August 1964 in Orvieto Cathedral.] *AAS* 56: 751–7.

(1965a) *Mysterium Fidei*. [Encyclical letter of 3 September 1965 on the Eucharist.] *AAS* 57: 753–74. (C).

(1965b) *Integrae servandae*. [Apostolic Letter *motu proprio* of 7 December 1965 re-ordering the 'Holy Office' and re-naming it 'Congregation for the Doctrine of the Faith'.] *AAS* 57: 952–55.

(1968) *Humanae Vitae*. [Encyclical letter on the regulation of birth, of 25 July 1968.] *AAS* 60: 481–503. (C).

(1971) Eucharistic Preparation requires Faith, Grace, and Reconciliation. Address delivered to a General Audience, 9 June 1971. Reproduced from the *Osservatore Romano* in *Adoremus*. Vol. 53, no. 4 (October 1971): 139–42.

Pius IX, Pope (1863) *Tuas libenter*. [Letter of 2 December 1863 to the Archbishop of Munich.] DS 2875–80.

Pius X, Pope (1903a) *Tra le sollecitudini* [A *motu proprio* in Italian of 22 November 1903 on the restoration of sacred music; with attached instructions.] *ASS* 36: 329–39; a Latin translation is in *ASS* 36: 387–95.

(1903b) [Letter in Italian of 8 December 1903 to the Cardinal Vicar of Rome, on the restoration of sacred music.] *ASS* 36: 325–9. (C).

(1903c) *Fin dalla prima*. [A *motu proprio* in Italian of 18 December 1903, giving basic norms for popular Catholic action.] *ASS* 36: 339–45. (C).

(1931) *Quadragesimo Anno*. [Encyclical letter of 15 May 1931 on social matters.] *AAS* 23: 178–228. Extracts in DS 3725–44. (C).

Pius XII, Pope (1945) [Address in Italian of 2 June 1945 to the Cardinals.] *AAS* 37: 159–68. (C: the title is *The Pope Condemns the Nazis*).

(1947) *Mediator Dei et hominum*. [Encyclical letter of 20 November 1947 on the Sacred Liturgy]. *AAS* 39: 521–95. Extracts in DS 3840–55. (C).

(1950) *Humani Generis*. [Encyclical Letter of 12 August 1950 on some false opinions.] *AAS* 42: 561–78. Extracts in DS 3875–99. (C).

Quinn, E. (1983) Farewell to Rahner. *Downside Review* 101: 177–81.

Rahner, K. (1962) Theologisches zum Monogenismus. *SzT* 1: 253–322 [*TI* 1: 229–96; originally appeared in *ZkT* 76 (1954): 1–18; 187–223.]

(1965) *Hominisation: the Evolutionary Origin of Man as a Theological Problem.* London: Burns Oates. Translates a work which appeared in 1958.

(1967) Evolution and Original Sin. In *Concilium (Church and World).* Vol. 6 no. 3: 30–5.

(1969a) Original Sin. *SM* 4: 328–34 [The original appeared in 1967.]

(1969b) Monogenism. *SM* 4: 105–7.

(1970) Die Sünde Adams. *SzT* 9: 259–75 [*TI* 11: 247–62; address delivered in 1968.]

(1971) Replik. Bemerkungen zu: Hans Küng, Im Interesse der Sache. *Stimmen der Zeit* 187: 145–60. Reprinted in Rahner 1972, pp. 49–70.

ed. (1972) *Zum Problem Unfehlbarkeit. Antworten auf die Anfrage von Hans Küng.* Freiburg, Basel, Vienna: Herder.

(1977) Foreword, pp. 6–8 in Rahner, K., Modehn, C., Zwiefelhofer, H.

Rahner, K., Modehn, C., Zwiefelhofer, H. eds. (1977) *Befreiende Theologie: der Beitrag Lateinamerikas zur Theologie der Gegenwart.* Stuttgart: W. Kohlhammer.

Rashdall, H. (1920) *The Idea of Atonement in Christian Theology.* London: Macmillan.

Régis, S. (1704) *L'usage de la raison et de la foi.* Paris: Cusson.

Rilke, R. M. (1955) Das Buch vom mönchischen Leben (1899) In his *Werke in drei Bänden.* Vol. 1, pp. 7–57. Frankfurt am Main: Insel Verlag.

Rites, Congregation of (1815) *Decreta authentica Congregationis Sacrorum Rituum nunc primum edita.* Rome: apud Franciscum Bourlié.

(1879) *Decreta authentica Congregationis Sacrorum Rituum ex actis eiusdem…* Rome: Typis S. Cong. de Propaganda Fide.

(1967) *Instructio de cultu mysterii eucharistici.* [Instruction of 25 May 1967 on the cult of the eucharistic mystery.] *AAS* 59: 539–73. (C).

(1970) *De unica interpretatione textuum liturgicorum.* [Document of 6 February 1970 on uniformity in translations of liturgical texts.] Reprinted in Kaczyinski (1976), no. 2050.

Ritual, Roman (1870) *Rituale Romanum Pauli V Pontificis Maximi iussu editum, et a Benedicto XIV auctum et castigatum.* Mechliniae: H. Dessain.

Rivière, J. (1909) *The Doctrine of the Atonement. A Historical Essay.* Trans. L. Cappadelta. London: International Catholic library.

Ruskin, J. (1983) *Praeterita*: the autobiography of John Ruskin. With an introduction by Kenneth Clark. Oxford University Press.

Russell, B. A. W. (1943) *The Problems of Philosophy.* Oxford: Oxford University Press.

Sacks, J. (1991) The world might weep. *The Times*, 29 March 1991: 12.

Sacraments and Divine Worship, Congregation for – *see* Rites, Congregation of.

Schelfout, O. (1960) Bedenkingen bij een nieuwe transsubstantiatie-leer. *Collationes Brugenses-Gandavenses*, 6: 289–320.

Schillebeeckx, E. (1967) *Christus' tegenwoordigheid in de Eucharistie*. Bilthoven: H. Nelissen. [English translation is Schillebeeckx 1968.]

(1968) *The Eucharist*. Translated by N. D. Smith. London: Sheed & Ward. [English translation of Schillebeeckx 1967.]

Schoonenberg, P. (1959a) De tegenwoordigheid van Christus. *Verbum* 26: 148–57.

(1959b) Een terugblik: ruimtelijke, persoonlijke en eucharistische tegenwoordigheid. *Verbum* 26: 314–27.

(1964a) Eucharistische tegenwoordigheid. *De Heraut* 95: 333–6.

(1964b) Tegenwoordigheid. *Verbum* 31: 395–415.

(1965) Nogmaals: eucharistische tegenwoordigheid. *De Heraut* 96: 48–50.

Selvaggi, F. (1949) Il concetto di sostanza nel dogma eucaristico in relazione alla fisica moderna. *Gregorianum* 30: 7–45.

(1954) Fisica cosmologia metafisica. In *Studi filosofici intorno all' 'esistenza', al mondo, al trascendente*, pp. 195–201. Analecta Gregoriana. Series filosofica. Serie A, numero 6. Rome: Pontificia Università Gregoriana.

(1956) Realtà fisica e sostanza sensibile nella dottrina eucaristica. *Gregorianum* 37: 16–33.

(1957) Ancora intorno ai concetti di 'sostanza sensibile' e 'realtà fisica'. *Gregorianum* 38: 503–14.

Smits, L. (1964a) Van oude naar nieuwe transsubstantiatieleer. *De Heraut* 95: 340–4.

(1964b) Nieuwe zicht op de werkelijke tegenwoordigheid van Christus in de Eucharistie. *De Bazuin* 48: 9/4–9/5. [References to this journal are complicated by its beginning a new volume in the middle of the year, and by its distinctive pagination. I give what can be found on the pages themselves.]

(1965) Het dogma verschillend verduidelijkt. *De Bazuin* 48: 23/4–23/6.

Soskice, J. M. (1989) *Metaphor and Religious Language*. Oxford: Clarendon Press.

Spiegelberg, H. (1970). *The Phenomenological Movement*. 2 vols. The Hague: Nijhoff.

Steenberghen, F. van (1955) *Aristotle in the West*. Translated by L. Johnston. Louvain: Nauwelaerts.

(1966) *La philosophie au XIIIᵉ siècle*. Louvain: Publications Universitaires.

Studies, Congregation of (1914) [Some approved theses of Thomistic philosophy, 27 July 1914.] *AAS* 6: 383–6. Reprinted in DS 3601–24.

Sykes, S. (1980) Sacrifice in the New Testament and in Christian theology. In Bourdillon and Fortes (1980), pp. 61–83.

(1984) *The Identity of Christianity. Theologians and the Essence of Christianity from Schleiermacher to Barth*. Philadelphia: Fortress Press.

(1991) *Sacrifice and Redemption: Durham Essays in Theology*. Cambridge: Cambridge University Press.

Tillard, J. M. (1983) *The Bishop of Rome*. Translated by J. de Satgé. London: SPCK.

Tongiorgi, S. (1862) *Institutiones Philosophicae*. 3 vols. Brussels: Société Belge de Librairie.

Trent, Council of (1546) *Decretum de peccato originali*. [Decree of 17 June 1546 on original sin.] DS 1510–16.

(1551) *Decretum de ss. Eucharistia*. [Decree of 11 October 1551 on the Holy Eucharist.] DS 1635–61.

Trevelyan, G. O. (1908) *The Life and Letters of Lord Macaulay*. Enlarged and complete edition. London: Longmans, Green.

Trooster, S. (1963) De eucharistische tegenwoordigheid in de hedendaagse Protestantse en Katholieke theologie. [Followed by a discussion.] *Werkgenotschap Katholieke Nederlandse Theologie, Jaarboek* 1962: 113–36.

Tyrrell, G. (1908) *Medievalism: a Reply to Cardinal Mercier*. London: Longmans, Green.

Unbelievers, Secretariat for (1968) *Humanae Personae Dignitatem*. [Document of 28 August 1968 on dialogue with unbelievers.] *AAS* 60: 692–704 (F).

Vanneste, A. (1956) Bedenkingen bij de scholastieke transsubstantiatie-leer. *Collationes Brugenses-Gandavenses* 2: 332–5.

(1957) [Review in French of F. J. Leenhardt's *Ceci est mon corps*.] *Collationes Brugenses-Gandavenses* 3: 270–2.

(1960) Nog steeds bedenkingen bij de transsubstantiatie-leer. *Collationes Brugenses-Gandavenses* 6: 321–48.

Vatican, First Council of the (1870) *Pastor aeternus* [Dogmatic constitution on Christ's Church.] *ASS* 6: 40–7; DS 3050–75.

Vatican, Second Council of the (1965) *Lumen Gentium* [Dogmatic Constitution of 21 November 1964 on the Church.] *AAS* 57: 5–71 (AG, F).

(1966a) *Nostra Aetate* [Declaration of 28 October 1965 on the relation of the Church to non-Christian religions.] *AAS* 58: 740–4 (AG, F).

(1966b) *Optatam totius* [Decree of 28 October 1965 on the training of priests.] *AAS* 58: 713–27 (AG, F).

(1966c) *Dei Verbum* [Dogmatic Constitution of 18 November 1965 on divine revelation.] *AAS* 58: 817–35 (AG, F).

(1966d) *Dignitatis humanae* [Declaration of 7 December 1965 on religious liberty.] *AAS* 58: 929–46 (AG, F).

(1966e) *Gaudium et Spes* [Pastoral Constitution of 7 December 1965 on the Church in the modern world.] *AAS* 58: 1025–120 (AG, F).

(1966f) [One of the closing messages in French of 8 December 1965: that to men of thought and science.] *AAS* 58: 11–12 (AG).

Vaux, R. de (1961) *Ancient Israel: Its Life and Institutions*. Translated by John McHugh. London: Darton, Longman & Todd.

Ward, W. ed. (1913) *Newman's Apologia pro Vita Sua. The Two Versions of 1864 and 1865. Preceded by Newman's and Kingsley's Pamphlets*. With an Introduction by Wilfrid Ward. London: Oxford University Press.

Waugh, E. (1955) An open letter to the Hon[ble]. Mrs Peter Rodd (Nancy Mitford) on a very serious subject. *Encounter* 5: 11–16.

(1979) *The Diaries of Evelyn Waugh.* Edited by Michael Davie. London: Penguin Books.

Whately, R. (1870) *Elements of Logic.* London: Longmans, Green.

Wicker, B. (1966) *Culture and Theology.* London: Sheed & Ward.

Williams, J. A. (1967) Royal Declaration. *New Catholic Encyclopaedia*, vol. 12, p. 693. New York: McGraw-Hill.

Wittgenstein, L. (1953) *Philosophische Untersuchungen/Philosophical Investigations.* Translated by G. E. M. Anscombe. Oxford: Basil Blackwell.

(1969) *Über Gewissheit/On Certainty.* Edited by G. E. M. Anscombe and G. H. von Wright. Translated by D. Paul and G. E. M. Anscombe. Oxford: Basil Blackwell.

Wohlmuth, J. (1975) *Realpräsenz und Transsubstantiation im Konzil von Trient: eine historisch-kritische Analyse der Canones 1–4 der Sessio XIII.* 2 vols. Bern: Herbert Lang; Frankfurt: Peter Lang.

Young, F. M. (1975) *Sacrifice and the Death of Christ.* London: SPCK.

Selective Index

Under each heading and sub-heading, items are generally arranged in the order of their occurrence in the book.

Texts of Aquinas, cited or mentioned

(*for methods of citation*, see p. xix)